DISCARD

FOR REFERENCE

Do Not Take From This Room

D1410489

MAGILL'S
LITERARY ANNUAL
2019

*Essay-Reviews of 150 Outstanding Books
Published in the United States During 2018*

With an Annotated List of Titles

Volume I
A-K

Edited by
Jennifer Sawtelle

SALEM PRESS
A Division of EBSCO Information Services, Inc.
Ipswich, Massachusetts

GREY HOUSE PUBLISHING

Magill's Literary Annual, 2019, published by Grey House Publishing, Inc., Amenia, NY, under exclusive license from EBSCO Information Services, Inc.

∞ The paper used in these volumes conforms to the American National Standard for Permanence of Paper for Printed Library Materials, Z39.48-1992 (R2009).

Publisher's Cataloging-In-Publication Data
(Prepared by The Donohue Group, Inc.)

Names: Magill, Frank N. (Frank Northen), 1907-1997, editor. | Wilson, John D., editor. | Kellman, Steven G., 1947- editor. | Goodhue, Emily, editor. | Poranski, Colin D., editor. | Akre, Matthew, editor. | Spires, Kendal, editor. | Toth, Gabriela, editor. | Sawtelle, Jennifer, editor.
Title: Magill's literary annual.
Description: <1977->: [Pasadena, Calif.] : Salem Press | <2015->: Ipswich, Massachusetts : Salem Press, a division of EBSCO Information Services, Inc. ; Amenia, NY : Grey House Publishing | Essay-reviews of ... outstanding books published in the United States during the previous year. | "With an annotated list of titles." | Editor: 1977- , F.N. Magill; <2010-2014>, John D. Wilson and Steven G. Kellman; <2015>, Emily Goodhue and Colin D. Poranski; <2016>, Matthew Akre, Kendal Spires, and Gabriela Toth; <2017->, Jennifer Sawtelle. | Includes bibliographical references and index.
Identifiers: ISSN: 0163-3058
Subjects: LCSH: Books--Reviews--Periodicals. | United States--Imprints--Book reviews--Periodicals. | Literature, Modern--21st century--History and criticism--Periodicals. | Literature, Modern--20th century--History and criticism--Periodicals.
Classification: LCC PN44 .M333 | DDC 028.1--dc23

FIRST PRINTING
PRINTED IN THE UNITED STATES OF AMERICA

CONTENTS

CONTENTS

PUBLISHER'S NOTE

Magill's Literary Annual, 2019 follows a long tradition, beginning in 1954, of offering readers incisive reviews of the major literature published during the previous calendar year. The *Magill's Literary Annual* series seeks to critically evaluate 150 major examples of serious literature, both fiction and nonfiction, published in English, from writers in the United States and around the world. The philosophy behind our selection process is to cover works that are likely to be of interest to general readers that reflect publishing trends, that add to the careers of authors being taught and researched in literature programs, and that will stand the test of time. By filtering the thousands of books published every year down to notable titles, the editors have provided librarians with an excellent reader's advisory tool and patrons with fodder for book discussion groups and a guide for choosing worthwhile reading material. The essay-reviews in the *Annual* provide a more academic "reference" review of a work than is typically found in newspapers and other periodical sources.

The reviews in the two-volume *Magill's Literary Annual, 2019* are arranged alphabetically by title. At the beginning of each volume is a complete alphabetical list of all covered books that provides readers with the title and author. In addition, readers will benefit from a brief description of each work in the volume. Every essay is approximately four pages in length. Each one begins with a block of reference information in a standard order:

- Full Book Title, including any subtitle
- *Author:* Name, with birth year, and death year when applicable
- *First published:* Original foreign-language title, with year and country, when pertinent
- Original language and translator name, when pertinent
- Introduction, Foreword, etc., with writer's name, when pertinent
- *Publisher:* Company name and city, and the number of pages
- *Type of work* (chosen from standard categories):

Anthropology	Fine arts
Archaeology	History
Autobiography	History of science
Biography	Language
Current affairs	Law
Diary	Letters
Drama	Literary biography
Economics	Literary criticism
Education	Literary history
Environment	Literary theory
Essays	Media
Ethics	Medicine
Film	Memoir

Miscellaneous	Psychology
Music	Religion
Natural history	Science
Nature	Short fiction
Novel	Sociology
Novella	Technology
Philosophy	Travel
Poetry	Women's issues

- *Time:* Period represented, when pertinent
- *Locale:* Location represented, when pertinent
- Capsule description of the work
- *Principal characters* (for novels, short fiction) or *Principal personages* (for bibliographies, history): List of people, with brief descriptions, when pertinent

The text of each essay-review analyzes and presents the focus, intent, and relative success of the author, as well as the makeup and point of view of the work under discussion. To assist readers further, essays are supplemented by a list of additional "Review Sources" for further study in a bibliographic format. Every essay includes a sidebar offering a brief biography of the author or authors. Thumbnail photographs of book covers and authors are included as available.

Three indexes can be found at the end of volume II:

- Category Index: Groups all titles into subject areas such as current affairs and social issues, ethics and law, history, literary biography, philosophy and religion, psychology, and women's issues.
- Title Index: Lists all works reviewed in alphabetical order, with any relevant cross references.
- Author Index: Lists books covered in the Annual by each author's name.

A searchable cumulative index, listing all books reviewed in *Magill's Literary Annual* between 1977 and 2019, as well as in *Magill's History Annual* (1983) and *Magill's Literary Annual, History and Biography* (1984 and 1985), can be found at online.salempress.com.

Our special thanks go to the outstanding writers who lend their time and knowledge to this project every year. The names of all contributing reviewers are listed in the beginning of Volume I, as well as at the end of their individual reviews.

COMPLETE ANNOTATED LIST OF CONTENTS

VOLUME I

After examining humanity's distant past in Sapiens *(2014) and its long-distance future in* Homo Deus *(2016), Israeli historian and scholar Yuval Noah Harari focuses his attention upon problems and solutions for the human species in the present and near future in* 21 Lessons for the 21st Century *(2018).*

The 7½ Deaths of Evelyn Hardcastle, *Stuart Turton's first novel, mimics the form and setting of a vintage Agatha Christie murder mystery, but with a twist: his narrator jumps from body to body, witnessing the same events from different characters' perspectives as he attempts to solve—or prevent—a murder.*

Though Nina Browning's life seems to be perfect on the surface, she is beginning to realize how much of a lie she has been living. When her son pulls what he considers a foolish prank on an innocent girl, Nina must choose to continue denying her unhappiness or confront the problems in her marriage and family.

American Histories *is a short-story collection that explores the legacy of slavery. It is written by the prolific African American author John Edgar Wideman.*

Terrance Hayes's sixth collection of poems, American Sonnets for My Past and Future Assassin, *explores American life after the election of Donald Trump to the presidency.*

Tayari Jones examines race, class, gender, and the nature of love and relationships in this deeply affecting novel, which focuses on an African American couple whose young marriage is upended after the husband is wrongly imprisoned.

Lisa Halliday's debut novel Asymmetry *is told in three disparate parts: in one, a young woman has an affair with a famous, older writer; in another, an Iraqi American economist navigates immigration at Heathrow; and finally, a famous novelist gives a radio interview.*

The Best Cook in the World *depicts the hardscrabble Southern life and cuisine of author Rick Bragg's family. It is his tenth book.*

Xhenet Aliu's debut novel, Brass, *tells the story of a mother and daughter, each coming-of-age in working-class Waterbury, Connecticut.*

David Chariandy's award-winning second novel, Brother, *highlights the large trials and small triumphs of growing up black in urban Canada. A family of Trinidadian heritage fights to survive in an ethnically diverse, economically challenged, and politically scapegoated enclave of Scarborough, a section of Toronto.*

Call Me American *is a memoir by Abdi Nor Iftin with Max Alexander. It chronicles Iftin's life growing up in Somalia during the wars of the 1990s before immigrating to the United States as well as contemplations about life in his adopted country.*

Journalist Rebecca Solnit's latest collection of essays, Call Them by Their True Names: American Crises (and Essays), *presents pieces about American politics, police brutality, and climate change that she published between 2016 and 2018.*

In Calypso, *David Sedaris shares his humorous yet often insightful observations on family, death, grief, aging, and other aspects of his everyday life.*

Former US poet laureate Donald Hall followed up his celebrated 2014 volume Essays after Eighty *with another collection of short essays reflecting on his long life and contemplating his approaching death.*

The Carrying, *Ada Limón's fifth poetry collection and the follow-up to her acclaimed* Bright Dead Things *(2015), explores the depths of human emotion and experience as felt through the natural world and relationships with other people. As Limón contemplates how humans sustain their place in the world—whether through creative expression, battles with infertility, or inspiration found in nature—her poetry stacks experience upon experience and creates a record of a woman's quest for connection. Rich descriptions coupled with raw emotion bring the poems to life.*

In The Feather Thief: Beauty, Obsession, and the Natural History Heist of the Century, *Kirk Wallace Johnson details the 2009 theft of hundreds of priceless specimens from the Natural History Museum in Tring, England, and the complex history underlying the robbery.*

Feel Free *is a collection of essays that explores topics ranging from politics to pop culture. It is British writer Zadie Smith's seventh book.*

Written by the best-selling American author Meg Wolitzer, The Female Persuasion *examines the state of contemporary feminism through the experiences of an idealistic young woman and her mentor.*

Lydia Millet's darkly comic, insightful, and superbly crafted collection of linked short stories set in Los Angeles, Fight No More, *focuses on characters who are either searching for or fleeing from their homes. Nina, the real estate agent who brokers their transactions, prompts them to contemplate the meaning of home as they struggle with relationships, abuse, and grief, yet rarely give up on the possibility of a brighter future.*

The Fighters *offers a view on the ground of the drawn-out US conflicts in Iraq and Afghanistan. Eschewing policy pronouncements from generals and government officials, author C. J. Chivers instead records the experiences of six service members in both countries up close.*

Celebrated Polish novelist Olga Tokarczuk creates a mosaic work in 116 sections, loosely based around the travels of an unnamed narrator, which relate a variety of stories and meditations on travel, grotesquerie, and what it means to be human.

Florida, *author Lauren Groff's newest collection of short stories, explores dread and time through the lens of the state of Florida.*

In Flunk. Start., *Sands Hall describes the ten years of her life during which she was influenced by Scientology. While under the group's influence, she struggled with many of its philosophies, but she was drawn to the commitment of the individual members. Though she often thought of leaving, she was also running away from family issues that her involvement both complicated and soothed.*

*In this English translation of Austrian author Christoph Ransmayr's 2006
German-language blank verse novel, two Irish brothers embark on an epic journey
to the land of Kham in eastern Tibet, where they seek to find and conquer a mythical
unmapped mountain.*

*Alice Russell is sharing information with federal agents Aaron Falk and Carmen
Cooper regarding fraud at BaileyTennants. However, her disappearance during a
company team-building exercise in the wilderness leads to a mystery: Did she leave
of her own accord or did someone make her disappear? Since Falk was the last
person she attempted to contact, he and his partner set off to help find the missing
woman.*

Frankenstein in Baghdad *is a loose retelling of Mary Shelley's classic horror
novel. Set in Iraq's capital during the city's occupation by American forces, it offers
insight into the terrible effects of pervasive violence on society.*

Sigrid Nunez's seventh novel, The Friend, *explores grief and companionship
through a woman's relationship with a Great Dane following its owner's suicide.
Told through a series of flashbacks to the narrator's interactions with her mentor—the dog owner in question—and her present-day attempts to make sense of the
loss and wrangle a giant dog in the cramped spaces of New York City,* The Friend
*is as much a meditation on art, connection, and mortality as it is a tale of loss and
recovery.*

In former ambassador Michael McFaul's memoir From Cold War to Hot Peace:
An American Ambassador in Putin's Russia, *the author recalls his career as a policymaker and diplomat in Russia.*

Ingrid Rojas Contreras's debut novel, Fruit of the Drunken Tree, *is a fictionalized
account of her family's difficulties in violence-wracked Bogotá, Colombia. Set during
the reign of drug king Pablo Escobar, the story is narrated by characters from vastly
different backgrounds who are both simply trying to survive.*

With Fryderyk Chopin, *the distinguished musicologist Alan Walker presents a comprehensive biography of the great composer of piano music. Walker*

painstakingly sifts fact from fiction in Chopin's life, illuminating the many facets of the composer's life, including his famous and complicated relationship with the novelist George Sand. He also provides insightful commentary on Chopin's extensive catalogue of works.

In The Future of Humanity: Terraforming Mars, Interstellar Travel, Immortality, and Our Destiny beyond Earth, *Michio Kaku explores the ways in which evolving technology may enable humans to leave Earth, their own physical bodies, or even the universe itself.*

A survivor of the Rwandan genocide, Clemantine Wamariya reckons with her experiences as a child refugee, offering a rare, first-person glimpse of a child's experience of atrocity. Moving back and forth between past and present, The Girl Who Smiled Beads *explores her long road toward stability in a new, American life.*

With Girls Burn Brighter, *debut novelist Shobha Rao tells the harrowing story of two young people from a poor village in India who become fast friends. They are traumatically separated, endure a series of hardships, undergo horrific ordeals, and survive by clinging to the hope of an eventual reunion.*

Megan Abbott's noir thriller Give Me Your Hand *follows the intertwining lives of two ambitious scientists.*

Pulitzer Prize–winning author, journalist, and longtime Texan Lawrence Wright explores the mythology of his home state in God Save Texas: A Journey into the Soul of the Lone Star State.

In this follow-up to her blockbuster The Nightingale *(2015), Kristin Hannah follows a family of three as they move from Seattle to Alaska hoping to leave behind the demons the father brought back with him from Vietnam.*

Christopher J. Yates' second novel, Grist Mill Road, *examines the hidden causes behind a traumatic incident and focuses on its effects on the lives of three people, both at the time of the event and more than quarter-century afterward when their paths intersect again.*

life, his relationships with family, friends, and lovers, and the path that he took to becoming a writer.

Part memoir, part true crime story, Michelle McNamara's gripping posthumous best seller, I'll Be Gone in the Dark *(2018), connects a series of violent crimes committed between 1974 and 1986 in central California. The result is a chilling portrait of the notorious Golden State Killer, who may have been brought to justice in 2018.*

A Jewish family saga with supernatural undertones, The Immortalists *follows the lives of four siblings who, as children, visit a fortune-teller in New York City. Upon request, the woman tells the children the exact date they will die, and the novel illustrates their different reactions to the information.*

The turbulent personal and professional life of internationally acclaimed journalist Marie Colvin is chronicled by a friend, fellow journalist Lindsey Hilsum, who examines Colvin's contributions to unmasking atrocities in several conflicts between 1987 and 2012.

In his debut poetry collection, Indecency *(2018), Justin Phillip Reed presents an exhilarating political poetry, experimenting with an elaborate formalism that impinges on its content. Implied by the book's title, Reed's incisive methodology transforms insolence into a fine art. Reed casts the constitutive tensions between body, identity, and their social and political determinants in sharp—and then even sharper—relief.*

Lynn Vincent and Sara Vladic offer a vividly thrilling and meticulously researched look at the deadliest maritime disaster in US naval history. Drawing on extensive survivor testimonies, this history focuses heavily on the story of Indianapolis's *final captain, Charles B. McVay III, who was unfairly court-martialed for the ship's sinking.*

Alisa Roth investigates police departments, courts, jails, and psychiatric facilities across the country to expose how the criminal justice system provides care—or lack of it—to people with mental illness.

COMPLETE ANNOTATED LIST OF CONTENTS

Tana French, author of the best-selling Dublin Murder Squad crime series, uses her stand-alone novel The Witch Elm *to explore themes of memory, identity, privilege, and luck in contemporary Dublin, Ireland.*

The Wizard and the Prophet, *by American journalist Charles C. Mann, explores the work of environmentalists Norman Borlaug and William Vogt and how it continues to inform pressing environmental debates.*

A. J. Finn's debut novel, The Woman in the Window, *follows Dr. Anna Fox, a former psychologist who refuses to leave her luxurious Harlem home, after she witnesses a crime that no one else believes happened.*

Journalist Elaine Weiss's second book, The Woman's Hour, *examines the weeks leading up to the ratification of the Nineteenth Amendment.*

When detective Daniel Hawthorne approaches author Anthony Horowitz to write a novel about his work, Horowitz reluctantly agrees. As a result, he is drawn into a murder mystery that might be more dangerous than he could anticipate.

You Think It, I'll Say It *is a collection of short stories that explores the contemporary experiences of middle-aged Americans. It is Curtis Sittenfeld's fifth book.*

CONTRIBUTING REVIEWERS

Pegge Bochynski

Joy Crelin

Chris Cullen

Robert C. Evans, PhD

Jack Ewing

Melynda Fuller

Molly Hagan

Frank Joseph

Mark S. Joy, PhD

Kathryn Kulpa, MA, MLIS

Laurence W. Mazzeno, PhD

Daniel P. Murphy

Lindsay Rohland

Marybeth Rua-Larsen

Julia A. Sienkewicz

Andrew Schenker

Theresa L. Stowell, PhD

Emily Turner

Thomas Willard, PhD

21 Lessons for the 21st Century

Author: Yuval Noah Harari (b. 1976)
Publisher: Spiegel & Grau (New York). 400 pp.
Type of work: Current affairs
Time: Present and near future
Locale: Global

After examining humanity's distant past in Sapiens *(2014) and its long-distance future in* Homo Deus *(2016), Israeli historian and scholar Yuval Noah Harari focuses his attention upon problems and solutions for the human species in the present and near future in* 21 Lessons for the 21st Century *(2018).*

#1 *NEW YORK TIMES* BESTSELLING AUTHOR OF SAPIENS

Yuval Noah Harari

21 Lessons for the 21ˢᵗ Century

Courtesy of Random House

In his third book, 2018's *21 Lessons for the 21st Century*, Yuval Noah Harari interprets the current social, political, and technological landscape to predict the significant, perhaps existential, challenges humanity will face in the next several decades. In many cases, his outlook is quite bleak: as technology advances inexorably, and swift communication pushes apart or pulls together groups of people with conflicting views, the pressure on individuals will grow. Some will not survive the resulting chaos. Others will be forced to subsist in reduced circumstances. However, Harari is not wholly negative. He suggests that those capable of adapting in a thoughtful, timely fashion will form the vanguard of a changed but resilient species. And, as his title suggests, he presents a variety of considerations he believes will help individuals and societies prepare for the serious changes ahead.

   21 Lessons is, in many ways, a follow-up to Harari's books *Sapiens: A Brief History of Humankind* (2014) and *Homo Deus: A Brief History of Tomorrow* (2016), which explore humanity's past and potential future, respectively. Both proved highly successful and propelled the author to acclaim as a popular guru of both history and futurism for general audiences. Harari then turned his attention to the trends of the mid-to-late 2010s and their impact on the near future. Sections of *21 Lessons* previously appeared as articles in various periodicals, examining particular aspects of modern society that contribute directly or indirectly to human welfare. Gathered into a collection, amended as necessary, given structure, and tied thematically, Harari's writing forewarns of an era fraught with uncertainty and filled with potential global upheaval. While the book discusses little that others have not already thought or expressed before, Harari's clear and engaging style draws in readers regardless of familiarity with the subjects at hand. He provides concrete examples to illustrate concepts and uses pithy sentences that drive home points, such as this telling observation: "Humans were always far better at inventing tools than using them wisely."

As the author reminds readers, doomsayers have been proclaiming about impending disaster since the dawn of time. Turns of the millennia, plagues of disease, history-changing inventions like gunpowder or steam engines, worldview-altering atomic bombs, and other natural or human-made phenomena have all engendered feelings of foreboding as possible harbingers of the end of the world. The difference now, Harari suggests, is the rapid pace of events unfolding in the twenty-first century compared to all the centuries of civilization that came before, as well as the sheer mass of humanity potentially affected by changes soon to materialize. The world has shrunk. Journeys that not long ago took days or weeks can now be accomplished in hours. People anywhere on the globe can connect with one another instantly at the touch of a button. Ideas, good or bad, can be exchanged at the speed of light.

A consequence of this modern way of life—and a major problem, Harari argues—is information overload. Humans have become obsessed with data-gathering, lately through sophisticated portable internet-capable devices, as a means of keeping in constant touch with the world and bringing relevance into their otherwise humdrum lives. And as individuals collect information, other entities with different motives (such as governments and corporations) are collecting information about them: personal history, health issues, food preferences, political affiliation, sexual proclivities, and much more, all conveniently broken down into demographic categories. The trouble is, humans are not necessarily equipped evolutionarily or emotionally to live in such mentally overwhelming conditions. The proto-humans who emerged as hunter-gatherers long ago developed brains structured to handle simple binary choices (e.g., kill or be killed). Though *Homo sapiens* has learned much and progressed far over time, the species remains biologically limited, wired for the analog rather than the digital age, and as such has difficulties processing and analyzing complicated data. Humans faced with a bewildering plethora of modern considerations linked to behavior, or reactions to sensual stimuli—Is something morally right? Is it socially acceptable? Is there profit to be made?—impulsively make decisions based on ancient intuitions and are prone to error. Individually and socially, these errors can have sweeping consequences.

21 Lessons is Harari's attempt to show ways in which even primitive, flawed brains can be applied to contemporary issues. The work is split into five main parts: the technological challenge, the political challenge, despair and hope, truth, and resilience. These parts are divided into a total of twenty-one chapters—the "lessons" of the title—that each examine a contemporary issue such as equality, war, or education. However, as many reviewers noted, the work is ultimately structured less like a series of prescriptive lessons than as general points to ponder and reflect on. While some might be disappointed in the lack of recommended actions with proven results, awareness and consideration of the issues Harari outlines is surely beneficial, even if one disagrees with some of his ideas.

Part 1, titled "The Technological Challenge," the longest section in the book, focuses mainly on the anticipated effects of biotech and infotech on humanity in the near future. Harari begins, however, with "Disillusionment: The End of History Has Been Postponed," a far-ranging chapter about how humans tend to think: in stories, tales, and myths, rather than in facts. He argues that this is a relic from when information could only be passed along from generation to generation orally, among members of separate tribes. All tribes had their own stories and like-minded groups banded together, united by common beliefs and ideals, a custom that held true from antiquity until modern times. For example, Harari maintains, the twentieth century was dominated by three major and largely incompatible movements that coalesced out of tribalism: fascism, communism, and liberalism.

Harari largely sympathizes with liberalism, which he identifies as the dominant remaining ideology in the early twenty-first century and defines most broadly as a belief in the value of liberty. Liberalism faced a major challenge from fascism—characterized by rabid nationalism under the leadership of dictators who ruthlessly suppress dissenting voices and ideas and rigidly control all aspects of society—but seemingly overcame it in World War II. Communism, which advocates a publicly owned society, then became the main threat to the liberal order,

Yuval Noah Harari is an Israeli historian affiliated with the Hebrew University of Jerusalem. His books Sapiens: A Brief History of Humankind *(first published in Hebrew in 2011 and translated into English in 2014), and* Homo Deus: A Brief History of Tomorrow *(2016) became international best sellers.*

but this threat faded following reforms in China and the breakup of the Soviet Union in the early 1990s. With liberalism apparently victorious, Harari notes flaws in the system, such as the fact that ongoing economic liberalization and globalization have failed to ensure peace and alleviate poverty. Indeed, the "disillusionment" the author discusses is with the very liberal principles many take for granted, as demonstrated by widespread backlash apparent in the mid-2010s.

Encapsulating this backlash for Harari are the US presidency of Donald Trump and Great Britain's vote to leave the European Union. Yet he is clear that these are just two pertinent examples of a general trend, one in which liberalism is being fractured to the point that it can no longer be considered a coherent driving story of humanity. He suggests that the concepts of liberty and equality are increasingly given to individual interpretation, with leaders such as Trump and proponents of Brexit mixing in illiberal ideas. The qualities of certain liberal principles—democracy, civil rights, religious freedom—have seemingly become arguable. This shift is aided by disruptive technological development, including channels that exacerbate confusion between opinion and fact, as well as by societal apprehension caused by events such as the global financial crisis, massive population movement, and devastating natural disasters. The result is a widespread resurgence of nationalism, an earlier and more localized guiding story than liberalism, communism, or fascism (though it played into all three). And while nationalism can take many forms, Harari warns against the apparent rise of inequality and prejudices based on factors including skin tone, national origin, mental or physical handicaps, gender identity, and religion.

After establishing many of the broad themes and concerns in the introduction and first chapter, Harari subsequently tackles narrower subjects, though all are complex and intertwined. In general, the author lays out his view of the current state of each issue, forecasts the challenges and choices ahead, and then discusses potential ways to prepare for and cope with what the future holds. Lesson number two, for instance—titled "Work: When You Grow Up, You Might Not Have a Job"—examines the impact of increasing automation on the job market. As proves typical throughout the book, the warnings are nothing new: the rise of robotics will eventually supplant humans in the performance of repetitive labor, while the advantages of artificial intelligence (AI) in storing and comparing data will make inroads into human cognitive superiority. It is highly possible that soon millions of human employees will become obsolete. Harari's discussion of solutions for the problem are also not particularly groundbreaking: individuals must become more creative in finding niches and concentrate on supplemental roles related to the advanced technologies, while governments should be prepared and consider legislative measures such as a universal basic income (UBI) that might help ease the transition to a heavily automated economy. Instead, it is the author's coherent and thought-provoking presentation of the issues at play, especially for general audiences, that is the real strength of the book.

Parts 2 through 5 continue to build upon the premises established in the first part. Harari touches upon dozens of tangential facets of the human experience that may or may not be relevant for individual readers, but it is probable that everyone will find something to latch onto. There are discussions of community and personal identity, religion versus science, and the ownership of data as the new standard of wealth. The author ventures far and wide in his arguments, drawing upon diverse resources—from Confucius and Buddha to Mark Zuckerberg and Joseph Goebbels—in an effort to give shape to abstract ideas. Fittingly, his final lesson comes the closest to truly imparting a teaching, as he advocates for meditation and mindfulness as a way to approach any situation or eventuality. Though this practice may not help all readers achieve peace of mind, it is arguably the clearest step any individual can take to face the many challenges of the present and future.

The tone of *21 Lessons* varies from pedantic to philosophical to jocular; in his passion to bring understanding to his theses, Harari sometimes explains too much. Other times, his thoughts turn generic or simplistic, giving the reader nothing to grasp. These flaws were noted in many reviews, which also tended to note the overlap between the book and Harari's previous works. Gavin Jacobson, in a review for *New Statesman*, even considered *21 Lessons* a failure on the whole. Yet though the book is inconsistent, it is seldom completely uninteresting, as indicated by the overall largely positive critical reception. Harari has an ability to startle with a well-expressed truth or controversial opinion. And most reviewers agreed that his skillful writing outweighs any missteps, especially as a primer for general readers rather than an academic-focused work.

Jack Ewing

Review Sources

Gates, Bill. "What Are the Biggest Problems Facing Us in the 21st Century?" Review of *21 Lessons for the 21st Century*, by Yuval Noah Harari. *The New York Times*, 4 Sept. 2018, www.nytimes.com/2018/09/04/books/review/21-lessons-for-the-21st-century-yuval-noah-harari.html. Accessed 23 Jan. 2019.

Jacobson, Gavin. "Yuval Noah Harari's 21 Lessons for the 21st Century is a Banal and Risible Self-Help Book." Review of *21 Lessons for the 21st Century*, by Yuval Noah Harari. *New Statesman America*, 22 Aug. 2018, www.newstatesman.com/culture/books/2018/08/yuval-noah-harari-s-21-lessons-21st-century-banal-and-risible-self-help-book. Accessed 23 Jan. 2019.

Lewis, Helen. "21 Lessons for the 21st Century by Yuval Noah Harari Review—A Guru for Our Times?" *The Guardian*, 15 Aug. 2018, www.theguardian.com/books/2018/aug/15/21-lessons-for-the-21st-century-by-yuval-noah-harari-review. Accessed 23 Jan. 2019.

O'Toole, Fintan. "'21 Lessons for the 21st Century': A Wake-Up Call about Humanity's Future." Review of *21 Lessons for the 21st Century*, by Yuval Noah Harari. *The Irish Times*, 13 Oct. 2018, www.irishtimes.com/culture/books/21-lessons-for-the-21st-century-a-wake-up-call-about-humanity-s-future-1.3644653. Accessed 23 Jan. 2019.

Review of *21 Lessons for the 21st Century*, by Yuval Noah Harari. *Publishers Weekly*, 25 June 2018, www.publishersweekly.com/978-0-525-51217-2. Accessed 23 Jan. 2019.

The 7½ Deaths of Evelyn Hardcastle

Author: Stuart Turton
First published: *The Seven Deaths of Evelyn Hardcastle*, 2018, in the United Kingdom
Publisher: Sourcebooks Landmark (Naperville, IL). 432 pp.
Type of work: Novel
Time: Early twentieth century
Locale: Blackheath Estate, near the village of Abberly, England

The 7½ Deaths of Evelyn Hardcastle, Stuart Turton's first novel, mimics the form and setting of a vintage Agatha Christie murder mystery, but with a twist: his narrator jumps from body to body, witnessing the same events from different characters' perspectives as he attempts to solve—or prevent—a murder.

Principal characters

AIDEN BISHOP, body-shifting narrator
LORD PETER AND LADY HELENA HARDCASTLE, owners of Blackheath House
EVELYN HARDCASTLE, their daughter
MICHAEL HARDCASTLE, their surviving son
THOMAS HARDCASTLE, their youngest son
ANNABELLE "ANNA" CAULKER, a mysterious woman
DANIEL COLERIDGE, a professional gambler
PLAGUE DOCTOR, a strange figure dressed in the beak-like mask of a seventeenth-century doctor
THE FOOTMAN, a Blackheath servant
TED STANWIN, a former gamekeeper rewarded for trying to save Thomas
SEBASTIAN BELL, a doctor
ROGER COLLINS, the butler

The 7½ Deaths of Evelyn Hardcastle, published in the United Kingdom as *The Seven Deaths of Evelyn Hardcastle* (2018), is a clever and twisty first novel that Carrie O'Grady for the *Guardian* described as "*Quantum Leap* meets Agatha Christie," with elements of the board game Clue and a British manor house setting that brings to mind the popular PBS television series *Downton Abbey* (2010–15). Like the classic Agatha Christie mystery *And Then There Were None* (1939), *The 7½ Deaths of Evelyn Hardcastle* begins with a group of people of different ages and backgrounds who have been brought together at an English country estate, Blackheath House, for a

Stuart Turton is a freelance British journalist with a degree in English and philosophy. He spent five years traveling the world, working along the way as a bookseller, writing teacher, and travel writer. He was the winner of the Brighton and Hove Short Story Prize. The 7 1/2 Deaths of Evelyn Hardcastle is his first novel.

party. Blackheath had been abandoned by the Hardcastle family years ago and now has a derelict, decaying appearance, despite attempts to spruce it up for the party. Nearly twenty years ago, tragedy struck the Hardcastles when their youngest child, Thomas, was senselessly murdered by a drunken groundskeeper, Charlie Carver. Rumors, however, suggest that there was more to the story. Some say that Carver was having an affair with Lady Helena Hardcastle; some even suggest that she was responsible for her son's death, but that Carver took the blame for her. Others say Helena blames her daughter, Evelyn, for Michael's death, because Evelyn was supposed to be keeping an eye on her young brother.

Now, nineteen years later, friends and family are gathered at Blackheath to celebrate Evelyn's engagement. What should be a happy occasion is instead a time of tension and resentment. Because of the family's financial troubles, Evelyn is being married off to the much older Lord Ravencourt, a wealthy banker. Desperately unhappy with her situation, and still feeling guilt from her brother's death, Evelyn pulls out a pistol in front of all the guests and shoots herself through the heart. Or at least, that is what seems to happen. Aiden Bishop, the protagonist of *The 7½ Deaths of Evelyn Hardcastle*, believes Evelyn was murdered, and he is determined to find out who killed her. In fact, he has to find out who murdered her, or he will be forced to relive the day's events again and again, each time inhabiting a different guest's body.

As the story opens, Bishop inhabits the body of drug-dealing doctor Sebastian Bell. He is being chased through the woods at night by an unknown killer, while trying to find and help a woman named Anna. He has no idea where he is or even who he is. He hears a shot. A silver compass is dropped into his pocket. A voice whispers in his ear: "East." The tense, highly suspenseful opening of the novel might make readers expect a taut, fast-paced thriller, but a great deal of the middle section of the book is spent examining issues of identity, showing Bishop adjusting to different host bodies, and filling in the increasingly complicated backstory of both Thomas Hardcastle's murder nineteen years ago and Evelyn Hardcastle's mysterious death. When Bishop finds himself in the body of Sebastian Bell, he is amnesiac and completely disoriented; not only does he not remember his original identity, he knows nothing about his host. As he moves into different hosts, Bishop's own past remains largely a mystery to him, but he gains a greater awareness of lives of the people he inhabits. He learns to work with the gifts and limitations of each host to solve Evelyn's murder. Sometimes he is able to think ahead and leave clues for a future host to find. In other cases, as with the profligate, lustful Jonathan Derby, he finds it hard to control the impulses of the bodies he inhabits.

The 7½ Deaths of Evelyn Hardcastle comes with a map of Blackheath and a facsimile invitation that lists some of the guests. There are many more characters than those listed, however, which can occasionally lead to some confusion. The plot twists and turns are also so complicated that readers may find themselves looking back, trying to remember what happened several hosts ago. Turton told *Publishers Weekly* that he set out to devise "the most complicated murder mystery imaginable," one that required a spreadsheet, multiple notebooks, and "the world's largest supply of Post-it notes" to craft. About halfway through, the momentum of the story seems to slow a little, caught up in the constant character changes and multiple subplots, but the final third of the novel returns to form, heightening the time constraints and pushing the pace to solve the mystery as Bishop understands more about who he is, who Anna is, and what is at stake for both of them. We also, for the first time, get a glimpse of the larger world beyond Blackheath and learn that Bishop's strange identity-hopping is not an accident.

The American hardcover dust jacket of *The 7½ Deaths of Evelyn Hardcastle* recalls the 1920s with an eye-catching art deco design, shades of black, gold, and red, with small, iconic images of elements from the book: including the murder weapon, a chess piece, and a compass. With its rambling country estate complete with boathouse and stables, a huge house staffed by servants, and upper-class characters who seem to have all the time in the world for sipping cocktails and exchanging gossip, *The 7½ Deaths of Evelyn Hardcastle* may appeal to nostalgia for the early years of the twentieth century, much as *Downton Abbey* did. Turton, however, has stated that he did not intend to glorify the golden age of the British aristocracy, but in fact cast a critical eye on the social inequities of the era. Many of the upper-crust characters who inhabit the world of Blackheath, while outwardly glamorous, are revealed as corrupt, selfish, weak, or even downright evil. In an early scene, Evelyn tells Sebastian about her parents' plan to bring her back to the site of her brother's death. When he asks why they would be so cruel, she replies, "Wealth is poisonous to the soul."

The 7½ Deaths of Evelyn Hardcastle presents a confusing mirror world where things and people are not always what they seem. Foes may turn into allies, and those who seem to be victims may turn out to be villains. Bishop must solve a murder that is going to happen, and even though his conscience tells him he should prevent it, he also knows that in another timeline, it has already happened. Turton's narrative touches lightly on some common aspects of the time travel paradox and whether it is possible to alter the future, but for the most part, he avoids discussion of the how and why of the body swapping and repeating events, whether they are science or magic. Some revelations do come at the end about who is orchestrating Bishop's continuous return, as well why the Plague Doctor is encouraging Bishop to find Evelyn's killer, but readers are still likely to be left with questions. *The 7½ Deaths of Evelyn Hardcastle* is neither fantasy nor science fiction, but primarily a mystery that few readers are likely to solve until the end.

The *7½ Deaths of Evelyn Hardcastle* was named to the October 2018 IndieNext List by the American Bookseller's Association. The British edition was shortlisted for the 2018 Costa First Novel Award and the 2018 Historical Writers' Association Debut Crown Award. Reviews of both the British and American editions were almost universally positive in praising the book's originality, unusual structure, intricate plotting, and ability to keep readers guessing until the very end. Many reviewers compared Turton to Agatha Christie, whose stylized mysteries often featured multiple plot twists, along with murders committed in an upper-class drawing-room setting. *Library Journal* recommended the novel, praising Turton's expert handling of the complicated plot. *Booklist*'s review also commended Turton's ability to keep the reader immersed in a complex plotline with multiple characters.

While most reviewers felt that *The 7½ Deaths of Evelyn Hardcastle* was ingeniously constructed, a few found it lacking in character development and emotional resonance. *Kirkus Reviews* acknowledged that the novel was "fiendishly clever and amusing . . . with explosive surprises," but thought that Turton's writing lacked "genuine feeling," and so failed to connect with the audience emotionally. O'Grady called the novel an "intellectual thriller," comparing it to a dazzling fireworks display, but also noted an emotional distance in the writing. *Publishers Weekly* wrote that the complicated plot twists might delight readers who love solving puzzles while frustrating others. Of course, the same might be said for many classic mysteries, and most reviews seem to agree that Turton accomplished what he set out to do: write the most complicated murder mystery ever.

Kathryn Kulpa, MA, MLIS

Review Sources

Jorgenson, Jane. Review of *The 7½ Deaths of Evelyn Hardcastle*, by Stuart Turton. *Library Journal*, 1 July 2018, p.57. *Literary Reference Center Plus*, search. ebscohost.com/login.aspx?direct=true&db=lkh&AN=130388480&site=lrc-plus. Accessed 28 Dec. 2018.

McMahon, Fiona. Review of *The 7½ Deaths of Evelyn Hardcastle*, by Stuart Turton. *Booklist*, 1 May 2018, p.20. *Literary Reference Center Plus*, search.ebscohost. com/login.aspx?direct=true&db=lkh&AN=129481505&site=lrc-plus. Accessed 28 Dec. 2018.

O'Grady, Carrie. "The Seven Deaths of Evelyn Hardcastle by Stuart Turton Review—Quantum Leap Meets Agatha Christie." Review of *The 7½ Deaths of Evelyn Hardcastle*, by Stuart Turton. *The Guardian*, 3 Mar. 2018, www.theguardian. com/books/2018/mar/03/the-seven-deaths-of-evelyn-hardcastle-by-stuart-turton-review. Accessed 28 Dec. 2018.

Review of *The 7½ Deaths of Evelyn Hardcastle*, by Stuart Turton. *Kirkus Reviews*, 15 July 2018, p.1. *Literary Reference Center Plus*, search.ebscohost.com/login.as px?direct=true&db=lkh&AN=130679903&site=lrc-plus. Accessed 28 Dec. 2018.

Review of *The 7½ Deaths of Evelyn Hardcastle*, by Stuart Turton. *Publishers Weekly*, 9 July 2018, pp.66–67. *Literary Reference Center Plus*, search.ebscohost. com/login.aspx?direct=true&db=lkh&AN=130580783&site=lrc-plus. Accessed 28 Dec. 2018.

"Spotlight on Stuart Turton." *Publishers Weekly*, 11 May 2018, www.publishersweekly.com/pw/by-topic/authors/profiles/article/76860-spotlight-on-stuart-turton.html. Accessed 28 Dec. 2018.

All We Ever Wanted

Author: Emily Giffin (b. 1972)
Publisher: Ballantine Books (New York).
  352 pp.
Type of work: Novel
Time: Present day
Locale: Nashville, Tennessee

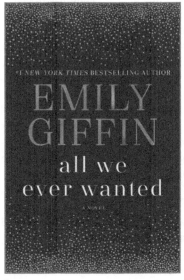

Courtesy of Random House

Though Nina Browning's life seems to be perfect on the surface, she is beginning to realize how much of a lie she has been living. When her son pulls what he considers a foolish prank on an innocent girl, Nina must choose to continue denying her unhappiness or confront the problems in her marriage and family.

Principal characters
NINA BROWNING, wealthy socialite wife and mother
KIRK BROWNING, her husband
FINCH BROWNING, her son
LYLA VOLPE, victim of bullying
TOM VOLPE, Lyla's father

In a year when the #MeToo movement has raised awareness of sexual harassment, when Bill Cosby has been found guilty of sexual assault, and a Supreme Court nominee has been accused of sexual misconduct from his high school years, Emily Giffin's ninth novel seems predestined to become a best seller, as *All We Ever Wanted* confronts this same problem alongside issues of privilege and racism.

When Lyla Volpe, a scholarship sophomore at a local private high school in Nashville, attends a party at the home of one of the popular senior boys, she becomes the victim of a terrible situation. At some point in the party, she has drunk so much that she passes out on the boy's bed. Someone at the party takes advantage of her lack of consciousness and takes a photo using the phone of another popular and wealthy senior, Finch Browning. The picture of a drunk girl, however, is not the only problem. The fact that her breast shows in the picture takes it squarely into the realm of sexual harassment. The photo's caption—"Looks like she got her green card"—takes it into the realm of racism. When the photo goes viral, it potentially becomes a legal issue. Giffin's novel presents the repercussions of this action on the Browning and Volpe families.

These events are presented through a structure of short chapters narrated in first person by the main characters of the novel: Nina Browning, Tom Volpe, and Lyla Volpe. The main character, Nina, narrates nineteen chapters. As the mother of the accused teen, Nina's chapters show a mother struggling to understand where her parenting went wrong and how or why her only son could do something so vile. These chapters also give readers the main insight into her husband, Kirk, and a realistic look at her son, Finch. A second focus is on Tom Volpe, who narrates nine chapters. Tom's passages introduce a single dad who is doing his best to raise a teenage daughter. Giffin also gives the teenage victim a voice, and Lyla narrates eight chapters, including the epilogue. Lyla's chapters provide the teenage victim's point of view. This interchange between the mother of the accused, the father of the victim, and the victim herself shows the different ways people process an abusive situation.

From a thematic angle, the novel addresses a variety of topics. The most obvious would be the actual problem of the sexually charged bullying. Nina recognizes the problem immediately, surprisingly sympathizing

All We Ever Wanted *is Emily Giffin's ninth novel. After graduating from Wake Forest University and the University of Virginia School of Law, Giffin worked as a lawyer for several years before turning to writing full time.*

with Lyla rather than with her own son. As she struggles with trying to comprehend what would make Finch do such a horrible thing, Nina faces the reality that her marriage is failing, and that her relationship with her son has irrevocably changed. Her sympathy for Lyla forces Nina to deal with a situation from her own youth: she was raped by an acquaintance while in college. She begins to admit that she made life choices based on that rape and her refusal to admit it publicly. In contrast, Nina's husband, Kirk, cannot understand his wife's desire to make sure a teenage girl they do not know is handling the situation in a healthy way. He even shrugs off the seriousness of the situation, telling his wife, "C'mon, Nina. This wasn't a *dick* pic. It was a little side boob." Finch sees his mother's empathy for the girl as a way to manipulate both Nina and Lyla. He acts remorseful, leading his mother to take him to Lyla's home to apologize. His act is good enough that both Nina and Tom believe that he wants to make amends, so when he asks to talk to Lyla alone, they allow it. Lyla has had a crush on Finch for quite some time, and he uses her attraction to become closer to her, encouraging her to believe that his girlfriend jealously took the photo with his phone. This manipulation confuses Lyla, who is so embarrassed by the whole thing that she just wants it to go away. She does not want to pursue charges against Finch; instead, she allows her crush to overwhelm her common sense, and she not only spends time alone with him without letting her dad or Finch's mother know, she eventually has sex with him, something she will later regret. Tom's involvement is on the sidelines. The single dad wants to protect his daughter, but he recognizes that a gap has grown between them, so he is not sure how to handle the situation. As a result, he often lets

© Emmanuelle Choussy

anger and frustration reign, alienating his daughter.

The racial bullying reflected in the caption that went out with the picture is problematic as well. Kirk tries to brush the photo's caption aside by noting that "it's a *little* racist," and Lyla's reaction is not strong either. She simply says it "was so rude to immigrants." Tom, Nina, and the school's headmaster are among the few who recognize the depth of the racial comment, so it takes distant second place behind the sexual and social problems evidenced in the other themes.

Another noteworthy theme focuses on the contrast between wealthy and working-class people. Nina, who comes from a middle-class family, understands the depth of the problem behind Finch's behavior, hoping that "he wouldn't lie, that he'd instead launch into a heartfelt apology for mocking a defenseless female peer, hurling a racist insult at her, insinuating that she was beneath him or somehow did not belong." Her husband and son, on the other hand, seem oblivious to the damage that Finch's actions have caused. Instead, Kirk uses his great wealth to try to buy his way out of any punishment for Finch, reminding the school's headmaster that the Brownings have donated large sums to the school. He also offers Tom a $15,000 bribe to forget that the photo was taken. Tom refuses to keep the money, returning it to Nina at a later time. Kirk's elitist attitude has rubbed off on Finch, who thinks nothing about spending hundreds of dollars on concert tickets which, in his own way, works as a bribe to keep Lyla from pursuing a complaint. Even the woman that Nina feels is one of her closest friends suggests that the Volpes are beneath notice because Tom is a working man and Lyla a scholarship student. This kind of entitlement, in combination with other marital problems, eventually leads Nina to decide that her marriage is over.

Marriage and parenting are additional thematic concerns addressed in the novel. Nina's realization that the comfortable life she has been living is not as wonderful as other people believe forces her to take action to change. She is frightened by a "glint of determination in Finch's eyes. Something that channeled his father and made me shiver a little inside." However, her husband's attitude bothers her more: "It was a foreign concept to Kirk—that something would actually be out of his *control*—and although in the past I'd found this quality attractive, it now filled me with disdain bordering on disgust." She makes a final decision about the end of her marriage when, in addition to Kirk's attitude problems, she faces the reality that he has had several affairs. Nina also feels guilty about Finch's actions based on the simple fact that she is his mother. She wants to believe in her son, but the evidence against him is overwhelming.

Tom's marriage and parenting are also highlighted. Though he is currently a single father, he was married when Lyla was small. His relationship with Lyla's mother was passionate, but when she chose to spend time flirting with another man rather than tending after their then four-year-old child, the marriage ended. In the following years, Lyla's mother only popped into her life at unexpected moments, complicating the girl's relationship with her strict father. Tom is never abusive, but he does have a hard time controlling his temper when his daughter's well-being is at stake. He learns to tamp down his anger as he realizes that his volatile reactions have the potential to damage her emotional state.

Friendship is a final key thematic idea in the novel. Nina has two women she considers close friends: Melanie and Julie. Melanie is a member of the same wealthy class as Nina and her husband, and she lives in Nashville. The two women have raised their children together, working together on school and charity events. In contrast, Julie is Nina's childhood friend. She is a middle-class lawyer who lives in Nina's less prestigious hometown. It does not take long to determine that Julie is the real friend, the one who will stick by Nina and be honest with her as the events unfold. Tom only has one real friend, Bonnie, an older woman for whom he had done some carpentry work in exchange for quiet counseling. Lyla's friendship with a classmate as well as a potential friendship with Finch's girlfriend are also explored. The most important friendship, however, is an unexpected one that develops between Nina and Tom.

The combination of well-developed, plausible characters who narrate their own versions of the events alongside relevant contemporary themes will keep the interest of readers despite the somewhat predictable aspect of the answers to the questions of what really happened.

Theresa L. Stowell, PhD

Review Sources
Review of *All We Ever Wanted*, by Emily Giffin. *Kirkus Reviews*, 15 May 2018, www.kirkusreviews.com/book-reviews/emily-giffin/all-we-ever-wanted/. Accessed 24 Sept. 2018.
Review of *All We Ever Wanted*, by Emily Giffin. *Publishers Weekly*, June 2018, www.publishersweekly.com/9780399178924. Accessed 24 Sept. 2018.
Marry, Jan. Review of *All We Ever Wanted*, by Emily Giffin. *Library Journal*, 15 June 2018, pp. 64–65. *Academic Search Complete*, search.ebscohost.com/login.as px?direct=true&db=a9h&AN=129963573. Accessed 24 Sept. 2018.
Walthen, LynnDee. Review of *All We Ever Wanted*, by Emily Giffin. *Booklist*, 15 May 2018, p. 20. *Academic Search Complete*, search.ebscohost.com/login.aspx?d irect=true&db=f6h&AN=129728607. Accessed 24 Sept. 2018.

American Histories

Author: John Edgar Wideman (b. 1941)
Publisher: Scribner (New York). 240 pp.
Type of work: Short fiction
Time: Unknown
Locale: United States

American Histories *is a short-story collec-*
tion that explores the legacy of slavery. It is
written by the prolific African American au-
thor John Edgar Wideman.

In many ways, *American Histories* (2018) is
an extension of its author's previous work.
John Edgar Wideman is a writer who, prior
to *American Histories*, was best known for
his Homewood trilogy. The book series ex-

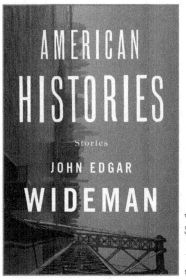

Courtesy of Scribner

plores the day-to-day life of the African American community in Pittsburgh, Pennsylvania, where Wideman grew up. Consisting of the novels *Hiding Place* (1981) and
Sent for You Yesterday (1983) as well as the short-story collection *Damballah* (1981),
the Homewood trilogy established Wideman's reputation as one of the most important
literary voices of his generation. Much of this acclaim stemmed from Wideman's incredible talent for providing intimate, nuanced insight into the experience of being an
African American man. *American Histories* continues this tradition powerfully.

    American Histories examines the legacy of slavery in the United States through a
collection of short stories. The author makes this clear in the book's first chapter, titled
"A Prefatory Note." Written as a letter, Wideman makes a plea to the current unnamed
president to eradicate slavery. He notes that although the Thirteenth Amendment tech-
nically abolished slavery in 1865, it endures as a social condition. To this day, the color
of someone's skin determines the oppression that they experience and, subsequently,
the quality of their life. Wideman writes that "history tells as many lies as truths." The
rest of the book aims to prove just this—that despite what scholars say, slavery never
ended. The author posits that unless something is done, it will continue until there are
"only two human beings left alive, neither one strong enough to enslave the other." Ultimately, the sentiments of "A Prefatory Note" establish *American Histories'* purpose:
using short stories to rewrite the lies that are accepted as historical fact.

    The twenty-one short stories that make up *American History* are linked by this goal
as well as the theme of slavery's legacy. Beyond these two commonalities, however,
they feel completely disparate. Some of the book's stories revolve around famous
historical figures such as Nat Turner, the leader of a slave revolt. Others are more like
biographical essays and focus on Wideman's family. One critiques the Korean film
The Yellow Sea (2010) and the American film *Precious* (2009). Another is told from

the first-person perspective of a suicidal man thinking about jumping off the Williamsburg Bridge in New York City. No matter the topic, however, the issue of race is omnipresent, inescapable—as it is for many African American men. Ultimately, Wideman is writing about being a human being onto whom the world continues to push discriminatory labels.

Another factor that prevents *American Histories* from feeling like a traditional collection of short stories is Wideman's literary style, which continues to evolve throughout the book. Some stories are no more than a couple paragraphs in length, while most go on for pages. Similarly, the tone, perspective, and structure change depending on the story. This decision effectively keeps readers on their toes—it is impossible to acclimate and sink into the book's flow because this flow is disrupted continually. Furthermore, by resisting an overarching feeling, each story can function as a standalone piece and be analyzed independently. "JB & FD," for example, is written as an imagined conversation between the white abolitionist John Brown and the African American abolitionist orator Frederick Douglass. Brown argues that abolitionists and enslaved people must pick up arms and fight to end slavery. Douglass counters that Brown's intentions are good, but his solution to the problem may be wrong. It is essentially a think piece that explores the options of violence and nonviolence as potential solutions to the problem of slavery.

In "Writing Teacher," Wideman goes in quite a different direction by depicting the experience of an African American professor trying to help a white student named Teresa McConnell improve her story about a woman of color experiencing racism. "Writing Teacher" is written in the first person with a confessional tone, making it easy to assume that Wideman himself is the narrator considering his teaching career at Brown University. The purpose of this piece is to question whether white people should ever write the stories of people of color—even if their intentions are good. Contrarily, the narrator wonders if it is even possible for him to help Teresa. Unlike "JB & FD" and many of the book's other stories, "Writing Teacher" seems grounded in the present and feels like an essay rather than a work of fiction.

Although each story within the collection is completely different than the others, Wideman's voice maintains a powerful connective thread. His distinct writing style has a kind of musicality to it. His sentences are poetic and rhythmic, such that they emanate a performative quality. Many passages seem as though they are written to be read aloud rather than just sit on the page. The short story "Dark Matter" demonstrates this. It is a series of passages that all begin with the words "we go out to dinner," and then Wideman describes what he and his unnamed companion subsequently discuss. Each passage is a single run-on sentence encapsulating everything they talk about in that evening. The passages are separated by asterisks, one of the author's favorite tools, which gives a stop-go cadence to his writing. Critics have long described Wideman's writing as lyrical and noted its celebration of the African American vernacular; this style continues in *American Histories*.

There is a raw, vulnerable quality to much of the book thanks to the fact that Wideman puts so much of himself into each installment. Sometimes, the presence of his life is there on the fringes, indirectly informing the story; other times it is the focus.

© Jean-Christian Bourcart

John Edgar Wideman is the author of some twenty books and professor emeritus of Africana studies and literary arts at Brown University. He is a two-time winner of the PEN/Faulkner Award for Fiction and a recipient of the MacArthur genius grant.

"My Dead" is a personal essay that begins with the author listing the full names, birth dates, and death dates of his family members who have died, including his mother, father, two brothers, and niece. "Lines" describes a character waiting to see someone in prison and experiencing déjà vu at a motel nearby. "Maps and Ledgers" is about a black man just launching an academic career when he learns that his father has been accused of murdering a friend. The untimely deaths and incarceration of family members are personal to Wideman, whose brother and son were both incarcerated for murder. Furthermore, they happen disproportionately more to African American citizens and are a part of slavery's legacy.

American Histories is difficult to compare to other books because it is so unique. In some ways, it feels like Zadie Smith's *Feel Free* (2018), a collection of essays that explore diverse topics and life experiences from an academic perspective. Both *American Histories* and *Feel Free* have an ambitious scope and are intent on getting to the truth about what it means to be human. However, *Feel Free* is more traditional and does not contain any short stories. The fiction of *American Histories* can be compared to the work of Toni Cade Bambara, an author best known for her short stories. Wideman and Bambara both use the medium to capture small moments of African American life with colorful vernacular and vivid descriptions.

Reviews for *American Histories* have been predominantly positive. Most critics have praised Wideman's talent for seamlessly blending autobiographical anecdotes with fiction. *Kirkus Reviews* highlighted this by stating, "Wideman's recent work strides into the gap between fiction and nonfiction as a means of disclosing hard, painful, and necessary truths." Similarly, the reviewer for *Publishers Weekly* remarked, "Each story feels new, challenging, and exhilarating, beguilingly combining American history with personal history." Readers looking for a new kind of short story, one that provides them with an in-depth experience of what it means to be African American today, will find *American Histories* to be fulfilling. Wideman uses his stories to depict racism in new ways. He presents small moments of prejudice with the same gravity as slavery and, in turn, demonstrates the way that racism creeps into every corner of life. It is difficult to finish *American Histories* without feeling as though the country is in desperate need of change.

Wideman's experimental literary style has been most well received by critics; however, it may deter some readers. Anyone interested in reading *American Histories* casually because they enjoy short stories might find the unorthodox style, meandering prose, and unusual structure to be somewhat impenetrable. In her review for the *New York Times*, Martha Southgate concluded, "I found the digressiveness of this collection frustrating at times—it's not a likable or easily accessible book. But in this case, that's not a criticism. 'American Histories' is not here to be liked. It's here to challenge you. And that it does." Simply put, Wideman makes his readers work to get to the meaningful messages he is trying to express. Not everyone will enjoy this labor. Others will find it deeply rewarding and appreciate his ability to take them somewhere they have never been.

Overall, Wideman has accomplished something remarkable with *American Histories*: he has blended history with fiction and biography to craft a collection of powerful short stories that are arguably some of the most important of the year. In addition to pushing the genre into an experimental direction, these short stories are likely to reshape the way readers think. As Colin Grant wrote for the *Guardian*, "The acutely immersive world of American Histories is irresistible, and these profoundly moving stories will haunt you long after you've finished reading." Intelligent, challenging, and poetic, *American Histories* not only showcases the formidable talent of Wideman but also presents the legacy of slavery in a new and important way.

Emily Turner

Review Sources

Review of *American Histories*, by John Edgar Wideman. *Kirkus Reviews*, Feb. 2018,
    p. 61. *Literary Reference Center Plus*, search.ebscohost.com/login.aspx?direct=tr
    ue&db=lkh&AN=127646376&site=lrc-plus. Accessed 23 Jan. 2019.
Review of *American Histories*, by John Edgar Wideman. *Publisher Weekly*, Jan.
    2018, p. 164. *Literary Reference Center Plus*, search.ebscohost.com/login.aspx?di
    rect=true&db=lkh&AN=127654710&site=lrc-plus. Accessed 23 Jan. 2019.
Grant, Colin. Review of *American Histories*, by John Edgar Wideman. *The Guard-
    ian*, 30 May 2018, www.theguardian.com/books/2018/may/30/american-histories-
    john-edgar-wideman-review. Accessed 23 Jan. 2019.
Southgate, Martha. "In Stories about Slavery and Its Legacy, Hints of the Author's
    Life." Review of *American Histories*, by John Edgar Wideman. *The New York
    Times*, 13 Apr. 2018,   www.nytimes.com/2018/04/13/books/review/john-edgar-
    wideman-american-histories.html. Accessed 23 Jan. 2019.

American Sonnets for My Past and Future Assassin

Author: Terrance Hayes (b. 1971)
Publisher: Penguin Books (New York). 112 pp.
Type of work: Poetry

Terrance Hayes's sixth collection of poems, American Sonnets for My Past and Future Assassin, *explores American life after the election of Donald Trump to the presidency.*

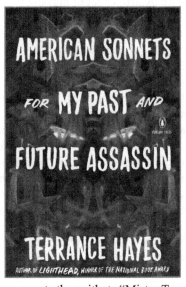

Courtesy of Pegasus

New York Times critic Parul Sehgal described Terrance Hayes's new poetry collection, *American Sonnets to My Past and Future Assassin*, as one of "the first fully-fledged works to reckon with the presidency of Donald Trump." None of the seventy poems in the collection call Trump out by name—unless one counts the epithets "Mister Trumpet," "Humpty-Dumpty," or "failed landlord with a people of color complex"—but rather they explore the changed atmosphere of the country following his 2016 election through Hayes's eyes. His vision is full of contradictions. The collection is both, as Hayes writes, "a record of my raptures" and a lamentation for "all the black people I'm tired of losing." As Sehgal wrote, this duality suggests a deeper ambivalence. Of America, he writes: "It is not enough / To love you. It is not enough to want you destroyed."

In *American Sonnets*, pain is expressed in the classic form of the love poem, though other elements of the sonnet are invoked and subverted according to Hayes's vision. A sonnet, from a word meaning a "little song," traditionally contains fourteen lines and a volta, or turn, "that introduces into the poem a possibility for transformation, like a moment of grace," Phyllis Levin wrote in the introduction to the book *The Penguin Book of the Sonnet: 500 Years of a Classic Tradition in English* (2001). Hayes was inspired by Wanda Coleman's *American Sonnets*, which were published in 1994 and influenced by jazz rhythms. The book's epigraph ("bring me / to where / my blood runs") comes from a Coleman poem. By design, the title of every poem in the book is "American Sonnets for My Past and Future Assassin," and the questions at the heart of each, Hayes told Don Share and Lindsay Garbutt on a podcast for *Poetry* magazine in September 2017, are "what is an American sonnet and who is the assassin?"

A recipient of a MacArthur "genius" grant, Hayes grew up in South Carolina, the son of a prison guard and a veteran, and went on to study poetry in graduate school with Toi Derricotte, the cofounder of the Cave Canem Foundation, at the University of Pittsburgh. His first book, *Muscular Music* (1999), won the Kate Tufts Discovery Award. His other collections include *Hip Logic* (2002) and *Wind in a Box* (2006).

Hayes's fourth book of poems, *Lighthead* (2010), won the National Book Award for Poetry in 2010. Both of his next books, 2015's *How to Be Drawn* and *American Sonnets*, were finalists for the National Book Award. All of his books have featured sonnets, and all of those sonnets explore the limits of the form. For example, one sonnet in *Hip Logic* consists of the line "We sliced the watermelon into smiles" repeated fourteen times. The phrase is iambic pentameter, a common sonnet stipulation. Critic Stephen Burt, who wrote a profile of Hayes for the *New York Times Magazine* in March 2015, observed that when students talk about Hayes "they talk about the underlying seriousness of poems about lynchings, fistfights or rape. But when poets talk about Hayes, they tend to address his invented forms."

As in much of Hayes's early work, *American Sonnets* explores fathers and fatherhood (the poet did not meet his biological father until he was an adult) and his frustrations with the limits of masculinity. In one such sonnet, which opens with "Sometimes the father almost sees looking," Hayes describes looking at his son's face "an openness / Like a wound before it scars." To share features with one's ancestors, Hayes writes, is "To be dead & alive at the same time." In another, he excoriates Trump for his hatred of women. "You ain't allowed to deride / Women when you've never wept in front of a woman / That wasn't your mother," he writes.

Hayes chose to write a collection of sonnets because the form offered a reassuring constraint, a concrete structure in an uncertain time. (Near the beginning of the book, he describes the form as "part music box, part meat / Grinder.") This, of course, does not mean that Hayes is not playful with the form. As Dan Chiasson wrote in his review for the *New Yorker*, "There are formal and rhetorical puzzles in nearly every one of Hayes's poems." One poem invites the reader to guess a word, while another, discreetly alphabetized, as Chiasson pointed out, lists threatening things and people: "All cancers kill me, crashes, cavemen, chakras / Crackers . . ." Following Coleman's lead, Hayes occasionally lets the sounds of words guide him. In one sonnet beginning "The umpteenth thump on the rump of a badunkadunk," Hayes uses the blunt sounds of Trump's name to convey his thudding distaste for the politician.

By contrast, in the collection's first poem, Hayes musically riffs on the beginning of the century for the black poet, writing, "It began with all the poetry weirdos & worriers, warriors / Poetry whiners & winos falling from ship bows, sunset / Bridges & windows." Still, he warns, "In a second I'll tell you how little / Writing rescues." Hayes's poems may not save him, or even help him understand a cruel and unjust world, he writes. To paraphrase the end of the poem, Hayes writes that Orpheus, the musician and poet of Greek myth who appears several times in *American Sonnets*, "was alone when he invented writing." The character drew a picture of an eye with an X drawn through it. "He meant *I am blind without you*. She thought he meant / *I never want to see you again*. It is possible he meant that, too."

Often Hayes's poems require careful unpacking, like the one that begins "I'm not sure how to hold my face when I dance." It evokes the legacy of Jimi Hendrix, a guitarist in the tradition of black music who is best remembered among the ranks of predominantly white hippies. Chiasson identified subtle references to Beat poet Allen Ginsberg's "Howl," a poem that enumerates how Ginsberg and his bohemian friends went mad and, among many other things, "leaped on negroes." "The white bohemians have the freedom to go on benders and sprees, while Hayes must wonder how 'to hold my face,'" Chiasson wrote. "He is not afraid of looking goofy; he is afraid of being murdered."

The collection contains tributes to figures like poet Emily Dickinson, Congresswoman Maxine Waters, poet Amiri Baraka, the musical artist Prince, and writer James Baldwin's face. There are also sonnets that explore other figures in a more somber light. One poem reckons with the legacy of Derek Walcott, a Nobel Prize–winning poet who died in 2017 and reportedly had sexually harassed at least two of his female students. Hayes's elegiac poem takes into full account the #MeToo movement that has sought to reckon with such abuses. Another poem references Emmett Till, a fourteen-year-old boy who was brutally lynched in Money, Mississippi, in 1955. Hayes writes, "a clutch of goons drove you through Money / Stole your money, paid you money, stole it again." He is referencing the historic cycle of America, a country built on stolen (slave) labor that continues to exploit black people.

Terrance Hayes's Lighthead *(2010) won the National Book Award for Poetry, and his collections* How to Be Drawn *(2015) and* American Sonnets for My Past and Future Assassin *(2018) were both finalists for the award. He received a MacArthur Fellowship in 2014.*

American Sonnets for My Past and Future Assassin received enthusiastic reviews when it was published in 2018. A reviewer for *Publishers Weekly* wrote, "Inventive as ever, Hayes confronts America's myriad ills with unflinching candor, while leaving space for love, humor, and hope." Sehgal praised Hayes's love of language, writing in the *New York Times*, "He loves to stuff a line full of sound . . . to write for the ear as well as the eye. His words call to be read aloud, to be tasted." She similarly praised the "different registers" of Hayes's joy and pain. Faraz Rizvi described the book for the *Millions* as "a gift in a fraught moment." The poems within, he wrote, "are timeless, by which I mean these sonnets annihilate any difference between past and future." Rizvi also illuminates one of Hayes's motifs—the recurring line, "There never was a black male hysteria." The phrase comes from a book poet Anthony Butts once wished to write called *Male Hysteria*, but never did. "In a book unwritten, there is neither future nor past—only the possibilities of both," Rizvi wrote.

Cameron Barnett wrote in the *Pittsburgh Post-Gazette* that *American Sonnets* skillfully examines what a world in which a divisive figure like Trump can rise to the nation's highest office means for "Blackness, for fatherhood, for freedom, and for the self." Hayes gives the old sonnet "new agency," he wrote, particularly in his deft voltas. Barnett highlighted two transformative lines within a single poem: "After blackness was invented / People began seeing ghosts," and "Something happens everywhere in this country / Every day. Someone is praying, someone is prey." Barnett also noted that for Hayes, the elusive and ubiquitous assassin can also be found in the self. "Through these poems, readers find themselves caught squarely in the unbeatable peril of the speaker, at once chased by a past America rearing up old ugliness and by a future that appears more mirror than canvas," he wrote.

Molly Hagan

Review Sources

Review of *American Sonnets for My Past and Future Assassin*, by Terrance Hayes.
Publishers Weekly, vol. 265, no. 16, Apr. 2018, p. 70. *Literary Reference Center
Plus*, search.ebscohost.com/login.aspx?direct=true&db=lkh&AN=129089301&sit
e=lrc-plus. Accessed 21 Feb. 2019.

Barnett, Cameron. "'American Sonnets for My Past and Future Assassin' by Terrance Hayes: Pain and Poignancy Collide." Review of *American Sonnets for My
Past and Future Assassin*, by Terrance Hayes. *Pittsburgh Post-Gazette*, 17 June
2018, www.post-gazette.com/ae/books/2018/06/17/American-Sonnets-for-My-
Past-and-Future-Assassin-by-Terrance-Hayes-Pain-and-poignancy-collide/sto-
ries/201805150050. Accessed 21 Feb. 2019.

Chiasson, Dan. "Sonnets and Bullets: The Politics and Play of Terrance Hayes." Review of *American Sonnets for My Past and Future Assassin*, by Terrance Hayes.
The New Yorker, vol. 94, no. 19, 2018, p. 64. *Literary Reference Center Plus*,
search.ebscohost.com/login.aspx?direct=true&db=lkh&AN=130289376&site=l
rc-plus. Accessed 26 Feb. 2019.

Rizvi, Faraz. "A Hole in Time: On Terrance Hayes's 'American Sonnets for My
Past and Future Assassin.'" Review of *American Sonnets for My Past and
Future Assassin*, by Terrance Hayes. *The Millions*, 13 June 2018, themillions.
com/2018/06/a-hole-in-time-on-terrance-hayess-american-sonnets-for-my-past-
and-future-assassin.html. Accessed 21 Feb. 2019.

Sehgal, Parul. "Sonnets That Reckon with Donald Trump's America." Review of
American Sonnets for My Past and Future Assassin, by Terrance Hayes. *The New
York Times*, 19 June 2018, www.nytimes.com/2018/06/19/books/review-terrance-
hayes-american-sonnets-for-my-past-and-future-assassin.html. Accessed 21 Feb.
2019.

An American Marriage

Author: Tayari Jones (b. 1970)
Publisher: Algonquin Books (Chapel Hill, NC). 320 pp.
Type of work: Novel
Time: Present day
Locales: Eloe and Jemison, Louisiana; Atlanta, Georgia

Tayari Jones examines race, class, gender, and the nature of love and relationships in this deeply affecting novel, which focuses on an African American couple whose young marriage is upended after the husband is wrongly imprisoned.

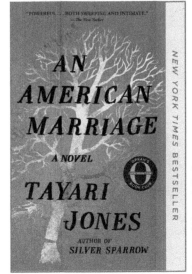

Courtesy of Algonquin Books

Principal characters

ROY HAMILTON, a black man who is wrongly imprisoned for rape
CELESTIAL DAVENPORT, his wife, an artist
ANDRE TUCKER, he and Celestial's friend
ROY "BIG ROY" HAMILTON SR., his father
OLIVE HAMILTON, his mother
FRANKLIN DAVENPORT, his father-in-law
GLORIA DAVENPORT, his mother-in-law

The specter of imprisonment looms large in the lives of African Americans all over the United States, which boasts the highest incarceration rate in the world. According to statistics posted on the website of the National Association for the Advancement of Colored People (NAACP), black Americans made up at least one-third of the US prison population in 2014 and are five times more likely to be arrested than white people. Such racial disparities have long plagued the US criminal justice system but have generally come to be accepted as a disturbing yet often inescapable part of the African American experience. This frightening cultural landscape forms the backdrop of Tayari Jones's fourth novel, *An American Marriage* (2018), which unflinchingly explores what happens to those who are directly affected by that historically unjust system, from the individuals imprisoned to the families, friends, and loved ones left behind.

The premise of Jones's novel treads familiar ground. Roy Hamilton and Celestial Davenport are a young, upwardly mobile black professional couple living in Atlanta, Georgia. Roy is an ambitious, successful representative for a textbook company, and Celestial is a talented and promising artist who specializes in creating high-end bespoke baby dolls called "poupées." They have been married for only eighteen months,

© Nina Subin

Tayari Jones is the author of four novels, including Leaving Atlanta *(2002), which won the Hurston/Wright Legacy Award for Debut Fiction. She was a founding member of the MFA program in creative writing at Rutgers-University–Newark. In 2018, she joined the English faculty at Emory University's College of Arts and Sciences.*

but their partnership is already on shaky ground, dogged by problems not unusual to other new couples. Celestial has suspicions about Roy's fidelity, but she is still grateful for his support and encouragement. Regardless, the couple are undeniably in love, bound by a palpable passion for each other that is "still burning blue hot," as Roy relates in the opening pages.

That love is put to the ultimate test, however, after Roy and Celestial visit Roy's parents, Big Roy and Olive, in his fictional hometown of Eloe, Louisiana, during Labor Day weekend. The visit is already an uneasy one for Celestial, who has not exactly been warmly embraced by Roy's traditional, working-class mother. Unlike Roy, Celestial hails from a privileged background. Her father, Franklin Davenport, is a former high school chemistry teacher who earned millions after inventing a compound that aids in the processing of orange juice, and her mother, Gloria, worked as an assistant superintendent of a school district. She wears "her pedigree like the gloss on a patent-leather shoe" and exhibits a fierce independent streak that, in Olive's eyes, limits her potential for motherhood.

Mother-in-law issues aside, Celestial senses that something is indeed wrong at the outset of the drive to Roy's native Eloe. Roy and Celestial spend the day and have dinner at Roy's parent's house, but instead of sleeping there, they decide to stay at a local hotel. There, the two get into a minor squabble after Roy drops a major revelation about his personal life. To cool off, Roy makes a run to the ice machine, where he has a chance encounter with a woman his mother's age. The woman is impaired by a shoulder injury, prompting Roy to help her with her ice and other matters before returning to his room. Roy and Celestial reconcile but their sleep is violently interrupted after police officers burst into their hotel room and arrest Roy, who is falsely accused of rape by the woman at the ice machine. Despite vigorously maintaining his innocence, Roy is ultimately convicted and sentenced to twelve years in prison.

It is here where Jones subverts reader expectations. Rather than easily turning her novel into a polemic about the institutional oppression of black men, she opts for a more personal and intimate story, one that reveals the devastating effects of forced separation on a married couple. Whatever problems Roy and Celestial had before his wrongful imprisonment are exacerbated tenfold. After opening the novel with separate chapters told from Roy and Celestial's first-person perspectives, Jones chronicles the couple's slow and painful dissolution in the form of letters between the two, an effective and practical creative choice that provides some of the most powerful passages in the novel. The author breathes new life into the lost art form by illustrating the difficulty in translating visceral feelings and emotions into words.

This process proves especially difficult for Roy. In his first letter to Celestial from Louisiana's Parson Correctional Center, he writes, "A love letter is supposed to be like music or like Shakespeare, but I don't know anything about Shakespeare. But for real, I want to tell you what you mean to me, but it's like trying to count the seconds of a day on your fingers and toes." Roy admittedly values actions more than words and his attempts at expressing the latter are at times awkward. As more time passes, however, his letters painfully reflect the helplessness and whirlwind of uncertainty felt by a man unjustly held in prison against his will.

Much of Roy's uncertainty stems from his relationship with Celestial, who herself does not know what the future holds for them. "I'm alone in a way that's more than the fact that I am the only living person within these walls," she writes in her first letter, composed at her and Roy's kitchen table. "Up until now, I thought I knew what was and wasn't possible. Maybe that's what innocence is, having no way to predict the pain of the future." Although shattered by this unfortunate turn of events, Celestial still has career ambitions of her own and is eager to realize them. Jones, consequently, poses an important question to readers that lies at the heart of her novel: should a wife be allowed to pursue her dreams and aspirations, regardless of circumstances surrounding her husband, however horrible they may be?

Early during the novel's epistolary section, it is apparent to readers that the answer to this question, at least as far as Celestial is concerned, is emphatically that she should be allowed to. In the wake of Roy's incarceration, Celestial dives headlong into her art and it is not long before she graduates from private commissions to a public retail space; she is profiled in *Ebony* magazine after winning a contest for a prison-inspired doll. In the interim, Celestial finds solace in her best friend and confidant, Andre, whom she has known since she was three months old. Andre was Roy's dormitory neighbor at Morehouse College, in Atlanta, and was the person who first introduced him to Celestial, who attended nearby Spelman College. It would be four years after that initial meeting, however, before Roy and Celestial started dating seriously.

Although Roy has long been under the impression that Celestial and Andre's relationship is a platonic one, that status is repeatedly called into question as the novel progresses. Letters and visits from Celestial become increasingly irregular, and at one point, Roy is forced to reach out to her father after going several months without hearing from her. Lost in a cloud of agonizing uncertainty, Roy turns to his older cellmate, Walter, for advice and comfort. Besides their relationship, Jones largely does not delve into the minutiae of prison life (though poignant descriptions, such as Roy's efforts to secure a pear he deeply craved, highlight his struggle), instead focusing mostly on Roy and Celestial's dissolving marriage.

Significant plot developments are gradually revealed through their correspondence, and eventually, Celestial writes Roy a letter explaining that she can no longer be his wife, after which Roy breaks off communication with her. Roy serves a total of five years in prison before having his conviction suddenly overturned, thanks in part to the efforts of his lawyer, Mr. Banks, who is a close friend of Celestial's family. When Roy is released, it has been some time since he last talked to Celestial. However, because she has yet to divorce him, he is still hopeful that their marriage can be salvaged.

It is at this point in the novel that Jones introduces a third narrator in Andre, who immediately sheds insight into what has become of his relationship with Celestial. "My affection for her is etched onto my body," he confesses, "like the Milky Way birthmark scoring my shoulder blades." Celestial and Andre, readers learn, have indeed become lovers during Roy's time in prison and have spent at least two years together. Both are beset with guilt after receiving news of Roy's impending release, but they remain committed to each other, so much so that the two, at Andre's urging, get engaged. News of their engagement, however, is met with protest from Celestial's father during an uncomfortable Thanksgiving Day dinner. The rest of Jones's novel alternates between the perspectives of Andre, Celestial, and Roy as each character pleads their case to the reader, filling in more backstory along the way.

Jones, who studied race and the American criminal justice system during a fellowship at Harvard University, has said that she got the idea for *An American Marriage* after witnessing a real-life confrontation between a couple during a routine trip to an Atlanta shopping mall. A man named Roy had ostensibly spent the previous seven years in prison and was calling out a woman, perceived to be his estranged wife or girlfriend, for being unfaithful to him during that time. Struck by the pained intensity of their argument, Jones used this incident as a starting point for what became an epic love story set against the modern realities of racial injustice.

Similar to Jones's previous works—*Leaving Atlanta* (2002), *The Untelling* (2005), and *Silver Sparrow* (2011)—the novel, which took six years to complete, is held together on the strength of its developed characters, namely its three central protagonists. Through the use of the first-person perspective, readers are allowed firsthand insight into their thoughts and actions. Torn by conflicting desires and intentions, Roy, Celestial, and Andre are all indeed flawed and imperfect, but they speak to the reader with an urgency and conviction that highlight the complexity of their situation. By design, Jones makes it hard for readers to pick sides, as her protagonists are afforded varying degrees of understanding. But it is the novel's ambiguous sense of culpability that makes it "so compelling," as critic Ron Charles opined in his *Washington Post* review.

While many of the novel's plot revelations are a little too on the nose, arriving neatly and perfectly packaged like Celestial's life-like poupée dolls, its flaws are far outweighed by its strengths, which prompted widespread praise from critics. In a representative review for the *Los Angeles Review of Books*, author Tina McElroy Ansa called the novel "truly masterful" and commented that it "is like a roller coaster that gains speed and intensity through turn after turn of information and backstory, illuminating all our human frailty and complexity along the way." With *An American Marriage*, which was long-listed for the 2018 National Book Award for Fiction, Jones trenchantly probes the various facets of marriage and the multitude of challenges it brings. More importantly, she offers readers a chilling glimpse into what it is like to be a black married couple in America, for whom the threat of injustice lurks at every turn.

Chris Cullen

Review Sources

Review of *An American Marriage*, by Tayari Jones. *Kirkus Reviews*, 12 Nov. 2017, www.kirkusreviews.com/book-reviews/tayari-jones/an-american-marriage/. Accessed 19 Aug. 2018.

Review of *An American Marriage*, by Tayari Jones. *Publishers Weekly*, 11 Dec. 2017, www.publishersweekly.com/978-1-61620-134-0. Accessed 19 Aug. 2018.

Ansa, Tina McElroy. "Injustice and Intimacy in Tayari Jones's *An American Marriage*." Review of *An American Marriage*, by Tayari Jones. *Los Angeles Review of Books*, 6 Feb. 2018, lareviewofbooks.org/article/injustice-and-intimacy-in-tayari-joness-an-american-marriage/#!. Accessed 19 Aug. 2018.

Charles, Ron. "Oprah's Newest Book Club Pick: *An American Marriage*, by Tayari Jones." Review of *An American Marriage*, by Tayari Jones. *The Washington Post*, 30 Jan. 2018, www.washingtonpost.com/entertainment/books/an-african-american-couple-torn-apart-by-the-justice-system/2018/01/30/eab5bd02-0524-11e8-8777-2a059f168dd2_story.html. Accessed 19 Aug. 2018.

Watts, Stephanie Powell. "A Marriage Upended, a Life Destroyed." Review of *An American Marriage*, by Tayari Jones. *The New York Times*, 6 Feb. 2018, www.nytimes.com/2018/02/06/books/review/american-marriage-tayari-jones.html. Accessed 19 Aug. 2018.

Asymmetry

Author: Lisa Halliday
Publisher: Simon and Schuster (New York).
  288 pp.
Type of work: Novel
Time: Early 2000s—2010s
Locales: New York, London

Lisa Halliday's debut novel Asymmetry *is told in three disparate parts: in one, a young woman has an affair with a famous, older writer; in another, an Iraqi American economist navigates immigration at Heathrow; and finally, a famous novelist gives a radio interview.*

Courtesy of Simon & Schuster

Principal characters
ALICE, a twenty-five-year-old publishing
    editor and aspiring writer
EZRA BLAZER, a celebrated novelist; seventy years old
AMAR JAFAARI, an Iraqi American economist

Lisa Halliday's debut novel *Asymmetry* is written in three parts. In the first, "Folly," Alice, a twenty-five-year-old editor at a New York publishing house, begins an affair with an elderly celebrated novelist named Ezra Blazer in 2003. In the second part, "Madness," an Iraqi American economist named Amar Jaafari contemplates his life while detained at Heathrow Airport in London in 2008. The novel's brief third act, "Ezra Blazer's Desert Island Discs," imagines novelist Blazer giving an interview to a public radio show in which he must choose seven songs to bring with him on a hypothetical desert island in 2011. The three parts chime together but never fully harmonize. *Asymmetry* is less a straightforward novel than a meditation on how novels are made with examples. Annalisa Quinn, who reviewed the book for National Public Radio (NPR), put it this way: "To what extent can we inhabit each other? What can we know about each other? How do we think about the suffering of others, and where do we put the blame? Can Alice inhabit Kurdistan, and Amar inhabit Alice? *Asymmetry* is a novel not only about the creation of that novel, but about the borders of empathy."

Halliday, like Alice, began her career working for a New York publishing house. She also, like Alice, had an affair with a famous novelist, the late Pulitzer Prize winner Philip Roth. Ezra Blazer is a thinly veiled Roth, and critics and literary insiders have delighted in the prurient details of what a secret affair with the famous author might have looked like. The placid "Folly," Katy Waldman of the *New Yorker* wrote, benefits from "the voyeuristic thrill" of this firsthand account of daily life with a literary legend. The description of everything from seemingly mundane tasks to sex is unavoidably filtered through Halliday's actual life experience.

However, Halliday does not rely entirely on her proximity to celebrity to power the novel, which Roth read and gave his blessing to before it was published in early 2018. (Roth died of congestive heart failure in May the same year.) Before *Asymmetry*, Halliday published a short story called "Stump Louie" in the *Paris Review* in 2005. After quitting her job in publishing, she worked as a freelance writer, editor, and translator in Milan. She won the Whiting Award in 2017, indicating her acknowledged strength as a writer in her own right.

The first part of *Asymmetry* can be described as autofiction, a lightly fictionalized form of autobiography—or an autobiographically influenced work of fiction. The definition is nebulous because the genre is meant to question how fact and fiction are separated at all. The novel as a whole deals explicitly with this theme, but "Folly" demonstrates it in a familiar form. Other famous examples of autofiction include Sheila Heti's *How Should a Person Be?* (2010), Ben Lerner's *10:04* (2014), and Karl Ove Knausgaard's multivolume novel *My Struggle*. Waldman, meanwhile, compared the sparsely realized character of Alice to the narrator of Rachel Cusk's contemporaneous autofiction trilogy beginning with *Outline* (2014). In those books, the story of the narrator is drawn entirely by the stories of the people around her; she is the negative space between their words. Halliday employs a similar technique for Alice to interesting effect.

Some of Alice's internal turmoil bubbles to the surface, but mostly, in the manner of Cusk, it does not. Her deep feelings for Ezra—of romantic love, but also admiration and poignantly, platonic friendship—manifest themselves in her willingness to come when he calls for her. She is the lens through which the story is told, but Ezra is undoubtedly its subject. Their bond is forged by their unique power dynamic: Ezra is Alice's mentor and benefactor, but Alice becomes Ezra's caretaker. He instructs her in things such as how to pronounce the name of the French existentialist Albert Camus and pays off her student loan debt, but in the end, Alice is the one who must gently remind her charge to close his mouth when it is inadvertently hanging open.

Ezra has wealth and acclaim, but Alice has time. Time passing, aging, and mortality are ever-present themes of their relationship. At Ezra's summer house outside of the city, Alice marvels at an antique wooden calendar on the mantel. Dowels with linen scrolls note the day and date. Halliday skillfully creates deep layers of meaning through rich description: "The dowels were pale and smooth and whenever passing Alice could not resist twisting one ever so slightly . . . although she never dared shift SATURDAY all the way to SUNDAY, or 2 to 3, or AUGUST to SEPTEMBER, for fear of not being able to shift them back."

It is suggested that Alice wants to be a writer and at one point, she muses on the ability of a Massachusetts-born choirgirl to inhabit the mind of a Muslim hot dog seller. In the second part, Halliday (or, in the conceit of the novel, Alice) puts this quandary to the test. "Madness" works as a short story in its own right, with a clear and complete trajectory and form. Amar Jaafari is Muslim, but he is not a hot dog seller. Born in airspace above the United States to an Iraqi Kurd family, he was raised in the working-class Bay Ridge neighborhood of Brooklyn. En route to Iraq, Amar is detained at Heathrow Airport in London. Between rounds of interrogation, Amar looks back on his life thus far.

In his reflection, Amar attempts to fill in sections of his life that he cannot remember, filling the time of his detention with almost philosophical musings. The faultiness of memory preoccupies him. Still, the memories he does have are fairly vivid. He describes his childhood apartment and annual trips to see family in Iraq. He recalls the gummy nature of time in Baghdad in the 1980s, when it took him and his cousins ten days to learn who had won the Super Bowl. He relives his most intense romantic relationship, begun in college and ended in London, where Amar was living alone, working as an intern at a think tank and volunteering at a children's hospital. He thinks of his older brother, Sami, a doctor and amateur pianist. Sami has recently been kidnapped and is being held for ransom. Even before the grievous event, Amar seems to have been struck by his own dual consciousness, being both Iraqi and American. How can so many terrible things be happening in one place, while life goes on, unperturbed, in another?

Halliday closes the novel with the short third act "Ezra Blazer's Desert Island Discs." It consists of a radio interview transcript in which an interviewer asks Ezra which seven songs he would take with him were he stranded on a desert island. The songs spring from important moments in Ezra's life, giving him an opportunity to expound on his own trajectory from a working-class kid in Pittsburgh, Pennsylvania (a nod to Roth's industrial Newark, New Jersey) to world-renowned author. He is surprisingly candid about his past loves and gestures toward his relationship with Alice. There is no revelatory conclusion to *Asymmetry*, but Ezra's interview neatly brings together some of Halliday's larger themes about empathy and the brevity of life.

Critics enthusiastically embraced *Asymmetry* when it was published in February 2018. Waldman argued that the novel was one of the best books of the year, writing, "Like music, *Asymmetry* possesses the mysterious quality of a created thing moving through time, expressing its own patterns, its meaning subsumed in the shifting symmetries of its form." Quinn, of NPR, called *Asymmetry* "a guidebook to being bigger than ourselves." In a review for the *New York Times*, Alice Gregory described the book as "a transgressive roman à clef, a novel of ideas and a politically engaged work of metafiction." A reviewer for *Kirkus* concluded: "A singularly conceived graft of one narrative upon another; what grows out of these conjoined stories is a beautiful reflection of life and art." Adam Kirsch of the *Atlantic* pointed out Halliday's prepublication admission of her affair with Roth, suggesting it played into the book's conceit more than as just a marketing stunt. "Halliday is not simply fanning the flames of readerly curiosity," he wrote. "Rather, she is opening a door into the labyrinth that she has designed in *Asymmetry*, a book whose unusual structure is part of its fascination. Like Roth himself, who inveterately mixes up literature and life, Halliday encourages real-world identifications so that she can play with them and subvert them."

Lisa Halliday is a Whiting Award–winning writer and translator. She published a short story called "Stump Louie" in the Paris Review *in 2005. Asymmetry is her first novel.*

Indeed, Alice's story is bolstered by its relationship to the author's real life. Arguably, it only works as thinly veiled autobiography, just as Amar's section is made more dynamic with the understanding that it was written by Alice. Reviewers also suggested that the book works as a response to Roth's 1979 novel *The Ghost Writer*, in which a young writer visits his older idol (supposedly modeled after Bernard Malamud). In it, the young writer aims to outdo his mentor, creating a story in which Anne Frank returns from the dead. Yet above all, the voices in *Asymmetry* reveal Halliday flexing her hard-won literary and imaginative skills. As Kirsch concluded, "*Asymmetry* is a 'masterpiece' in the original sense of the word—a piece of work that an apprentice produces to show that she has mastered her trade."

Molly Hagan

Review Sources

Review of *Asymmetry*, by Lisa Halliday. *Kirkus*, 28 Nov. 2017, www.kirkusreviews. com/book-reviews/lisa-halliday/asymmetry/. Accessed 18 Sept. 2018.

Gregory, Alice. "Three Lives, and the Tenuous Ties That Bind Them." Review of *Asymmetry*, by Lisa Halliday. *The New York Times*, 12 Feb. 2018, www.nytimes. com/2018/02/12/books/review/lisa-halliday-asymmetry.html. Accessed 18 Sept. 2018.

Kirsch, Adam. "*Asymmetry*: A Mentorship Tale, with Surprises." Review of *Asymmetry*, by Lisa Halliday. *The Atlantic*, 18 Feb. 2018, www.theatlantic.com/entertainment/archive/2018/02/lisa-halliday-asymmetry-review/553139/. Accessed 18 Sept. 2018.

Quinn, Annalisa. "'Asymmetry' Is a Guide to Being Bigger Than Yourself." Review of *Asymmetry*, by Lisa Halliday. *NPR Books*, 15 Feb. 2018, www.npr. org/2018/02/15/583438115/asymmetry-is-a-guide-to-being-bigger-than-yourself. Accessed 18 Sept. 2018.

Waldman, Katy. "Why 'Asymmetry' Has Become a Literary Phenomenon." Review of *Asymmetry*, by Lisa Halliday. *The New Yorker*, 12 Apr. 2018, www.newyorker. com/books/page-turner/why-asymmetry-has-become-a-literary-phenomenon. Accessed 18 Sept. 2018.

Baby Teeth

Author: Zoje Stage (b. 1969)
Publisher: St. Martin's Press (New York).
320 pp.
Type of work: Novel
Time: Present day
Locale: Pittsburgh, Pennsylvania

Mother and daughter, Suzette and Hanna Jensen, both crave the love and attention of husband and father Alex Jensen. When seven-year-old Hanna begins to plot against her mother, however, Suzette begins to wonder just how dangerous Hanna is.

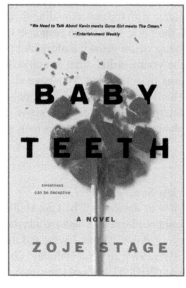

Courtesy of St. Martin's Press

Principal characters
HANNA JENSEN, a seven-year-old
SUZETTE JENSEN, her mother, an artist
ALEX JENSEN, her father, an architect
DR. BEATRIX YAMAMOTO, her psychologist
MARIE-ANNE DUFOSSET, her imaginary friend, a historical witch figure
MR. GUTIERREZ, principal at Tisdale School

Zoje Stage's debut novel, *Baby Teeth*, is a psychological thriller that explores family dynamics amid the effects of psychological and physical health problems. Throughout the novel, Stage raises the questions of how much love is enough. The novel's point of view bounces between seven-year-old Hanna and her mother, Suzette, providing a fractured structure that gives insight into the minds of the two main characters. In fact, Hanna's first-person narration, which both starts and ends the novel, is the only place where Hanna's thoughts are truly exposed. In these chapters, the novel explores the depth of the child's psychotic thought structure. Hanna is shown to be extremely intelligent, and her narration provides an explanation for her complicated behavior, promoting understanding and sympathy. Suzette's chapters would seem to provide a breath of adult reasoning, but they often fall into self-deprecating or angry rants about her own childhood, her marriage, and her role as a mother to a seemingly vindictive child. The result of these intertwined narrations is sympathy and disdain for both adult and child, blurring the lines between protagonist and antagonist throughout the novel.

The biggest theme addressed in the novel is psychological health. At seven years old, Hanna, for the most part, does not speak. Her mutism is based partially on a misconception of language. She remembers having tried to speak as a toddler, but she imagined the words turning into insects. Hanna describes, "The bugs fell from her mouth, frighteningly alive, scampering over her skin and bedclothes. She flicked them away. Watched them escape under her closed door. Words, ever unreliable, were no one's friend." When she does finally decide to talk, she only uses language to frighten her mother. For example, while Suzette tries to practice spelling words with Hanna, the child writes the word "hate," profanity, and that her mother is "week and stupid." Her first verbal words to Suzette are a response to her mother's anger after the child has interrupted some alone time. After her mother demands to know why Hannah does not listen, the child pretends to be possessed by her imaginary friend—Marie-Anne Dufosset, a French girl who was burned at the stake for being a witch centuries earlier—in order to scare Suzette. Stage writes, "Her eyes rolled back until they were solid white. Dead nothingness in the sockets. 'Because I'm not Hanna.'"

Further, Hanna's thoughts often demonstrate her disconnect with reality. She frequently focuses on the ways she believes Suzette has hurt her and formulates plans to injure or even kill her mother. In some ways, her behavior is a reaction to Suzette. Early in the novel, Hanna worries, "Mommy wanted to get rid of her; she was always trying to leave her behind." Hanna's obsessive love for her father, Alex, is another excuse for her twisted thinking, and her often violent actions further reveal a child who does not deal with reality in healthy ways. The physical attacks on her mother include cutting Suzette's hair while she sleeps, scattering thumbtacks on the floor next to her mother's bed, attempting to attack Suzette with a hammer, and thrusting a flaming stick into her mother's face. Suzette is not the only recipient of Hanna's physical wrath, though; the child aggressively barks and growls at one principal, physically attacks a toddler in a grocery store, and goads a child with disabilities into injuring himself so badly that he is sent to a hospital.

Suzette's own mental health is shown as fairly problematic. She struggles with depression and anxiety as a result of a childhood that was filled with physical illness and the diagnosis and effects of Crohn's disease. Her emotional weakness often shows that Suzette is intolerant of, and sometimes spiteful toward, Hanna's behavior. She is often just as jealous of Hanna's relationship with Alex as Hanna is of Suzette's relationship with him. As a result, she is occasionally physically and verbally abusive. Hanna points to a moment when she was two years old that first created her hatred of her mother. Suzette tells the younger child, "I didn't think it would be so lonely. I didn't think you'd be so hard to spend so much time with. You make me miss Alex, Daddy, who he was before." In the same moment, she almost causes the toddler to choke. As years passed, Hanna continued to act out, and Suzette continued to spew hurtful words at the girl, justifying her anger as a normal reaction to the child's behavior. Though the two-year-old Hanna did not completely comprehend her mother's words, seven-year-old Hanna is smart enough to understand the meaning behind them.

Suzette also childishly taunts her daughter when Hanna's behavior is observed by someone else. Though she feels vindicated by the fact that other people are acknowledging that Hanna is actually a problem, she is not content. In one instance, she tells Hanna, "Daddy pretends to himself that Hanna's still a little girl, a baby. The picture he keeps of her on his desk at work is so old, from when Hanna was three—back when we still thought she might turn out all right. Hanna's been a disappointment." These emotional taunts show that Suzette can be, at least partially, blamed for Hanna's opinion of her.

In addition to the psychological issues developed in the two main characters, *Stage* introduces physical problems as well. The most notable issue is Suzette's Crohn's disease. In a flashback to Suzette's childhood and teen years, she explains that she was not diagnosed in time to prevent lasting physical problems caused by the symptoms of Crohn's disease. As an adult, Suzette is still immersed in her own illness. This ongoing physical struggle is paralleled in Alex and Suzette's search to find a physical reason for Hanna's mutism, resulting in multiple tests and doctors' visits for the child. As Hanna's behavior climaxes in a dangerous attack on Suzette, Dr. Yamamoto, the girl's psychologist, even suggests that lesions on her brain may be part of the problem behind the sociopathy the girl exhibits.

Another thematic issue *Stage* raises is that of parenting. Both Suzette and Alex question themselves as parents. Suzette frequently wonders whether it was her bad parenting that caused Hanna's behavior, while Alex often retreats from the reality of what is happening at home by working. In some ways, Suzette's fears are true, as Hanna's antics are often in retaliation for things Suzette does that Hanna does not like. When Suzette tries to send Hanna to school, Hanna acts out, believing that Suzette is trying to get rid of her for good. Although Suzette is only trying to send Hanna to school, this has not been explained clearly and leads to a disconnect in the child's mind. This disconnect is reinforced as Suzette's patience is limited and she craves a time when she can spend time alone to rediscover herself and reconnect with Alex. Suzette admits her ambivalence as a parent to Dr. Yamamoto: "I needed to look at her and see Alex—I wanted baby Alex. But she looked like me, like my mother. I let him pick her name, so I'd always remember she was Alex's child." Alex, on the other hand, appears to be the perfect father. He reads Hanna bedtime stories, calls her "lilla gumman," and often takes her side against her mother. It is not until he witnesses Hanna physically attacking Suzette that he realizes that his daughter's problems are deeper than he has wanted to admit. Even after Alex accepts Hanna's need for professional intervention and he and his wife take her to a treatment facility where she can be treated for her psychopathy, his self-centered attitude reigns. Stage does not allow Suzette and Alex complete happiness, and she ends the novel with an unexpected twist.

Suzette often uses her bitterness about her mother's parenting to excuse her own parenting. In one memory of her own youth, Suzette's mother took her to a hospital after an attack of her Crohn's. Suzette remembers, "They arrived at the hospital, and her mother played her best parlor trick and transmogrified into a commonplace person." Her mother then proceeded to lie to the nurse about how long Suzette's health had been a problem. Suzette blames her mother's emotional distance for her own inability to unconditionally love her child. Despite Suzette's complaints about her mother, however, the older woman's actions do suggest that she, in at least a limited way, cared about her daughter. For instance, after a surgery to attempt to repair Suzette's bowel, the teen developed a fistula. Her mother faithfully tended the girl, taking care of her

Baby Teeth is the first novel for Zoje Stage. Stage's previous experience is in the world of film and theater. She has written and produced several films, including a documentary short that received praise from the New York Times*.*

physical needs for years without complaint. Suzette even remembers her mother as being an engaged grandmother when Hanna was first born, but when her mother died while Hanna was still small, Suzette thinks of her death as a betrayal and abandonment. Though she recognizes that her child-parent relationship with her mother probably influenced her reactions to her daughter, she does not care enough about Hanna to stop the cycle of parental selfishness.

Baby Teeth received mostly positive reviews. A reviewer for *Publishers Weekly* called the novel "deviously fun" and wrote that it "takes child rearing anxiety to demented new heights." A review in *Library Journal* noted that *Baby Teeth* is "deliciously creepy" and serves as an "exploration of the dark side of modern motherhood." The well-structured novel has enough twists and turns to keep readers engaged in wondering what fiendish action Hanna will take next and questioning whether Suzette should take more responsibility for the child's actions or if she is justified in her reactions.

Theresa L. Stowell, PhD

Review Sources

Review of *Baby Teeth*, by Zoje Stage. *Kirkus Reviews*, 16 Apr. 2018, www.kirkusreviews.com/book-reviews/zoje-stage/baby-teeth/. Accessed 1 Feb. 2019.

Review of *Baby Teeth*, by Zoje Stage. *Publishers Weekly*, 16 Apr. 2018, p. 64. *Literary Reference Center Plus*, search.ebscohost.com/login.aspx?direct=true&db=lkh&AN=129089282&site=lrc-plus. Accessed 1 Feb. 2019.

Parrott, Kiera. Review of *Baby Teeth*, by Zoje Stage. *Library Journal*, 1 Apr. 2018, p. 50. *Literary Reference Center Plus*, search.ebscohost.com/login.aspx?direct=true&db=lkh&AN=128688161&site=lrc-plus. Accessed 1 Feb. 2019.

Back Talk

Author: Danielle Lazarin
Publisher: Penguin Books (New York). 256
  pp.
Type of work: Short fiction
Time: Present day
Locales: New York, Paris, San Francisco

Back Talk *is a collection of sixteen short stories which explore the daily lives of women.
Lazarin's characters, who range in age and
gender, struggle with such issues as first romance, divorce, family dysfunction, and loss
of a parent.*

Courtesy of Penguin

Principal characters

CLAUDIA, *a teenager whose mother has died*
CAITLIN, *a teen with divorced parents who
  feels left out by her older siblings*
ANNA, *a young woman exploring life in Paris*
NICK, *a police officer who cares for his sister and nieces*
ALISON, *a single mom who wants the best for her daughters*
NOAH, *a widower with children*
VANESSA, *a child who wants to believe in the supernatural*

Danielle Lazarin's debut story collection, *Back Talk*, begins with the epigraph "It was
different for a girl," a quote from Susan Minot's 1989 short story "Lust." This quote
prepares readers for the kinds of stories the author will present: stories about women
of all ages and walks of life dealing with the kinds of issues that many women face.
These issues include growing up, sibling relationships, romance, lies, loneliness and
loss, and friendships.

Many of the stories present tales of the emotions involved in growing up. In "Appetite," the first story in the collection, a teenager falls into her first relationship and
deals with the changes that the loss of her mother has brought into the family. Though
the story seems to focus on Claudia's romantic experiences, her relationships with
her sister Michelle and her father are intertwined into a tale that explores the different
ways people deal with grief. One of Claudia's ways of coping has been to cling to her
boyfriend, George, who "won't ask me what I want but he will give me what I need."
While Claudia tries to relax into a relationship with a boy who cares for her, Michelle
finds solace from heartbreak in cooking. Claudia also clings to this action, finding
security in "coming home to find her in the kitchen; I like eating her food, sitting with
her while she makes it." Claudia's grief, however, often overwhelms her. After discovering her father in bed with a woman, she hides from her sister, thinking, "I want to

tell her it's not George, that it's Dad, that it's a woman who will always be a stranger to us, that I am scared I'll never remember our mother correctly, but I'm so afraid of breaking Mich's heart any further that I don't, not that night, not ever." Claudia cannot even allow herself a long-term happiness for fear of loss, and she breaks up with George to save herself later pain; ironically, her memories just "fill the apartment with more ghosts."

"The Holographic Soul" also points to the way life changes subtly, as it depicts the Oliver sisters, Hannah and Vanessa, growing up. They are so close that they seem to share a psychic connection. As they move toward adulthood, they learn to accept changes that allow their mother to find herself again, becoming a stronger, happier person as a result. The positive ending suggests that Vanessa follows in her mother's footsteps and "never outgrow[s] the belief that there is something to see beyond this world." In "Dinosaurs," teenaged Claire struggles to figure out whether she should break up with her boyfriend and turns to the father of the children she babysits for advice.

Sibling relationships are a common theme in the stories. The first tale shares the changed relationship between Claudia and her older sister after their mother's death. Claudia finds comfort in watching her older sister fulfill simple household duties, but also hides her own grief from Michelle, whose grief often seems to overpower the emotional atmosphere of the house. "Spider Legs," the third piece in the collection, also explores a strained sibling relationship. In this story, seventeen-year-old Caitlin travels to Paris, where she spends a portion of the year at her mother's home after her parents' divorce. Caitlin says of her older siblings, Jack and Jill, "They always stand behind one another, no matter who stands against them. To me, their fierce loyalty is the inaccessible nucleus of our family." While Jack and Jill attempt, during the course of the story, to include Caitlin in several outings, they have left her on the outside for so long that she cannot find a way to stop hurting.

In contrast to Caitlin's existence on the edges of her family, Hannah and Vanessa in "The Holographic Soul" are "the only siblings in the neighborhood who don't try to leave each other at home, or sacrifice each other during the backyard games that always end in someone else's tears. V and I only need each other." In "Hide and Seek," Lazarin explores the relationship between two adult siblings, a brother and a sister, as well as the connection between the woman's two daughters. In each relationship, the siblings take turns caring for each other.

Many of the stories also deal with romance. Claudia experiences her first love in "Appetite," while Robin struggles with the end of a marriage in "Floor Plans." Anna is torn between holding onto a safe love at home and new possibilities in Paris in "American Men in Paris I Did Not Love." The unnamed narrator of "Landscape No. 27" is bitter over both her husband's and her lover's "collective failure of . . . imaginations, by your inability to follow me into the hard place I was going with anything other than the offer to fuck me anyway." She contemplates the distance between herself and both men; they do not understand each other and have not made much effort to do so. Meanwhile, in "Lover's Lookout," a chance meeting between two lonely people leads a young woman to think about what went wrong in her recently ended relationship and what she really wants in the future.

Lies and secrets are another common set of themes among the stories. In "Appetite" Claudia relates hearing her sister on the phone with friends: "She's never been better, I hear her tell them, another lie in our house." When Franny, the main character of "Weighted and Measured," is dealing with growing apart from high school friends Lucia and Patrick, she is asked why she never cries when they fight. But Franny, the story notes, is a silent crier, "so if she ever had, on the other end of a call with Lucia or Patrick, they might never have known it was happening at all." Instead, she lets their relationships die in silence. Anna, of "American Men in Paris," lies when writing to a friend: "I tell him I miss him, but not Paris, that it's a shame he's fallen for it like every other sucker out there." The narrator of "Landscape No. 27" calmly states that she began an affair with an artist because she "needed a secret."

Loneliness and loss seep through the characters in many of the stories. Eight years after her parents' divorce, Caitlin, in "Spider Legs," says of living with her father, "I've never shaken the feeling that he thinks my stay is just temporary." At the end of the story, she has come to an understanding about herself and her family: "I am the piece that belongs in a different box, that comes from a different puzzle altogether." Anna, in "American Men in Paris," is not sure whether to let go of her relationship with Sam, a boy from home, when he visits her in Paris, and they realize that they cannot hide their "mutual feelings of failure at how to be with each other." Though she has friends in her

© Sylvie Rosokoff

Back Talk is Danielle Lazarin's debut collection of short stories, many of which have been published previously in other venues. She also writes nonfiction. She has degrees from Oberlin College and the University of Michigan and has been awarded grants from the New York Foundation for the Arts and the Northern Manhattan Arts Alliance.

new home, Anna sometimes feels lonely and homesick, which she describes as an "ache to return to a place I already know won't feel like home anymore." Lost love and death plague many of the characters in the collection as well. For instance, Alison's ex-husband Michael has been killed in "Hide and Seek" and Noah's wife has died in "Dinosaurs." Claudia's mother's death changed her family dynamics in "Appetite," leaving three people in grief.

Friendships are another thematic offering in the collection. In "Floor Plans," Robin, following her divorce from her husband, becomes friends with her neighbor Juliet. In "Weighted and Measured," Franny's and Lucia's friendship is a tie that provides stability throughout their childhood but cannot withstand changes when one goes away to private school, leaving the other behind.

Lazarin keeps the readers' attention not only through the development of multiple thematic issues faced by women but also by varying the points of view. The majority of the stories are told in first person, focusing on one female character. "Weighted and Measured," "Hide and Seek," "Dinosaurs," and "Looking for a Thief" are told from a limited omniscient point of view. In "Hide and Seek," for the first time in the collection, Lazarin makes Nick, a man, the viewpoint character, something she does again in "Dinosaurs." "Back Talk" takes another direction, using second person pronouns when referring to the main female character, striking out against the girl's silence.

The collection's critical reception was primarily positive. Carmen Maria Machado pointed out, in a review for the *New York Times*, that it could be seen as an issue that Lazarin's protagonists are almost exclusively middle- or upper-class, educated white women, but concludes that part of the reason the stories are so effective is that they show "the grind of the patriarchy on even the most privileged of women." *Kirkus* referred to it as an "exquisite debut short story collection," while *Publishers Weekly* lauded the book as "confident," "exhilarating," and "uniformly excellent." Emily Park, for *Booklist*, pointed to Lazarin's "poignant imagery" and "fresh voice," further stating "Her exceptional craftsmanship speaks to the heart, as she paints these tales with empathy and a compassion that extends to all humankind."

Theresa L. Stowell, PhD

Review Sources

Review of *Back Talk*, by Danielle Lazarin. *Kirkus Reviews*, 15 Jan. 2018, p. 1. *Book Review Digest*, search.ebscohost.com/login.aspx?direct=true&db=brd&AN=1273 03522&site=ehost-live. Accessed 8 Aug. 2018.

Review of *Back Talk*, by Danielle Lazarin. *Publishers Weekly*, 23 Oct. 2017, p. 60. *Book Review Digest,* search.ebscohost.com/login.aspx?direct=true&db=brd&AN =125843319&site=ehost-live. Accessed 8 Aug. 2018.

Hong, Terry. Review of Back Talk, by Danielle Lazarin. *Library Journal*, 15 Apr. 2018, p. 37. *Book Review Digest*, search.ebscohost.com/login.aspx?direct=true&d b=brd&AN=128930639&site=ehost-live&scope=site. Accessed 8 Aug. 2018.

Machado, Carmen Maria. "If It's a Man's World, Let's Escape It . . . or Subvert It." Review of *Back Talk*, by Danielle Lazarin. *The New York Times*, 20 Mar. 2018, www.nytimes.com/2018/03/20/books/review/back-talk-danielle-lazarin.html. Accessed 1 Nov. 2018.

Park, Emily. Review of *Back Talk*, by Danielle Lazarin. *Booklist*, 15 Nov. 2017, p. 23. *Book Review Digest*, search.ebscohost.com/login.aspx?direct=true&db=brd& AN=126410521&site=ehost-live. Accessed 8 Aug. 2018.

Bad Blood
Secrets and Lies in a Silicon Valley Startup

Author: John Carreyrou (b. ca. 1973)
Publisher: Alfred A. Knopf (New York).
352 pp.
Type of work: Current affairs, medicine, technology
Time: 2003–18
Locales: Palo Alto, California, and environs; other US locations

In this suspenseful investigative master-piece, journalist John Carreyrou details the rise and fall of Theranos, a high-tech company founded on the bright hope of making lives better. Because of incompetence, paranoia, and greed, Theranos over time was transformed into a criminal enterprise that endangered lives.

Courtesy of Knopf Doubleday

Principal personages

ELIZABETH HOLMES, cofounder and chief executive officer of Theranos
SHAUNAK ROY, a chemical engineer and cofounder of Theranos
RAMESH "SUNNY" BALWANI, Holmes's boyfriend and a senior Theranos executive
DAVID BOIES, lawyer for Theranos
CHANNING ROBERTSON, associate dean of Stanford School of Engineering and Theranos board member
RICHARD FUISZ, an entrepreneur and medical inventor
ALAN BEAM, a lab director at Theranos
TYLER SHULTZ, a Theranos employee who blew the whistle on the company
JOHN CARREYROU, the author, a Wall Street Journal investigative reporter

There once was an up-and-coming Silicon Valley company called Theranos. The brainchild of charismatic Stanford University dropout Elizabeth Holmes, Theranos was incorporated in Palo Alto, California, in 2003 and, according to its own publicity, was a medical technology innovator with the potential to change the world. Key to this mission was its core product, a sophisticated miniaturized portable device supposedly capable of quickly and accurately analyzing human blood. While basic handheld blood analyzers were already on the market, the Theranos version would purportedly perform dozens of different types of blood tests, for everything from vitamin C levels to diabetes to malaria. Better still, the device worked effectively with small sample sizes, mere drops produced by pricking a finger, rather than requiring syringes full of blood drawn from a vein.

The possibilities of such a machine were myriad. It was so simple to operate it could be used painlessly in a patient's home. Economics of scale increased benefits and profits: retail chains could employ the snazzy machine in-store to check customers' blood (potentially saving lives) while they shopped. Pharmaceutical firms could make quick medication adjustments according to analysis data, reducing costs significantly when conducting clinical trials of new drugs.

However, there was a major problem with these idealized scenarios, as journalist John Carreyrou's book *Bad Blood: Secrets and Lies in a Silicon Valley Startup* meticulously uncovers. Despite the optimistic outlook and much positive attention from investors and the media, Theranos as an organization was fragile and unstable. The chief executives envisioned a futuristic product, but in fact had no clue about how—or if—it could be built, and were too aggressively stubborn, too greedy, or too arrogant to admit their incompetence. The device Theranos finally produced, the Edison (and its flawed descendants), did not live up to the company's lofty promises. A jumble of jury-rigged components wrapped in a sleek tamper-proof package, the company's product was eventually exposed as one of the most extreme examples of the Silicon Valley trend known as vaporware—hardware or software that is vigorously promoted but mired in perpetual development.

As the struggle to produce a workable device lengthened, and queries from clients and investors multiplied, Theranos executives, long experts at distorting truth, resorted to outright deceit. They spoke of contracts they did not have (such as the US military, which the company alleged was using their device as a tool in the field of battle). They shunned or fired or threatened employees who expressed doubt about the product or raised concerns about ethics. They lied shamelessly in public. They fudged results, aided by the fact that they operated in a zone where there were regulatory gaps. It was Carreyrou's investigative reporting on Theranos for the *Wall Street Journal* beginning in 2015 that brought the company's pervasive fraud to light. The resulting scandal rocked the medical technology industry the way the Enron affair had shaken the energy/commodity world in 2001. *Bad Blood* brings the full scope of Carreyrou's investigation, and his skillful journalistic writing style, to book form.

Carreyrou carefully explains Theranos's background, illustrating how the concept of its technology was so appealing that many people bought in despite significant warning signs. Chemical engineers, hardware and software designers, lab technicians, and other specialized professionals were drawn to join the exciting new company touting its mission to radically reshape healthcare to the benefit of all. Investors—including media mogul Rupert Murdoch and other notable names—enthusiastically funded Theranos, enabling it to grow rapidly from a one-person idea into a $10 billion enterprise with hundreds of employees during the fifteen-year arc of its precipitous rise and ignominious fall. The company's board of directors attracted illustrious figures including venture capitalist Donald L. Lucas, former statesmen Henry Kissinger and George Shultz, military leader James Mattis, Stanford professor Channing Robertson, and star lawyer David Boies. Major retailers were convinced to such a degree by the Theranos story that they spent millions to have the company install and operate untested (and ultimately unworkable) devices in hundreds of stores, where they were used to perform unauthorized tests on thousands of unsuspecting individuals.

The initial success of Theranos, as Carreyrou emphasizes throughout *Bad Blood*, was largely due to the persuasive but amoral genius of cofounder Holmes. Entrepreneurship and medicine were both part of her family heritage. She was descended from Charles Louis Fleischmann, who in the 1860s founded the company that made Fleischmann's Yeast and left a lasting family fortune, while her great-great-grandfather established Cincinnati General Hospital and the University of Cincinnati medical school. Even as a child, Holmes felt the tug of ambition, reportedly telling relatives that she wanted to be a billionaire when she grew up. While she eventually achieved her hope, Carreyrou builds much of his narrative around the questionable decisions she made to get there, and how it began to fall apart.

Holmes's original business idea sounded terrific. While a student at Stanford University in the early 2000s, she envisioned a miniature blood-testing device that could both diagnose and treat a range of medical conditions. The concept, combined with her mesmerizing promotional skills, proved irresistible to many. Though Holmes had virtually no scientific or technical training, she saw herself as a visionary along the lines of tech pioneers Steve Jobs and Bill Gates. Her pitch managed to attract an impressive collection of the brainy, the well-connected, and the wealthy, and Holmes dropped out of college to build the company.

While Holmes quickly and masterfully built Theranos into a thriving company, creating a working version of her visionary device proved more difficult. Blood is a tricky substance to analyze, as Carreyrou explains in easy-to-follow terms, because many tests can only be performed after solids are separated from blood plasma. Even in the best of circumstances, such as a sterile laboratory environment, blood is easily contaminated; in a tiny portable device of the sort Holmes envisioned, crowded with pipettes and tubes and chemicals, contamination is almost guaranteed, invalidating test results. Theranos's goal of using miniscule amounts of blood (the result of Holmes's morbid fear of needles) created an additional problem: a few drops simply do not provide enough material to perform a variety of tests. Company lab technicians, chemical engineers, and designers were charged with overcoming these challenges.

Undeterred by a constant succession of setbacks, Holmes continued promoting the benefits of a nonexistent device. She and her cohorts—primarily her boyfriend and top company executive Ramesh "Sunny" Balwani—made projections for future sales and profits that were not just unrealistic (overblown optimism is a common practice in Silicon Valley and elsewhere), but completely bogus without an actual working product. As Carreyrou documents, it is one thing to delude oneself about the viability of an idea. It is an entirely different matter to purposely deflect scrutiny, exaggerate, fake results, conceal facts, or otherwise perpetrate increasingly transparent falsehoods in order to dupe people. Theranos leaders conducted their swindle inside and outside the organization, dragging countless others along in the nightmare pursuit of an impossible dream.

Theranos did eventually produce versions of a blood-testing device, though they were a far cry from the original concept. The so-called Edison machines were never as capable as claimed, and many supposed tests were run on industry standard equipment. A later device, called the mini-Lab, consisted of a credit card-sized unit into which a patient's sample was supposed to be collected. The card was then to be inserted into a toaster-like reader for analysis. The exterior appearance of the miniLab and its alleged capabilities were good enough that supermarket giant Safeway and pharmacy chain Walgreens each committed tens of millions of dollars and signed lucrative contracts agreeing to use the devices in many stores. In actuality, the miniLab was a disaster. It frequently did not work at all. It required more than a nominal amount of blood to produce readings. When it did work, it typically produced wildly inaccurate results. The development of the device, in Carreyrou's hands, is a thrilling adventure story with many twists and turns. The details can be both shocking and humorous; for example, the author relates an amusing Potemkin village–type incident in which Theranos dummies up a nonfunctional automated laboratory to show US vice president Joe Biden during his tour of the corporate headquarters.

© Michael Lionstar

John Carreyrou is an investigative journalist who long reported for the Wall Street Journal. *He won Pulitzer Prizes for his work with the newspaper in 2003 and 2015, among other awards.*

The seeds of Theranos's downfall were sown almost from the beginning of the enterprise. Many people involved with various aspects of the company had misgivings about the product or the questionable principles of the executives. Yet such individuals were usually cowed by the prospect of facing off against the powerful company executives or made mute by internal security measures such as spy cameras, sophisticated locks, and e-mail monitoring software. Nobody wanted to be party to a lawsuit based on violation of nondisclosure agreements protecting trade secrets. However, former employee Tyler Shultz—grandson of former US secretary of state George Shultz, a onetime Theranos board member—contacted Carreyrou after attempts to bring up his misgivings about the company's activities with Holmes and other executives proved fruitless.

So began the reporting that led to the exposure of Theranos's fraud and eventually to *Bad Blood*. Carreyrou adeptly casts himself as a player in the narrative, noting the legal threats he and his sources received from the company. And indeed, he had a significant role in Theranos's fate: the once $9 billion company began to collapse after Carreyrou's initial articles appeared in 2015, and, by the publication of his book in 2018, was headed into bankruptcy. Later that year Holmes and Balwani were both indicted on federal fraud charges and Theranos was officially dissolved.

As a crisp, clear documentation of the history of Theranos from beginning to end, *Bad Blood* could serve as the template for what investigative journalism should be. Carreyrou's research is impeccable and thorough, as he interviewed more than 150 people, including some 60 former Theranos employees, to expose the whole sordid story. He makes complex, technical processes understandable and paints vivid scenes with plain, unadorned prose. His inclusion throughout the entire narrative of biographical sketches and pithy quotations from those who participated in some capacity in the Theranos experiment underscores the human element behind the corporate façade.

Carreyrou's newspaper reporting on Theranos won him several awards, and *Bad Blood*, too, was met with strong critical acclaim. The work was named the Financial Times and McKinsey Business Book of the Year. It was also quickly optioned for film, indicating the dramatic strength of the core story.

Jack Ewing

Review Sources
Crow, David. Review of *Bad Blood: Secrets and Lies in a Silicon Valley Startup*, by John Carreyrou. *Financial Times*, 8 July 2018, www.ft.com/content/20855a62-803d-11e8-8e67-1e1a0846c475. Accessed 4 Jan. 2019.

Lowenstein, Roger. "'Bad Blood' Review: How One Company Scammed Silicon Valley. And How It Got Caught." Review of *Bad Blood: Secrets and Lies in a Silicon Valley Startup*, by John Carreyrou. *The New York Times*, 21 May 2018, . Accessed 4 Jan. 2019.

Nguyen, Kevin. "'Bad Blood' Review: The Biggest Scam in Silicon Valley." Review of *Bad Blood: Secrets and Lies in a Silicon Valley Startup*, by John Carreyrou. *GQ*, 21 May 2018, www.gq.com/story/bad-blood-review. Accessed 4 Jan. 2019.

Perkowitz, Sidney. "Bad Blood, Worse Ethics." Review of *Bad Blood: Secrets and Lies in a Silicon Valley Startup*, by John Carreyrou. *Los Angeles Review of Books*, 7 Sept. 2018, lareviewofbooks.org/article/bad-blood-worse-ethics. Accessed 4 Jan. 2019.

Zarley, B. David. "Silicon Valley Has a Blind Spot, and John Carreyrou's 'Bad Blood' Exposes It." Review of *Bad Blood: Secrets and Lies in a Silicon Valley Startup*, by John Carreyrou. *Paste Magazine*, 28 May 2018, www.pastemagazine.com/articles/2018/05/bad-blood-by-john-carreyrou.html. Accessed 4 Jan. 2019.

Barracoon
The Story of the Last "Black Cargo"

Author: Zora Neale Hurston (1891–1960)
Editor: Deborah G. Plant (b. 1956)
Publisher: Amistad (New York). 208 pp.
Type of work: Biography, history, memoir
Time: ca. 1841–1935
Locales: Kingdoms of Takkoi and Dahomey,
West Africa (now in Benin); Alabama

In Barracoon, *Zora Neale Hurston recounts most of the biography of Cudjo Lewis, an African man who was enslaved by a hostile nation and then sold to American slavers. Lewis, who was brought illegally to the United States just before the Civil War on perhaps the last slave ship ever to enter the country, told Hurston about his life and times both before and after his arrival in the US.*

Courtesy of HarperCollins

Principal personages
CUDJO LEWIS, a.k.a. Oluale Kossola, an African man enslaved and brought to the antebellum United States
ABILE "CELIA" LEWIS, his wife
ZORA NEALE HURSTON, an African American author who interviewed him
TIMOTHY MEAHER, the principal owner of the slave ship that brought Lewis to the US
JAMES MEAHER, one of Meaher's brothers
PATRICK BYRNES "BURNS" MEAHER, another of Meaher's brothers

Although Zora Neale Hurston's fascinating book *Barracoon* was begun in the late 1920s and completed in 1931, its publication was delayed for close to a century. One reason for this fact is already suggested by the volume's epigraph, taken from Hurston's memoir *Dust Tracks on a Road*: "But the inescapable fact that stuck in my craw, was: my people had *sold* me and the white people had *bought* me. . . . It impressed upon me the universal nature of greed and glory." Writer Alice Walker, in her frank foreword to this volume, does not flinch from this depressing truth. "Reading *Barracoon*," she writes, "one understands immediately the problem many black people, especially black intellectuals and political leaders, had with it." After all, the book "records the atrocities African peoples inflicted on each other, long before shackled Africans, traumatized, ill, disoriented, starved, arrived on ships as 'black cargo' in the hellish West."

Indeed, the most gruesome passages in Cudjo Lewis's account of his life as one of the last black slaves to arrive in the United States deal not with being callously enslaved

Courtesy of Barbara Hurston Lewis and Faye Hurston

Zora Neale Hurston, an anthropologist and prolific writer, is widely considered one of the greatest American authors of the twentieth century. Her famous novel, Their Eyes Were Watching God, *has received great acclaim, as have many of her other works of fiction and nonfiction.*

by white Americans but with being brutally conquered by black Africans. Lewis's tribe suffered a surprise attack by the king of Dahomey, who had established a lucrative trade in captured Africans and whose truly fearsome warriors—both male and female—showed no mercy to the people they slaughtered or enslaved. Heads were lopped off, parents were killed in front of their children, and captives endured long forced marches with pauses mostly to give the captors time to smoke the decaying severed heads to eliminate their nauseating stench. After arriving at the capital of Dahomey, the captives saw mounds and mounds of bleached skulls before being thrust into huge enclosures called barracoons and then stripped of their clothes as they were forced onto the waiting American slave ship.

This nakedness was a huge torment to Lewis, especially after he and his fellow slaves arrived in America. Much to his surprise, the newly enslaved were often treated contemptuously by enslaved people who had already become Americanized or were American-born. The nakedness of the new arrivals made them seem "primitive" to the African Americans, as did their inability to speak English and their strange religious customs. Lewis spends much time reporting the indignities he and the "Africans" suffered at the hands of black Americans, both before and after the official end of slavery. He and his fellow tribe members saw themselves as Africans first and foremost and, after being freed, long hoped to save enough money to return to their native continent. They established their own Africatown community in southern Alabama, near Mobile, and although many of them soon converted to Christianity, their relations with other blacks in the area were often frosty. Lewis's Christianity soon became intense, and it is clear that a deep faith that helped him and other members of his community survive the challenges they faced, from both black and white Americans. Eventually they gave up their dreams of returning to Africa and not only adapted to their new conditions but, in some ways, prospered to the extent that they could. Lewis recounted with special pride how he and the other Africans did not wait for government help, as others did, to establish a school for their children. Their self-reliance was (and is) impressive, and the courage they displayed is one of the most inspiring aspects of an often-depressing book. Many readers will come away from this volume with a renewed appreciation of the bravery, resilience, and inventiveness human beings can demonstrate when pushed to their limits.

One of the most surprising, and endearing, qualities Lewis displayed was a real sense of humor. He emerges from his interviews with Hurston as an immensely like-able and compassionate man. He loved his wife and children and was severely pained by their deaths, especially that of his wife, who predeceased him by thirty years. Over the course of this book, Cudjo goes from being an innocent, naive teenager to a wise old man and pillar of his local community. It is easy to see why Hurston sought him out and enjoyed talking to him. She was not, however, the first or only person to show an interest in him and in Africatown, and in fact early versions of her tale depended heavily on or even plagiarized preceding accounts, especially those of a woman named Emma Langdon Roche. But Hurston, in her long-unpublished manuscript, displays all the talents that made her a leading anthropologist of the black community and among the best American writers.

One reason her book remained unpublished is that she refused to alter Lewis's style of speech. He spoke a kind of pidgin English that might have sounded primitive to publishers and to some of her fellow intellectuals but that, today, sounds convincingly authentic and often extremely poignant. At one point, for instance, Lewis describes the Dahomians' attack on his village:

"I see de great many soldiers wid French gun in de hand and de big knife. Dey got de women soldiers too and dey run wid de big knife and make noise. Dey ketch people and dey saw de neck lak dis wid de knife den dey twist de head so and it come off de neck. Oh Lor', Lor'!

"I see de people gittee kill so fast! De old ones dey try run 'way from de house but dey dead by de door, and de women soldiers got dey head. Oh, Lor'! . . . Everybody dey run to de gates so dey kin hide deyself in de bush, you unnerstand me. Some never reachee de gate. De women soldier ketchee de young ones and tie dem by de wrist. No man kin be so strong lak de woman soldiers from de Dahomey. So dey cut off de head. Some dey snatch de jaw-bone while de people ain' dead. Oh Lor', Lor', Lor'! De poor folkses wid dey bottom jaw tore off dey face!"

Nothing later in the book approaches this kind of vivid horror, but Lewis's story re-mains fascinating throughout precisely because of the sheer variety of his experiences, from terrified teenager to beloved and respected elder.

Of course, the book also benefits from the sheer skill of Hurston's own phrasing as well. Although she generally lets Lewis speak for himself, every so often she nar-rates, showing in that process, her personal gift for creating memorable language. For instance, describing the captives' procession to the capital of Dahomey, she calls it "the first leg of their journey from humanity to cattle." Later she notes that most of "Africa's ambassadors to the New World have come and worked and died, and left their spoor, but no recorded thought." She calls the Americans' purchase of Lewis and his fellow captives a "last deal in human flesh," and instead of referring to the king of Dahomey's throne, she instead calls it his "stool of rank." Recounting an early meeting with Lewis in which he mentioned his long-dead wife, Hurston notes that his "smile faded into a wretched weeping mask." This book is valuable then not only for the historical facts it presents, but also for its status as perhaps the last major piece of Hurston's own writing to become widely available to her many admirers.

Deborah Plant, in editing the book, has done a splendid job. She not only sought out Alice Walker to provide an eloquent foreword but also wrote a brief but fact-filled introduction of her own. The volume is bookended by a photograph of the Door of No Return on Gorée Island, Senegal, and by a photograph of Cudjo Lewis in old age. The caption of this latter picture reads:

> Cudjo Lewis (Oluale Kossola), in front of his home in Africatown (Plateau), Alabama, circa 1928. To have his photograph taken, Kossola dressed in his best suit and removed his shoes: "I want to look lak I in Affica, 'cause dat where I want to be."

One wishes that more such photos and drawings had been included, but the prose in *Barracoon* is sharp and striking on its own.

The book concludes with various appendices by Plant, including an afterword in which she discusses Hurston's reliance on previous sources, a habit that an early Hurston biographer labeled plagiarism. Plant suggests that Hurston may not have been able to bring herself to describe, in her own words, the sheer horror of Lewis's captivity narrative: "Perhaps, rather than force herself to deal with such disorienting facts that stuck in her craw, Hurston chose, in the moment, to submit a narrative about the raid that had already been penned." Whatever the explanation, Hurston produced her own memorable account of Lewis's life, based on repeated personal interviews with him. Anyone who compares and contrasts her text with the earlier book by Emma Langdon Roche will recognize the extent of Hurston's originality, both in substance and in tone.

Plant's valuable edition closes with an abundance of helpful historical material, including a glossary of terms and a list of some of Cudjo's neighbors in Africatown. Students of literature and history will find *Barracoon* intriguing, and anyone who needs reminding of the strength of the human spirit cannot fail to be moved.

Robert C. Evans, PhD

Review Sources

Bancroft, Collette. "Review: In Zora Neale Hurston's 'Barracoon,' the Voice of Slavery's History Speaks." Review of *Barracoon: The Story of the Last "Black Cargo,"* by Zora Neale Hurston. *The Tampa Bay Times*, 9 May 2018, www.tampabay.com/features/books/Review-In-Zora-Neale-Hurston-s-Barracoon-the-voice-of-slavery-s-history-speaks_168017046. Accessed 30 Aug. 2018.

Jones, Tayari. "Zora Neale Hurston's Masterpiece, 'Barracoon,' Finally Sees the Light of Day." Review of *Barracoon: The Story of the Last "Black Cargo,"* by Zora Neale Hurston. *The Washington Post*, 7 May 2018, www.washingtonpost.com/entertainment/books/zora-neale-hurstons-masterpiece-barracoon-finally-sees-the-light-of-day/2018/05/07/654f9b50-5214-11e8-9c91-7dab596e8252_story.html. Accessed 30 Aug. 2018.

Muhammad, Ismail. "The Crushing Sorrow of *Barracoon*." Review of *Barracoon: The Story of the Last "Black Cargo,"* by Zora Neale Hurston. *Slate*, 7 June 2018, slate.com/culture/2018/06/zora-neale-hurstons-barracoon-reviewed.html. Accessed 30 Aug. 2018.

Womack, Autumn. "Contraband Flesh: On Zora Neale Hurston's *Barracoon*." Review of *Barracoon: The Story of the Last "Black Cargo,"* by Zora Neale Hurston. *The Paris Review*, 7 May 2018, www.theparisreview.org/blog/2018/05/07/contraband-flesh-on-zora-neale-hurstons-barracoon. Accessed 30 Aug. 2018

Beastie Boys Book

Authors: Michael Diamond (b. 1965) and
Adam Horovitz (b. 1966)
Publisher: Spiegel & Grau (New York). 590
pp.
Type of work: Biography
Time: 1981–2012
Locales: New York, Los Angeles

Courtesy of Random House

In Beastie Boys Book, *Michael Diamond
and Adam Horovitz, the two surviving Beastie Boys, provide an affectionate retrospective on their legendary hip-hop group. In a
volume jammed with photographs and other
visual memorabilia of Beastie Boys history,
Diamond and Horovitz successfully evoke
the fun-loving and irreverent spirit that characterized the group's music.*

Principal personages

ADAM YAUCH, member of the Beastie Boys who died of cancer in 2012
MICHAEL DIAMOND, member of the Beastie Boys
ADAM HOROVITZ, member of the Beastie Boys
KATE SCHELLENBACH, member of the Beastie Boys in their early punk rock days, and
later a member of the group Luscious Jackson
RICK RUBIN, producer of early Beastie Boys records and cofounder of Def Jam
Recordings
RUSSELL SIMMONS, cofounder of Def Jam Recordings and musical entrepreneur
MARIO CALDATO JR., producer of four Beastie Boys albums

A goodly portion of the members of Generation X—those who were teenagers during
the 1980s—spent part of those teen years banging their heads to "(You Gotta) Fight
for Your Right (To Party!)," the iconic Beastie Boys ode to adolescent rebellion. Along
with other 1980s anthems to partying and rock and roll, like Twisted Sister's "We're
Not Gonna Take It," this song became a staple on MTV, the new and hugely influential
music video network that shaped the tastes and imaginations of a generation. Exposure like this made the Beastie Boys, for an evanescent moment, the face of youthful
rebellion in the Reagan era. But the Beasties were more than just pop cultural bad
boys, though they made the most of that image for years. The Beastie Boys were also
hip-hop pioneers who helped bring rap music into the mainstream; they also became
the first white stars in a predominantly African American genre.

For this contribution alone, the Beastie Boys would have earned themselves at least
a footnote in the history of popular music. But the group survived its wild and crazy

phase in the 1980s and aged well. The Beastie Boys never stopped experimenting and taking risks with their music. They built an impressive discography and branched out into other aspects of the music business. They earned respect, as well as lots of money, and began garnering awards, including three Grammy Awards. In 2012, the Beastie Boys—Adam Yauch, Michael Diamond, and Adam Horovitz—were inducted into the Rock and Roll Hall of Fame. Perhaps to their surprise, the Beastie Boys had become an institution.

Sadly, Yauch died of cancer just a few weeks after the Rock and Roll Hall of Fame ceremony. *Beastie Boys Book* begins with words of tribute to him. Yauch was slightly older than Diamond and Horovitz, and was seen by them as something of an older brother. He was a leader in the group, a technological innovator, and also someone interested in ideas and the wider world. Yauch also fostered the group's social conscience. His embrace of Tibetan Buddhism inspired the Beastie Boys to help organize Tibetan Freedom Concerts in the 1990s. Yauch's premature death led to the dissolution of the Beastie Boys.

Perhaps unsurprisingly, it was originally Yauch's idea to do a book about his and his friends' experiences as the Beastie Boys; but it was left to Diamond and Horovitz to make the project a reality. The result is a quintessentially Beastie Boys production. *Beastie Boys Book* is as wackily eclectic as any of the group's albums. It is thick and bursting with color, packed with photos of the Beasties at various stages of their career, as well as drawings, diagrams, and other bits of ephemera from their years in the music business. Also enlivening the book are contributions from a range of their friends. The distinguished writer Luc Sante provides an essay on the New York City music scene in 1981, the year the teenaged Beasties first came together as a band. The comedian Amy Poehler provides a mock review of the Beastie Boys' music videos. Filmmaker Spike Jonze offers a photo essay on working with the Beastie Boys. Celebrity chef Roy Choi provides a brief cookbook of Beastie-inspired dishes. Beastie Kate Schellenbach, of the band's initial punk incarnation, offers up a memoir of their early days and a tribute to an enduring friendship with the Boys. These are just a sampling of the guest essays that provide interesting and sometimes eccentric perspectives on the Beastie Boys phenomenon.

The main burden of carrying the book, though, falls on Diamond and Horovitz. They do not attempt to coauthor the text; each takes individual responsibility for a roughly equal number of chapters. That does not stop them and others from making acerbic comments on each other's narrative in notes printed in different colored ink. The result is a text that often reads like an ongoing conversation, heightening both the sense of fun and the immediacy of the book. A conscious decision to strive for informality may account for the exceedingly casual tone that both Diamond and Horovitz display in their sections of the book. The authors' prose reads as if directly transcribed from a tape recorder. This goes beyond the "as told to" approach of many purportedly first-person memoirs. Diamond and Horovitz are both now in their early fifties. As they make clear in their book, they have long since left behind their wild rock-and-roller days, and have settled into a more sedate and responsible lifestyle with wives and children. Yet their texts come across as if narrated by the twenty-year-old rappers they once were. In addition to being deliberately and juvenilely ungrammatical, they are free with expletives. Perhaps the authors actually still speak this way, although they may just be trying to connect with their fan base. In *Beastie Boys Book*, the boys will ever remain the Beasties of yore. Although Diamond and Horovitz don't explicitly make this point, cool calculation was always integral to their success.

The Beastie Boys began life as privileged white kids in New York City. All three attended progressive schools that made few demands that got in the way of their real interests. Diamond and Horovitz write with some genuine wonder at the forbearance of their parents, who let their teenaged children stay out late at night, wandering from one hole-in-the-wall night spot to another listening to hardcore punk. A good chunk of the early part of *Beastie Boys Book* is a celebration of the New York music scene at the dawn of the 1980s. Sante provides an overview, and Diamond and Horovitz fill in the personal blanks. It was the edgy and effervescent musical environment of the Big Apple, with its unending cross-fertilization of styles and rhythms, that nurtured the Beastie Boys and shaped their distinctive sound. They began as a wannabe punk band, a group of kids having fun practicing in each other's homes and playing in microscopic venues to audiences made up mostly of their friends. The original Beastie Boys lineup eventually settled down to Yauch, Diamond, Horovitz, and Schellenbach. The band achieved something of a breakthrough with their song "Cooky Puss," inspired by a Carvel ice cream cake. This became a hit with club DJs in New York. Part of another Beastie Boys song, the reggae-inflected "Beastie Revolution," was incorporated into a British Airways commercial. When the members of the group discovered what had happened, they sued and received $10,000 each, a fabulous sum to them, which made possible the purchase of better instruments.

Michael Diamond, known by his stage name Mike D, was a rapper and drummer for the Beastie Boys. Adam Horovitz, known by his stage name Ad-Rock, was a rapper and guitarist for the Beastie Boys. Beastie Boys Book is the first book for both of them.

By 1983, Yauch, Diamond, and Horovitz were falling under the spell of hip-hop music, which was beginning to emerge from its origins in the streets and underground clubs. They started experimenting with rapping. This led them in quest of a DJ. The person they found was Rick Rubin, a student at New York University. Much more than a DJ, Rubin was branching into music production. That year, with Russell Simmons, he launched Def Jam Recordings; together, these youthful entrepreneurs would ride the hip-hop wave to fame and fortune. Rubin encouraged Yauch, Diamond, and Horovitz in their rapping. The chauvinistic rap persona Rubin crafted for the Beastie Boys left no room for a young woman, and Schellenbach was dropped from the group. The hip-hop Beastie Boys—now sporting the stage names MCA, Mike D, and Ad-Rock—began recording with Def Jam, which was also producing the work of rap artists like LL Cool J and Run-DMC. This raised the group's profile. They were even booked to open for Madonna on her 1985 tour in support of *Like a Virgin*.

The great breakout for the Beastie Boys came with their 1986 debut full-length album *Licensed to Ill*. This was the record on which they claimed their right to party and perfected their image as pop music bad boys. The fruit of their labors was an album that reached number one on the Billboard charts and became a money-making machine for them and Def Jam. Wildly successful in their early twenties, the trio of Beasties had attitude to spare. They relished their rock star status and gave even more when they performed live on stage. Onstage antics began to catch up with them, however, during a tour of Great Britain, when members of the group were accused (unjustly) of insulting children with disabilities and throwing a full can of beer at a concertgoer. None of this derailed the Beastie Boys. In subsequent years, they parted ways with Def Jam Recordings and began working with collaborators like producer Mario Caldato Jr. They toned down the party guy hijinks, took up Tibetan Buddhism, and at some thirty years together, became not only a long-lasting group but an institution.

Long before this book appeared, Yauch, Diamond, and Horovitz regretted and apologized for the juvenile sexism of their hydraulic phallus days. They made amends with Schellenbach, releasing records by her band Luscious Jackson through the label they founded, Grand Royal. Rebels no more, the Beastie Boys became thoroughly domesticated members of the entertainment establishment; the Beastie Boys grew up. *Beastie Boys Book* is a chronicle of that process. It is also, with its wealth of illustrations and anecdotes, a rollicking time capsule that recaptures the energy and excitement of American popular music in the 1980s and 1990s.

Daniel P. Murphy

Review Sources

Review of *Beastie Boys Book*, by Michael Diamond and Adam Horovitz. *Kirkus Reviews*, 27 June 2018, www.kirkusreviews.com/book-reviews/michael-diamond/beastie-boys-book/. Accessed 4 Feb. 2019.

Review of *Beastie Boys Book*, by Michael Diamond and Adam Horovitz. *Publishers Weekly*, 30 July 2018, www.publishersweekly.com/9780812995541. Accessed 4 Feb. 2019.

Beller, Thomas. "A Capacious New History of the Beastie Boys by the Two Who Remain." Review of *Beastie Boys Book*, by Michael Diamond and Adam Horovitz. *The New York Times*, 30 Nov. 2018, www.nytimes.com/2018/11/30/books/review/beastie-boys-book-michael-diamond-adam-horovitz.html. Accessed 4 Feb. 2019.

Ruzicka, Michael. Review of *Beastie Boys Book*, by Michael Diamond and Adam Horovitz. *Booklist*, 15 Oct. 2018, www.booklistonline.com/Beastie-Boys-Book-Michael-Diamond/pid=9678167. Accessed 4 Feb. 2019.

Scott, A. O. "The Beastie Boys Put Down the Mic and Pick Up the Pen." Review of *Beastie Boys Book*, by Michael Diamond and Adam Horovitz. *The New York Times*, 24 Oct. 2018, www.nytimes.com/2018/10/24/arts/music/beastie-boys-book-interview.html. Accessed 4 Feb. 2019.

Vozick-Levinson, Simon. "Inside the Beasties' Wild, Moving Memoir." Review of *Beastie Boys Book*, by Michael Diamond and Adam Horovitz. *Rolling Stone*, Oct. 2018, www.rollingstone.com/music/music-features/beastie-boys-book-interview-adam-horovitz-michael-diamond-738703/. Accessed 4 Feb. 2019.

54

Bellewether

Author: Susanna Kearsley (b. 1966)
First published: *Bellewether*, 2018, in Canada
Publisher: Sourcebooks Landmark (Naperville, IL). 448 pp.
Type of work: Novel
Time: 1759, present day
Locale: Millbank, New York

Charley Van Hoek finds more than she bargained for when she takes over as curator of a small house museum on Long Island. Secrets are hidden in the history of the family who owned the house, but someone wants those stories told. As Charley discovers mysterious hints, she will uncover the truth behind a family's legend.

Principal characters

CHARLOTTE "CHARLEY" VAN HOEK, curator of the Wilde House Museum
NIELS VAN HOEK, her brother, a real estate lawyer
RACHEL, her teenage niece, Niels's daughter
THEO VAN HOEK, her father
BENJAMIN WILDE, a Revolutionary War hero
LYDIA WILDE, his sister
JOSEPH WILDE, one of his three brothers, a Loyalist
FRANK WILDE, present-day descendent of the Wilde family, board member at the museum
LIEUTENANT JEAN-PHILIPPE DE SABRAN DE LA NOYE, French-Canadian officer billeted with the Wilde family
VIOLET, enslaved African American woman living in the Wilde home
SAM ABRAMS, a contractor working on the museum

Author Susanna Kearsley is known for romance novels that contain at least one of the following: a touch of the paranormal, a hint of mystery, and a connection to the past. For instance, *Mariana*, which won the Catherine Cookson Fiction Prize in 1993, tells the story of a young woman who travels back to the seventeenth century. In *The Rose Garden*, published in 2011, Eva confronts the ghosts of those who lived in the house that she visits after her sister's death. After falling in love with a man from the past, she struggles to decide where she belongs. Kearsley's 2015 novel *A Desperate Fortune* also addresses the past; in this case, however, the main character stays firmly in the present while the past is related through the journal of an earlier woman.

In a similar manner, *Bellewether*, Kearsley's thirteenth novel, also carries readers on a journey through time as present-day Canadian American Charley Van Hoek moves to Millbank, New York, on Long Island, where her father's family, the Van Hoeks, are from. Her brother, Niels, has died and she is taking care of his teenage daughter, Rachel. Charley has also taken a job as a curator at the local Wilde House Museum. Unlike *Mariana* or *The Rose Garden*, Charley herself does not travel back in time; however, *Bellewether* takes readers back to the eighteenth century through the story of Lydia Wilde and Jean-Philippe de Sabran de la Noye, two unlikely lovers whose tale began in the house which has become Charley's museum.

The novel is framed, like a house, with a "Threshold" and a "Postern," chapters that essentially serve as a prologue and epilogue. The "Threshold" introduces the Wilde House and its architectural history, briefly establishing the reason it would become a museum in Charley's time. The rest of novel's structure is arranged around three narrators: Charley, Lydia, and Jean-Philippe. Charley's twelve present-day chapters start and finish the action of the novel. Charley narrates her chapters from a first-person point of view. Except for Charley's last chapter, each of her chapters are immediately followed by a narrative from Lydia and then one from Jean-Philippe, both told in limited omniscient narration. The chapters are tied together by small details; the weather or a twenty-first century object that appears at the end of one of Charley's chapters may resurface as a similar condition or object in the beginning of the following Lydia chapter. The chapters are also linked by the paranormal. The Wilde House comes with a mysterious but harmless ghost as well as a ghost story involving Lydia, Jean-Philippe, and Joseph.

Romance provides a thematic link between the present and past. At the beginning of the novel, Charley laments the distance between herself and the man she has been dating. So, when she finds herself attracted to contractor Sam Abrams, she struggles with her feelings. It is not surprising that her boyfriend leaves her; her niece and friends tell her they did not like him anyway, and her attraction to Sam goes into overdrive. The romance between Lydia and Jean-Philippe takes more time to grow. When they first meet, Lydia is still grieving the loss of her fiancé, her brother Joseph's best friend, at a battle in Canada, and she despises the very sight of the two French officers who had surrendered and have been sent to the Wildes' home as prisoners on a parole of honor. Lieutenant de Brassart easily fits the stereotype that she expects of the French, that "no Frenchman could ever be counted a gentleman," but Jean-Philippe surprises her with his gentle attitude. Over the months the men stay with the family, Jean-Philippe comes to care for Lydia and his careful attention to her family wins her heart as well.

The ghost story further encourages romance and mystery in the novel's present day. Frank Wilde, a descendant of Lydia's family, tells Charley the tale of a tragic romance between Lydia and Jean-Philippe. According to Frank, the lovers' attempted to sneak away from the Wilde's house one night, intending to board a waiting boat and move to Canada. When Jean-Philippe lights a lamp the couple are spotted by Joseph, who shoots Jean-Philippe. Lydia subsequently dies of heartbreak. On some nights, a light moves through the forest to the water where the two had planned to meet. The tale of the ghostly lieutenant is enhanced by several ghostly encounters Charley experiences

Susanna Kearsley is the author of thirteen novels. Though she studied politics and international development, her work experience includes being a curator at a museum. She has won the Romance Writers of America RITA Award, two RT Reviewers' Choice Awards, National Readers' Choice Awards, and the Catherine Cookson Fiction Prize.

while working in the museum. This legend, reinforced by a limited biography of Lydia's life, leads Charley on a quest to make the ill-fated couple's story known.

Kearsley's romances are often intertwined with carefully researched historical events and period details, and *Bellewether* is no different. The novel's narrative raises several historical issues, including the presence of slavery in the northern states in the eighteenth century. The Wilde family reportedly did not own slaves, but the presence of Violet, a black woman, in the house belies that story. Violet's background, her mother's life, and her father's identity come out as the story progresses, telling of abuse that affects the lives of the extended Wilde family. Jean-Philippe also reveals that his Canadian family owned slaves, something of which he disapproved. The French and Indian War is another historical tie throughout the novel. Joseph, Lydia's brother, fought for the British in the battles, but the loss of his best friend at the hands of the French damages him and leaves him bitter. This bitterness adds a layer of conflict when Jean-Philippe and de Brassart are sent to stay at the Wildes' home.

The titular *Bellewether* itself plays only a minor part in the story. The ship, which is one of several owned by Lydia's brother William, limps into the harbor near the Wilde House after having been attacked in the West Indies by Big Headed Tom, a pirate. As Lydia learns what happened to the *Bellewether*, she begins to question the relationships that she has always trusted, and she learns to let go of resentments that she has long held. The ship serves as a positive symbol when Joseph, who was trained to build ships, once again finds something to interest his mind; thus, the ship serves as a turning point for him as well.

Another war-related theme that is introduced, but not fully developed, is draft evasion. Joseph fought for the British in the French and Indian War before the action of the novel, but Frank tells Charley, "Joseph was the one who turned a traitor in the Revolution and went up to Canada." Charley's father also left the United States for Canada to avoid being sent to war. Charley says, "My father called himself a draft resister, though most other people, I had learned, preferred the more alliterative 'draft dodger.'" Her father's flight from service in the Vietnam War causes long-term family issues that Charley confronts as she tries to find healing.

In addition to the historical and war issues, there are a few more universal themes. Grief is a theme for many of the characters in the novel. Charley's grief over her brother Niels's death is clear from the beginning when she laments "Missing my brother, for me, was a physical pain. Three months on, it still felt as though some vital organ inside me had been ripped away and the wound stitched up badly, the edges too ragged to heal." Though Charley is able to function despite her grief, her niece, Rachel, struggles more heavily. She tries to go back to college after Charley comes to stay with her, but she cannot handle even simple everyday activities like showering and sleeping, so she drops out, returning to her father's home where Charley can keep an eye on her. The novel's eighteenth-century characters also grieve for loved ones they have lost. Lydia grieves for her mother and her lost fiancé. Joseph grieves for his best friend and his lost innocence, both lost in battle. French Peter, a neighbor to the Wilde family, loses a child. Jean-Philippe holds onto his grief over the death of Angélique, an enslaved West Indian woman who had been like a mother to him. Violet grieves the loss of her mother, Phyllis.

The importance of family is another theme that ties the narratives together. Charley's relationship with her niece and her love for her deceased brother are the reason for her move to Millbank, but her parents are mostly absent from the novel, remaining in Canada because of her father's health and his legal status as a draft resister. Since the museum is in the town where her father grew up, however, Charley learns about her extended family. Her wealthy grandparents had disowned Theo years before and ignored Niels' and Rachel's presence in their town, so Charley's expectations of a relationship with her grandmother are limited. Charley seeks out a meeting with her grandmother anyway, and a rift begins to heal.

Readers who are interested in colonial historical novels will find this book an enjoyable and fast read. Those who enjoy time travel, romance, and a touch of the supernatural will also find that it fits their expectations.

Theresa L. Stowell, PhD

Further Reading

Greenburg, Karin. Review of *Bellewether*, by Susanna Kearsley. *School Library Journal*, July 2018, p. 80. *Education Research Complete*, search.ebscohost.com/login.aspx?direct=true&db=ehh&AN=130382013&site=eds-live. Accessed 5 Dec. 2018.

Maguire, Susan. Review of *Bellewether*, by Susanna Kearsley. *Booklist*, 15 May 2018, pp. 20–21. *Literary Reference Center Plus*, search.ebscohost.com/login.aspx?direct=true&db=lkh&AN=129728616&site=lrc-plus. Accessed 5 Dec. 2018.

Renfro, Crystal. Review of *Bellewether*, by Susanna Kearsley. *Library Journal*, 1 July 2018, pp. 67. *Literary Reference Center Plus*, http://search.ebscohost.com/login.aspx?direct=true&db=a9h&AN=130388519&site=ehost-live. Accessed 5 Dec. 2018.

Beneath a Ruthless Sun
A True Story of Violence, Race, and Justice Lost and Found

Author: Gilbert King (b. ca. 1962)
Publisher: Riverhead Books (New York).
432 pp.
Type of work: History
Time: Primarily 1957–1971
Locale: Lake County, Florida

Pulitzer Prize–winning author Gilbert King tells the true story of Jesse Daniels, who was framed for rape by a notorious Florida sheriff, and the quest of journalist Mabel Norris Reese for Daniels's release.

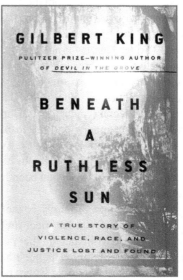

Courtesy of Penguin

Principal personages

JESSE DELBERT DANIELS, a white, intellectually disabled teenager, a fruit picker

WILLIS MCCALL, a racist sheriff who had him criminally committed

BLANCHE KNOWLES, the wife of a citrus grower, whom Daniels was accused of raping

MABEL NORRIS REESE, a small-town newspaper publisher who followed his case

Pulitzer Prize winner Gilbert King's book *Beneath a Ruthless Sun: A True Story of Violence, Race, and Justice Lost and Found* tells the story of Jesse Daniels, an intellectually-disabled teenager who was framed for rape in the rural Lake County, Florida, town of Okahumpka in the late 1950s. Daniels's tale is at the center of a sprawling tableau that touches on the unchecked power of Florida's citrus barons and the state's stark refusal to integrate schools in the wake of the Supreme Court case *Brown v. Board of Education* in 1954. In one of many textual asides, King recalls Dr. Martin Luther King Jr.'s harrowing 1964 visit to St. Augustine, Florida, which the civil rights leader described as "the most segregated city in America." The book's primary personage may be white, but as the author and legal journalist Jeffrey Toobin noted in his *New York Times* review, *Beneath a Ruthless Sun* "exposes the sinister complexity of American racism." Race, power, and wealth are the real themes of King's book.

Daniels's story also provides a unique lens for examining the myriad abuses of the county's murderous and corrupt Lake County sheriff Willis McCall. Toobin described McCall as "a figure of nearly incomprehensible evil." In a *New York Times* article about King's previous book, *Devil in the Grove: Thurgood Marshall, the Groveland Boys, and the Dawn of a New America* (2012), William Grimes described McCall as a "one-man reign of terror in Lake County" and quoted King as saying that McCall made the notorious Alabama lawman Bull Connor seem tame. "Connor used dogs and fire hoses," King wrote. "McCall actually killed people." McCall's unlikely foil in the book is a middle-aged white journalist named Mabel Norris Reese. Despite pressure from the state and the vigilante Ku Klux Klan, Reese doggedly pursued justice for those wronged by McCall, first in her small, self-published Mount Dora newspaper and then later from a larger outfit in Daytona Beach. Working with Daniels's indigent mother, Pearl, Reese dutifully followed the case for nearly twenty years, first proclaiming Jesse's innocence and then lobbying for his release from a notoriously barbaric mental institution, where Daniels served fourteen years for a crime he did not commit.

King's first book, *The Execution of Willie Francis: Race, Murder, and the Search for Justice in the American South* (2008), is set in Louisiana. In it, a black teenager named Willie Francis was convicted of murdering a white man and was sentenced to death. However, his execution by electric chair went awry and he did not die. The book follows Francis's subsequent Supreme Court case, in which he argued that a second execution attempt would be cruel and unusual punishment. King is best known, however, for *Devil in the Grove*, winner of the 2013 Pulitzer Prize for General Nonfiction. It too takes place in Lake County and features Sheriff Willis McCall—Toobin described *Ruthless Sun* as "a sequel of sorts" to *Devil*, which documents four black men accused of raping a white woman in 1949. Their lawyer was a young Thurgood Marshall, later a groundbreaking Supreme Court justice.

King again touches on that case in *Ruthless Sun*, noting how McCall shot two of the men after their convictions were overturned by the Supreme Court. One man was killed; the other survived to tell how McCall led the men into a grove while transporting them from the state prison to the county jail ahead of their retrial. In *Ruthless Sun*, the story serves to underscore McCall's cruelty, but also, and more disturbingly, his uncanny ability to escape responsibility for his crimes, even after flouting the highest court in the land. King did not initially intend to write another book about McCall or Lake County, but after meeting Noel "Evvie" Griffin, a former Lake County police deputy, at a reading of *Devil in the Grove*, King felt compelled to tell Jesse Daniels's story.

Ruthless Sun details how late one night in December 1957, Blanche Knowles, the thirty-one-year-old wife of wealthy citrus baron Joe Knowles, called her family lawyer. She told him that a black man had broken into her house—her husband was out of town visiting his mistress—and raped her. Within hours, McCall and his deputies rounded up nearly every young black man in Lake County. These included Bubba Hawkins, the nephew of Virgil Hawkins, who led a series of court battles, including a successful Supreme Court case, to integrate the University of Florida law school. Framing the young Hawkins for Knowles's rape would have been exactly the kind of race retribution favored by McCall and his men, yet after days of interrogation, Bubba and most of the other young men were released, and a white nineteen-year-old, Jesse Daniels, was arrested instead.

Reese, the newspaper reporter, had been following the Knowles rape case since the early morning hours after the crime took place. Daniels's arrest surprised and disturbed her. Daniels, who could not afford a lawyer, was held for days until McCall announced that Daniels had confessed to the rape. In short order, Daniels was deemed unfit to stand trial, precluding him from defending himself, and was shipped off to a notoriously brutal mental institution in Chattahoochee, Florida. He remained there for fourteen years. The second half of *Ruthless Sun* follows Reese's attempts to free Daniels, but it also complicates the story of the rape itself. King offers strong evidence that a black eighteen-year-old named Sam Wiley Odom really did rape Knowles and that McCall knew it. Odom was later tried for the rape of another woman and, according to the Florida law as it applied to black men, was sentenced to death. Most provocative, however, is the rumor that Odom was hired by Joe Knowles to kill Blanche—though the theory remains unproven.

The most remarkable aspect of King's book is the system of complicity employed by the state and federal government to satisfy the whims of powerful men. Working with state attorney Gordon Oldham, McCall insisted on Daniels's guilt for years—purely to protect the reputation of a wealthy white family, who did not want the stigma of one of their own having been raped by a black man. "The plot against Daniels seems baffling, verging on nonsensical—until you begin to see the community the way King does . . . deformed by racial animus and misogyny," Jennifer Szalai wrote in her *New York Times* review. Szalai did criticize King's tendency to include tangential anecdotes, like the case of the Platt children, members of an ethnic Irish Indian family, who looked too much like black children to be admitted to white Lake County schools. (McCall, of course, played an important role in the Platt case.) "This isn't to say that King's digressions are uninteresting, or even irrelevant," Szalai wrote. "It's just that combined with the baroque twists of the Daniels case, the book begins to get unwieldy." *Ruthless Sun*, she opined, lacks the momentum of *Devil* because its hero, Mabel Norris Reese, appears only through her newspaper editorials. (Reese died in 1995.) Still, Szalai concluded that King's argument about the embedded racism and corruption in Lake County "is timely and important, even if one sometimes wishes it were more clearly made."

Gilbert King is the author of The Execution of Willie Francis: Race, Murder, and the Search for Justice in the American South *(2008) and the Pulitzer Prize–winning* Devil in the Grove: Thurgood Marshall, the Groveland Boys, and the Dawn of a New America *(2012).*

Other critics offered similar praise, and *Beneath a Ruthless Sun* received starred reviews from *Publishers Weekly* and *Kirkus*. The reviewer for *Publishers Weekly* also described the book as "labyrinthine" but concluded, "Packed with riveting characters and startling twists, King's narrative unfolds like a Southern gothic noir probing the recesses of a poisoned society." The critic for *Kirkus* described the book as a "page-turner," writing that King "documents the lawless ferocity" with which Florida resisted granting black people their rights. "By turns sobering, frightening, and thrilling, this meticulous account of the power and tenacity of officially sanctioned racism recalls a dark era that America is still struggling to leave behind," the Kirkus reviewer asserted. Author Gary Krist described the book for the *Washington Post* as an "expertly told saga," writing that King "recounts this perplexing story with compassion and a vibrant sense of time and place." He noted, however, that though Daniels is eventually freed, true justice seems to have eluded the villains of Lake County. McCall, who was tried for and acquitted of the second-degree murder of a mentally ill black man in 1972, was voted out of office that year after serving seven consecutive terms as county sheriff. Oldham, who put more than fifty people on death row, retired with honor in 1984 and was memorialized in 2000 with a bench at the local courthouse.

Molly Hagan

Review Sources

Review of *Beneath a Ruthless Sun: A True Story of Violence, Race, and Justice Lost and Found*, by Gilbert King. *Kirkus*, 6 Feb. 2018, www.kirkusreviews.com/book-reviews/gilbert-king/beneath-a-ruthless-sun. Accessed 24 Oct. 2018.

Review of *Beneath a Ruthless Sun: A True Story of Violence, Race, and Justice Lost and Found*, by Gilbert King. *Publishers Weekly*, 12 Feb. 2018, www.publishersweekly.com/978-0-399-18338-6. Accessed 24 Oct. 2018.

Krist, Gary. "A Riveting Tale of Small-Town Southern Prejudice—with an Unusual Twist." Review of *Beneath a Ruthless Sun: A True Story of Violence, Race, and Justice Lost and Found*, by Gilbert King. *The Washington Post*, 11 May 2018, www.washingtonpost.com/outlook/a-riveting-tale-of-small-town-southern-prejudice--with-an-unusual-twist/2018/05/10/c57dbc24-38e1-11e8-9c0a-85d477d9a226_story.html. Accessed 24 Oct. 2018.

Szalai, Jennifer. "A True-Crime Mystery from the 1950s, Fueled by Racism and Corruption." Review of *Beneath a Ruthless Sun: A True Story of Violence, Race, and Justice Lost and Found*, by Gilbert King. *The New York Times*, 25 Apr. 2018, www.nytimes.com/2018/04/25/books/review-beneath-ruthless-sun-gilbert-king.html. Accessed 24 Oct. 2018.

Toobin, Jeffrey. "How a Racist Sheriff Railroaded a Disabled Teenager and Got Off." Review of *Beneath a Ruthless Sun: A True Story of Violence, Race, and Justice Lost and Found*, by Gilbert King. *The New York Times*, 3 May 2018, www.nytimes.com/2018/05/03/books/review/gilbert-king-beneath-ruthless-sun.html. Accessed 24 Oct. 2018.

The Best Cook in the World
Tales from My Momma's Table

Author: Rick Bragg (b. 1959)
Publisher: Alfred A. Knopf (New York).
  512 pp.
Type of work: Memoir
Time: 1960s
Locale: Alabama

The Best Cook in the World *depicts the hard-scrabble Southern life and cuisine of author Rick Bragg's family. It is his tenth book.*

Principal personages
RICK, the author
JIMMY JIM, his great-great-grandfather
AVA, his grandmother, who learned to cook
  during the Depression
CHARLIE, his grandfather and Ava's husband
MARGARET, his mother and the book's primary focus
AUNT JUANITA, Margaret's sister

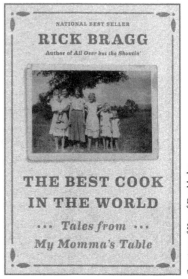

Courtesy of Knopf Doubleday

It is hard to know what genre *The Best Cook in the World* belongs to. Written by the celebrated journalist Rick Bragg, the five-hundred-page-plus tome is both a cookbook and a memoir. The book is filled with stories about Bragg's family members and their lives in Alabama throughout the early twentieth century, with each chapter punctuated by a beloved recipe or two. Although it is hard to put a label on such a literary mashup, *The Best Cook in the World* can be enjoyed by epicureans and historical biography lovers alike.

As a journalist, Bragg has established himself as an important representative of the American South. A former correspondent for the *New York Times* and regular contributor to *Gun & Garden* magazine, he won a Pulitzer Prize for his work in 1996. *The Best Cook in the World* reflects Bragg as a writer in that it goes back to his roots and focuses on one of his most favorite subjects: being "poor white trash." It is a designation that Bragg has used to describe his family in previous works including his critically acclaimed first book, *All Over but the Shoutin'* (1997).

With *All Over but the Shoutin'*, Bragg examined his experience growing up with an alcoholic father, who was dead by the age of forty, and his hardworking mother, Margaret, who did everything in her power to provide for her children. The book can essentially be described as an homage to Margaret and the sacrifices she made to ensure that Bragg and his siblings could escape poverty. Indeed, by picking cotton and taking on every odd job that came her way, Margaret was able to help her son go on to Harvard University and a successful career as a writer.

In many ways, *The Best Cook in the World* is a spiritual sequel to *All Over but the Shoutin'*. Rather than focus on his mother Margaret's sacrifices, however, it celebrates her cooking. At one point, Bragg suggests that the reason he never felt as poor as he actually was growing up was because of Margaret's food and his family's tradition of storytelling. Through delicious home-cooked meals and outrageous stories around the dinner table, the Braggs were rich in culture, tradition, and love. While a book that explores these themes has the potential to be cloying, Bragg masterfully ensures the tone is one of darkly comedic sentimentality and is never saccharine. He creates this balanced feeling by highlighting the beauty that exists in life's hardest moments.

One of the central ideas of *The Best Cook in the World* is that food is an essential part of familial identity. Recipes are comparable to heirlooms and should be passed down from generation to generation. This point is reinforced by the book's chronological organization, in which each chapter shares a story about one of Bragg's ancestors. The timeline begins in the 1920s and continues through 2017. The family stories typically include descriptions of the food they were eating at the time and occasionally detail how certain recipes came to be. Other times, they are simply amusing anecdotes loosely connected to Bragg's family meals. The chapter "Clementine," for example, showcases a recipe for fried chicken, green beans, and yellow potatoes. The story leading up to the recipe is about his father racing home to be on time for supper. When he arrived home, he told a young Bragg that he was driving so fast that he hit and killed "Clem Ritter" and left her body next to the road. Bragg believed his father had committed homicide until it was later revealed that Clem Ritter was his Aunt Juanita's dog, which survived.

Throughout the book, Bragg uses the kind of warm, colorful language that seems reminiscent of Alabama. Overall, the author's literary style has a distinctly Southern flavor with a pace that can be described as unrushed and meandering. The stories also have a below the Mason Dixon line feeling in that they focus largely on the funny twists and turns in otherwise everyday life. Each chapter is centered on a different character from Bragg's family. Sometimes he writes the stories from his perspective. Other times, he assumes their perspective and writes in the third person. The result feels like pages from a Mark Twain novel in that the stories follow fascinating, unusual Southern people and are brimming with irony.

Despite the fact it contains descriptive prose and character-driven narratives, *The Best Cook in the World* occasionally reads like a work of historical nonfiction. Through

© Steven Forster

An Alabama native, Rick Bragg is best known for his book All Over but the Shoutin' *(1997). He is a Pulitzer Prize– and James Beard Award–winning journalist. A regular contributor to* Gun & Garden *magazine, he teaches at the University of Alabama.*

Bragg's family, readers are provided with an in-depth look at what life was like for poor white Southerners throughout the first half of the twentieth century. Their lives were shaped by the Depression, wars, and Prohibition. There was not much work to be had and resources were limited. For anyone interested in this time and place, the book proves to be a fascinating read, especially when it comes to just how creative Bragg's family had to be to survive.

The family recipes shared in the book reflect such creativity. For example, Bragg shares instructions for making one of his mother's favorites, "poke salad," which is made from a toxic weed and is poisonous if not prepared carefully. Of course, if the family had not been so poor they would not have bothered to try and eat a potentially deadly plant. But it was something they had at their disposal, and so they found ways to circumvent the poisonous side effects. Another recipe that demonstrates the family's resourcefulness is "baked possum." To prepare a possum, Bragg reveals, it is necessary to first trap it and then tie it up for a week while feeding it corn. As their diet consists of carrion, this process helps flush all the dead animal meat from their bodies. It is a lot of work for what results in only a few pounds of meat, but that did not stop them.

While foods such as poke salad, baked possum, and snapping turtle soup may not sound appetizing to some readers, Bragg somehow successfully makes a case for their culinary importance. He reveals that his mother still makes poke salad, even though she can afford nicer ingredients. And the story of how his Aunt Juanita ate an entire baked possum, to her family's shock, and it ended up curing her of an illness is convincing of the meat's nutritional value. These are foods that are distinctly American, and yet have not been celebrated by chefs or reintroduced into restaurants the way many other poor Southern dishes have. By the end of the book, many readers will conclude that the exclusion of these types of foods is a mistake.

Reception of *The Best Cook in the World* has been overwhelmingly positive. Most critics have praised Bragg's ability to use cooking tips to transport them to the rural twentieth-century South. Jonah Raskin writes in his review for *New York Journal of Books*, "You can read this book for the stories, or the recipes, or for the language. Or for all of the above. It's likely that you'll find this book mouth-watering and likely, too, that you'll want to eat traditional Southern cooking of the sort that Rick Bragg's 'momma' made." It is true that one of the book's greatest qualities is how seamlessly Bragg blends personal stories with recipes. Bragg is an exceptional storyteller who truly knows how to capture characters, heart, and humor on the page. His writing is warm, intimate and highly engaging. It is easy to get lost in his family's stories.

Still, *The Best Cook in the World* has its shortcomings. For one, the book's length at times can feel overwhelming and in need of stronger editing. Bragg could have easily trimmed a hundred pages from it without much being lost. Although the anecdotes and recipes are brilliantly written, they share similar qualities and as such can feel a little repetitive after a while. Furthermore, the meandering style that Bragg writes in may not suit people who are looking for a more traditional memoir or cookbook. However, *The Best Cook in the World* is intended to reflect the oral storytelling tradition of Bragg's family and it succeeds in this goal. While this will delight readers who want to feel immersed in Southern culture, others may find it hard to follow.

Another aspect of the book that should be considered in a critical light is the way that the book handles the issue of race—or, more accurately, how it does not handle race. Bragg sets out to write about the experience of his family, which means that he is depicting the lives of poor white Alabamians; black Alabamians are not mentioned. There is nothing wrong with this fact, but it does seem like a missed opportunity for Bragg to not provide readers with a look into the racial dynamics of the South during this time. Considering that he states early on that he is interested in telling the stories of poor, working class people, there is no reason why he should not have explored what that meant to other racial groups who are in this category, especially considering how intertwined race and Southern food are, as the development of Southern cuisine is intertwined with the development of African American soul food to a significant extent.

Despite its flaws, however, *The Best Cook in the World* is unique and engrossing. In addition to capturing what life was like for his family in rural Alabama, Bragg has succeeded in writing a delicious cookbook. Margaret Bragg's penchant for butter, lard, fried foods, gravy, and fresh garden vegetables means that the resulting recipes will appeal to many as comfort food. Furthermore, the style in which Bragg writes his mother's recipes feels so intimate and special—they are essential transcribed from conversations that he has had with her. Ultimately, readers will get an education on Southern life, culture, and food with Rick Bragg's masterful *The Best Cook in the World.*

Emily Turner

Review Sources

Review of *The Best Cook in the World*, by Rick Bragg. *Kirkus Reviews*, 23 Jan. 2018, www.kirkusreviews.com/book-reviews/rick-bragg/the-best-cook-in-the-world. Accessed 5 Dec. 2018.

Review of *The Best Cook in the World*, by Rick Bragg. *Publishers Weekly*, 1 Jan. 2018, www.publishersweekly.com/978-1-4000-4041-4. Accessed 5 Dec. 2018.

Holahan, David. "The Best Cook: In Rick Bragg's Book About Momma's Table, It's All Over but the Eatin'." Review of *The Best Cook in the World*, by Rick Bragg. *USA Today*, 23 Apr. 2018, www.usatoday.com/story/life/books/2018/04/23/best-cook-rick-braggs-new-book-mommas-table-its-all-over-but-eatin/490711002/. Accessed 5 Dec. 2018.

Raskin, Jonah. Review of *The Best Cook in the World*, by Rick Bragg. *New York Journal of Books*, 24 Apr. 2018, www.nyjournalofbooks.com/book-review/best-cook. Accessed 5 Dec. 2018.

Brass

Author: Xhenet Aliu
Publisher: Random House (New York). 304
pp.
Type of work: Novel
Time: 1996 and present day
Locale: Waterbury, Connecticut

Xhenet Aliu's debut novel, Brass, *tells the story of a mother and daughter, each coming-of-age in working-class Waterbury, Connecticut.*

Principal characters

ELSIE, an eighteen-year-old waitress; Luljeta's mother
LULJETA, a seventeen-year-old yearning to know her father
BASHKIM, an Albanian refugee; Elsie's boyfriend
MAMIE, Elsie's alcoholic mother

Xhenet Aliu's debut novel, *Brass*, is set in working class Waterbury, Connecticut. Home to a now-shuttered brass factory, the town's slogan—"What's more lasting than brass?"—has become an ironic taunt to the overworked, underpaid people that live there. There are two threads to Aliu's funny and heartbreaking novel. Told in alternating chapters, one thread follows the coming-of-age story of a young woman named Elsie Kuzavinas in 1996. The other thread follows Elsie's seventeen-year-old daughter, Luljeta, known as Lulu, in the recent present.

Aliu, who works as an academic librarian in Athens, Georgia, was born and raised in Waterbury. She is, like Luljeta, of Albanian and Lithuanian descent, though the book is not autobiographical. Aliu's first publication, a collection of short stories called *Domesticated Wild Things, and Other Stories* (2013), received the Prairie Schooner Book Prize in Fiction. The stories also take place in Waterbury, featuring gritty, working-class characters and situations often marked by economic struggles and abusive relationships. *Brass*'s Elsie, and Luljeta for that matter, would fit in with such a crowd. Elsie's mother, called Mamie, is a depressed, alcoholic woman who treats her daughters' strep throat with ice cream. As a mother herself, Elsie tells Luljeta that Santa Claus didn't stop at their house because it didn't have a chimney—not because they were too poor to afford presents. Poverty, and the stew of emotions and fears that come with it, is a dispiriting constant, actively consuming every aspect of both generations' lives. Thus, when Elsie and Luljeta are offered a means of escape—Elsie through the advances of a young Albanian man and Luljeta through the prospect of moving away—they both rush to take it.

The book opens with Elsie. She has recently graduated from high school and works as a waitress at a Greek restaurant called the Betsy Ross Diner. There, she meets Bashkim, an Albanian line cook who tells her, "I swear to Allah, you are the most beautiful girl I have ever seen." Elsie describes the line as less of a compliment and more of a "threat." When she protests, he follows it up with: "Unless you are ungrateful. Unless you are a b—h." Their courtship progresses, mostly in the front seat of Bashkim's sports car. He has a wife back in Albania, but Elsie thinks of her as a kind of phantom, not real in their everyday lives. Her past experiences with men are unsubstantial. She's had boyfriends, but she has little memory of her father. He walked out on Mamie, Elsie, and Elsie's younger sister, Greta, years ago. When Elsie was about ten, Mamie off-handedly mentioned that he died. The women in *Brass* don't expect much from their male partners, and receive even less. Elsie, who goes on to date a kind, community college professor as an adult, keeps him at arm's length, afraid she will ask for something that he will not give.

Months after Elsie and Bashkim begin their fling, Elsie becomes pregnant. She tells herself she will seek an abortion, but for weeks, remains caught between actually doing it and telling Bashkim. When she finally does tell Bashkim, his reaction surprises her. He wants to have the child and raise it with her. The bulk of Elsie's story takes place over the course of her pregnancy and her tumultuous relationship with Bashkim, who was raised in a labor camp and insists on investing money in Albania's budding, but ultimately ill-fated, new democratic government.

Luljeta's story is quite different. Luljeta is a shy, seventeen-year-old high school honor roll student. Her world is turned upside down, however, when she receives a rejection letter from New York University, her dream school and the emblem of her escape from Waterbury. Later, her nemesis, a bully named Margarita, punches her in the face—but not before Luljeta lets fly an uncharacteristic zinger. Facing a suspension for being on the receiving end of a fight, Luljeta decides she will become a new person, the core of which will be shaped by the father she has never known. Luljeta begins her quest to find her father at the Betsy Ross Diner, where she meets a young Albanian boy named Ahmet. She also meets Elsie's former employer, and Bashkim's relative, Yllka. Luljeta is both thrilled and terrified by this connection. The reader knows the complexity of Elsie's story, even though Luljeta does not. "They'll never see each other, or themselves, as clearly as the reader gets to see them both—that's the magic trick here," Julie Buntin wrote in her review of the book for the *New York Times*. "In granting the reader access to both women's interiority, Aliu brings to life the simple, heartbreaking fact that though our stories can intersect, we're ourselves alone."

Luljeta loves her mother but resents her mother's love: "It's infuriating, your mother's need for you." Luljeta's story is written in the second person, connecting the "you" to Luljeta, while leaving the impression that the narrative is universal. "It's not fair that you should serve as her primary motivation for getting out of bed in the morning, especially considering that you have no idea what the hell you want from your own life, other than to get out of this crap town and figure it out elsewhere." Luljeta is torn between wanting a different life for herself and pleasing her mother, who does not want her to care about her father. Buntin captured some of Luljeta's guilt when she

Xhenet Aliu is an author and academic librarian. She published a collection of short stories called Domesticated Wild Things *in 2013.* Brass *is her first novel.*

wrote in her review, "I both wanted Lulu to 'get out,' and to shake her for being so ungrateful."

This is a natural reaction, though it also might have something to do with the dominance of Elsie's storyline, which is arguably the more dynamic of the two. Luljeta's quest to meet her father is believably constructed but lacks the real-life urgency of Elsie's predicament. Elsie must navigate a new living situation in a room with Bashkim in the house of Yllka and her husband. She is a cultural outsider and occasionally a social outcast, viewed as Bashkim's mistress. She must find money to raise a child while also, heartbreakingly, trying to figure out how to have a child without much guidance. She is filled with love and gratitude for the ultrasound technician who shows her perfunctory kindness, telling her that the baby looks beautiful—"which up until then I thought was just a word someone called you when he wanted a blow job."

Some scenes with Bashkim and Mamie, eviscerating with a wine glass in her hand, are painful to read. Neither of these characters, though, are one-dimensional villains. Bashkim, a refugee who suffered a horrifying childhood in a labor camp, seems to truly care for Elsie, though he still chooses to abandon her. His background does not excuse his behavior, but it serves as a reminder that abuse begets abuse. The same can also be said for Mamie. She may be the matriarch in this story, but Aliu suggests she is one in a line of young, single mothers who have suffered at the hands of abusive partners. In one startling scene, Elsie and her middle-aged coworkers crack a series of misogynist jokes. The session quickly ends; even jokes confront them with their own perceived worthlessness. These moments might make *Brass* seem too bleak, but Aliu's voice is quite funny, easing moments of suffering.

Brass received positive reviews when it was published in early 2018. In a starred review for *Kirkus Reviews*, one critic described it as a "glimmering debut," adding that "Aliu's writing is polished and precise, bringing her characters glowingly to life." Many critics praised Aliu's character development, including David Canfield, who, reviewing the novel for *Entertainment Weekly*, wrote that "Aliu has introduced herself as a major new literary voice," and that she "draws her heroines with such wit, grace and complexity." Caroline Leavitt of the *San Francisco Chronicle* had more praise for Aliu's authorial skill. "The writing blazes on the page," she wrote. "The narrative is also incredible funny, sly and always popping with personality." A reviewer for *Publishers Weekly* called it "a captivating, moving story of drastic measures, failed schemes, and the loss of innocence." In the *New York Times*, Buntin seemed personally moved by the story. "The moment Elsie and Lulu meet for the first time . . . transformed what was already a unique coming-of-age story and an incisive reckoning with class in America to something unforgettably wise and powerful," she wrote of a surprising, climactic scene. "'Brass' simmers with anger—the all too real byproduct of working hard for not enough, of being a woman in a place where women have little value. . . . Aliu alchemizes that anger into love, and in doing so creates one of the most potent dramatizations of the bond between mother and daughter that I've ever read."

In addition to its positive critical reviews, *Brass* was longlisted for the 2018 Center for Fiction First Book Prize.

Molly Hagan

Review Sources

Review of *Brass*, by Xhenet Aliu. *Kirkus Reviews*, 15 Oct. 2017. *Literary Reference Center Plus*, search.ebscohost.com/login.aspx?direct=true&db=lkh&AN=126220 210&site=lrc-plus. Accessed 29 Aug. 2018.

Review of *Brass*, by Xhenet Aliu. *Publishers Weekly*, 30 Oct. 2017. *Literary Reference Center Plus*, search.ebscohost.com/login.aspx?direct=true&db=lkh&AN=12 5966565&site=lrc-plus. Accessed 29 Aug. 2018.

Buntin, Julie. "A Mother and Daughter and a Town Made of 'Brass.'" Review of *Brass*, by Xhenet Aliu. *The New York Times*, 7 Mar. 2018 www.nytimes. com/2018/03/07/books/review/brass-xhenet-aliu.html. Accessed 29 Aug. 2018.

Canfield, David. "*Brass* Is a Gritty, Dazzling Novel about Chasing the American Dream: EW Review." Review of *Brass*, by Xhenet Aliu. *Entertainment Weekly*, 26 Jan. 2018, ew.com/books/2018/01/26/brass-xhenet-aliu-book-review/. Accessed 29 Aug. 2018.

Leavitt, Caroline. Review of *Brass*, by Xhenet Aliu. *San Francisco Chronicle*, 17 Jan. 2018, www.sfgate.com/books/article/Brass-by-Xhenet-Aliu-12505735.php. Accessed 29 Aug. 2018.

Brother

Author: David Chariandy (b. 1969)
First published: *Brother*, 2017, in Canada
Publisher: Bloomsbury Publishing (New
York). 192 pp.
Type of work: Novel
Time: 1980s–1990s
Locales: Scarborough and Toronto, Ontario;
Sainte Madeleine, Trinidad

Courtesy of Bloomsbury USA

*David Chariandy's award-winning second
novel,* Brother, *highlights the large trials
and small triumphs of growing up black in
urban Canada. A family of Trinidadian heritage fights to survive in an ethnically diverse,
economically challenged, and politically
scapegoated enclave of Scarborough, a section of Toronto.*

Principal characters
MICHAEL JOSEPH, the narrator
FRANCIS JOSEPH, his older brother
RUTH JOSEPH, their mother, born in rural Trinidad
AISHA, a young woman who used to live in the neighborhood
JELLY, Francis's best friend, a talented disc jockey
SAMUEL, Aisha's father, a security guard

Michael Joseph, the narrator of *Brother*, informs readers that his community of Scarborough, Ontario, is locally nicknamed "Scarlem" and "Scarbistan," and was once
known as "Scarberia" for its distance from downtown Toronto. The nickname "Scarlem" suggests a fitting comparison: Scarborough, like Harlem, is an inner-city community that residents in the surrounding metropolis—Toronto and New York, respectively—periodically view with varying degrees of acceptance, disdain, suspicion, fear,
or alarm. Scarborough, like its American counterpart, contains a large concentration of
people of color. Many Scarborough residents come from South and Central America,
the Caribbean, the Middle East, China, and India, gravitating to the area where immigrants typically collect in Canada's largest city.

Michael's parents exchanged the poverty of a village in Trinidad for the poverty
endemic to a run-down urban Canadian neighborhood in Scarborough called the Park.
Michael and his older brother, Francis, have never known any life but that experienced
while residing in their no-frills unit in a building called the Waldorf, an ironic name
now that the structure is old and crumbling. The boys, born in Canada, only vaguely
remember their father, who deserted the family when they were just toddlers, but who

is rumored to live elsewhere in the city. The children are raised by their mother, Ruth, who once had ambitions of becoming a nurse. She toils long hours commuting to and from cleaning jobs at distant office buildings or shopping malls. From an early age, Michael and Francis are left alone with stern admonishments from Ruth to behave while she is gone (do not unlock the door; do not fiddle with the knobs on the stove). Led by curious, ingenious instigator Francis, however, the siblings manage to get into relatively harmless mischief: they escape outside, gorge themselves on sweets, and break things.

The existence of the Joseph family is difficult, but tolerable in an environment where the hard-working, neighborly residents greet one another daily, trade recipes, listen to music together, and generally look out for one another. Scarborough also has its attractions; its denizens live adjacent to Lake Ontario. Better still, the Rouge Valley, a national urban park carved out by retreating glaciers, is contained almost entirely within Scarborough's boundaries. The boys grow up playing frequently in the Rouge: splashing in creeks, building forts, or following the tracks of wild animals.

As Michael and Francis age, they develop quite different personalities. Michael is an introvert who often visits the library with a studious neighbor named Aisha. Francis, however, is outgoing and bold, popular with the girls, and respected by older, tougher kids for his brooding nature and explosive temper. Francis is afraid of nothing. His fearlessness is demonstrated in an incident at a bus stop when a gang led by a boy flashing a hunting knife threatens Michael. Without hesitation, Francis grabs the naked blade with his bare hand and, unconcerned about cutting himself, wrests the knife away.

By the time Francis reaches double-digits in age, he has become a surrogate father to Michael, often reminding his sibling to stand up for himself. Francis teaches Michael special skills he has learned on his own. For example, Francis shows Michael how to climb to the top of a utility power pole without being electrocuted by hazardous live wires. The purpose of Francis's exercise is to help Michael accept the risk inherent in pursuing a goal: from the lofty perch he can gain a new perspective about the place where he lives and see the patterns of the streets.

When the brothers reach their teenage years, they become physically separated. Michael, still a nerdy type who wants to be more like Francis but does not have the courage to emulate his brother, begins a relationship with Aisha after she introduces him to sex. Francis, who once enjoyed education, has a confrontation with a teacher in a high-school class, mouths off, is expelled, and never returns to school. Ashamed to have failed his family and unable to face his mother's disappointment, Francis leaves home—though he returns occasionally with groceries to help the struggling family. Francis begins hanging out with a group of other young men of questionable reputation at Desirea's, a strip-mall barbershop run by a man named Dru. Francis and the others spend days and nights at the shop, listening to music as played by his disc-jockey friend Jelly, and, it is rumored, smoking marijuana. Michael visits his brother there, where he is shown to Francis's tiny new living quarters, in the barbershop storage room. His cot is even smaller than the bunkbeds they had shared.

Though Francis does not have a driver's license and has never taken driving lessons, he co-owns a beat-up Honda convertible, and takes his brother for a harrowing ride around town. The car is transportation for the brothers and Jelly, who wants to compete in a disc-jockey competition for a possible contract from a powerful event promoter. In one of *Brother*'s most memorable passages, Jelly is shown to be a genius at what he does. With Francis handing records back and forth, Jelly auditions for the promoter and a well-known professional disc jockey, the Conductor. Jelly starts with a simple Somalian song, adds bass and drum lines, then seamlessly integrates many different types of music—soul, calypso, rhumba, blues, country-western, punk—to create a unique soundtrack that causes the Conductor to rise and applaud. After the audition, Francis, worried that the promoter does not have Jelly's contact information, attempts to re-enter the place where the contest was held, but is stopped by four large bouncers. In response to a black bouncer's insults, the much smaller Francis breaks the man's nose with a single punch. After Michael and scrawny Jelly are quickly eliminated from participating in the fight, Francis is viciously beaten and kicked to a bloody pulp. As the friends limp away, the promoter calls after them, warning that if they come back the police will be called to arrest them.

The Park neighborhood of Scarborough suddenly receives unwanted negative publicity following a shooting near the Joseph family's home. A casual acquaintance of Francis's is killed, several people are wounded, and a sleeping child is narrowly missed by stray bullets. Afterward, inflammatory editorials appear in newspapers condemning the suburb as a breeding ground for violence. The city government steps up police presence in the area, and the barbershop becomes a target. Squads of armed policemen in bulletproof vests make regular unannounced visits to hassle whoever they find. The young men are manhandled, told to turn out their pockets, made to produce identification, and otherwise harassed. Each visit by law enforcement is more threatening than the last and their arrival invariably turns the barbershop's atmosphere from relaxed and friendly to tense and dangerous.

The structure of *Brother* is nonlinear, which adds both to its suspense and its poignancy. The story opens in the 1990s with the reunion of Michael and Aisha, now both adults in their mid-twenties, whose careers are heading in opposite directions. Michael has worked for five years at the Easy Buy, a discount supermarket, "unloading skids, bagging groceries, cleaning up spills in aisles." By contrast, Aisha, who was granted a scholarship as a teen, is now a writer and freelance computer programmer who has worked and traveled around the world. While Aisha is in town, tending to her dying father, she stays at the Joseph's humble abode, sleeping on the bottom bunk, Michael's usual bed, while he sleeps on the living room couch. The top bunk has no mattress because it is no longer needed: Francis has been dead for ten years. By the end of the first chapter readers realize that Ruth—first seen watching television with the sound off—is not in her right mind. The plot, which unspools over the course of the novel, shows how the combination of Francis's volatile character, his unpredictable behavior, his associations, and the increasingly antagonistic attitudes of the surrounding community all contributed to his untimely demise. Francis's death, in turn, results in Ruth's madness, which manifests in frightening ways: when not carefully watched, she wanders away, often barefoot.

The bulk of Chariandy's semi-autobio-
graphical novel (the author was born and
raised in Scarborough) consists of vignettes
told in flashbacks as crisp as high-contrast
black-and-white snapshots that sharply etch
character-defining moments for members
of the Joseph family. The young boys are
seen, for example, conducting a heartbreaking search for their missing father. They ring
doorbells at random in a low-rise apartment
building where Mr. Joseph may have been
spotted until a man answers, telling them
over the intercom to go away. In another section, young Michael and Francis are taken
by their mother to Trinidad so they can meet
their relatives and experience their Caribbean heritage first-hand, the better to appreciate the food and the culture of the island once
they return to Canada.

Balanced against episodes from the past
is a secondary storyline set in the present.
Aisha plans to gather together as many of the

© Joy von Tiedemann

David Chariandy's debut novel, Sou-
couyant *(2007), won a Gold Independent
Publisher Award for Best Novel and was
nominated for several other major Canadian literary awards. His second novel,* Brother, *was awarded the $50,000
Writer's Trust Fiction Prize in 2017.*

old gang from a decade ago that can be found for a party to commemorate the life of
Francis on the tenth anniversary of his death. The hope is that the event will bring Ruth
back to reality.

Evocative, nuanced, and often lyrical, *Brother* contains powerful, startling imagery that underscores the novel's central theme: good, bad, or indifferent, life is worth
celebrating, even for those living on the fringes in hostile territory. Critics greeted the
novel with acclaim, and it received Canada's Writer's Trust Fiction Prize.

Jack Ewing

Review Sources

Donaldson, Emily. "David Chariandy's 'Brother.'" Review of *Brother*, by David
    Chariandy. *Canadian Notes & Queries*, Winter 2018, notesandqueries.ca/reviews/
    david-chariandys-brother-reviewed-by-emily-donaldson/. Accessed 15 Oct. 2018.

Eidse, David. Review of *Brother*, by David Chariandy. *The Winnipeg Review*, 15
    Oct. 2017, winnipegreview.com/2017/10/brother-by-david-chariandy/. Accessed
    15 Oct. 2018.

Grubisic, Brett Josef. "Brother a 'Poetic Vision' in the Heart of Scarborough."
    Review of *Brother*, by David Chariandy. *The Toronto Star*, 29 Sept. 2017, www.
    thestar.com/entertainment/books/reviews/2017/09/29/brother-a-poetic-vision-in-
    the-heart-of-scarborough.html. Accessed 15 Oct. 2018.

Nayeri, Dina. "'Brother" by David Chariandy Review—A Family on the Edge of Disaster." Review of *Brother*, by David Chariandy. *The Guardian*, 16 Mar. 2018, www.theguardian.com/books/2018/mar/15/brother-by-david-chariandy-review. Accessed 15 Oct. 2018.

Nurse, Donna Bailey. "Lives of a Brother: Love, Hope and Death in Scarberia." Review of *Brother*, by David Chariandy. *Literary Review of Canada*, Oct. 2017, reviewcanada.ca/magazine/2017/10/lives-of-a-brother/. Accessed 15 Oct. 2018.

Call Me American

Authors: Abdi Nor Iftin (b. 1985) with Max
  Alexander (b. 1957)
Publisher: Alfred A. Knopf (New York).
  320 pp.
Type of work: Memoir
Time: 1985–the present
Locales: Somalia, Kenya, United States

Call Me American *is a memoir by Abdi Nor
Iftin with Max Alexander. It chronicles Iftin's
life growing up in Somalia during the wars
of the 1990s before immigrating to the United States as well as contemplations about
life in his adopted country.*

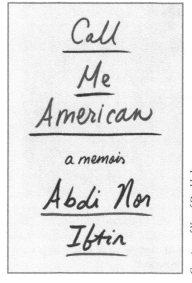

Courtesy of Knopf Doubleday

Principal personages
ABDI NOR IFTIN, narrator, the middle child
  of three
MADINAH IBRAHIM MOALIM, his mother, a traditional nomadic herder of the Rahanw-
  eyn clan
NUR IFTIN, a.k.a. Nur Dhere, his father, a traditional nomadic herder of the Rahanw-
  eyn clan who became a well-known Somali basketball player
HASSAN NOR IFTIN, his older brother
NIMA NOR IFTIN, his younger sister
MOHAMMED SIAD BARRE, Somalian dictator and president who came to power in
  1969
MOHAMMED FARRAH AIDID, Somalian army general; leader of the rebels
SICIID, the Iftins' neighbor in Mogadishu

Call Me American opens with the birth of author Abdi Nor Iftin under a neem tree in
Mogadishu, the capital of Somalia. He is unsure of the date but believes it must have
been around 1985. What is striking about this entry into the author's life is the way
he uses the opportunity to pull the reader into the landscape that surrounded him and
his family and the culture that is connected to it. "Neem trees grow everywhere in Somalia, with fragrant blossoms like lilacs and medicinal bitter sap that prevents sores,"
Iftin writes. "The trees have small leaves, but the limbs spread wide and give shelter
from the sun—a good place to have a baby. A good place to be born."

 Connection to land and culture drives Iftin's narrative. When his parents move
from their rural home to Mogadishu, due to drought and famine, they are thrust into
a whole new world and must adjust to life away from the land they know best. Iftin
chronicles their life in the city. His father becomes a well-known basketball star, recognizable to those in his community and a hero to his sons.

© Michael Lionstar

Call Me American *is Abdi Nor Iftin's first book. Iftin works closely with the Somali community in Maine as a medical translator.*

Iftin is six years old when civil war breaks out in Somalia between the Somalian government led by President Mohammed Siad Barre of the Darod clan and rebel militias led by Siad Barre's rival, army general Mohammed Farrah Aidid of the Hawiye people. The Iftin family flees Mogadishu for Baidoa, in the south-central Bay region where Iftin's parents are from, hoping to find safety with family, but the conflict is spreading. His father is forced to leave the family because families are safer without men, as soldiers are less likely to kill women and children. Iftin, his siblings, and his mother hide in the brush, foraging for whatever food they can find, all while his mother is pregnant. Eventually, the family returns to Mogadishu when it is deemed the safest place to settle, but even there, there is no guarantee.

The title *Call Me American* comes from Iftin's love of American culture. While in Mogadishu, US Marines enter the city hoping to quell the violence, and Iftin becomes enamored with them—with their power and their uniforms. Iftin describes one of the moments in which his fervor for the Americans stood out most significantly:

I stood on the beach, picking through the discarded camouflage uniforms with the American names sewn above the pockets. I held them up, hoping one would fit my skinny little body. My friends Mohammad, Bashi, and Bocow laughed. I looked at them and scowled.

"I'm not Somali," I said. "I am *Mareekan*. I was left behind by the marines. And they will come for me soon."

Before Iftin meets the marines, however, he begins to obsess over American culture through films. Iftin and his brother Hassan also go to a neighbor's home to watch American movies like *Die Hard* and *Terminator* on her small TV and stay up at night talking about the movies' stars, debating whether Arnold Schwarzenegger vacations in nearby Kenya.

When the Islamist extremist group al-Shabaab takes over the country during Iftin's teen years, his obsession with America becomes a point of danger. At one point, he is told to abandon his nickname and overt interest or risk death during an anonymous phone call. Iftin eventually escapes to Kenya. After winning the US visa lottery, he settles in Maine, where he works as a medical translator.

The language Iftin uses throughout *Call Me American* is both simple and effective. Poignant descriptions of his family allow Iftin to express what has been lost when the members are torn apart. At one point, when his newborn sister dies from malnutrition, he expresses jealousy, considering her the lucky member of the family who escaped the suffering endured by the others. Iftin juxtaposes his baby sister's death with a scene of his remaining sister, Nima, eating sand to fill her belly.

Iftin's detailed recounting of his family's struggle to survive during the civil war, in particular, allows him to open up his story. To provide water for their family, Iftin and Hassan must wait in line for hours to fill up a jug. Eventually, even this action becomes dangerous, as the two begin to sneak out at night to avoid the lengthy wait. The relationship between the brothers appears seamless, as if they are acting on a psychic level that allows them to navigate the dangerous landscape surrounding them.

The story is also timely in 2018, as President Donald Trump's administration has threatened to end the US diversity visa lottery and has imposed entry restrictions, commonly referred to as the travel ban, on people from Somalia and six other countries; of these, Somalia, along with Iran, Libya, Yemen, and Syria, are Muslim-majority countries. Iftin writes about the danger felt by the Somali community in Maine after Trump's election in 2016. The anti-Muslim rhetoric used by Trump's campaign to capture the presidency had Iftin and his friends on edge, and in many ways Iftin can no longer recognize the country he once loved, though he has not given up on it. Iftin wants his actions to serve as an example of why immigrants like him are important to the United States.

The political message of Iftin's work is not partisan, however, but rather that of a person who lives in one place yet longs for, and believes he belongs in, another—in this case, the United States. During the latter part of *Call Me American*, Iftin writes about the difficulty he had of fitting in as a recent immigrant and of how he endured the teasing of those around him. But he also recalls the changing of the seasons and the new people he has met. Because of the linear structure of the story, *Call Me American* is able to capture Iftin's journey more effectively than it could through flashbacks. As the reader follows Iftin from his birth to his adult life in the United States, the memories that make up his life begin to fit together like a puzzle.

Critical reception for the book was warm. More often than receiving a review, Iftin himself would appear on television and radio interviews, or give interviews to print and online outlets. Nearly unanimously, those who responded to the book commented on its simple but haunting structure and tale. In his review for the *Portland Press Herald*, Frank O Smith wrote, "It is an inspiration and a reminder, an especially timely one, of how powerful the American dream remains to legions of people across the globe, especially those caught in the grind of religious, political and tribal terror and destruction." For the *New York Review of Books*, Jane Constantineau wrote, "Iftin's account of his journey does not mince words or attempt to soften the worst atrocities he and his family experienced. Loyal and grateful to his mother, he shows particular sensitivity to the injustices suffered by women in Somalia." In fact, Iftin's relationship with his mother remains an important point to his life. Much of the money he earns as a translator goes back to her—she still lives in Somalia—and to his other family members.

Iftin ends *Call Me American* with meditations about his mother, Trump's presidency, and Islam. His mother, he writes, is getting older. She cannot see or hear as well as she once could. However, her body is still strong—she can still run and jump the way she did as a young woman—and her perseverance gives him strength in his new life. He also dreams of bringing her to the United States before her death so she can see the snowfall and try "the sweet drinks at Starbucks."

He also laments radical Islamism and how it continues to affect those living in Somalia. He writes, "Radical Muslims do not represent Islam. Nor do they represent the hopes and dreams of the Somali people." He then goes on to describe what Islam and his home mean to him and how the political landscape is changing in Somalia.

Iftin's book is one perfectly situated in this political and cultural moment. His ability to tell a hard story without becoming sentimental or nostalgic is a tremendous feat. At a time when nations are becoming more divided, stories like Iftin's bring the focus back to how an individual life can be impacted by the political landscape at home and abroad.

Melynda Fuller

Review Sources

Review of *Call Me American*, by Abdi Nor Iftin. *Kirkus*, 20 Mar. 2018, www.kirkus-reviews.com/book-reviews/abdi-nor-iftin/call-me-american/. Accessed 20 Nov. 2018.

Constantineau, Jane. Review of *Call Me American*, by Abdi Nor Iftin. *New York Journal of Books*, 19 June 2018, www.nyjournalofbooks.com/book-review/me-american. Accessed 20 Nov. 2018.

Dwyer, Dialynn. "A Somali Refugee Always Dreamed of Being American. Now, He Lives in Maine and He's Written a Memoir about His Journey." Review of *Call Me American*, by Abdi Nor Iftin. *The Boston Globe*, 18 June 2018, www.boston.com/news/books/2018/06/18/call-me-american-abdi-nor-iftin. Accessed 20 Nov. 2018.

Smith, Frank O. "Against Tremendous Odds, Abdi Nor Iftin Made It from War-Ravaged Somalia to America." Review of *Call Me American*, by Abdi Nor Iftin. *Portland Press Herald*, 13 July 2018, www.pressherald.com/2018/07/15/against-tremendous-odds-abdi-nor-iftin-made-it-from-war-ravaged-somalia-to-america/. Accessed 20 Nov. 2018.

Call Them by Their True Names
American Crises (and Essays)

Author: Rebecca Solnit (b. 1961)
Publisher: Haymarket Books (Chicago). 166 pp.
Type of work: Essays
Time: 2016–18
Locales: San Francisco, California; New York, New York; United States

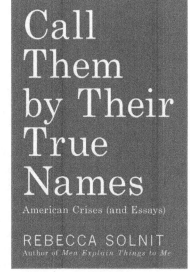

Journalist Rebecca Solnit's latest collection of essays, Call Them by Their True Names: American Crises (and Essays), *presents pieces about American politics, police brutality, and climate change that she published between 2016 and 2018.*

Author and essayist Rebecca Solnit has written on a broad range of subjects. One of her better-known works, an essay collection called *Men Explain Things to Me*, was published in 2014. The title essay, first published in 2008, was a viral sensation. In it, Solnit describes meeting a man at a party who, upon hearing that she is a writer, insists on condescendingly summarizing a review of a book for her. A friend tries to interrupt him several times, but ignorant and unfazed, the man proceeds to explain Solnit's own book to her. Reactions to the piece coined the popular term "mansplaining." Other essays in that book explore larger transgressions, and how women are often discredited, even when they are talking about their own lives. Solnit published a follow-up to that book, another collection of feminist essays, called *The Mother of All Questions,* in 2017.

Many of Solnit's earlier essay collection similarly examine social problems. *Hope in the Dark: Untold Histories, Wild Possibilities* (2004), originally published as a reaction to the US invasion of Iraq, was reissued in 2016. Marketed as a guide for activists in dark times, it enjoyed tremendous popularity among progressives after the 2016 presidential election. *A Paradise Built in Hell: The Extraordinary Communities That Arise in Disaster* (2009), explores how people come together in times of disaster, arguing that the communities formed in bad times offer hints about how society can function in good times. Solnit's other books include *Savage Dreams: A Journey into the Hidden Wars of the American West* (1994), about wars against indigenous people and nuclear testing in Nevada; *River of Shadows: Eadweard Muybridge and the Technological Wild West* (2003), about the converging histories of Hollywood and Silicon Valley; and *Wanderlust: A History of Walking* (1999), a book about walking as a pleasurable but also political act. Solnit also wrote an ongoing column for *Harper's Magazine* and was a regular contributor to publications such as the *Guardian* and the

London Review of Books.

Solnit's essay collection *Call Them by Their True Names: American Crises (and Essays)*, explores American politics, police brutality and climate change. All of the pieces included were written between 2016 and 2018. The title, Solnit explains in the book's foreword, was inspired by a fairy tale trope. The character Rumpelstiltskin, for example, was defeated when the woman at the heart of the story discovered his true name. In the same vein, Solnit encourages her readers to be direct about societal ills like racism. "Calling things by their true names cuts through the lies that excuse, buffer, muddle, disguise, avoid, or encourage inaction, indifference, obliviousness," she writes. "It's not all there is to changing the world, but it's a key step."

This concept is fruitfully explored in the essay "Break the Story," a revised version of a commencement address Solnit gave at her alma mater, the University of California, Berkeley's Graduate School of Journalism. In the piece, which appears in the fourth section of the book, she calls on journalists to examine the larger framework in which they tell stories. She questions common wisdom about objectivity, and writes about the impossibility of truly neutral ground. For example, she asks, why is choosing not to own a car considered political, but owning a car is not? She cites a quote from the late Ben Bagdikian, her ethics professor at UC Berkeley and a journalist who played a key role in the publication of the Pentagon Papers (documents that broke the story of presidential lies and the Vietnam War) and later published noted works about the threat of growing media monopolies. Bagdikian, Solnit writes, once said, "You can't be objective, but you can be fair." In these essays, and in her attempt to name things are they truly are, Solnit does well by this credo.

The first section of the book, "Electoral Catastrophes," explores the presidential campaign and 2016 election of Donald Trump. Solnit writes about Trump's misogyny and comments he made denigrating his hometown, New York City. She moves on to larger political ideas in the second section, "American Emotions." In the section's first essay, "The Ideology of Isolation," she argues that isolation, the idea "that people are not connected to other people, and that they are all better off unconnected," is the core of American right-wing ideology. She relates this isolationist worldview to conservative skepticism of climate change, a topic that she has covered in more detail in other works. Climate change, she argues, proves that people are inextricably linked to each other and to the earth itself. In the second section's last essay, "Preaching to the Choir," Solnit unpacks the title phrase. She argues that there is value in speaking, organizing, and parsing nuance among those who share similar views. "The primary assumption behind the idea that we shouldn't preach to the choir is that one's proper audience is one's enemies, not one's allies," she writes. She would rather follow the example of actual preachers, who rally their congregations and unite them in a common goal.

Solnit returns to the topic of climate change in the book's third section, "American Edges." In an essay called "Climate Change Is Violence," she draws a distinction between "hands-on violence" and "industrial-scale violence." Hands-on violence requires a direct exchange between perpetrator and victim, such as injuries inflicted by gun, knife, or car. The latter category includes events like nuclear war that destroy hundreds or thousands or even millions of lives at a time. Similar points have been made before, but Solnit was inspired to write the essay after coming across a press release warning of a "direct link" between climate change and a rise in violence. She was frustrated that the construction of the warning failed to address climate change itself as an act of violence. It suggests that the only type of violence we face is of the hands-on variety; companies that accelerate climate change are absolved by omission despite the fact that they perpetrate violence on an industrial scale. Her point relates to her larger thesis in "Break the Story," about how language shapes the way we see the world.

Two other essays in the third section of the book focus on specific people. In "Death by Gentrification: The Killing of Alex Nieto and the Savaging of San Francisco," first published in the *Guardian* in 2016, Solnit tells the story of Alejandro "Alex" Nieto, a resident of the Bernal Heights neighborhood of San Francisco who was murdered by police in 2014. The essay describes Nieto's killing, which occurred after a new neighborhood resident called 911, thinking that Nieto, who was eating lunch in the neighborhood's public park, was carrying a gun. Nieto had a Taser hooked to his belt for his job as a nightclub security guard. In "Bird in a Cage: Visiting Jarvis Masters on Death Row," Solnit writes about Masters, who was sentenced to death for conspiring to murder a guard while in prison. Despite evidence supporting his innocence, the fifty-seven-year-old Buddhist writer remained on death row at the time Solnit was writing.

Nadia Ismail, who reviewed the book for the *Columbia Journal*, deemed "Death by Gentrification" and "Bird in a Cage" the strongest essays in the collection. Solnit's "longtime knowledge of the San Francisco Bay Area and its communities comes through and breathes a freshness and complexity into her advocacy for vulnerable populations," Ismail wrote. "These essays felt more like stories rather than vehicles for rhetoric, although there is of course politics wrapped up into both." Ismail, who offered the book a mostly positive review, did criticize Solnit for including too many essays about rhetoric, and too few about people.

Call Them by Their True Names was longlisted for the 2018 National Book Award for Nonfiction and won a 2018 Kirkus Prize. In a starred review, the *Kirkus* reviewer wrote: "Solnit is careful with her words (she always is) but never so much that she mutes the infuriated spirit that drives these essays." A reviewer for *Publishers Weekly* wrote, "As always, [Solnit] opts for measured assessment and pragmatism over hype and hysteria."

© Adrian Mendoza

Rebecca Solnit is an award-winning author and essayist. Among her best-known books are Men Explain Things to Me *(2014),* Hope in the Dark: Untold Histories, Wild Possibilities *(2004), and* River of Shadows: Eadweard Muybridge and the Technological Wild West *(2003).*

Paul Constant, writing for the *Seattle Review of Books*, joked that he was depressed after finishing the book because other thinkers, particularly those on social media, seem "murky and grey" next to Solnit's exacting prose. "Arguments are less sharp, reality seems confusing in its moral complications," he wrote. "It's like going from a high-definition television to a grainy black-and-white set with a clothes-hanger antenna." Maria Popova, writing for the website *Brain Pickings*, described Solnit as "one of our era's boldest public defenders of democracy, and one of the most poetic," and placed the writer in a long line of cultural thinkers who have considered how best to use language to speak truth to power, including *Silent Spring* author and environmentalist Rachel Carson, novelist Virginia Woolf, author James Baldwin, and fantasy writer Ursula K. Le Guin. In particular, Popova praised *Call Them by Their True Names*, writing, " the pieces in the book furnish an extraordinarily lucid yet hopeful lens on the present and a boldly uncynical telescopic perspective on the future."

Molly Hagan

Review Sources
Review of *Call Them by Their True Names: American Crises (and Essays)*, by Rebecca Solnit. *Kirkus*, 16 July 2018, www.kirkusreviews.com/book-reviews/rebecca-solnit/call-them-by-their-true-names/. Accessed 25 Feb. 2019.
Review of *Call Them by Their True Names: American Crises (and Essays)*, by Rebecca Solnit. *Publishers Weekly*, 13 Aug. 2018, www.publishersweekly.com/978-1-60846-329-9. Accessed 25 Feb. 2019.
Constant, Paul. "Rebecca Solnit Calls Us by Our True Names, but Sometimes We Can't Hear Her." Review of *Call Them by Their True Names: American Crises (and Essays)*, by Rebecca Solnit. *Seattle Review of Books*, 6 Dec. 2018, www.seattlereviewofbooks.com/notes/2018/12/06/rebecca-solnit-calls-us-by-our-true-names-but-sometimes-we-cant-hear-her/. Accessed 25 Feb. 2019.
Ismail, Nadia. Review of *Call Them by Their True Names: American Crises (and Essays)*, by Rebecca Solnit. *Columbia Journal*, 6 Sept. 2018, columbiajournal.org/review-call-them-by-their-true-names-by-rebecca-solnit/. Accessed 25 Feb. 2019.
Popova, Maria. "Rebecca Solnit on Rewriting the World's Broken Stories and the Paradigm-Shifting Power of Calling Things by Their True Names." Review of *Call Them by Their True Names: American Crises (and Essays)*, by Rebecca Solnit. *Brain Pickings* 18 Oct. 2018, www.brainpickings.org/2018/10/18/rebecca-solnit-call-them-by-their-true-names/. Accessed 25 Feb. 2019.

Calypso

Author: David Sedaris (b. 1956)
Publisher: Little, Brown (New York). 272 pp.
Type of work: Essays, memoir
Time: 2012–17
Locales: West Sussex, England; Emerald Isle, North Carolina

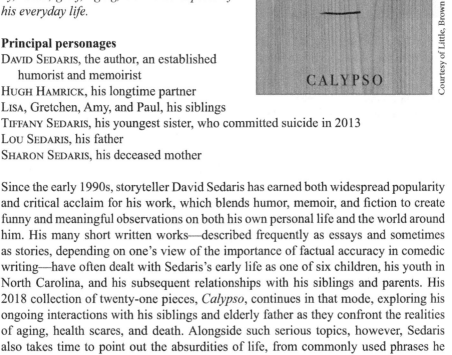

In Calypso, *David Sedaris shares his humorous yet often insightful observations on family, death, grief, aging, and other aspects of his everyday life.*

Principal personages
DAVID SEDARIS, the author, an established humorist and memoirist
HUGH HAMRICK, his longtime partner
LISA, Gretchen, Amy, and Paul, his siblings
TIFFANY SEDARIS, his youngest sister, who committed suicide in 2013
LOU SEDARIS, his father
SHARON SEDARIS, his deceased mother

Since the early 1990s, storyteller David Sedaris has earned both widespread popularity and critical acclaim for his work, which blends humor, memoir, and fiction to create funny and meaningful observations on both his own personal life and the world around him. His many short written works—described frequently as essays and sometimes as stories, depending on one's view of the importance of factual accuracy in comedic writing—have often dealt with Sedaris's early life as one of six children, his youth in North Carolina, and his subsequent relationships with his siblings and parents. His 2018 collection of twenty-one pieces, *Calypso*, continues in that mode, exploring his ongoing interactions with his siblings and elderly father as they confront the realities of aging, health scares, and death. Alongside such serious topics, however, Sedaris also takes time to point out the absurdities of life, from commonly used phrases he hates to the medical field's policies regarding disposal of excised tumors. While many of the twenty-one pieces in *Calypso* were previously published in venues such as the *New Yorker*, the *Guardian*, and the *Paris Review* and others are newly presented in the collection, the collection ultimately forms a cohesive whole that displays the signature wit and entertaining literary style Sedaris has cultivated over several decades.

    Calypso begins with the essay "Company Man," in which Sedaris discusses what he characterizes as one of the few perks of middle age: owning a home with a guest room. His home in West Sussex, England, in fact features multiple guest rooms, and Sedaris notes that he and his longtime partner Hugh often host guests. He focuses

© Ingrid Christie

David Sedaris is the author of numerous collections of fiction and nonfiction, including Barrel Fever *(1994),* Me Talk Pretty One Day *(2000),* Dress Your Family in Corduroy and Denim *(2004), and* Let's Explore Diabetes with Owls *(2013). A collection of his diary entries,* Theft by Finding, *was published in 2017.*

on one 2012 visit from his sisters Gretchen, Lisa, and Amy, which he had felt was potentially a "last hurrah" before he and his siblings, nearly all of whom were in their fifties by that point, began to risk being "picked off like figures at a shooting gallery" by diseases such as cancer, which had killed their mother decades before. As the first essay in the collection, "Company Man" serves as a useful introduction to Sedaris and his family, reacquainting readers familiar with his earlier work with familiar names and both easing new readers into the complexities of Sedaris's life and introducing them to his characteristic style and sense of humor. At the same time, the essay serves to create a false expectation for the events that will come next. Sedaris tells the reader that his sisters' visit may be the last time the four of them are all together and that the ailments that they will endure will be physical. Life, however, proves both of those points inaccurate.

The second essay in *Calypso*, "Now We Are Five," upends the expectations put forth in "Company Man" with its first sentence, which reveals that in May 2013, Sedaris's youngest sister, Tiffany, committed suicide at the age of forty-nine. While the essay focuses in part on Tiffany's personal history, it largely concerns the author's reaction to the death of his sister, to whom he had not spoken for eight years. Having previously identified heavily as one of six siblings, Sedaris grapples with the concept of becoming one of only five and struggles to understand why Tiffany would have taken her own life. Following that event, however, the bond between the remaining members of the Sedaris family appears to have strengthened. Sedaris recounts that shortly after Tiffany's death, the family gathered for a previously planned vacation in Emerald Isle, North Carolina, an area in which they had visited regularly earlier in life. Partway through the vacation, Sedaris spontaneously purchased a beach house that he named the Sea Section. The beach house serves as the setting for many of the subsequent pieces in *Calypso*, which make it clear that the 2012 visit mentioned in "Company Man" was far from the last hurrah for the Sedaris family. Over the subsequent years, the extended family gathered at the Sea Section on multiple occasions, many of which provided extensive inspiration for later essays documenting the family members' interactions and Sedaris's amusing insights. Encompassing both essays originally published elsewhere and brand-new works, *Calypso* can at times become slightly repetitive, such as when Sedaris introduces people and the location multiple times: the author reminds the reader that the Sea Section is the name of his North Carolina beach house on several occasions, for instance, and he reintroduces brother Paul's daughter, Madelyn, as his niece in several different essays. Nevertheless, such reminders are largely unobtrusive and help readers make sense of the large family that has featured prominently in much of Sedaris's writing.

In addition to Tiffany's suicide and its aftermath, *Calypso* tackles a number of emotionally fraught topics related to Sedaris's family. The author's elderly father is a major subject of concern as Sedaris seeks to navigate their relationship, which is hampered by a general lack of communication between father and son as well as by their incompatible political beliefs and the elder Sedaris's refusal to move into a retirement home or hire domestic help. Indeed, while many of the details of Sedaris's relationship with his father are specific to their relationship, the concerns about the welfare of aging relatives expressed in a number of *Calypso*'s essays will likely ring particularly true to readers who have experienced similar situations. Sedaris likewise delves into his mother's alcoholism, which became particularly troubling during the period between when the Sedaris children left home and her death in 1991, in the essay "Why Aren't You Laughing?" A powerful piece, the essay explores Sedaris's feelings of guilt for not acknowledging his mother's alcoholism for what it was during her lifetime or stepping in to help her. At the same time, he calls attention to the connection between him and his mother, a storyteller who—much like Sedaris himself—specialized in "the real-life story, perfected and condensed."

Alongside his discussions of his family's past and ongoing interactions, Sedaris devotes a significant portion of *Calypso* to the health issues that became some of his prominent concerns in middle age. In "Stepping Out," he chronicles the obsession with hitting his daily step goal that developed following his purchase of a Fitbit fitness tracker, which pushed him to shoot for even higher goals and drove him to range farther and farther from home in his daily mission of picking up litter from the sides of roads in West Sussex. "I'm Still Standing" deals with a gastrointestinal illness that plagued Sedaris during a speaking tour, the evocative description of which is both disgusting and all too realistic. Perhaps the most memorable incident in *Calypso* occurs in the title essay, in which Sedaris recounts the events surrounding a highly unorthodox surgery to remove a benign fatty tumor known as a lipoma from his abdomen. Determined to feed the tumor to a snapping turtle that lived near his beach house, Sedaris refused to have the lipoma removed by the first surgeon he visited, as the surgeon told him that it would be illegal to give Sedaris the tumor after it was removed. The author goes on to recount meeting a doctor at a public appearance in Texas and undergoing a clandestine surgery to remove the lipoma, which was then sent to one of his sisters for safekeeping. At the end of "Calypso," Sedaris is thwarted in his mission of feeding the lipoma to the turtle, having learned that the turtles are hibernating for the winter. In the essay "Sorry," however, Sedaris resumes his quest, undaunted by the death of the turtle he had previously selected, and recounts that he ultimately fed the lipoma to a group of turtles gathered behind a shopping plaza.

Dealing primarily with the period between 2012 and 2017, *Calypso* focuses largely on happenings concerning Sedaris and the members of his family but also delves somewhat into the political atmosphere during that period. In "A Modest Proposal," Sedaris recalls his response to the US Supreme Court's 2015 ruling legalizing same-sex marriage, which prompted him to propose to Hugh eighteen times in an attempt to take advantage of the tax benefits now available to them. "A Number of Reasons I've Been Depressed Lately" concerns the events leading up to and immediately following the 2016 US presidential election, while the final essay in the collection, "The Comey Memo," begins with the extended Sedaris family's realization that former Federal Bureau of Investigations director James Comey is vacationing at a house down the street from the Sea Section. While such essays ostensibly deal with current events and politics, they ultimately provide Sedaris with further opportunities to explore his relationships with the people around him and the complicated nature of being a family in the twenty-first century.

Upon its publication in 2018, *Calypso* received widespread critical acclaim, with many critics commenting on how the essays featured in the book dealt with somewhat darker topics than Sedaris's usual fare. In a positive review for the *Washington Post*, Rachel Manteuffel identified Sedaris's writing as "a touch crueler" than it has been in the past, while a reviewer for *Kirkus* identified the book as an example of Sedaris at both his darkest and his best. Sarah Crown, in a review for the *Guardian*, called *Calypso* Sedaris's "most truthful work yet," commenting on both the emotional truthfulness that she argues has always defined his work as well as the author's efforts to provide a more revealing look at "his former careful management of his and his family's stories." Indeed, reviewers particularly focused on elements of the book related to Sedaris's family, including Tiffany's suicide, his mother's alcoholism, and the Sedaris siblings' concerns about their aging father. At the same time, however, critics widely noted that despite *Calypso*'s focus on several serious topics, the essays collected in the book retain the signature humor for which Sedaris has long been known. The reviewer for *Publishers Weekly* called the book "sidesplitting," while in a review for NPR, Heller McAlpin wrote that "reading Sedaris' family stories is like tuning into a spectacularly well-written sit-com." Although McAlpin asserted in her review that not all of the pieces in *Calypso* are outstanding, she went on to identify Sedaris as the best contemporary American humorist.

Joy Crelin

Review Sources

Review of *Calypso*, by David Sedaris. *Kirkus*, 20 Feb. 2018, www.kirkusreviews. com/book-reviews/david-sedaris/calypso-sedaris/. Accessed 30 Sept. 2018.

Review of *Calypso*, by David Sedaris. *Publishers Weekly*, 19 Mar. 2018, www.publishersweekly.com/978-0-316-39238-9. Accessed 30 Sept. 2018.

Crown, Sarah. "*Calypso* by David Sedaris Review—A Family Affair." *The Guardian*, 26 July 2018, www.theguardian.com/books/2018/jul/26/calypso-david-sedaris-review. Accessed 30 Sept. 2018.

Cumming, Alan. "David Sedaris Has a New Essay Collection. It Changed Alan Cumming's Whole Worldview." Review of *Calypso*, by David Sedaris. *The New York Times*, 25 May 2018, www.nytimes.com/2018/05/25/books/review/david-sedaris-calypso.html. Accessed 30 Sept. 2018.

Manteuffel, Rachel. "After Nine Books, What More Could David Sedaris Have
    to Say? A Great Deal." Review of *Calypso*, by David Sedaris. *The Washington
    Post*, 29 May 2018, www.washingtonpost.com/entertainment/books/after-nine-
    books-what-more-could-david-sedaris-have-to-say-a-great-deal/2018/05/28/
    e5ea9d5e-5e90-11e8-b2b8-08a538d9dbd6_story.html. Accessed 30 Sept. 2018.
McAlpin, Heller. "In 'Calypso,' David Sedaris Blends Slime and the Sub-
    lime." Review of *Calypso*, by David Sedaris. *NPR*, 30 May 2018, www.npr.
    org/2018/05/30/613149372/in-calypso-david-sedaris-blends-slime-and-the-sub-
    lime. Accessed 30 Sept. 2018.

A Carnival of Losses
Notes Nearing Ninety

Author: Donald Hall (1928–2018)
Publisher: Houghton Mifflin Harcourt (Boston). 224 pp.
Type of work: Essays, memoir

Former US poet laureate Donald Hall followed up his celebrated 2014 volume Essays after Eighty *with another collection of short essays reflecting on his long life and contemplating his approaching death.*

Courtesy of Houghton Mifflin Harcourt

The closer a person gets to death, the more likely he or she is to look back pensively on life, especially if that person is already a reflective, thoughtful individual. Donald Hall, the legendary poet and occasional essayist, was such an individual, spending a lifetime putting feelings, thoughts, and reflections into words. When Hall, already in his eighties, gave up writing poetry in 2010, he began composing short pieces of prose, reminiscences of a life in literature and frank discussions of his deteriorating physical state. These pieces combined tenderness, humor, and piercing insight, proving Hall a master of the prose form that he turned to after he no longer had the energy for verse. A collection of these writings was published as *Essays after Eighty* in 2014, and the book's widespread acclaim led Hall to write a new series of essays. This second round of short reminiscences was then collected in *A Carnival of Losses: Notes Nearing Ninety*, a worthy follow-up that was published just weeks after Hall died at the age of eighty-nine.

As befitting a book written by a man very aware of his approaching demise, *A Carnival of Losses* is suffused with a sense of death and decay. For Hall, this confrontation with death is inevitable, but it is not new: his second wife, the poet Jane Kenyon, fell ill with terminal leukemia in the mid-1990s and died in 1995. Hall had previously written about his life with Kenyon and her untimely death, first in the celebrated poetry collections *Without* (1998) and *The Painted Bed* (2002), and later in the memoir *The Best Day the Worst Day: Life with Jane Kenyon* (2005). In *A Carnival of Losses*, Kenyon continues to cast a long shadow over Hall's writing. Her death not only foreshadows his own, but their former life together continually calls forth joyful reminiscences from the author as well.

In fact, this mixture of joy and sorrow is key to the method of *A Carnival of Losses*, and in the juxtaposition of playful anecdotes with deep-throttle meditations, the book achieves a successful combination of seeming opposites. As Hall writes, "Now I understood how death and desolation fit into the riotous joy and laughter. . . . The emotional intricacy and urgency of human life expresses itself most fiercely in contradiction. If any feeling makes a sunny interminable sky, the feeling is a lie and the sky is a lie." This formulation, which reflects Hall's method throughout the book, comes to the writer as a revelation after he attends a live performance of the popular radio program *This American Life* as a special guest of host Ira Glass. The performance contains a joyous dance number and then follows it up with an old audio recording of Hall discussing Jane Kenyon shortly after her death. The joyousness in the concert hall gives way to sorrow and then moves at least partway back as the audience erupts in laughter at a humorous anecdote that Hall told about Kenyon's last moments. This full juxtaposition of riotousness and sorrow deeply moves the author, as he insightfully documents.

Donald Hall was an award-winning poet, essayist, editor, and memoirist who served as the poet laureate of the United States from 2006 to 2007. He wrote over fifty books in numerous genres and received the National Medal of the Arts from President Barack Obama in 2011.

But not everything in *A Carnival of Losses* is so dramatic. Much of the pleasure of this deeply pleasurable book lies in listening to a highly intelligent, sympathetic individual offer up charming, seemingly tossed-off asides. Some of these reminiscences are extremely humorous, as when Hall describes receiving a communication from Boston University soliciting his papers for their archive, with the letter repeatedly referring to him as *David* Hall. Only later does he hear from several writer friends that they too have received an identical missive from the same BU administrator. Other anecdotes are simply charming, as in the many reflections back on the author's childhood and early family life, particularly those from his formative experience working on his grandfather's farm. But no matter how slight these short pieces are, they always contain larger hidden insights.

For example, in a brief piece on baseball and football, Hall's method seems to be just to describe to the reader straightforwardly his sports watching practices and then offer up a short reminiscence. But even this straightforward piece contains plenty of insight that enlightens the reader. For example, he contrasts the speed of baseball ("slow") and football ("fast") and leaves it at that, only to return to modify this conception at the end of the paragraph. Football, which contains far more waiting around than actual game play, only seems quick, he determines. When Hall finally concludes that football takes hours to convey just a few minutes of real action, he gets at something profound about the nature of time and how people react to time, both real and perceived, in daily life.

Because a book made up entirely of short essays about Hall's life, interests, and impending death would probably be a little too much of a good thing, *A Carnival of*

Losses is strategically divided into four sections to help keep things fresh. The first section, entitled "Notes Nearing Ninety," consists entirely of these short essays, but the second section, "The Selected Poets of Donald Hall," tweaks the approach. This section also consists of short reminiscences, but they all concern his encounters and friendships with various poets, many of them among the major writers of their time. Although many of the anecdotes that Hall tells are winning, and although the shift in approach does keep things fresh, this is perhaps the least interesting section of the book. It will certainly appeal to readers deeply familiar with the world of poetry but is of less general interest and of less depth than the other sections.

The third section of the book consists entirely of a strong standalone piece, "Necropoetics," that was originally published online in the *New Yorker*. A consideration of the poetry of death in relation to his own personal relation with death (specifically that of Kenyon), the piece makes an elegant case for the productive intersection of life and art. The book's final section, "A Carnival of Losses," returns to the anecdotal form of the first section. However, it differs a little in that a good portion of the section is taken up by a long penultimate essay, "Way Way Up, Way Way Down." This piece gives the reader a blow-by-blow account of a recent health emergency in which Hall thought he was going to die.

For all the variety and lightheartedness of much of the book, *A Carnival of Losses* is indeed ultimately about death: how people confront it, how they make their peace with it, its inexorableness. The opening essay, "You Are Old," sets the tone confidently and eloquently—and with humor. "You are old when you learn it's May by noticing that daffodils erupt outside your window," Hall begins. "You are old when someone mentions an event two years in the future and looks embarrassed. You are old when the post office delivers your letters into a chair in your living room and picks up your letters going out. You are old when you write letters." In this brilliant listing of observations, Hall cleverly communicates the circumstances of his own life, largely homebound, oblivious to time except when he is reminded of it by what he can see out his window. But by writing in the second person, directly addressing the reader, he universalizes his situation. You may be young now, he effectively tells the reader, but someday you will be like me, someday you will live with death every moment of your life.

This direct confrontation with death comes through most forcefully in the aforementioned essay, "Way Way Down, Way Way Up," which brings the reader nearly to the end of the book. Hall in the essay proceeds by an intense accumulation of detail. The piece describes a health crisis he experienced after attending a birthday party his children threw for him. Attending such a party takes a lot out of him, and the next day he wakes up feeling wretched. This feeling continues, and what follows over the next few months is a series of health emergencies that lead Hall to conclude he is dying. Rather than offer much in the way of reflection, here Hall is more concerned with taking the reader on an intensely detailed trip through his various visits to the hospital and his numerous bodily malfunctions. The result is a harrowing journey through what it means to have a body well into its ninth decade. Hall spares no detail and allows the reader to see that even if his or her body works well now, the reader is still subject to all the future decay that comes with being a person in an imperfect shell.

But this essay is not all despairing. Hall does make a recovery, even if, as it turned out, he was only to live another couple of years. He ends the piece with his reminiscences of the *This American Life* live show, and in following up the mostly narrative flow of the essay with his insights into the entwined nature of joy and despair, he asks the reader to view the proceeding narrative in a new light. Life, especially in old age, may be a bit of a wretched business, but there are always compensating joys. These joys kept Hall going strong well into his late eighties and they are at the heart of this final literary enterprise, sustaining the reader's attention with a series of delightful anecdotes that, even at their most charming, never lose sight of the central fact about human life being that it must come to an inevitable conclusion.

In working both sides of the human equation, *A Carnival of Losses* registers as a powerful entry in the literature of death. Critical response was strong, with many reviewers suggesting the book was a fitting capstone to a great career. In a starred review, *Publishers Weekly* expressed the consensus that it was a powerful continuation of the themes introduced in *Essays after Eighty*, particularly aging and mortality. Even in its preoccupation with humankind's final end, though, Hall's book is finally as much about life, in all its multifarious glory, as it is about death.

Andrew Schenker

Review Sources

Review of *A Carnival of Losses*, by Donald Hall. *Kirkus Reviews*, 19 Mar. 2018, www.kirkusreviews.com/book-reviews/donald-hall/a-carnival-of-losses. Accessed 3 Oct. 2018.

Review of *A Carnival of Losses*, by Donald Hall. *Publishers Weekly*, July 2018, www.publishersweekly.com/978-1-328-82634-3. Accessed 3 Oct. 2018.

Garner, Dwight. "A Poet Laureate Sends News From the End of Life." Review of *A Carnival of Losses: Notes Nearing Ninety*, by Donald Hall. *The New York Times*, 30 July 2018, www.nytimes.com/2018/07/30/books/review-carnival-of-losses-donald-hall.html. Accessed 3 Oct. 2018.

McAlpin, Heller. "Donald Hall's Parting Gift: Essays on Aging and Not Always Gracefully." Review of *A Carnival of Losses: Notes Nearing Ninety*, by Donald Hall. *The Washington Post*, 25 June 2018, www.washingtonpost.com/entertainment/books/is-it-possible-to-age-gracefully-insights-from-a-poet-on-the-cusp-of-90/2018/06/18/9e7c696a-680f-11e8-bea7-c8eb28bc52b1_story.html. Accessed 3 Oct. 2018.

The Carrying

Author: Ada Limón (b. 1976)
Publisher: Milkweed Editions (Minneapolis, Minnesota). 120 pp.
Type of work: Poetry

The Carrying, Ada Limón's fifth poetry collection and the follow-up to her acclaimed Bright Dead Things (2015), explores the depths of human emotion and experience as felt through the natural world and relationships with other people. As Limón contemplates how humans sustain their place in the world—whether through creative expression, battles with infertility, or inspiration found in nature—her poetry stacks experience upon experience and creates a record of a woman's quest for connection. Rich descriptions coupled with raw emotion bring the poems to life.

American poet Ada Limón achieved a breakthrough of sorts in 2015 with her collection *Bright Dead Things*, which was nominated for several prestigious awards including the National Book Award. It established her as a respected artistic capable of exploring the many complexities of life and identity. Her fifth book, *The Carrying*, follows up that success by continuing to showcase her signature themes, including the use of nature as a lens through which she examines her life and the lives of others. The often autobiographical poems in the collection also deal with subjects such as struggling to conceive a child and the connection to family, whether by blood or otherwise.

The poems of *The Carrying* are separated into three numbered sections. The collection begins with an epigraph from the poem "She Had Some Horses" by Joy Harjo, which cuts to the complicated feelings Limón goes on to examine in her own poems throughout the book. To Limón, nature is both beauty and brutality, and death is as much a part of life as is joy. She achieves this balance by exploring the human connection to both sides of such dualistic concepts, investigating why one side is necessary to reach the other.

In the first section of the book, Limón opens with a short poem called "A Name." The poem imagines Eve walking through the garden of Eden, naming the animals that surround her. The speaker then wonders about whether this Eve hoped the animals would in turn give her a name. In a few simple lines, Limón connects the human Eve to the animals around her, showing her vulnerability and her desire to become one with the natural world. In Limón's world, no hierarchy exists among living things.

The following poem, "Ancestors," finds Limón describing her own origins. Yet instead of descriptions of her family tree or the act of birth itself, the imagery is that of nature, of rocks and trees. Even a couch where she was born is described as green and placed "between / the vineyards and the horse pasture." Limón's narrator cannot remember the faces she saw first—her parents and brother are only briefly mentioned—but she recalls later seeing leaves seen through windows of cars, bedrooms, classrooms in different stages of life. She contemplates the fact that all the power of leaves derives from roots, and yet that roots also prevent the freedom of running. Clearly, the concept of ancestry hold deep meaning and primordial power that can be interpreted in several ways. Additionally, the scene of birth and trees continues from the depiction of Eve in the previous poem in developing themes of fertility and nature, which run throughout the book.

Two poems from the first section begin to touch upon some of the more immediate autobiographical issues Limón deals with in *The Carrying*. "Trying" explores Limón's connection to the dirt of her garden, how she is drawn to create things, juxtaposed with her and her husband's attempt to conceive a child. While the poem begins on a positive note and the relationship between the couple appears reasonably strong and healthy, there is a sense of disturbance and decline. There is mention of news of violence that limits their enthusiasm, and the sun begins to set. The concluding lines hint at an effort to strive against an underlying problem:

> Even now, I don't know much
> about happiness. I still worry
> and want an endless stream of more,
> but some days I can see the point
> in growing something, even if
> it's just to say I cared enough.

"The Vulture & The Body" finds Limón traveling to a fertility clinic. However, on her drive she passes five dead animals: a raccoon, a coyote, and three deer. Death and potential life are entwined in her world. "I want to tell my doctor about how we all hold a duality / in our minds: futures entirely different, footloose or forged," she writes. Her visit to the clinic shows the growth of follicles during a sonogram, and it seems she is getting closer to her dream of carrying a child, but she is preoccupied by the death she has seen. "What if, instead of carrying / a child, I am supposed to carry grief?" she asks herself. Yet grief—and perhaps also the creation of new life—can be framed as a natural response to death, as much a part of nature as the vulture Limón sees circling the roadkill on her way home.

At the heart of *The Carrying*, then, is the cycle of life. Aram Mrjoian noted this in a review for the *Chicago Review of Books*, writing that "Although the subject matter is often mournful, the endurance of nature also comes to light. Even though an individual may perish, there is consistency in the life cycles of bumblebees, dandelions, and race horses—all of which are examined with gorgeous language and imagery that makes Limón's collection hard to put down, even in the moments that cause a deep, sorrowful ache." This sentiment continues on in part two of the book. Limón further connects her current life with the natural world around her, even when momentum seems lost, or at least moving in an unexpected direction.

"The Burying Beetle" once again finds Limón tending to her garden, weeding for four hours straight and attending to her tomatoes, sweet potatoes, and Japanese maple. Her body is connected to the dirt, to the life springing up around her, but her spirit carries a heaviness. The longing is quickly pinpointed, as she identifies the need for the warmth and connection only found in empathetic physical connection with another. The importance of her marriage is again highlighted, as the absence of her husband along with other losses has caused deep pain. As emerges over the course of the collection, Limón and her husband are dealing with his father's declining mental state and the aging of their parents in general, so death haunts many of the poems beyond the couple's struggles with fertility.

"The Dead Boy" is one poem that encapsulates this sense of loss. In it, Limón remembers the death of a boy by overdose

© Lucas Marquardt

Poet Ada Limón is the author of several books of poetry. Her collection Bright Dead Things *(2015) was a finalist for the National Book Award, the National Book Critics Circle Award and the Kingsley Tufts Poetry Award. Her work has also appeared in publications including the* New Yorker, *the* Harvard Review, *and* Pleiades.

years before. Yet even in this example of senseless death, there is rich nature imagery that suggests life will continue. The poem is set during the spring, the time of rebirth, and includes lush descriptions of the grass and bugs, lemonade, and other details that seen incongruous with the pain of loss. Limón also acknowledges the symbolism of the dead boy's name, Griffin, in mythology an animal that is a hybrid of a lion and eagle. Still, she does not allow the ever-present sense of nature to dilute the intensity of her feelings in the moment of seeing the dead boy's body. As she writes, "He is etched in my mind, named / in language forever and only as: dead boy, / dead boy, and gone."

In "The Real Reason" Limón explores a body that is alive but still marked by tragedy. The poem, in a highly prose-like form, is framed as an explanation of the real reason she does not have a tattoo—a subject that might be light and humorous but quickly proves quite serious. When she was younger, she relates, she asked her artist mother if she would design a tattoo for her. Her mother's emotional resistance to the idea exposed to Limón how different her mother's relationship to her own body is, as a burn victim covered with scars. Limón's mother lost an unborn child in the disfiguring incident as well, connecting the story of the poem all the more deeply with the themes of Limón's collection.

By the third part of *The Carrying*, Limón is beginning to reckon with the potential of not ultimately becoming a mother and the fact that those around her will continue their decline. Nature, of course, helps in coming to terms with such things, and descriptions of plants and animals continue to abound. Horses in particular are a regular theme in Limón's work, and two poems in the third section use them to drive home some of her most poignant thoughts in the book. "Carrying" is about the narrator's connection to a mare she owns that is pregnant with a foal. This provides Limón space to discuss her own climb towards her forties without a child and what that means in a culture that prizes parenthood, motherhood, above all else. She describes the horse and herself in the optimistic closing lines:

> Ours, her coat/thicker with the season's muck, leans against
> the black fence and this image is heavy
> within me. How my own body, empty,
> clean of secrets, knows how to carry her,
> knows we were all meant for something.

The following poem, called "What I Didn't Know Before," begins with a tender description of a foal's first moments of life, how they come to the world fully formed and ready to walk. This description transitions into an address to the narrator's partner, recounting their love. The connection between the two scenarios is clearly laid out: "What was between / us wasn't a fragile thing to be coddled, cooed / over. It came out fully formed, ready to run."

As Mrjoian and other reviewers suggest, critical reception for The Carrying was highly positive. It received a starred review from *Publishers Weekly* and was included in roundups of notable new poetry from outlets such as the *Washington Post* and *The New York Times*. Writing for *Bustle*, E. Ce Miller called the book "a deeply intimate collection, and fans of Limón might likely consider it her most personal collection yet. It touches on everything from the current political climate and nature to love and grief." Limón herself noted the intimately autobiographical nature of the collection in interviews. Ultimately, *The Carrying* provides a new, deeper chapter in Limón's body of work, as she uses her poetic tools to unravel an increasingly confounding, sad, yet exhilarating world.

Melynda Fuller

Review Sources

McAndrews, Wila. Review of *The Carrying*, by Ada Limón. *PANK*, 4 Sept. 2018, pankmagazine.com/2018/09/04/review-carrying-ada-limon/. Accessed 7 Jan. 2019.

Miller, E. Ce. "Ada Limón's 'The Carrying' Is a Poetry Collection To Help You Make Sense of the State of the World Right Now." Review of *The Carrying*, by Ada Limón. *Bustle*, 14 Aug. 2018, www.bustle.com/p/ada-Limóns-the-carrying-is-a-poetry-collection-to-help-you-make-sense-of-the-state-of-the-world-right-now-10081122. Accessed 7 Jan. 2019.

Mrjoian, Aram. "'The Carrying' Is Ada Limón's Most Personal Poetry Yet." Review of *The Carrying*, by Ada Limón. *Chicago Review of Books*, 16 Aug. 2018, chireviewofbooks.com/2018/08/16/the-carrying-ada-limon-review/ . Accessed 7 Jan. 2019.

Neimark, Gillian. Review of *The Carrying*, by Ada Limón. *The Los Angeles Review*, Aug. 2018, losangelesreview.org/review-carrying-ada-limon/. Accessed 7 Jan. 2019.

Churchill
Walking with Destiny

Author: Andrew Roberts (b. 1963)
Publisher: Viking (New York). Illustrated. 1,152 pp.
Type of work: Biography
Time: 1874–1965
Locales: Great Britain, Western Europe, and the Middle East

Historian Andrew Roberts offers a detailed, comprehensive portrait of Winston Churchill, the British statesman who led his country in its struggle against the Axis powers during World War II.

Principal personages
WINSTON LEONARD SPENCER-CHURCHILL, British politician
CLEMENTINE HOZIER CHURCHILL, his wife

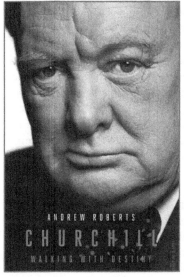

Courtesy of Penguin

HERBERT H. ASQUITH, Prime minister of the United Kingdom, 1908–16
DAVID LLOYD GEORGE, Prime minister of the United Kingdom, 1916–22
STANLEY BALDWIN, Prime minister of the United Kingdom for three terms between 1923 and 1937
NEVILLE CHAMBERLAIN, Prime minister of the United Kingdom, 1937–40
CLEMENT ATTLEE, Deputy prime minister under Churchill and later prime minister (1945–51)
ANTHONY EDEN, member of Churchill's War Cabinet and later prime minister (1955–57)
FRANKLIN DELANO ROOSEVELT, President of the United States, 1933–45
ADOLF HITLER, leader of Germany, 1933–45

"London will be in danger and in the high position I shall occupy," a brash sixteen-year-old Winston Churchill told a classmate at Harrow, "it will fall to me to save the capital and save the Empire." This boast is cited twice in *Churchill: Walking with Destiny*, veteran historian Andrew Roberts's biography of the British politician generally credited with having made good on these boasts a half-century later. For six years, beginning in 1939, Great Britain and the British Empire faced an existential threat from the forces of Germany and its allies under the leadership of Adolf Hitler, a warmongering dictator bent on expanding his own empire, the Third Reich, which he confidently predicted would last a thousand years. How Churchill came to occupy the position of savior that he had forecast for himself and what he did to prepare himself for the role is the subject of Roberts's carefully researched and gracefully written life story.

Churchill: Walking with Destiny has plenty of company on shelves housing books about Churchill. He is the principal subject or a major figure in at least one thousand titles. The official biography, running to eight volumes, was begun by Churchill's son, Randolph, and completed by Martin Gilbert in 1988. There were others before and numerous ones after, many focused on a particular aspect of Churchill's professional or personal life. Finding a new way to present a figure whose professional and personal life has been examined from almost every possible angle might deter most historians; Roberts embraces the task, however, creating a portrait of Churchill that is well rounded and sympathetic.

Son of a leading British politician (Randolph Churchill) and an American socialite (Jennie Jerome), Winston Churchill was in the public eye from the day he graduated Sandhurst in 1894 and began a military career that he acknowledged was to be a stepping stone into politics. For more than five years, he scurried around the globe from one military encounter to another, weapon in one hand and pen in the other, recording his experiences in articles and books that made him a household name before he first ran successfully for Parliament in 1900. Within less than a decade, he had become a government minister and served in positions under a succession of Conservative and Liberal politicians that included Herbert Asquith, David Lloyd George, and Stanley Baldwin. With each of them, he had a fractious relationship; they recognized his administrative talents and stood in awe of his public speaking ability but blanched at his tendency to pursue his own agenda at the expense of political unity.

To his credit, Churchill led reform movements in the ministries over which he presided with the same zeal (and sometimes reckless abandon) that he showed on the battlefield. His achievements in modernizing the British navy during his tenure as first lord of the admiralty (1911–15) are often overshadowed by Great Britain's disastrous attempts during World War I to seize the Dardanelles. While Roberts acknowledges Churchill's role in this military debacle, he makes certain Churchill's accomplishments as a government minister are brought to the forefront of his narrative.

Roberts identifies several driving forces behind Churchill's career. As the son of a successful politician and a descendant of a long line of political figures dating back to John Churchill, 1st Duke of Marlborough and hero of the Battle of Blenheim, Winston felt it his duty as well as his destiny to enter politics. From an early age, he felt—almost assumed—he would one day be prime minister; every career decision was made with calculation to prepare himself for this role. Though sometimes appearing to be self-serving, his actions were always motivated by his belief in the British Empire—and the superiority of English-speaking peoples over other nationalities and races.

If there is one quality that Roberts stresses throughout his narrative, it is Churchill's prescience. Churchill foresaw the need for a strong navy and championed development of a military air force. He was among the first to warn about the threat posed by Communism as a political movement. For nearly a decade, he railed against Germany's efforts to rebuild its military and expand its territory; almost alone among top-level British politicians, he warned of the dangers posed by Hitler and the Nazis, lobbying—usually without success—for Great Britain to rearm and prepare for inevitable conflict with Germany. Unfortunately, so strong was the sentiment for appeasement that Hitler's overt disregard for terms of the Treaty of Versailles that ended World War I, including land grabs in Austria and Czechoslovakia, failed to shift either political will or public opinion. Only when Germany invaded Poland in September 1939 did Churchill's colleagues in Parliament begin to pay attention to him.

Roberts devotes nearly half his narrative to the period between 1939 and 1945, the six years during which Great Britain fought—at times almost alone—against the Nazis. When Prime Minister Neville Chamberlain ultimately brought Great Britain into World War II in September 1939, Churchill returned to the government as first lord of the admiralty, a position he held until the following May, when Chamberlain stepped down and Churchill finally attained the position for which he had prepared himself all his life: prime minister. His first act was to create a coalition government that included members of his own Conservative Party and representatives of the Labour and Liberal Parties.

© Nancy Ellison

Andrew Roberts is a historian who has written several award-winning books, including Masters and Commanders: How Four Titans Won the War in the West, 1941–1945 *(2008),* The Storm of War: A New History of the Second World War *(2009), and* Napoleon: A Life *(2014).*

Members of his War Cabinet were drawn from these parties and included Labour leader Clement Attlee, who would succeed Churchill at the end of the war.

Even at the darkest moments, Churchill projected a sense of confidence in the ability of Great Britain (and eventually its allies as well) to overcome the German menace. Roberts points out how often Churchill's speeches before, but especially during, the war were aimed at two audiences: his countrymen in Great Britain and the American public. Long before anyone acknowledged the fact publicly, Churchill realized that the war against Hitler could be won only with assistance from the United States. He knew he had an ally in President Franklin D. Roosevelt but he also understood that the US Congress and the American public would have to be convinced that assisting Great Britain would be in their country's best interest. Churchill's and Roosevelt's joint efforts to develop a strategy for freeing Europe from Hitler and his allies is given ample coverage in Roberts's compelling account of the political and military dimensions of World War II.

When the war ended for Great Britain in May 1945, the immensely popular Churchill found himself summarily out of the job for which he had worked his whole life. In a stunning defeat, his Conservative Party lost a general election to Labour before the ink was dry on peace treaties. For the next two decades, Churchill was in and out of office, lecturing when not serving, taking another turn as prime minister (1951–55), and traveling the globe as a senior statesman. The dissolution of the British

Empire in the years immediately following the war pained him greatly; however, he had the good fortune of being prime minister when a youthful Princess Elizabeth ascended the throne upon the death of her father in 1952. Upon Churchill's death in 1965, he was mourned on both sides of the Atlantic as one of the greatest statesmen of the century.

As often happens, historical revision has taken its toll on Churchill's reputation; he has come in for criticism from a handful of historians and politicians for a host of actions and beliefs that may have been popular in the first half of the twentieth century but which are no longer held in high esteem. Roberts deals with these critiques directly, taking every opportunity to dispel the myths and misinterpretations that have been the source of criticism of Churchill over the course of his career. Roberts has a plausible retort to virtually every criticism leveled at Churchill by his colleagues or by historians who have not been taken in by the sheer force of Churchill's larger-than-life personality. Lest it seem that Roberts paint Churchill as a secular saint, however, there is sufficient criticism in his book to leave readers with a sense that Churchill had his share of faults, personal as well as political. Churchill's egotism, brusque treatment of subordinates and colleagues, and insistence on the correctness of his own views—often expressed in stentorian speeches and wicked personal barbs that made some despise him and even his supporters cringe occasionally—made him difficult to get along with. Only his wife, Clementine, seemed to have any influence in getting him to tone down his rhetoric and keep his focus on major issues (of which there were always many).

Roberts also explains how, on occasion, Churchill was on the wrong side of history. For example, he stood in the way of women's suffrage, earning the opprobrium of suffragettes, because he believed giving women the vote might damage the fortunes of his own party. He also opposed (quite strenuously) efforts to grant independence to India. Sadly, his political colleagues and the public gave greater credence to his mistakes than his sage predictions; Roberts implies that, had people listened to Churchill during the 1930s, the conflict with the Axis powers might have been shorter and less costly, especially in human lives.

No person exists solely through their work. As busy as Churchill was with politics, he was also a husband, father, and son, and these personal relationships are given due consideration in Roberts's biography. Churchill's courtship of Clementine Hozier is handled briefly but deftly, and their lifelong mutual love is presented as a constant that anchored Churchill even in the most trying times. A loving if not always present father, Churchill was often chagrined and sometimes embarrassed by the actions of his son Randolph—much as Churchill's father had been by the young Winston. Roberts is frank in discussing Churchill's need for money, noting on more than one occasion how book royalties or payments for articles paid the bills or helped reduce what seemed to be Churchill's incessant debt. The sheer volume of work Churchill published is remarkable—even more so when one considers it was often done as a sideline to a busy schedule as a government minister or soldier on the battlefield. When one considers the quantity and quality of Churchill's historical and political writing, it seems appropriate that he was awarded the Nobel Prize in Literature in 1953.

At over 1,100 pages, *Churchill: Walking with Destiny* is likely to appeal to a readership already intrigued by Churchill. However, Roberts's lively style and his ability to weave together a coherent portrait of his subject from thousands of source documents (including, according to Roberts, first-time access granted by Queen Elizabeth II to King George VI's records of his weekly meetings with Churchill during World War II) makes the book a rewarding read for anyone interested in domestic British politics, international relations, military history, or the life stories of great persons. The volume is copiously illustrated with photographs and illustrations from every period of Churchill's life as well as numerous maps that provide graphic representations of the major conflicts in which Churchill participated as either a combatant or political leader. The importance of *Churchill: Walking with Destiny* was expressed by Richard Aldous in his review of the book for the *New York Times*, as he described it as "the best single-volume biography of Churchill yet written."

Laurence W. Mazzeno

Review Sources

Aldous, Richard. "Is This the Best One-Volume Biography of Churchill Yet Written?" Review of *Churchill: Walking with Destiny*, by Andrew Roberts. *The New York Times*, 13 Nov. 2018, www.nytimes.com/2018/11/13/books/review/andrew-roberts-churchill-winston-biography.html. Accessed 15 Jan. 2019.

McCrum, Robert. Review of *Churchill: Walking with Destiny*, by Andrew Roberts. *The Guardian*, 29 Oct. 2018, www.theguardian.com/books/2018/oct/29/churchill-walking-with-destiny-andrew-roberts-review. Accessed 15 Jan. 2019.

Sempa, Francis P. Review of *Churchill: Walking with Destiny*, by Andrew Roberts. *New York Journal of Books*, www.nyjournalofbooks.com/book-review/churchill-walking-destiny. Accessed 15 Jan. 2019.

Circe

Author: Madeline Miller (b. 1978)
Publisher: Little, Brown and Company (New York). 400 pp.
Type of work: Novel
Time: Greek Heroic Age
Locales: Isle of Aiaia, Helios's palace

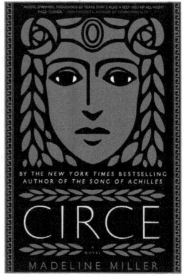

Courtesy of Little, Brown

This best-selling novel is a creative retelling of classical Greek mythology and Homer's Odyssey, *focusing on the witch Circe and her motivations after she is forced into exile after a foolish choice. In the ensuing years, Circe must come to accept herself and embrace her strengths as well as the powers hidden within.*

Principal characters
CIRCE, a goddess and witch
HELIOS, Circe's father, the Titan sun god
GLAUCOS, Circe's first lover, originally a human
DAEDALUS, inventor and captive of Pasiphaë
ODYSSEUS, prince of Ithaca, lover of Circe
TELEGONAS, Circe's son by Odysseus
TELEMACHAS, son of Odysseus and his wife, Penelope

Circe is Madeline Miller's second novel. It follows the critically acclaimed *The Song of Achilles* (2011), which is a retelling of the hero tale about the prince Patroclus and hero Achilles, loosely based on Homer's *Illiad*. In *Circe*, Miller returns to the Greek age of heroes, but this time her protagonist is Circe, the daughter of the Titan sun god Helios and the nymph Perse. Like her debut piece, *Circe* pulls from classical literature, particularly Homer's *Odyssey* and Ovid's *Metamorphoses*, as well as traditional Greek mythology about the Olympians and Titans. Despite well-known roots, Miller's original version of Circe's tale brings the character to life through a deeper exploration of her loves, her legends, and her ultimate fate.

Similar in form to the bildungsroman story line, the novel begins with Circe's childhood. The firstborn child of the Helios and Perse, Circe is not quite the boon that her mother expected, and within moments of meeting her new daughter, Perse says to her husband, "Come . . . Let us make a better one." Circe is described by her father as a goddess worthy of only a human prince as a husband. The child's self-image is further damaged by her parents' lack of attention, the barbed insults given by her younger siblings Pasiphaë and Perses, and her invisibility to the other gods in her father's realm. Her desire for attention leads her to break the unspoken rules of the immortal realm. Her first rebellion happens after Zeus, the leader of the competing Olympian gods, chooses Helios's palace as the location for the beginning stage of the Titan Prometheus' punishment. Circe brings Prometheus a drink after he has been beaten and left hanging while the rest of the gods feast. Though her compassion could be interpreted as treason and restart the old war between the Olympians and Titans, no one notices because she is of so little value. This simple act of compassion and her uncle's response that "Not every god need be the same" foreshadow how Circe later views her place in the world.

When her favorite brother, Aeetes, also abandons her, Circe begins to escape to the shore of a deserted land where she and Aeetes played as children. There, she meets Glaucos, a young fisherman. Lonely, Circe craves his attention and falls in love with him. She makes deals to bless his catches and finds a way to turn him into a god. Despite Circe's sacrifices for Glaucos, as a god, he rejects her. Driven by grief and jealousy, Circe changes Glaucos' new love interest, Scylla, into a monster with multiple heads and tentacles. Though Scylla's change is a reflection of her own inner truth, Circe later struggles with guilt over the lives lost to the monstrous creature. This act—proving her ability to manipulate the power of herbs—identifies Circe as a witch. Her siblings also share her abilities, and their collective power inspires fear in the Olympians.

While her siblings are only put under observation, Circe receives a harsher punishment. Her father declares, "She is a disgrace to our name. An ingrate to the care we have shown her. It is agreed with Zeus that for this she must be punished. She is exiled to a deserted island where she can do no more harm." The exile ironically reveals a strength that Circe did not know she possessed, and she turns her banishment to her advantage: "I will not be like a bird bred in a cage, I thought, too dull to fly even when the door stands out. I stepped into those woods and my life began."

Circe's new life on the island of Aiaia presents a deeper characterization of an empowered woman who, for the most part, chooses her own path. She takes Hermes as a lover despite the earlier fear that she would never have company on her solitary island, and she is given a respite when her sister calls her to help deliver the Minotaur. While aiding her sister, Circe befriends and becomes lovers with the inventor Daedalus, who is Pasiphaë's captive. Angry about the way her sister has treated Daedalus, as well as Pasiphaë's treatment of Circe herself, the goddess learns to stand up for herself. After returning to the island, she feels both the light and weight of her exile. She knows that Aiaia is, for her, "the wildest, most giddy freedom," while also remembering that "A golden cage is still a cage."

Circe uses her time on the island to polish her witchcraft, learning the powers of the local wildlife and using it to create potions that will add to her power. This power is illustrated most strongly when a ship full of sailors lands on her shore. She welcomes them, feeds them, and turns them into pigs after the captain of the crew rapes her. She refuses to allow others to direct her life at this point. More sailors come, and more men are turned to pigs over the following years. Only when Odysseus's ship lands on her shore does Circe realize how lonely she has been. His confidence and seemingly straightforward personality draw her to the hero, and they soon become lovers.

Since the novel is more character driven than plot focused, it is important to note that the characterization of Circe is further developed through her relationship with Odysseus. She has known fear, grief, and frustration in the long years of her life, but she has also found joy and contentment despite her exile. Loneliness, however, has become an unwelcome companion, so when Odysseus bargains with her, she agrees. In the year that Odysseus spends with Circe, she learns of the outside world and begins to better understand mortals. She also realizes as his tenure on the island draws to a close that she is tired of being alone, and she allows herself to become pregnant with his child, a fact that she does not share with him.

Though lovers, Circe does not truly love Odysseus. She learns what love truly means when she bears a mortal child. Just before her son, Telegonus, is born, Athena appears and threatens the child's life. Circe's strength grows even stronger in her defiant refusal to let the Olympian take her child, and she sets a protection over the island. Telegonus is not an easy baby, but Circe bears the trials of childrearing on her own, never asking for help. When the boy reaches his teen years, she learns she must let him to make his own mistakes. She allows Telegonus to travel to Ithaca to meet his father. Tragic circumstances lead to the fulfillment of Athena's earlier prophecy, and the boy returns home with Odysseus's wife, Penelope, and older son, after having accidentally served as a catalyst in Odysseus's death.

The final relationship that Circe forms is

Madeline Miller was awarded the Orange Prize for Fiction for her first novel, The Song of Achilles. *She holds a BA and MA in the classics.*

with Telemachus, the son of Odysseus and Penelope. Telemachus and Circe bond over the stories about and failures of Odysseus, and Circe realizes that she is more attracted to his straightforward son than the adventure and glory seeking hero. Circe then allows her own son to become Athena's new hero and she takes a final stand. She demands release from her exile and blackmails her father. Circe also kills Scylla, releasing herself from the guilt over the multitudes of deaths caused by the monster. Her final act in the story is paradoxically both surprising and expected as she faces the years ahead, knowing: "My divinity shines in me like the last rays of the sun before they drown in the sea. I thought once that gods are the opposite of death, but I see now they are more dead than anything, for they are unchanging, and can hold nothing in their hands." Her strength is made whole as she refuses to bow to those expectations, choosing to change her own fate in a way that no other god would choose. The character development displays a woman who is completely different from the insecure child that was introduced at the beginning of the novel.

Threaded through Circe's story is a variety of other literary and mythological characters that readers will easily recognize. In addition to the tales of Prometheus's punishment, Scylla's transformation, and the Minotaur's birth, Circe learns that her niece Ariadne has aided the hero Theseus in killing her sister's beastly spawn. She is also visited by another niece, Medea, with her human lover Jason of the Argonauts, and Odysseus shares the tales of Helen of Troy and the Trojan Horse. These familiar tales move the plot along while aiding in the deeper development of the main character herself. Miller's presentation of Circe can be heavy at moments, but the author is able to add a lighter tone at several points, including the passages about turning sailors into pigs.

Critical reviews of the novel provided mostly positive feedback. For instance, *Publishers Weekly* lauded Miller, who "paints an uncompromising portrait of a superheroine who learns to wield divine power while coming to understand what it means to be mortal." *Kirkus Reviews* noted that "the supernatural sits intriguingly alongside 'the tonic of ordinary things'" and suggested "the spell holds fast." The plot was also extolled by many reviewers. Wilda Williams for *Library Journal* called it "beautifully written and absorbing," while Sarah Johnson for *Booklist* found "poetic eloquence . . . and fine dramatic pacing." Jane Henriksen Baird, a reviewer for *School Library Journal*, commented that "Miller deftly weaves episodes of war, treachery, monsters, gods, demigods, heroes, and mortals," calling the book an "absorbing and atmospheric read." The few negative comments suggest a tendency toward melodrama at points throughout the novel and a specific line that "seems jarringly modern," as mentioned by *Kirkus Reviews*. Regardless, *Circe* reached number one on the New York Times Best Sellers: Hardcover Fiction list.

Theresa Stowell

Review Sources

Baird, Jane Henriksen. Review of *Circe*, by Madeline Miller. *School Library Journal*, Apr. 2018, www.slj.com/?detailStory=circe-madeline-miller-slj-review. Accessed 25 July 2018.

Review of *Circe*, by Madeline Miller. *Kirkus Reviews*, 1 Feb. 2018. *Literary Reference Center Plus*, search.ebscohost.com/login.aspx?direct=true&db=lkh&AN=127646593&site=lrc-plus. Accessed 25 July 2018.

Review of *Circe*, by Madeline Miller. *Publishers Weekly*, 5 Feb. 2018. *Literary Reference Center Plus*, search.ebscohost.com/login.aspx?direct=true&db=lkh&AN=127810205&site=lrc-plus. Accessed 25 July 2018.

Johnson, Sarah. Review of *Circe*, by Madeline Miller. *Booklist*, 15 Feb. 2018. *Literary Reference Center Plus*, search.ebscohost.com/login.aspx?direct=true&db=lkh&AN=128157207&site=lrc-plus. Accessed 25 July 2018.

Williams, Wilda. Review of *Circe*, by Madeline Miller. *Library Journal*, 15 Feb. 2018, p. 56. *Literary Reference Center Plus*, search.ebscohost.com/login.aspx?direct=true&db=lkh&AN=127946543&site=lrc-plus. Accessed 25 July 2018.

Clock Dance

Author: Anne Tyler (b. 1941)
Publisher: Knopf (New York). 304 pp.
Type of work: Novel
Time: 1967, 1977, 1997, 2017
Locales: Lark City, Pennsylvania; San Diego, California; Phoenix, Arizona; Baltimore, Maryland

In Clock Dance, *a woman whose life has been defined by others finds a new purpose and surrogate family in Baltimore, Maryland.*

Principal characters
WILLA DRAKE, later known as Willa MacIntyre and Willa Brendan, the protagonist
MELVIN DRAKE, her father
ALICE DRAKE, her mother
ELAINE DRAKE, her younger sister
DEREK MACINTYRE, her first husband
SEAN MACINTYRE, her son with Derek
IAN MACINTYRE, her son with Derek
PETER BRENDAN, her second husband
DENISE CARLYLE, Sean's ex-girlfriend
CHERYL CARLYLE, Denise's daughter

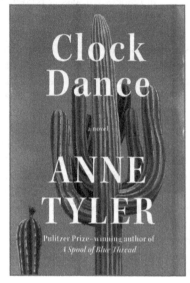

Courtesy of Knopf Doubleday

Over the course of her long career as a novelist, which began with the 1964 publication of the novel *If Morning Ever Comes*, Anne Tyler has become known for books that deal with both the details of everyday life and the dramatic relationships and events found within dysfunctional families. She has explored topics such as marriage, parenthood, and self-discovery through myriad characters over more than half a century of writing. The city of Baltimore, Tyler's home for many decades, serves as a key setting in many of her novels, including the Pulitzer Prize winner *Breaking Lessons* (1988) and the 2015 novel *A Spool of Blue Thread*, a finalist for the prestigious Man Booker Prize. With her twenty-second novel, *Clock Dance*, Tyler builds upon her previous works to create a thought-provoking narrative that calls attention to the role the past plays in shaping the present as well as the daunting nature of breaking free from predictability and passivity.

    Clock Dance is divided into two parts, encompassing roughly the first third and the latter two-thirds of the book, respectively. The first part is itself divided into three portions, each set in a different year and setting the stage for the events of the book's later narrative. The novel begins in 1967, when its protagonist, Willa Drake, is eleven years old and living in the small town of Lark City, Pennsylvania. Life in the Drake family is challenging. Willa's mother, Alice, is subject to abrupt and unpredictable changes in mood—or "flare-ups," as Willa calls them—that periodically cause her to run away from home, shout at her family, and even hit her young daughters. Willa's father, Melvin, is understanding and patient to the point of passivity and does little to address his wife's apparent struggles with mental illness. When Alice unexpectedly leaves home for more than a day, Willa takes a larger role in caring for her younger sister, Elaine. Although Alice eventually returns home, Willa's assumption of the caretaker role shapes her future trajectory, pushing her down a path of caring for others—often at the expense of her own fulfillment.

Willa's trajectory is solidified further in the second section of Part I, which takes place in 1977. A twenty-one-year-old college junior, Willa becomes engaged to her boyfriend, Derek MacIntyre, a senior who already has a job lined up in California for after graduation. Derek attempts to convince Willa to marry him within a matter of months and transfer from her current college, where she has a scholarship and plans to pursue further studies in foreign languages, to a school in California. He disregards her own wishes as well as her account of a frightening experience on the airplane when they fly to visit Willa's parents for Easter, but Willa nevertheless agrees to marry him.

The marriage comes to an abrupt and tragic end in the third section of part 1, set in 1997, in which Derek dies in a car accident that he caused during an incident of road rage. Having herself survived the accident, Willa is forced to adjust to life as a widow while continuing to care for her teenage sons, one of whom is set to leave for college only a few months after his father's death. In this portion of the narrative, Tyler stresses the effects Willa's own childhood has had on her approach to parenting. She notes that Willa "tried her best to be a good mother—which to her meant a predictable mother" and was "the only woman she knew whose prime objective was to be taken for granted." This section also reveals that despite Derek's assurances twenty years before, Willa had not, in fact, been able to continue her studies as planned and had instead stopped attending college after she became pregnant with her first child.

Part 2 of *Clock Dance* begins in July 2017, when Willa is sixty-one years old. She receives a phone call from a stranger, who informs her that a woman named Denise has been shot and, believing Willa to be Denise's mother-in-law, asks her to come care for the injured woman's daughter, Cheryl. While Denise had previously been in a relationship with Willa's son Sean, the two had broken up some time before, and he is not Cheryl's father. Despite having no obligation to care for Cheryl, Willa agrees to travel from her new home in Arizona to Baltimore, Maryland, to step in. Her second husband, Peter, accompanies her on the trip despite his belief that Willa—whom he often refers to as "little one"—is being unreasonable.

After arriving in Baltimore, Willa quickly bonds with nine-year-old Cheryl, an incongruously mature child who reminds Willa of her younger self. While Denise remains in the hospital to recover from the operation she underwent after the shooting, Willa and Peter settle into Denise's home alongside Cheryl and her dog, Airplane, and meet some of the many memorable characters who live in the neighborhood. Impatient

Courtesy of Knopf Doubleday

Anne Tyler is an acclaimed, best-selling author of numerous novels and short stories. Her best-known works include Dinner at the Homesick Restaurant *(1982),* The Accidental Tourist *(1985), the Pulitzer Prize–winning* Breathing Lessons *(1988), and* A Spool of Blue Thread *(2015), which was short-listed for the Man Booker Prize.*

to get back to Arizona and convinced that Willa is "going to pieces," Peter urges Willa to leave Baltimore as soon as Denise returns home from the hospital. Despite her deeply engrained need to be as accommodating as possible, she refuses to return home with him immediately, instead choosing to remain in Baltimore until Denise, whose leg is in a cast, is capable of getting around on her own. Over the subsequent days, Willa bonds further with her newfound surrogate family and feels increasingly at home in their neighborhood. As the novel moves toward its conclusion, the long-established patterns of Willa's life come into conflict with her desire for a more meaningful and fulfilling existence, propelling her toward a rebellion that has been decades in the making.

Like many of Tyler's novels, which often feature extensive flashbacks and multiple generations of family relationships, *Clock Dance* is heavily shaped by the passage of time and the links between past and present. That is most apparent from the structure of the novel, especially the division between part 1 and part 2 and the additional divisions within part 1. While the events featured in part 1 could be considered mere backstory, and some readers might find that portion of the narrative to be overly lengthy, Tyler makes it clear throughout the latter portion of the novel that the events of part 1 were essential in shaping the Willa presented in part 2. Without the insights given in part 1, elements of Willa's personality and behavior—including her passive and accommodating nature and her degree of learned helplessness—might frustrate readers who prefer a more assertive protagonist. However, by addressing Willa's troubled childhood, her history of taking a subordinate role to condescending older husbands, and her frequently thwarted professional aspirations, Tyler clearly explains the roots of the character's later hunger for a new role in life and subsequent rebellion. As *Clock Dance* clearly illustrates, the Willa of 2017 has been shaped by all of the Willas who came before, each of whom is, in some ways, still alive within her. While her eventual rebellion is a quieter one than some readers may prefer, it is consistent with both the Willa of 2017's personality and with the character arc presented over the course of the novel.

In addition to Willa, Tyler populates the world of *Clock Dance* with an intriguing cast of supporting characters. Most memorable are those who, even when mentioned rarely, contribute to the overall spirit of the Baltimore neighborhood in which much of the book takes place. Indeed, while Tyler does not delve particularly deeply into the lives of the secondary characters, each one further develops the personality of the neighborhood, which essentially functions as a character of sorts itself. The world of the novel at times can seem somewhat old fashioned or anachronistic, particularly in the portion set in 2017. That is particularly evident in regard to nine-year-old Cheryl, whose language, opinions, and even name do not necessarily seem to belong to a child born in 2008. However, such details further support the developing bond between Cheryl and Willa, who sees the girl as a sort of kindred spirit. Such potential anachronisms also emphasize the timeless nature of the novel's focus on breaking free from old patterns and building a new family based on choice rather than obligation.

Reviews of *Clock Dance* were mixed, with some critics enjoying Tyler's latest work and others identifying it as disappointing in comparison to her earlier novels. The structure of the narrative was a key point of contention, as some reviewers found part 1 in particular to be disjointed or superfluous. In her review for the *Independent*, Lucy Scholes described the beginning of the novel as "jerky," while Carol Memmott wrote for the *Chicago Tribune* that the beginning section is "at times a long slog." Memmott further noted that some of the characters and situations in those sections have no immediately apparent role in the later sections of the book. Other critics, however, highlighted the ways in which the brief glimpses into key portions of Willa's early life inform the reader's understanding of her personality and actions in part 2.

Critics also disagreed about the quality of the narrative as a whole. Writing for the *Guardian*, Julie Myerson called attention to similarities between *Clock Dance* and other of Tyler's books and argued that the novel's plot was at times too convenient and lacked adequate conflict. *USA Today* reviewer Charles Finch likewise identified weak points, noting that "secondary characters are wispy, some of the beats are a little pat." Despite such criticisms, however, many still found *Clock Dance* to be another compelling offering from Tyler. Finch ultimately described the novel as "a powerful, stirring work," while Memmott praised Tyler's ability to create realistic characters and make ordinary, everyday activities and situations particularly interesting. In this way, *Clock Dance* carries on some of the key features of Tyler's acclaimed body of work.

Joy Crelin

Review Sources

Charles, Ron. "*Clock Dance*, Anne Tyler's 22nd Novel, Feels Familiar—for Better and Worse." Review of *Clock Dance*, by Anne Tyler. *The Washington Post*, 3 July 2018, www.washingtonpost.com/entertainment/books/clock-dance-anne-tylers-22nd-novel-feels-familiar--for-better-and-worse/2018/07/02/c0842a70-7d9f-11e8-bb6b-c1cb691f1402_story.html. Accessed 1 Nov. 2018.

Finch, Charles. "Time Heals Family Wounds in Anne Taylor's Lovely New Novel, *Clock Dance*." Review of *Clock Dance*, by Anne Tyler. *USA Today*, 9 July 2018, www.usatoday.com/story/life/books/2018/07/09/book-review-clock-dance-anne-tyler/753148002/. Accessed 1 Nov. 2018.

Memmott, Carol. "In Anne Tyler's Latest Novel, a Woman Learns to Dance, Not Sleepwalk, through Life." Review of *Clock Dance*, by Anne Tyler. *Chicago*

Tribune, 16 July 2018, www.chicagotribune.com/lifestyles/books/sc-books-clock-dance-anne-tyler-0718-story.html. Accessed 1 Nov. 2018.

Myerson, Julie. "*Clock Dance* by Anne Tyler Review—an Old Friend Stuck in Neutral." Review of *Clock Dance*, by Anne Tyler. *The Guardian*, 24 July 2018, www.theguardian.com/books/2018/jul/24/clock-dance-anne-tyler-review. Accessed 1 Nov. 2018.

Scholes, Lucy. "*Clock Dance* by Anne Tyler, Review: Less Nuanced than her Best Work, but You Still Root for Tyler's Heroine." Review of *Clock Dance*, by Anne Tyler. *Independent*, 19 July 2018, www.independent.co.uk/arts-entertainment/books/reviews/clock-dance-anne-tyler-book-review-breathing-lessons-spool-of-blue-thread-a8454726.html. Accessed 1 Nov. 2018.

Tuttle, Kate. "Anne Tyler's Latest Heroine Quits Cushy Arizona for Quirky Baltimore." Review of *Clock Dance*, by Anne Tyler. *The New York Times*, 1 Aug. 2018, www.nytimes.com/2018/08/01/books/review/clock-dance-anne-tyler.html. Accessed 30 Sept. 2018.

The Day the Sun Died

Author: Yan Lianke (b. 1958)
First published: *Ri xi*, 2015, in Taiwan
Translated: from the Chinese by Carlos Rojas
Publisher: Grove Press (New York). 352 pp.
Type of work: Novel
Time: 2016
Locale: Gaotian, Zhaonan County, China

Courtesy of Grove Atlantic

In author-provocateur Yan Lianke's novel The Day the Sun Died, *fourteen-year-old narrator Li Niannian, whose parents sell funerary items for a living, recounts in one day, hour after meticulous hour, the grizzly details of a village torn asunder by the rare affliction of mass somnambulism.*

Principal characters
LI NIANNIAN, the narrator, fourteen years old
LI TIANBAO, his father
SHAO XIAOMIN, his mother
SHAO DACHENG, a.k.a. Uncle Zhang, his maternal uncle
YAN LIANKE, famous writer

Yan Lianke's novel *The Day the Sun Died* (2018; *Ri xi*, 2015) is deliberately provocative, complicated, and fever-inducing. Told through the first-person perspective of fourteen-year-old Li Niannian, the story's callow protagonist recounts what Julian Gewirtz, writing for the *New York Times*, called "a relentless and even brutal experience." Over the course of twenty-four delirious hours, struggling to bear the torrid heat of June, residents of Gaotian, a small agrarian town nestled amid the Central Plains in China's Funiu Mountain Range, must face the ghastly horrors of a "once-in-a-century" occurrence when a bizarre epidemic of sleepwalking, or rather "dreamwalking," a literal translation of the Chinese word for somnambulism, plagues the region.

Li Niannian's maternal uncle, Uncle Zhang, is in charge of the local crematorium, enforcing state regulations that oblige people to abandon traditional burial customs and begin practicing cremation. Li Niannian's father, Li Tianbao, is an informant for his brother-in-law, earning extra money on the side (an extra four hundred yuan, to be exact) by spying and ratting on the townspeople who are brazen enough to break the law and clandestinely bury their deceased family members. After Tianbao reports these transgressors to Uncle Zhang, the "enforcement brigade" arrives. "Every village and town," Li Niannian explains, has "its own enforcement brigade, which would appear wherever there was a corpse that had not been cremated." Using explosives, the brigade cumbersomely exhumes graves and cremates on site. Not surprisingly, the townspeople grow to loathe Uncle Zhang and the world of compulsory cremation he represents.

When Li Tianbao discovers that Uncle Zhang, too, has been making money on the side—lots of it—selling corpse oil to an index of corporate buyers, Li Tianbao is morally outraged and convinces his wife to open the New World funerary shop. The Li family produces and sells ceremonial items, such as wreaths, flower bouquets, and papercuts that grieving families use to honor their dead and make sure they have everything they need in the afterlife. In turn, Li Tianbao uses New World's earnings to buy up all the corpse oil from Uncle Zhang and hides it in a nearby cave.

Mayhem and upheaval ensue, as the "great somnambulism" rushes into Gaotian, and the afflicted residents act out their repressed fantasies and desires. As the only person to remain unafflicted, Li Niannian calmly, though pessimistically, narrates the horrible spectacles that he sees, and shares with the reader the rumors that circulate through town as quickly as the dreamwalking hysteria does. Neighbors kill neighbors. Some of the dreamwalkers jump in the nearby canal to take their own lives. One woman almost goes into labor, while others fornicate or run around naked. An older woman is cremated alive. A wife confesses to murdering her husband. Uncle Zhang and his wife cook up poison to serve to their wealthy neighbors. The mayor and other town officials begin enacting scenes from the old imperial court. Meanwhile, the police are practically asleep. As the hours pass, and as the town slips deeper into moral decay, outsiders take advantage of the town's affliction. They flock in to pillage and loot, fomenting violent insurrections and near-interminable battles.

Because the story is told through a fourteen-year-old's perspective, one who, furthermore, is a proclaimed "idiot," Yan's prose is simple but astoundingly clear. His words are freighted with sagacity and profundity without ever betraying the measured voice of a disaffected teenager whose expectations are far from optimistic. That said, Yan balances such despondent simplicity with poetic inflection, as he wields a variety of literary devices ranging from alliteration to synesthetic metaphors and similes. Yan also fashions himself into a metafictional device, appearing as a salient character whose debilitating writer's block ends after he survives dreamwalking, and pledges to write about the day's outstanding events.

At times, *The Day the Sun Died* is fragmented and disjointed. But so are dreams, which infect and inflect waking life. The implication of such a fluid boundary is that personal experience may be no less fragmented and disjointed, especially when intruded upon by a series of traumas. Li Niannian strongly alludes to this when he says in the preface, before venturing to tell his story, that he is unable to provide a rational articulation of the sequence of events; that he has "no choice" but to tell the story of how the great somnambulism happened to him. His story is scattered, arresting, and at times static while at other times roiling with disturbances. For what unfolds hour after painstaking hour, stretching to what seems like an eternal endurance of incongruous elements and outrageous acts, is indeed markedly unusual. Its cause, never really explored, seems to inhere only in effects that continually disrupt any sense one might make of the situation. In a world in which everybody suddenly and mysteriously starts dreamwalking, waking life becomes an inescapable nightmare.

Yan is known for his daring prose and has faced harsh censorship in China. He experiments with the absurd and has a penchant for writing dark satire. *Dream of Ding Village* (2005), which was banned by the Chinese government, tells the chilling story of a lucrative blood-selling racket that leaves thousands of impoverished farmers in Henan province infected with AIDS. As expected, Yan dims the lights even more in this modern gothic allegory about self-determination in a rural, twenty-first-century China that is fast becoming the world's economic center. Having modernized, it has joined the global economy, is entwined in complex technology transfers, engages in dubious appropriation of intellectual property, pursues unfair trade practices, and so forth. Conversely, and not unlike much of rural China, Gaotian is provincial, structured by uneven relations between peasants and property owners. Subsisting primarily off its wheat fields, Gaotian is steeped in the mixed composition of the present. At once modern and premodern, it is caught up in a provisional state of dissolution. Its denizens both passively and reactively tarry with change, engaging historical forces germane to "capitalism with Chinese characteristics," as writer Yasheng Huang and others have framed China's economy, its sociopolitical trends, and its attendant new technologies.

Courtesy of Grove/Atlantic

The Day the Sun Died, which received largely positive reviews, is arguably not just about President Xi Jinping's Chinese Dream as both a vision of national renewal and an anticipated nightmare for anyone dreading potentially being left behind. Nor is it only about somnambulists who loot, kill, and confess as they carry out what otherwise, in their waking state, would be safely repressed drives and desires. Rather, Yan's latest book serves as remarkable social commentary with universal scope. Sean Hewitt, writing for the *Irish Times*, noted that the novel em-

Yan Lianke is an award-winning writer of more than twenty satirical novels and story collections. He has received numerous literary honors in China and internationally, including the Lu Xun Prize, the Lao She Award, and the 2014 Franz Kafka Prize. He was a Man Booker International Prize finalist in 2013 and 2016.

ploys "a strange elegance and dark, masterful experiment," one that will perhaps pique interpreters, critics, and reviewers for some time. Using well-crafted irony, *The Day the Sun Died* is an oblique, albeit smart, report on China's political-economic landscape as it has developed, and continues to develop, into the twenty-first century. Of the book's ability to get such significant themes across, Hewitt further stated, "This is a brave and unforgettable novel, full of tragic poise and political resonance, masterfully shifting between genres and ways of storytelling."

Arguably, however, it also aims its allegorical function toward rampant nationalism, corruption, hypocrisy, avarice, cowardice, and helplessness that are found not only in China but everywhere. Such unflattering attributes and more reverberate throughout the pages, gathering together in a collective dream state that enables selfish acts and selfless delusions. An anonymous reviewer for *Publishers Weekly* stated that "the interweaving of politics and delusion creates a powerful resonance" that ripples across the surface of a complexly layered story. If Yan's earlier novel *Lenin's Kisses* (2012; *Shou huo*, 2003) served to scorn China's transition to capitalism, *The Day the Sun Died* is his attempt to legitimize, by further contextualizing, said scorn. Effectively depicting the conditions by which one, like the dreamwalkers, may come to "see only the people and things they care about . . . as if nothing else exists," Yan's latest novel reveals just how nightmarish things may possibly get when whole populations are subjected to, and ensnared by, the unbreakable, oneiric spell of late capitalism and its strata of ideologies.

Frank Joseph

Review Sources

Review of *The Day the Sun Died*, by Yan Lianke. *Kirkus Reviews*, 17 Sept. 2018, www.kirkusreviews.com/book-reviews/yan-lianke/the-day-the-sun-died/. Accessed 16 Jan. 2019.

Review of *The Day the Sun Died*, by Yan Lianke, *Publishers Weekly*, 1 Oct. 2018, www.publishersweekly.com/978-0-8021-2853-9. Accessed 16 Jan. 2019.

Gewirtz, Julian. "In a Brutal Chinese Satire, Villagers Surrender to Their Worst Impulses." Review of *The Day the Sun Died*, by Yan Lianke. *The New York Times*, 28 Dec. 2018, www.nytimes.com/2018/12/28/books/review/yan-lianke-the-day-the-sun-died.html. Accessed 16 Jan. 2019.

Hewitt, Sean. "The Day the Sun Died, by Yan Lianke: A Brave, Masterful Novel." Review of *The Day the Sun Died*, by Yan Lianke. *The Irish Times*, 28 July 2018, www.irishtimes.com/culture/books/the-day-the-sun-died-by-yan-lianke-a-brave-masterful-novel-1.3558083. Accessed 16 Jan. 2019.

Hilton, Isabel. "The Day the Sun Died by Yan Lianke Review—The Stuff of Nightmares." Review of *The Day the Sun Died*, by Yan Lianke. *The Guardian*, 29 July 2018, www.theguardian.com/books/2018/jul/29/the-day-the-sun-died-yan-lianke-review-china. Accessed 16 Jan. 2019.

"Yan Lianke's Dark Satire of Modern China." Review of *The Day the Sun Died*, by Yan Lianke. *The Economist*, 26 July 2018, www.economist.com/books-and-arts/2018/07/26/yan-liankes-dark-satire-of-modern-china. Accessed 16 Jan. 2019.

The Death of Mrs. Westaway

Author: Ruth Ware
Publisher: Gallery/Scout Press (New York).
384 pp.
Type of work: Novel
Time: Present day
Locales: Brighton and Penzance, England,
and environs

*In best-selling author Ruth Ware's fourth
novel,* The Death of Mrs. Westaway, *a young
tarot card reader in dire straits is unexpectedly invited to the reading of a will. Though
she believes she has been mistakenly named
a beneficiary, she decides to take advantage
of the opportunity to acquire some much-
needed cash.*

Courtesy of Gallery/Scout Press

Principal characters
HARRIET MARGARIDA "HAL" WESTAWAY, a twenty-one-year-old orphan who works as
a tarot card reader
HESTER MARY WESTAWAY, a.k.a. Mrs. Westaway, a wealthy woman recently deceased
ROBERT TRESWICK, the estate attorney for Mrs. Westaway
ADA WARREN, the aged housekeeper at Trepassen House, the Westaway residence
HARDING WESTAWAY, Mrs. Westaway's eldest son
ABEL WESTAWAY, Mrs. Westaway's middle son
EZRA WESTAWAY, Mrs. Westaway's youngest son
EDWARD ASHBY, Abel's romantic partner, a doctor
MITZI WESTAWAY, Harding's sympathetic wife and mother of their three teenaged
children

Ruth Ware's *The Death of Mrs. Westaway* establishes the novel's sinister tone from
the very first page by quoting a popular nursery rhyme about magpies, scavenger birds
often associated in folklore with evil or bad luck. The verse begins "One for sorrow
/ Two for joy" and ends ominously with "Seven for a secret / Never to be told." The
symbolism is immediately reinforced by a diary entry that serves as a preface, dated
November 29, 1994. The unidentified writer, looking out a window, observes a fox
stalking a flock of magpies. Further entries, inserted into the novel at key intervals, reveal details of the narrator's personal history, relationships, and current circumstances
that, over time, dovetail into the plot.

The main narrative leaps forward more than two decades with the introduction of
the colorful central character, Harriet "Hal" Westaway. Described as skinny and pale,
the twenty-one-year-old wears glasses and has short black hair, a large earring in the

shape of a thorn, and tattoos (including one of a large magpie on her back). Hal was born, raised, and still lives in Brighton, a popular seaside resort on England's south coast about fifty miles from London.

Hal lives modestly, residing in the only living quarters she has ever known: a small, shabby walk-up apartment. She has few acquaintances, and no living relatives of whom she is aware. Since her beloved mother, Margarida "Maggie" Westaway, was killed instantly in a hit-and-run incident three years earlier, Hal has earned a meager living practicing the craft her mother taught her: telling fortunes, especially by reading tarot cards. Though she occasionally also reads palms, Hal usually employs tarot cards because she enjoys the symbolism, though she does not believe the cards have any supernatural powers. Hal is a skilled "cold reader," able to discern clues without conducting research (this person is wearing run-down shoes so may be experiencing financial woes, that one has an untanned space on the ring finger, thus might be divorced or widowed) to assist her in creating plausible scenarios about a client's past, present, and future. Hal operates under the name and sign her mother used—Madame Margarida—and sees clients in a small leased kiosk on Brighton's West Pier.

While survival has been a struggle for Hal since her mother died, her existence is becoming increasingly perilous. During a particularly rough time, she borrowed five hundred pounds from a loan shark known as Mr. Smith. A year later, after repaying approximately two thousand pounds, she is further in debt than ever. After Hal missed or was tardy with a few payments, Mr. Smith sent vaguely threatening notes. Eventually, he sends a large, bald, bulky representative to Hal's kiosk as a personal reminder to pay up, or else. The smiling thug smashes some of Hal's possessions and notes that bones and teeth can just as easily be broken. She is told to pay the full amount she owes within a week or to expect another, less friendly, visit from the collector.

Fortunately for Hal, when she had arrived home the night before, among a stack of bills in the mail she had found a formal letter from an attorney, Robert Treswick of Penzance. The letter informed her of the death of her octogenarian grandmother, Hester Mary Westaway, who left behind a sizable estate. Hal has been named a beneficiary and would learn details after Mrs. Westaway's funeral in St. Piran. Hal thinks she has been contacted in error: her mother said her grandparents died many years ago. (Maggie also claimed that Hal was the product of a one-night stand with a man whose name she did not know.) However, with little to lose, and plenty of incentive to get out of town, Hal decides to travel to hear the reading of the will. She figures she might be able to use her specialized people skills to bluff her way into a large-enough financial legacy to pay off her bills, especially her debt to Mr. Smith.

Using a nearly maxed-out credit card, Hal buys a train ticket to Penzance. Most of her small supply of cash is spent taxiing to St. Piran, where she attends Mrs. Westaway's funeral. Afterward, Hal, Mr. Treswick, and the Westaway clan gather at the family residence, Trepassen House. This is a huge, dilapidated mansion dating from the eighteenth century, with wings added over the years. The structure is sprawled across extensive, overgrown grounds that include a garden maze, a weed-choked lake, and a copse of trees where magpies gather. Inside, the mansion seems even larger and gloomier. The place features high ceilings, dim lighting, filthy windows, and thousands

of dark corners. There is only a single bathroom in the entire house. As little heat issues from inadequate fireplaces, it proves quite chilly. Cobwebs drape across ancient
furniture, and dust lies in thick layers in unused rooms.

Hal soon meets the others named in Mrs. Westaway's will. Present are the dead
woman's three adult sons, who were estranged from their unlikable mother. Harding, the oldest, has a wife, Mitzi, and three teenaged children in attendance. Abel, the
middle son, is there with his partner, Edward. Ezra, the youngest, owns a photographic
gallery in southern France. The longtime housekeeper of Trepassen House, Ada Warren, bears a close resemblance in character and description to that of Mrs. Danvers in
Daphne du Maurier's *Rebecca* (1938) and dresses all in black.

At the appropriate time, Mr. Treswick provides details of the estate and the dis-
bursement of funds: Mrs. Westaway had "some three hundred thousand pounds in cash
and securities." The house alone, even in its present run-down state, is worth as much
as £2 million. Mrs. Warren is bequeathed the sum of £30,000 for her long service,
the other three grandchildren are granted £10,000 apiece, the three sons have been
bypassed, and the remainder of the estate has been willed to Hal. While the other sons,
who hated their mother, act indifferent about being left out of the inheritance, Harding
is outraged. Hal, meanwhile, is distressed; she had hoped to gain just a little cash to
bail herself out of financial difficulty and had no aspirations of becoming a wealthy
heiress. She feels guilty about usurping a fortune from the rightful heirs. Her major
goal then is to forget about profiting illegally while deftly extricating herself from the
situation before she can be accused of attempted fraud.

The bulk of the second half of *The Death of Mrs. Westaway* is consumed by Hal's
dilemma as it plays out over the next several days, with movement complicated by
unusually harsh winter weather. On one hand, Hal tries to back away to avoid possible
legal consequences. On the other hand, she becomes more involved: during her stay
at Trepassen, she uncovers evidence that sheds new light on various members of the
Westaway family and on the connections that led to her being named in the will. As
revelations mount, the plot twists in unexpected directions. Tension increases and the
danger level rises, yet Hal continues the pursuit of the truth, unwittingly placing her
life at risk.

As in Ware's previous novels, also psychological thrillers often inspired by the
likes of classic mystery writers such as Agatha Christie, *The Death of Mrs. Westaway*
incorporates numerous Gothic literary tropes to effectively create a sense of suspense.
The lead characters in all the author's books to date, for example, are women in some
sort of distress and whose lives are placed in jeopardy. *In a Dark, Dark Wood* (2015)
has Leonora Shaw, an amnesiac who has suffered a head wound. For *The Woman
in Cabin 10* (2016), it is Lo Blacklock, a victim of a break-in who must deal with
post-traumatic stress as she attempts to unravel a mystery while at sea on a cruise
ship. Meanwhile, *The Lying Game* (2017) features four women, friends who share a
dark secret from the past. However, Ware's protagonists are more likely to internalize
anguish, rather than screaming or crying, as in Gothic novels of old, and often utilize
modern technology (such as computers, cell phones, and social media). While secondary characters are often underdeveloped or stereotypical—Harding is a stock stuffy,

upper-class character while Mrs. Warren is a du Maurier homage—Ware's strength lies in creating relatable protagonists of depth. Hal Westaway, for all her flaws, is resourceful, demonstrates maturity beyond her years, and exhibits a conscience that makes her attempt to do what is right.

British author Ruth Ware burst upon the literary scene with her best-selling debut novel, In a Dark, Dark Wood *(2015). Since then, she has earned acclaim for her ability to create suspense while publishing a novel per year:* The Woman in Cabin 10 *(2016),* The Lying Game *(2017), and* The Death of Mrs. Westaway *(2018).*

Ware is likewise skilled in carefully creating a brooding, mysterious Gothic setting. The atmosphere is fraught with hidden secrets and undisclosed crimes that come to light and exert seismic, engaging shifts throughout the course of the story, leading the reviewer for *Kirkus Reviews* to describe the novel as "expertly paced, expertly crafted." Most of the action unfolds in or around big, creepy Trepassen House, which serves as an inanimate but dominating presence. The house emits noises—floors creak, plumbing shrieks, and Mrs. Warren's cane-assisted gait produces its own malevolent rhythm. The structure and grounds together seem to incorporate evil intent. There are rumors that a maid hanged herself and someone drowned in the dark waters of the little lake. House doors stick at inopportune times. Poor lighting disguises traps for the unwary: missing steps, sudden drops, and other obstacles. Hal is accommodated in a tiny attic room where it would be easy to become trapped (there are sliding locks on the door's exterior and bars over the windows), and where someone has etched "HELP ME" into the glass. The magpies provide a constant and ominous presence as Hal pieces together clues and spirals toward the truth.

Jack Ewing

Review Sources

Corrigan, Maureen. "Ruth Ware's New Thriller Is a Classic." Review of *The Death of Mrs. Westaway*, by Ruth Ware. *The Washington Post*, 24 May 2018, www.washingtonpost.com/entertainment/books/why-ruth-wares-new-thriller-is-a-classic/2018/05/23/ac2a1a62-5d10-11e8-9ee3-49d6d4814c4c_story.html. Accessed 2 Aug. 2018.

Review of *The Death of Mrs. Westaway*, by Ruth Ware. *Kirkus*, 3 Apr. 2018, www.kirkusreviews.com/book-reviews/ruth-ware/the-death-of-mrs-westaway. Accessed 2 Aug. 2018.

Review of *The Death of Mrs. Westaway*, by Ruth Ware. *Publishers Weekly*, 2 Apr. 2018, www.publishersweekly.com/978-1-5011-5621-2. Accessed 2 Aug. 2018.

Scholes, Lucy. "*The Death of Mrs. Westaway* by Ruth Ware, Review: A Dark Tale by One of the Best Thriller Writers Around." Review of *The Death of Mrs. Westaway*, by Ruth Ware. *Independent*, 27 June 2018, www.independent.co.uk/arts-entertainment/books/reviews/the-death-of-mrs-westaway-review-ruth-ware-thriller-novel-lying-game-a8420001.html. Accessed 2 Aug. 2018.

The Desert and the Sea
977 Days Captive on the Somali Pirate Coast

Author: Michael Scott Moore (b. 1969)
Publisher: Harper Wave (New York). 464 pp.
Type of work: Autobiography, history
Time: 2012–14
Locales: Somalia, Germany, United States

Moore recounts his years as a captive of pirates in Somalia, where he went as a journalist to report on the development of piracy in northeast Africa. He describes his captors, their motives, their behavior, and his own reactions to his ordeal.

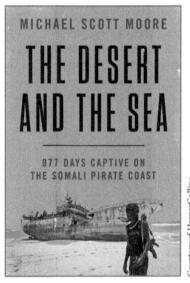

Courtesy of HarperCollins

Principal personages

MICHAEL SCOTT MOORE, author; American journalist and historian of surfing

MARLIS SAUNDERS, his mother

ASHWIN RAMAN, his mentor and friend; an Indian documentary filmmaker and war correspondent

MOHAMMED SAHAL GERLACH, his translator, a Somali elder living in Berlin

MOHAMED AHMED ALIN, his host, regional president of Galmudug, Somalia

MOHAMMED GARFANJI, pirate boss

ROLLY TAMBARA, his fellow captive, a fisherman from the Seychelles

By the time Michael Scott Moore decided, in late 2011, to report on the problem of piracy in Somalia, he had published a highly praised book on international surfing and had established a reputation as a well-respected reporter. Although he was born in the United States, he had been living for years in Germany, where he covered the trials of ten captured Somalian pirates and became intrigued by the whole phenomenon of early twenty-first-century piracy off the coast of Africa. "The rise of modern pirates buzzing off Somalia was an example of entropy in my life time, and it seemed important to know why there were pirates at all," Moore writes. He was supported in his plan to cover the pirates by several respected journalistic organizations, including the Pulitzer Center on Crisis Reporting. Moore's memoir, by "the only Western journalist to witness everyday life on a ship captured by Somali pirates" according to the book cover flap copy, has been extolled by reviewers for providing a vivid, first-person account of 977 days in captivity, an experience which at least two reviewers have described as "harrowing."

Some readers, however, may be more skeptical about Moore's motives for working in an area where he knew there was a good and growing chance of being taken prisoner. They may wonder why Moore needed to report from the ground instead of interviewing relevant subjects by phone and having filming done by a local crew. They might question why he would risk causing his friends and loved ones so much anguish not only in worrying about him but also in trying to raise the enormous sums Somali kidnappers typically demanded. And, perhaps most importantly, they may wonder why he saw a need to risk the lives of others if he ever needed to be rescued, especially given the possibility that rescuers risked facing torture and death to come to his aid.

At least a few skeptics may ask questions such as these, but most readers and reviewers seem to have taken Moore pretty much as he presents himself: as an intrepid reporter determined to see things for himself while investigating the "underreported aspects of Somali piracy." They have been fascinated by his day-by-day descriptions of his captivity, his word-by-word recollections of conversations with his captors and other captives, and his meticulously specific reporting about the tedium of life as a prisoner, punctuated by occasional attempts at escape, possibilities of rescue, and bouts with sickness and despair. Moore recalls the personalities of the captors and other captives and the complex relationships they developed with him and with each other, and reviewers have especially admired the minute fidelity of his memory. At times the book reads like a screenplay, with its long stretches of dialogue between Moore and those he met during his many months as a prisoner.

Moore grows frustrated that the Marines are not coming to rescue him and that the US government (or some other responsible party) seems in no special hurry to pay his kidnappers the $20 million that they think he is worth, along with letters of exoneration from President Barack Obama. The book reads like a piece of fiction in the sense that settings, conversations, tones of voice, and details of thought are presented and rendered, though it is never clear that Moore was taking the exceptionally thorough notes that would have been necessary to reconstruct events as they are reconstructed here. The book has sometimes been praised for being almost a novelistic page-turner, but some readers may feel that it is not an especially reflective book, except for a few attempts at quoting the stoics, nor is it particularly rich in any kind of historical or cultural insight. Moore offers a few pages, near the beginning, about the history of Somalia and Somali piracy, and he does give some sense, in those pages, about the nature of life in Somalia before he was captured. Most of the book, however, is devoted to recollections of his own captivity, including almost two years in solitary confinement.

Moore was in Somalia for less than two weeks before being threatened with kidnapping. Rumors were circulating that potential captors thought he would bring in fifteen million dollars in ransom. He briefly considered flying out of the country at once but decided that he needed to visit just one more place to do a bit more reporting. Potential kidnappers thought he might be a spy intent on helping the European Union's ongoing, well-publicized antipiracy initiative, even after he explains that he is simply a journalist. Having refused to leave the country and having reached his destination, he asks such questions as "How did your career as a pirate start?"—the kind of interview that some cynics, perhaps, may think could have been conducted just as successfully by cell phone from Europe.

Courtesy of HarperColllins

Michael Scott Moore is the author of Sweetness and Blood *(2010), a well-regarded book on international surfing, and* Too Much of Nothing *(2003), a novel about a brooding ghost in Los Angeles. He was written for the German magazine* Spiegel Online *and has won various prizes for his nonfiction.*

In the meantime, Moore shows his awareness that almost anything (such as a dispute over the cost of lunch) could lead to a kidnapping. He knows about kidnappings that have taken place just prior to his arrival. Nevertheless, when his mentor and traveling companion, Ashwin Raman, decides to fly out of Somalia sooner rather than later, Moore decides not to accompany him. Instead, he decides to stay around for another crucial research trip. As it happens, it is on his way back from the airport that he is captured. He cannot believe it while it is happening, although some readers will be wondering, by this point, how it could *not* have happened. During the kidnapping, the terrorists beat him and broke his glasses. Moore's reaction is typical: "'Somebody *help* me.' Of course, nobody did." This, some cynics will say, is frequently his reaction throughout the book: he is in a jam, and nobody seems to be acting quickly enough, for him, to get him out of it.

By page 48, Moore has been taken hostage. For the next 350 or so pages, he remains one. Those pages give him plenty of time to show his varied emotions—ranging from fear to anger to sarcasm to frustration, but especially devil-may-care stoicism and writerly wit. Moore recalls his tone and attitude in every conversation he describes, which are many. Often the book is well written, and it has been highly praised for the quality of its prose, although some readers may find it somewhat tedious. After all, on most days not much happened to the captives except continuing captivity. At one point, Moore does make an exciting effort to escape by jumping into the sea, but mainly he talks to and about his captors. Occasionally he reflects on the life and premature death of his father, who committed suicide when Moore was twelve. Moore, in contrast, dreamed of a life involving (among other things) "exotic" travel. For him, standard existence in the United States was deeply flawed: "I would never have to deal with Californian banality again. By 'banality' I meant marriage and divorce, but also drugstores, U.S. politics, TV news, rush-hour traffic, vast American supermarkets, and everything that reminded me of the painful and tedious past." By the end of his captivity and the book, he develops a much richer and fuller appreciation for a culture he had disparaged before being taken hostage.

Ironically, during his captivity, Moore spent most of his time depending on that culture to somehow save him, either by paying large sums of money or by sending Marines to free him from the pirates. Every time a plane or helicopter is heard, Moore and his captors suspect a military rescue mission. FBI agents meet regularly with his mother, trying to reassure her that the less his capture is publicized, the more likely he is to be ransomed at a relatively reasonable price. In the meantime, Moore depicts his own bravery: "I gave [Abdul, a captor] a cold stare. If helicopters were coming, I wanted to be seen, and he had no weapon, no authority beyond his frantic tantrum. I was not about to 'make myself small' for Abdul."

Occasionally, Moore expresses regrets. After his brief escape attempt, he learns that a comrade has been beaten on the feet with the flat blade of a knife in front of the entire crew: "I should have realized Rolly might also be punished, and thinking about it was worse punishment, for me, than the beating I took." This may *sound* modest, but some readers may think that it implies Moore's emotional generosity as well as his physical toughness.

Moore also candidly concedes that his skepticism about Western civilization was naïve and even stupid. He feels sorry for his mom, Marlis Saunders, and foolish when an anticipated ransom payment does not happen. At one point he concedes that he "screwed up" by extending his stay in Somalia and seems genuinely grateful to the brave ex-military man who flew into danger to fly Moore out after the ransom was eventually paid. Moore spends a paragraph near the end of the book briefly thanking various people, and another paragraph reporting his own newfound humility.

Moore rarely comes across as less than heroic, and, since all the people who captured him were later killed in a gunfight with other terrorists, no one is alive to dispute his account—or at least no other account is reported in the book. It would have been fascinating, in fact, if Moore had interviewed his surviving fellow captives in detail and included their interviews in the book, so that their narratives could counterpoint and enrich his own. Instead, the book's focus is on Moore, and it is this focus that has intrigued and pleased so many readers who have appreciated his account of bravery, resilience, psychological toughness, and philosophical maturity. For some readers, however, the true hero of this volume will not be Michael Scott Moore, but his devoted mom, who raised his $1.6 million ransom from family, friends, magazines he worked for, and other institutions.

Robert C. Evans, PhD

Review Sources

Review of *The Desert and the Sea: 977 Days Captive on the Somali Pirate Coast*, by Michael Scott Moore. *Kirkus Reviews*, 1 June 2019, p. 1. *Literary Reference Center Plus*, search.ebscohost.com/login.aspx?direct=true&db=lkh&AN=130386 047&site=lrc-plus. Accessed 7 Jan. 2019.

Dziuban, Emily. Review of *The Desert and the Sea: 977 Days Captive on the Somali Pirate Coast*, by Michael Scott Moore. *Booklist*, 1 June 2018, p. 16. *Literary Reference Center*, search.ebscohost.com/login.aspx?direct=true&db=lkh&AN=13 0237986&site=lrc-plus. Accessed 7 Jan. 2019.

Hoffert, Barbara. Review of *The Desert and the Sea: 977 Days Captive on the So-mali Pirate Coast*, by Michael Scott Moore. *Library Journal*, 15 Feb. 2018, p. 44. *Literary Reference Center*, search.ebscohost.com/login.aspx?direct=true&db=lkh &AN=127946489&site=lrc-plus. Accessed 7 Jan. 2019.

Keymer, David. Review of *The Desert and the Sea: 977 Days Captive on the Somali Pirate Coast*, by Michael Scott Moore. *Library Journal*, 1 June 2018, p. 101. *Literary Reference Center*, search.ebscohost.com/login.aspx?direct=true&db=lkh &AN=129811217&site=lrc-plus. Accessed 7 Jan. 2019.

McConnell, Tristan. "Almost Dying for the Story: On Michael Scott Moore's "The Desert and the Sea: 977 Days Captive on the Somali Pirate Coast." Review of *The Desert and the Sea: 977 Days Captive on the Somali Pirate Coast*, by Michael Scott Moore. *Los Angeles Review of Books*, 28 July 2018, lareviewofbooks.org/ article/almost-dying-for-the-story-on-michael-scott-moores-the-desert-and-the-sea-977-days-captive-on-the-somali-pirate-coast/#!. Accessed 7 Jan. 2019.

Directorate S
The C.I.A. and America's Secret Wars in Afghanistan and Pakistan

Author: Steve Coll (b. 1958)
Publisher: Penguin Press (New York). 784 pp.
Type of work: History, current affairs
Time: 2001–16
Locales: Afghanistan, Pakistan, and Washington, DC

As he came into office, President Donald Trump reiterated the American determination to win in Afghanistan. The war will continue with no immediate end in sight. Coll's Directorate S *serves as a useful primer for anyone bewildered by the long history of the Afghan War. He also makes a compelling case that this conflict will not be resolved until the Pakistani riddle is solved and addressed.*

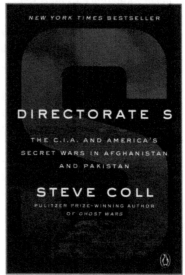

Courtesy of Penguin

Principal personages

GEORGE W. BUSH, president of the United States, 2001–9

BARACK OBAMA, president of the United States, 2009–16

CONDOLEEZZA RICE, US secretary of state, 2005–9

HILLARY CLINTON, US secretary of state, 2009–13

GEORGE TENET, Central Intelligence Agency (CIA) director, 1997–2004

PORTER GOSS, CIA director, 2004–6; former member of Congress and chair of the House Intelligence Committee

MICHAEL HAYDEN, CIA director, 2006–9; former director of the National Security Agency

LEON PANETTA, CIA director, 2009–11; US secretary of defense, 2011–13

DAVID PETRAEUS, CIA director, 2011–12; former commander of US and NATO forces in Afghanistan, coalition forces in Iraq

JOHN BRENNAN, CIA director, 2013–17

BENAZIR BHUTTO, leader of the Pakistan People's Party, 1988–2007

ZALMAY KHALILZAD, ambassador to Afghanistan, 2003–5; ambassador to Iraq, 2005–7; US permanent representative to the United Nations, 2007–9

RICHARD HOLBROOK, US special representative for Afghanistan and Pakistan, 2009–10

AMRULLAH SALEH, official in the Northern Alliance, head of Afghanistan's National Directorate of Security, 2004–10

HAMID KARZAI, first elected president of Afghanistan, 2004–14

PERVEZ MUSHARRAF, president of Pakistan, 2001–8
ASHFAQ KAYANI, director general of Pakistan's intelligence agency, 2004–7; chief of
army staff, 2007–13

In *Directorate S*, the distinguished journalist Steve Coll provides a sequel to *Ghost Wars* (2004), his Pulitzer Prize–winning account of covert American involvement in Afghanistan from the 1979 Soviet invasion through the summer of 2001. In this somber follow-up narrative, he traces the efforts of the administrations of Presidents George W. Bush and Barack Obama to hunt down al-Qaeda terrorists and protect the US-sponsored Afghan government from Taliban insurgents. Coll persuasively argues that US policy in Afghanistan has been foiled by the hostility of elements in the government of Pakistan and its intelligence agency, Inter-Services Intelligence (ISI). Coll's book takes its title from the ISI's secret operations wing, which US intelligence officers and diplomats referred to as Directorate S.

Viewers of the fourth season of the popular American spy melodrama *Homeland* (2011–19) were treated to a dark portrayal of ISI, whose members actively sponsor a ruthless terrorist leader and permit a bloody assault on Americans in their capitol. This fictionalized depiction of the Pakistanis reflected a deterioration of relations between the Obama administration and Islamabad that had culminated in May 2011, when US special forces killed the September 11 attack mastermind, Osama bin Laden, in a compound next door to the Pakistani military academy in Abbottabad. The embarrassing discovery that the world's most-wanted terrorist had been residing peacefully in the same neighborhood as Pakistan's military elite highlighted but did nothing to resolve the intractable complexities of an increasingly dysfunctional US-Pakistani "partnership."

The conundrum of Pakistan lies at the heart of *Directorate S*. Coll and his assistants conducted dozens of interviews and pored through mountains of available documents, including those released by Wikileaks. That there are still gaps in Coll's coverage is a measure of the complexity of the situation in South Asia, where the United States, Pakistan, India, Iran, and China are all pursuing varying interests. It also reflects the enigmatic role of the Pakistanis in the post–September 11 War on Terror. Coll is unable to penetrate a Pakistani military and intelligence establishment that is opaque to the best and the brightest in the United States government. But as a first draft of history, Coll has made a splendid contribution to our understanding of the war in Afghanistan.

Directorate S makes for fascinating but depressing reading. American troops first entered Afghanistan in the fall of 2001; they remain there today. What was originally meant to be a brief punitive strike has turned into the United States' longest war. Coll's chronicle of this conflict is a scathing indictment of US policy in Afghanistan. He sees the Afghan quagmire as a humbling reminder of the limits of American power. Coll reveals that he shares the Beltway media's disdain for George W. Bush and Republicans. Yet his narrative makes clear that Obama and his team did no better in resolving the political and military dilemmas facing the United States in Afghanistan. Equally disturbing, Coll demonstrates that neither president was well served by the professionals of the US military and intelligence services, which he argues, pursued their own tightly focused missions at the expense of a more coherent strategy in Afghanistan as the emphasis of the war shifted from hunting al-Qaeda terrorists to battling a Taliban insurgency. The State Department and National Security Council also proved incapable of articulating and executing an effective policy for resolving the Afghan conflict. As a result, all too often, different branches of the United States government were waging their own uncoordinated wars in Afghanistan.

It is easy to criticize American actions in Afghanistan. It is harder to offer plausible alternatives to American intervention and ongoing involvement in that war-torn land. In the wake of the September 11 attacks, it was imperative to bring to justice those responsible for the murders of nearly three thousand Americans. The al-Qaeda perpetrators of the attack were headquartered in Afghanistan, where al-Qaeda leader Osama bin Laden and his associates were honored guests of the Taliban, an Islamic fundamentalist movement that had ruled most of nation since late 1996. The Taliban rebuffed American demands to arrest the al-Qaeda leaders in their midst. Only Pakistan, which had long supported the Taliban, stood by their Afghan protégés diplomatically and urged the United States government to negotiate with the Kabul regime. Fed up with what it perceived to be obstruction and bad faith on the part of the Taliban, the Bush administration and the United Kingdom launched air attacks on October 7, 2001. The ensuing campaign was in some ways a military triumph. With a minimal number of boots on the ground, the United States and local allies such as the Northern Alliance overthrew the Taliban regime in a matter of weeks. Unfortunately, the United States failed to muster enough troops to trap Osama bin Laden and other key al-Qaeda leaders in the mountain stronghold of Tora Bora. Bin Laden and a significant number of al-Qaeda fighters escaped to Pakistan. There, in conjunction with refugee Taliban forces, they became a destabilizing force in both Afghanistan and Pakistan for years to come.

The light American footprint in Afghanistan was deliberate. The Bush administration was interested in hunting terrorists and spared little thought for nation-building in the country it had conquered. The United States sponsored the establishment of a new government, headed by Hamid Karzai. Well-intentioned at the top but wracked by corruption on the local level, the Afghan government proved unable to generate much support in large stretches of the country. A resurgent Taliban appealed to the Islamic fundamentalism of many Afghans, portraying the government as a pack of renegades in cahoots with the "crusaders." As the Taliban began to make inroads into the Afghan countryside, the United States gradually increased its military commitment to Karzai's regime. American force and firepower failed to bring battlefield victory because the Taliban could always retreat across the border to sanctuary in Pakistan. Increasingly frustrated, Karzai demanded that the United States address the Pakistani toleration of Taliban refugees within their border, but the Americans kept resisting his pleas.

Ostensibly, Pakistan was an ally. Pakistani president Pervez Musharraf had reluctantly enlisted his country in the War on Terror. The Pakistanis rounded up al-Qaeda operatives in their larger cities and turned them over to the United States. Yet other al-Qaeda figures as well as the Taliban operated with impunity in the Pakistani provinces bordering Afghanistan. The government's ambivalent attitude toward wanted terrorists reflected profound divisions within the Pakistani state.

Since independence in 1947, Pakistan had alternated between periods of civilian rule and military dictatorship. Musharraf himself had taken power in a coup in 1999. Pakistan was a powerful, heavily armed nation, yet its political and social structure was fractious and fragile. From its inception, Pakistan had identified itself as an Islamic state, and over time many political and military leaders increasingly adopted a fundamentalist approach to Islam. Obsessed by its historic rivalry with India, the Pakistani military supported Islamist terrorists who operated in the disputed province of Kashmir. The terrorists who in 2008 carried out a murderous rampage in Mumbai, India, that left 164 people dead, were based and trained in Pakistan.

Steve Coll is the Henry R. Luce Professor of Journalism and dean of the Graduate School of Journalism at Columbia University and a staff writer at the New Yorker. *He won the 1990 Pulitzer Prize for explanatory journalism while working at the* Washington Post. *He has authored eight books, including the Pulitzer Prize–winning* Ghost Wars *(2004) and* Private Empire: ExxonMobil and American Power *(2012).*

During the Russian occupation of Afghanistan and the subsequent Afghan civil wars, the ISI, the Pakistani military intelligence service, had supported the Taliban. The ISI's Directorate S continued to support its old clients after the US intervention in Afghanistan. The Pakistanis doubted that the United States would stay in Afghanistan long, and they saw the Taliban as their best instrument for dominating Afghanistan and warding off potential Indian influence. The dangerous penchant of the Pakistani military for fostering Islamist radicalism would come to haunt them in the wake of the American war. Islamist extremists turned on the Pakistani government, launching terrorist attacks across the country. The military found itself drawn into a bloody and indecisive war against radicalized tribesmen in the northern province of Waziristan. These Pakistani troubles raise profound but intractable questions that Coll ultimately cannot answer. Was the Pakistani government duplicitous from the start of the War on Terror, secretly supporting the Taliban and elements of al-Qaeda? Or was Pakistan an anarchic state, with different parts of the military elite pursuing different policies, making it possible for General Ashfaq Kayani, the head of the Pakistani Army to claim in 2011 that he genuinely had no idea that Osama bin Laden was living next door to his military academy? Whatever the truth may be, a mixture of Pakistani intrigue, obfuscation, or incompetence crippled the American war effort in Afghanistan.

The United States put up with this uncertainty because the federal government was committed to engagement with Pakistan. Even as Pakistan was sheltering the Taliban, it was also crucial to maintaining the supply routes that sustained US forces in Afghanistan. The Bush administration believed that cultivating Pakistan was imperative because it is a nuclear power. Similar calculations motivated the Obama administration. Vice President Joe Biden once told an unhappy President Karzai that Pakistan was fifty times more important than Afghanistan. President Obama increased troop levels but simultaneously announced a withdrawal date, putting the Taliban on notice that all they had to do was wait out the US offensive. An effort was made to begin negotiations with the Taliban, but that ended in diplomatic humiliation.

As he came into office, President Donald Trump reiterated the American determination to win in Afghanistan. The war will continue with no immediate end in sight. Coll's *Directorate S* serves as a useful primer for anyone bewildered by the long history of the Afghan War. He also makes a compelling case that this conflict will not be resolved until the Pakistani riddle is solved and addressed.

Daniel P. Murphy

Review Sources

Bacevich, Andrew J. "The War That Will Not End." Review of *Directorate S: The C.I.A. and America's Secret Wars in Afghanistan and Pakistan*, by Steve Coll. *The New York Times Book Review*, 31 Jan. 2018, www.nytimes.com/2018/01/31/books/review/steve-coll-directorate-s.html. Accessed 26 Nov. 2018.

"Digging a Hole in the Ocean: A Gripping Account of America's Longest War." Review of *Directorate S: The C.I.A. and America's Secret Wars in Afghanistan and Pakistan*, by Steve Coll. *The Economist*, 8 Feb. 2018, www.economist.com/books-and-arts/2018/02/08/a-gripping-account-of-americas-longest-war. Accessed 26 Nov. 2018.

Greenberg, Karen J. "Shadow Warriors." Review of *Directorate S: The C.I.A. and America's Secret Wars in Afghanistan and Pakistan*, by Steve Coll. *The American Scholar*, Spring 2018, pp. 114–16. *Literary Reference Center Plus*, search.ebscohost.com/login.aspx?direct=true&db=lkh&AN=128250199&site=lrc-plus. Accessed 26 Nov. 2018.

Luttwak, Edward N. "War of Error: The Incompetence of American Intelligence Services in Afghanistan." Review of *Directorate S: The C.I.A. and America's Secret Wars in Afghanistan and Pakistan*, by Steve Coll. *The Times Literary Supplement*, 26 June 2018, www.the-tls.co.uk/articles/public/directorate-s-steve-coll-luttwak. Accessed 26 Nov. 2018.

Mazzetti, Mark. "The Pakistan Trap." Review of *Directorate S: The C.I.A. and America's Secret Wars in Afghanistan and Pakistan*, by Steve Coll. *The Atlantic*, Mar. 2018, pp. 38–40. *Literary Reference Center Plus*, search.ebscohost.com/login.aspx?direct=true&db=lkh&AN=127722885&site=lrc-plus. Accessed 26 Nov. 2018.

Powers, Thomas. "The War without End." Review of *Directorate S: The C.I.A. and America's Secret Wars in Afghanistan and Pakistan*, by Steve Coll. *The New York Review of Books*, 19 April 2018, www.nybooks.com/articles/2018/04/19/cia-war-without-end. Accessed 26 Nov. 2018.

Dopesick
Dealers, Doctors, and the Drug Company That Addicted America

Author: Beth Macy
Publisher: Little, Brown (New York). Illustrated. 384 pp.
Type of work: Current affairs
Time: Largely present day
Locale: United States

Dopesick *is a top-down exploration of the American opioid crisis. It is longtime journalist Beth Macy's third book.*

Principal personages

RONNIE JONES, a heroin dealer who recognized the market opportunity for heroin that the abuse of prescription painkillers created

TESS HENRY, a young mother whose fight against addiction comes to a tragic end

DR. ART VAN ZEE, a physician in Virginia's Lee County trying to help addicts; he recognized the addictive power of OxyContin early on and called for the drug to be removed from the market and reformulated

ED BISCH, the father of a son who died from an overdose; he cofounded the nonprofit Relatives Against Purdue Pharma

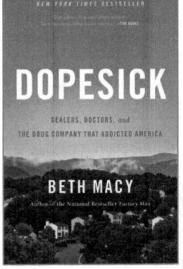

Courtesy of Little, Brown

Beth Macy has a reputation for being the kind of journalist who seeks out the types of people and stories that reflect the more unseen parts of America. Her talent for this became evident in her first book, *Factory Man* (2014), which profiled the furniture maker John Bassett III. A colorful character, Bassett successfully fought off the onslaught of foreign competition and was able to save his small town. The book became a best seller, lauded for the spotlight it shone on the plight of struggling American factories. Macy's second book, *Truevine* (2016), tells the incredible story of two brothers who were kidnapped and forced to perform in circus sideshows because they were albino African Americans. It is an examination of the Jim Crow South and, like all of Macy's books, largely focuses on events that take place in her home state of Virginia.

Macy cut her teeth working as a cub reporter for the *Roanoke Times* and stayed with the paper for over twenty years, subsequently harboring a vested interest in the people living there. While a lesser author's work might feel too specific and regional, Macy manages to find the bigger, universal picture in her stories. Her third book, *Dopesick: Dealers, Doctors, and the Drug Company That Addicted America* (2018), illustrates this skill especially well. Although it is mainly set in central Appalachia, it reflects a crisis that is affecting the entire country.

An in-depth depiction of the opioid epidemic that has contributed to the more than seventy thousand deaths from drug overdoses in 2017 alone, according to the National Institute on Drug Abuse, *Dopesick* aims to identify the causes of this crisis in the United States. Macy begins by looking at the country's previous experience with heroin addiction. In 1898, the narcotic was released to the public and marketed as a painkiller that could serve as a stronger alternative for morphine. Just two years later, 250,000 citizens had become addicted to such pain-relieving drugs derived from opium. This is not the only time in history that a wave of drug addiction has destroyed the lives of thousands of Americans—after all, the 1980s were famously a time when crack ravaged inner cities. However, Macy looks to the early twentieth century specifically because she wants to draw an important connection to the current crisis as an opioid epidemic that was essentially started legally by pharmaceutical companies.

Much of *Dopesick* is an indictment of the Purdue Pharma company, which pushed doctors in the 1990s to prescribe OxyContin as a painkiller for minor aches and pains. A powerful narcotic, OxyContin proved to be highly addictive and soon consumed the lives of tens of thousands of people from every walk of life. When such prescription opioids became more difficult and expensive to acquire, addicts continued to turn more to heroin. The diversity of those impacted is one of the most important points of the book. It is not just the poor, jobless, and disenfranchised who have become addicts but also middle-class communities of housewives, students, and working professionals. In some capacity, everyone in rural America is being influenced by opioids, including heroin. Macy describes the first time she realized this was such a widespread, all-reaching phenomenon as when she met the mother of Jesse Bolstridge, a former football star who died of an overdose at age nineteen. Bolstridge's mother wanted to know how her once happy, healthy, and responsible son ended up dead on a stranger's bathroom floor. Their meeting ultimately inspired Macy to turn *Dopesick* into a top-down investigative piece of journalism.

There are many qualities that make *Dopesick* a compelling read, but perhaps none stand out as much as Macy's thoroughness. The book provides a complete picture of all the forces and factors behind the opioid epidemic. To accomplish this, Macy adopts an almost Charles Dickensian view by interviewing dozens of members from the diverse swathe of people affected. This includes doctors, police officers, addicts, the family members of addicts, health activists, and even pharmaceutical executives. By presenting the perspectives of everyone involved, Macy imbues readers with an honest and thorough understanding of the issue. While the situation is undeniably grim, such an in-depth understanding is key to developing an effective solution.

A large part of what makes *Dopesick* so resonant is the fact that it is brimming with fascinating figures. Macy treats all of her subjects with humanity—even individuals who might not seem like they deserve it. Such is the case with Ronnie Jones, a heroin dealer who is almost singlehandedly responsible for bringing the drug to the Shenandoah Valley. After getting out of prison, Jones attempted to find work in computer repair but ended up working the line at a chicken factory. Discouraged and looking to make money, Jones soon realized that many of his neighbors were addicted to painkillers but could not afford black market pills. He viewed it as a business opportunity and started importing heroin from New York City by using runners to transport the drugs on Chinatown buses. Although his actions would result in the deaths of hundreds of people in the area, Macy does not paint him as a black-and-white villain. Instead, she shows glimpses of the man behind these crimes, someone who initially tried to turn his life around after getting out of prison.

While Jones is a divisive character, most of the other people depicted in *Dopesick* fall into clearer designations. Macy demonstrates how the pharmaceutical executives knew that their products were highly addictive and still lied about it to doctors, pushing them, including through various incentives, to prescribe opioid pills for moderate pain. The discussion of rural Virginia doctor Art Van Zee's desperate fight against the marketing of OxyContin provides further insight into the severity of the situation. Meanwhile, the dozens of addicts and their families who

Beth Macy spent over twenty years as a journalist for the Roanoke Times. *She was awarded a Nieman Fellowship at Harvard University. She is also the author of* Factory Man *(2014) and* Truevine *(2016).*

are interviewed are presented in a more sympathetic light. Their plight is embodied by Tess Henry, who appears relatively frequently throughout the book. A young mother and addict, Henry struggled back and forth between pills, heroin, and sobriety over the years that Macy followed her. Eventually, she overdosed and died.

Henry is arguably the most important character in *Dopesick* because, as a captivating subject Macy followed over time, she successfully challenges the addict stereotype. As Macy demonstrates, there is a societal stigma attached to addiction that prevents many people from getting help. This stigma suggests that all addicts are degenerate, untrustworthy individuals somehow deserving of the suffering that they are enduring. Henry was an addict; however, she was also a young mother who wanted more than anything to get her life back on track. And yet, this goal proved to be impossible. There were not enough people and resources to help her get through the treacherous phase of "dopesickness," a state of withdrawal in which people become violently ill. By getting to know Henry, readers are provided with a better understanding of just how easily good people can get caught up in opioid addiction as well as how hard it is for them to escape. The takeaway is clearly that the hundreds of thousands of people like Henry need more help, resources, and treatments if the epidemic is ever going to end.

Reception of *Dopesick* has been overwhelmingly positive. For many critics, Macy has become the go-to expert on the opioid epidemic. As written in *Kirkus Reviews*, the book is "an urgent, eye-opening look at a problem that promises to grow much worse in the face of inaction and indifference." It is true that for readers who are interested in developing an understanding of the crisis, there is no better resource than *Dopesick*.

Macy leaves no stone unturned as she seeks out the truth about how the crisis started, how it spread, its far-reaching effects, and potential solutions.

One of the most lauded qualities of *Dopesick* has been the way in which it provides an essential snapshot of the struggle that so many Americans, particularly in vulnerable rural areas, are currently grappling with. In her review for the *Washington Post*, Susan Okie stated, "Although Macy's stories are set in Virginia, they could happen anywhere in the United States. Most compelling are the characters she was able to follow over time." Okie's review touches on another part of what makes *Dopesick* such an important book—however regional the problem may seem, ultimately it is something that is gutting the entire country. Many of the people who die from opioid overdoses every day come from similar backgrounds as the relatable, "compelling" people featured in the book. Macy's investigation suggests that in order for this issue to be taken care of, the United States must start taking it seriously by curbing the power of "Big Pharma" and developing jobs for the rural unemployed.

Beyond the informative nature of *Dopesick*, it is a captivating read thanks to Macy's intrepid writing style. The author's decision to write in the first person and thereby insert herself as a figure in the story makes *Dopesick* even more engaging. Readers will feel as though they are along for the ride, discovering facts and truths at the same time as Macy does. It is an exciting, dynamic choice that makes the exploration of an especially distressing topic more palatable and human.

If there is any negative criticism about the book, it is that, for some, its focus may feel somewhat redundant. The issue of the opioid epidemic became a topic of national discussion several years before the 2018 publication of *Dopesick*. The book is not breaking a new, shocking story but rather reiterating an ongoing one that has frustratingly not improved much. As Jennifer Szalai wrote in her review for the *New York Times*, "Macy captures an Appalachian landscape in a state of emergency and in the grip of disillusionment, but there's little here that's new. Indeed, that's part of her point—not enough has changed." Although some readers may initially feel that the book is old news, it adopts a unique angle and is never boring or too depressing. In fact, it can be quite hopeful and galvanizing, thanks to Macy's decision not to spend time in drug dens, witnessing people shooting up or overdosing. Instead, she focuses much of the book on the people who are fighting back, the addicts, doctors, and activists who are working hard to put an end to this epidemic once and for all. The result is an essential and inspiring piece of journalism.

Emily Turner

Review Sources

Review of *Dopesick: Dealers, Doctors, and the Drug Company That Addicted America*, by Beth Macy. *Kirkus*, 10 May 2018, www.kirkusreviews.com/book-reviews/beth-macy/dopesick/. Accessed 17 Nov. 2018.

Review of *Dopesick: Dealers, Doctors, and the Drug Company That Addicted America*, by Beth Macy. *Publishers Weekly*, 11 June 2018, www.publishersweekly.com/978-0-316-55124-3. Accessed 17 Nov. 2018.

Okie, Susan. "Heartbreaking Stories of Lives Lost and Families Crushed in the Opioid Epidemic." Review of *Dopesick: Dealers, Doctors, and the Drug Company That Addicted America*, by Beth Macy. *The Washington Post*, 28 Sept. 2018, www.washingtonpost.com/outlook/heartbreaking-stories-of-young-lives-lost-and-families-crushed-in-the-opioid-epidemic/2018/09/28/8e6858b8-af36-11e8-9a6a-565d92a3585d_story.html. Accessed 17 Nov. 2018.

Szalai, Jennifer. "*Dopesick* Traces the Opioid Crisis, from Beginning to Blow Up." Review of *Dopesick: Dealers, Doctors, and the Drug Company That Addicted America*, by Beth Macy. *The New York Times*, 25 July 2018, www.nytimes.com/2018/07/25/books/review-dopesick-beth-macy-opioid-crisis.htm. Accessed 17 Nov. 2018.

Educated

Author: Tara Westover (b. 1986)
Publisher: Random House (New York). 352 pp.
Type of work: Memoir
Time: 1986–present
Locales: Idaho; Brigham Young University, Provo, Utah; University of Cambridge, England; Harvard University, Cambridge, Massachusetts

Tara Westover's coming-of-age-story chronicles her struggle to break away from the emotional and physical abuse she suffered at the hands of some members of her survivalist family and redefine herself through the pursuit of higher education.

Courtesy of Random House

Principal personages
TARA WESTOVER, the author
GENE, her father
FAYE, her mother
SHAWN, her abusive older brother
AUDREY, her sister, whom Shawn also abused

Early on in her memoir *Educated*, Tara Westover relates how her father's account of the 1992 Ruby Ridge incident, in which federal law enforcement laid siege to the northern Idaho property of Randy Weaver and his family, was etched into her memory. Weaver, an antigovernment survivalist who lived a spartan life off the grid, failed to show up to a court date on gun charges, and US marshals attempted to arrest him. However, the operation was botched and resulted in the deaths of a marshal and Weaver's fourteen-year-old son; a long standoff ensued in which Weaver's wife was also killed. The incident became a national scandal and drew attention to the survivalist lifestyle. But for other survivalists—such as Westover's family—it was a cautionary tale that only furthered distrust in federal authorities.

Westover's father impressed on his children that they would likely face a government invasion much like the Weavers did. His extreme views shaped the lives of his wife and seven children in ways that scarred them emotionally, psychologically, and sometimes physically. Yet *Educated* shows how a wholly different outcome is possible thanks to the power of learning. This disturbing yet triumphant memoir presents a harrowing story of growing up in a toxic environment of domination, abuse, and ignorance—and finally escaping to chart a new course in the wider world. The book is a window into the decidedly non-mainstream survivalist way of life, as well as a personal story of success through hard work, dedication, and the benefits of an open mind.

Westover writes in a relatively standard memoir format, generally progressing from her early life to the present. Along the way she establishes the background that led her family to the survivalist lifestyle. Her parents, Gene and Faye (both pseudonyms, as Westover uses for all those family members with whom she eventually became estranged), held nonconformist ideas born from an extreme interpretation of their Mormon religion and from resentment of what they viewed as "socialist" influences in mainstream American society. Her mother came from a middle-class family who lived in the valley near Buck's Peak in Idaho's Rocky Mountains. Her father came from a farm family with a history of violence. According to Westover, Faye rebelled from her own family by marrying Gene, and the couple began a hardscrabble life on his family's property at the foot of Buck's Peak. They had seven children, of which Westover was the youngest.

Gene, the unquestioned patriarch of his family, owned a small construction company and a junkyard. He drove the family's survivalism, believing the apocalypse was imminent and that the Illuminati, a supposed secret cadre of powerful elites, were conspiring to take over the world. News such as the Ruby Ridge incident only fueled his religious fundamentalism and paranoia. He stocked an underground bunker with guns and food, and instructed his children to prepare to resist federal authorities.

Gene also insisted that Faye become a midwife. At first she was timid about practicing her new profession. Yet as she grew more skilled, she was much in demand. Home births were popular in their rural community, and few bothered about legalities such as birth certificates. In fact, Westover and several of her siblings went years without such a document. Later in Faye's career, she branched out into homeopathic medicine, finding success with homemade herbal remedies and essential oils. Her formulations were guided by "muscle testing" and other pseudoscientific techniques.

Because Gene was suspicious of public education, Westover and her siblings were ostensibly homeschooled. However, any efforts at standard education ended at learning to read. Instead the girls' education consisted of assisting their mother at home births and helping her produce healing tinctures. The boys entered the construction and junkyard businesses with their father. If the boys could not assist Gene for any reason, then Westover and her sister, Audrey, were expected to step in.

Junkyard work was hazardous and dirty. Westover describes several serious accidents, some of which could have been fatal. For example, as her father and brother Luke were preparing cars for the crusher, Luke unintentionally soaked his jeans with gasoline. Later, when he was using a cutting torch, a spark hit his pants and flames engulfed his leg. In another instance, Gene was attempting to cut a tank from a vehicle but neglected to remove the fuel. A spark from the torch he was using ignited the gasoline and severely burned his face, torso, and fingers. Westover describes his injuries in such explicit detail that one can almost smell his charred flesh, which Faye nursed back to health.

Westover is not excused from the backbreaking work because of her sex. On one occasion she expresses her fears of getting injured to her father, which he dismisses

Tara Westover graduated from Brigham Young University in 2008 and was granted a scholarship to Trinity College, Cambridge, where she earned a master's degree. In 2014 she was awarded a PhD in history from the University of Cambridge. Her memoir, Educated, *is her first book.*

by saying that God and his angels will watch over her. Soon afterward, she topples off a loader with an iron spike impaled in her leg. For most of these injuries, no one in the family seeks medical help, as they distrust doctors and lack medical insurance.

The dangers of the junkyard are challenging enough, but the physical, verbal, and psychological abuse Westover endures at the hands of her older brother Shawn is far more damaging. When she was a child, he tolerated and sometimes protected her, and she viewed him as her hero. Yet around the time she enters puberty, his behavior toward her changes. When she engages in normal teenage behavior like wearing lip gloss, he calls her a "slut" and worse. One night, as their mother watches silently, he physically attacks Westover. Another time, he drags her to the bathroom and holds her head under water in the toilet. This shocking abuse continues for a decade. It is disturbing reading, made even more so by the fact that other family members ignore Shawn's behavior.

One distinctive characteristic of Westover's writing is that it sometimes serves as a commentary on the reliability of our memories. By definition, writing a memoir is a subjective exercise where material is filtered through emotional and temporal lenses that in turn color memory. Westover acknowledges that other family members may recall things differently than she does. This is evident in the way Westover and her brothers remember details of Luke's junkyard accident, for example. As she reflects on the incident she questions whether she has gotten the story right, admitting to being unsure of certain parts in the chain of events. Many of her uncertainties involve the role played by her father, whom she cannot interview due to their estrangement. When Westover asks her brothers Richard and Luke to share their recollections with her, their memories of the details vary from hers and from one another's. Could the unique relationship each has with their father cause them to recall events differently? These questions are not necessarily solved, but raising them adds to the honesty and complexity of the narrative.

The vagaries of memory again come into play when Westover attempts to expose Shawn's abuse to her parents. When she and Audrey are adults, Audrey confesses to Westover that Shawn had physically abused her as well. The sisters agree to tell their parents, but Audrey backs out. Westover confronts them on her own, which opens a Pandora's box of recriminations, denials, and deadly threats from Shawn. Their parents steadfastly deny that Shawn could have done the things Westover accuses him of—in spite of the fact that Faye had witnessed his cruelty firsthand. Their denial becomes the basis for their embrace of a less sinister, more acceptable memory of Shawn's behavior.

Although Westover's memories are deeply entangled with her family's during the first section of the book, her recollections gradually become her own as she struggles to follow in her brother Tyler's footsteps and attend Brigham Young University (BYU) in Provo, Utah. College seems like an unattainable dream for a young woman who lacks a high school diploma and has little knowledge of the world. She studies the few books she has access to—mainly the Bible and texts on Mormon religion and history—but still faces an uphill battle to prepare for higher education. Eventually, however, she teaches herself algebra and trigonometry so she can pass the math portion of the ACT college entrance test. Her drive to learn is an "obscenity" to her father, but she learns that it is possible to defy him. She discovers in herself what she later identifies as a crucial skill: "the patience to read the things I could not yet understand."

Accepted to BYU, Westover arrives on campus and discovers overwhelming intellectual and social barriers. Although her roommates at the generally conservative school are Mormons, by her family's standards their way of dressing is highly immodest. For their part, her roommates are hard pressed to understand a young woman who, at least at first, sees no reason to wash her hands after using the toilet. Westover also finds herself at a loss in the classroom. For example, she has to raise a hand to ask what the Holocaust was, to the disbelief of her professor and fellow students. However, the great rush of new information also sheds a light on parts of her home life. When she studies the civil rights movement, she understands for the first time a racial slur Shawn had used to demean her. In a psychology class, a professor's description of the symptoms of bipolar disorder makes her wonder about her father's mental health.

Westover's adjustment to college life is difficult, and she often finds herself in a perpetual tug-of-war between her new life and her family's extreme values. Her developing sense of independence and self-worth is often derailed when she goes home for summers and is confronted by Gene and Shawn for what they perceive as her "uppity" attitude. But with each successful step in academia—her graduation from BYU with honors, a Gates Scholarship that leads to a master's degree in philosophy at the University of Cambridge, a fellowship at Harvard University, and her return to Cambridge to earn a doctorate—she puts some distance between her oppressive upbringing and her new reality.

Westover's success comes at a cost, however. She and her two brothers who also earn college degrees grow increasingly different from their parents and siblings who remain uneducated. The divide between the two groups is starkly illustrated when Westover returns to Idaho for her grandmother's funeral. For Westover, the confrontation over Shawn's abusiveness leads to full estrangement from several of her family members.

The real-life family conflict behind *Educated* led to some controversy upon its publication. Indeed, Westover's parents reportedly hired an attorney to rebut her portrait of them in the book, though no direct legal action was immediately taken. Nevertheless, *Educated* was met with impressive critical attention for a debut work and garnered much acclaim. Reviewers praised both the revealing, gripping nature of the underlying story and Westover's compelling writing style. The book was long-listed for the Carnegie Medal for Excellence in Nonfiction and selected on recommended reading lists by many outlets. It also met with commercial success, reaching number one on the New York Times Best Seller list.

Pegge Bochynski

Review Sources

Review of *Educated*, by Tara Westover. *Kirkus Reviews*, 12 Nov. 2017, www.kirkus-reviews.com/book-reviews/tara-westover/educated. Accessed 3 Oct. 2018.

Review of *Educated*, by Tara Westover. *Publishers Weekly*, Feb. 2018, www.publishersweekly.com/978-0-399-59050-4. Accessed 3 Oct. 2018.

Hong, Terry. Review of *Educated*, by Tara Westover. *Library Journal*, 15 June 2018, p. 47. *Literary Reference Center*, search.ebscohost.com/login.aspx?direct=true&db=lfh&AN=129963457&site=eds-live. Accessed 3 Oct. 2018.

Hulbert, Ann. "Educated Is a Brutal, One-of-a-Kind Memoir." Review of *Educated*, by Tara Westover. *The Atlantic*, Mar. 2018, www.theatlantic.com/magazine/archive/2018/03/tara-westover-educated-a-memoir/550919. Accessed 3 Oct. 2018.

Schwartz, Alexandra. Review of *Educated*, by Tara Westover. *The New Yorker*, 18 June 2018, www.newyorker.com/recommends/read/educated-by-tara-westover. Accessed 3 Oct. 2018.

The Emissary

Author: Yoko Tawada (b. 1960)
First published: *Kentoshi*, 2014, in Japan
Translated: from the Japanese by Margaret Mitsutani
Publisher: New Directions (New York). 128 pp.
Type of work: Novel
Time: Unspecified time in the future
Locale: Tokyo, Japan

The Emissary

Yoko Tawada

Courtesy of New Directions

Celebrated Japanese novelist Yoko Tawada creates an atypical vision of a post-apocalyptic future, delivering a short, surprisingly quiet work that mirrors many of the trends and anxieties of the present day.

Principal characters
YOSHIRO, a centenarian living in post-apocalyptic Tokyo
MUMEI, his great-grandson, a kindly, sickly boy

As awareness of the potential dire effects of climate change has increased in the twenty-first century, along with the continuing threat of nuclear war and the ever-expanding world population on a planet with limited resources, the popularity of novels envisioning an apocalyptic future has grown. The 2010s especially saw an abundance of new novels, often similar in concept, in the post-apocalyptic genre. Many popular visions of the apocalypse involve intensive violence and a war-like or desolate environment. However, some take a tamer approach, envisioning rebuilding and cooperation over fighting. One such approach is seen in celebrated Japanese writer Yoko Tawada's short novel *The Emissary*. Tawada, who writes, in the words of Parul Sehgal for the *New York Times* (17 Apr. 2018), "tender, screwy parables about outsiderism," applies this aesthetic to the world of post-disaster Japan and the results are quite different than most other books about an apocalyptic future. While her other most celebrated books, *The Bridegroom was a Dog* (2012) and *Memoirs of a Polar Bear* (2016), were outwardly ambitious books—the latter followed three generations of a literary polar bear family—*The Emissary* is deliberately dialed back, dedicated to quiet observation and giving only glimpses of larger picture.

While Tawada does not give specific details about the novel's underlying setting, the plot is satisfying. In the wake of an unnamed disaster—reminiscent of the 2011 Fukushima Daiichi nuclear disaster—Japan and other countries have completely isolated themselves from each other, creating country-specific policies and approaches to the situation. Much of the land is poisoned and the majority of animals have disappeared. Tokyo is largely abandoned as the southern parts of Japan are deemed more desirable in the wake of the disaster. Most strikingly, the conditions caused by the disaster have introduced an inversion in the relative constitutions of the young and the old. Children born after the disaster are sickly, have difficulty with everyday tasks like eating, walking, and breathing, and face short lifespans, while the elderly remain in good health that seems to improve the older they get.

The two main characters of the book represent these two poles, with the centenarian Yoshiro doomed to live on while his beloved great-grandson, Mumei, deteriorates. Mumei, like most of his fellow children, accepts his fate and is a most warm-hearted and sensitive boy. Yoshiro, sad at the prospect of outliving his great-grandson, wanders through his days while spending as much time with the boy as possible. The book, while sticking to the third person, shrewdly shifts back and forth between the perspectives of these two characters, highlighting both the innocent way Mumei looks at the world and the melancholy reflections of Yoshiro, who recalls the events of his past life while looking forward to an uncertain future.

In crafting an imagined world of the future, Tawada touches on several disturbing trends of the modern world. Most obviously, her vision encompasses environmental disaster, an extremely relevant consideration in the wake of both Fukushima and general climate change. In her vision of the isolationist policies that every country enacts in the wake of the disaster, she extrapolates from the late-2010s trend, present in many countries, towards extreme nationalism. Although this trend took off in earnest in the years following the book's original publication in Japan, it was already a very prevalent tendency present in the policies created by Japanese prime minister Shinzō Abe. Finally, in portraying the sickliness of the children, and in particular their inability to process many different kinds of food, Tawada mirrors the increasing sensitivities that many people are developing to what they eat and their environments in general.

Another characteristic of *The Emissary* that reflects the contemporary state of the world is the devolution of language. In post-apocalyptic Japan, in keeping with the country's isolationist policy, all foreign words have been banned. For example, on the book's first page, Yoshiro says that the word "jogging" has been all but forgotten as a result of "foreign words falling out of use." Instead, this sort of running is now referred to as "loping down." While older people like Yoshiro remember the old words, they are completely meaningless to the younger generation. This creates some odd situations which reveal both the complexity and the arbitrariness of language. When the younger generation sees the word "made" on a pair of shoes, they interpret the English word as being the Japanese word "made" which means "to" or "until."

Language has always been a particular concern of Tawada's, who writes alternatively in Japanese and German, sometimes in the same book. Furthermore, as Sehgal pointed out, translation is often a principal theme in her novels, whether that involves translating animal-speak to human language or mediating between different world tongues. "When you learn a language," Sehgal quoted Tawada as saying, "you don't just learn words but also how to make them, you learn the mechanism of the language, and you can keep making new words." In *The Emissary*, the work of translation continues, as Yoshiro, who has the vocabulary of the older generation—which is that of the early twenty-first century—has to translate his way of speaking in order to be comprehensible to the younger generation. The world of *The Emissary*, though, is not one in which language is enriched but rather enfeebled. While the younger generation does create new vocabulary, they live in an inevitably diminished linguistic state uninfluenced by other languages.

The Emissary is a quietly imagined telling of a post-apocalyptic world that lacks much in the way of specific events. In so much as a there is a central plot, it is late-developing and treated somewhat obliquely. This plot involves the efforts of a group of citizens, including Mumei's great-grandmother, Marika, and his schoolteacher, to locate the ideal child to serve as an emissary to foreign countries. What the duties of this emissary will be is left vague, but it becomes clear that Mumei is the perfect candidate for the job and that he will inevitably be chosen.

This central narrative does come to prominence at the end of the novel, but the treatment of the conflict remains somewhat

© Nina Subin

Yoko Tawada is the celebrated author of Memoirs of a Polar Bear *(2012),* The Bridegroom was a Dog *(2016), and multiple other novels. She has won numerous awards including the Akutagawa Prize and the National Book Award. She writes in both Japanese and German.*

secondary, and a final section that jumps forward several years into the future may be seen by some readers as unsatisfying. Nonetheless, what the book is most focused on, and what makes it so appealing, is its exploration of the relationship between the two central characters. It is a surprisingly warm-hearted area of focus for a book that takes place in such bleak circumstances, with the winningly good-natured characters both showing a genuine respect and concern for each other, even beyond their obvious familial bonds. Yoshiro inevitably gives in to a certain amount of bitterness and disillusion, having seen the world he knew for most of his life completely disintegrate, but he fruitfully turns his focus to looking after Mumei. "Unable to foresee what sort of fate awaited Mumei in the future," Tawada writes, "Yoshiro kept his eyes open, taking each day as it came, hoping the present wouldn't crumble under his feet." Given the state of the world and Mumei's poor health, this is about all he can do.

Mumei also serves the important role of making strange the world that Tawada presents. Whereas Yoshiro's perspective represents that of someone who grew up in a world that resembles the realistic 2010s, Mumei only knows the post-apocalyptic landscape. Therefore, those sections that stick close to Yoshiro's perspective allows the reader to align their perspective with someone highly identifiable; Yoshiro serves as an accessible guide to exploring the new world. Mumei's perspective, on the other hand, is one that is perpetually strange and illuminating. "Mumei never forgot for an instant that food was dangerous," Tawada explains, drawing attention to the fact that something often taken for granted, the consumption of food, has been completely changed for the younger inhabitants of the future because of the effects of the disaster.

Mumei's perspective is also highlighted through his unique way of using language, allowing Tawada to once again translate between different modes of seeing, thinking, and writing. For example, Mumei declares, "lemon is so sour it makes you see blue." Tawada uses the device of synesthesia, translating one sense (taste) into another (sight), to illustrate how the younger generation differs from the older generation. In addition to this unexpected translation, Mumei also subverts normal color associations which would lead the reader to think of lemon in terms of yellow. By aligning the reader with this strange perspective, then, in which one sense bleeds into another and the color palette becomes completely upset, it becomes clear that the changes that have occurred to the world creates an unbridgeable gulf between those born before and after the apocalypse, a gulf that comes down to the very act of existing consciously in the universe. That Yoshiro and Mumei cannot bridge this gulf makes *The Emissary* a perpetually sad undertaking; that they keep trying, no matter what, makes it a hopeful and moving work of literature.

The Emissary received mainly positive reviews, with critics citing Tawada's use of language as particularly engaging. Sehgal noted the powerful effect of the carefully constructed prose: "Tawada seems content to evoke mood. . . . Her language has never been so arresting." A review of the novel for *Kirkus Reviews* (15 Feb. 2018) agreed, calling it "An ebullient meditation on language and time that feels strikingly significant in the present moment." In addition, many critics highlighted the complex and emotional relationship between Yoshiro and Mumei as one of the best aspects of the novel. Reviewers were not without criticism however, with some believing that parts of the book lacked substance. Sehgal, for example, felt that despite the beauty of Tawada's writing, *The Emissary* showed "a flickering brilliance that never kindles into more."

Andrew Schenker

Review Sources

Review of *The Emissary*, by Yoko Tawada. *Kirkus Reviews*, 15 Feb. 2018, p. 183.
    Literary Reference Center Plus, search.ebscohost.com/login.aspx?direct=true&db
    =lkh&AN=127960985&site=lrc-plus. Accessed 28 Jan. 2019.
Review of *The Emissary*, by Yoko Tawada. *Publishers Weekly*, 29 Jan. 2018, pp.
    164–66. *Literary Reference Center Plus*, search.ebscohost.com/login.aspx?direct
    =true&db=lkh&AN=127654711&site=lrc-plus. Accessed 28 Jan. 2019.
Hungate, Andrew. "Yoko Tawada's Dystopian Novel 'The Emissary' Delivers a
    Bitingly Sharp Satire of Present-Day Japan." Review of *The Emissary*, by Yoko
    Tawada. *Words Without Borders*, Feb. 2018, www.wordswithoutborders.org/book-
    review/yoko-tawada-dystopian-novel-the-emissary-is-a-bitingly-smart-satire-
    japan. Accessed 28 Jan. 2019.
Keeley, Matthew. "Atomic Aftermath: Yoko Tawada's Mysterious New Novel, *The
    Emissary*." Review of *The Emissary*, by Yoko Tawada. *Tor.com*, 29 June 2018,
    www.tor.com/2018/06/29/book-reviews-yoko-tawada-the-emissary/. Accessed 28

Jan. 2019.

Sehgal, Parul. "After Disaster, Japan Seals Itself Off From the World in 'The Emissary.'" Review of *The Emissary*, by Yoko Tawada. *The New York Times*, 17 Apr. 2018, www.nytimes.com/2018/04/17/books/review-emissary-yoko-tawada.html. Accessed 28 Jan. 2019.

Empire of Sand

Author: Tasha Suri
Publisher: Orbit (New York). 496 pp.
Type of work: Novel
Time: Unknown
Locale: Ambhan Empire

Tasha Suri's debut novel, Empire of Sand, *is the first of a projected series called the Books of Ambha. It introduces the magical Ambhan Empire, based on Mughal India.*

Principal characters
MEHR, *a young woman of the Amrithi, a shunned magic-using clan; the daughter of the governor of Irinah*
AMUN, *her husband, a bound Amrithi*
LALITA, *her surrogate mother, an Amrithi courtesan*
MAHA, *her nemesis, a powerful mystic who manipulates the dreams of the gods*
ARWA, *her younger sister*
MARYAM, *her stepmother*

Tasha Suri's debut, *Empire of Sand*, is a fantasy novel set in the fictional Ambhan Empire, inspired by Indian history. In the book, a young woman named Mehr discovers the power inherent in her blood. She is a noblewoman, the daughter of a governor, but her mother was Amrithi. The Amrithi are the undesirables of the Ambhan Empire. Elements of their culture are shunned, so Mehr must practice her rites—ritualistic dances honoring the gods—in secret. Mehr's life, at the outset of the novel, is complicated. She resides in her father's palace but lives as an outsider. Her stepmother, Maryam, goes out of her way to separate Mehr from her younger sister Arwa. Maryam believes that doing so will somehow expunge Arwa of her Amrithi nature. Mehr's only friend is an older woman, a courtesan, named Lalita. Lalita is Amrithi, though she pretends she is not, and acts as a surrogate mother to Mehr, teaching her the rites. Mehr's real mother left nearly ten years before to return to her nomadic clan. The Amrithi clans, descended from immortal spirits called daiva, roam the vast desert of the empire. Mehr would like to be with her own people, particularly as it becomes clear that the emperor intends to rid the empire of Amrithi for good. Through an accidental act of magic during a dream storm—a sandstorm caused by the disquieting dreams of the sleeping gods—her wish is partially granted, and her life takes an exhilarating but dangerous turn. Suri presents an intricate world, full of palace intrigue and complicated mythology involving the mercurial daiva and the magical nature of vows. The world expands over the course of the novel and, in the end, changes totally, laying the groundwork for the next books in a planned series called the Books of Ambhan. The second book in the series, *Realm of Ash*, is slated for publication in November 2019 and will feature Arwa as its protagonist.

Suri, a librarian who lives in London, was born to Punjabi parents, and the book draws on this cultural heritage. The world of the Ambhan Empire is based heavily on the Mughal Empire in India, which lasted from about the sixteenth to the eighteenth century. The belief system draws from Hinduism, and the Amrithi rites are influenced by Indian classical dance. When Mehr dances the rites, she creates sigils, or magic symbols, through movement. In the world of fantasy novels, a reviewer for *Kirkus* wrote, "there is something undoubtedly refreshing about a form of magic that is expressed in gesture instead of words." *Empire of Sand* also explores colonialism and forced assimilation. The Ambhan Empire subjugates the Amrithi people while simultaneously, as Mehr learns, using Amrithi magic to bolster its power. The Amrithi are, Suri writes, "the kindling wood that [feeds] the fire of the Empire's strength." The Maha, a mystic priest figure, enslaves Amrithi to dance rites compelling the gods to dream favorably of the empire, extending its influence and granting the Maha immortality. Creating imbalance in the empire's favor, however, is against the instinct of the Amrithi because it forces them to drive away the mercurial spirits of their ancestors, the animal-like daiva. (One reviewer compared the daiva to djinn, or genies.)

Early in the book, Mehr's only understanding of "dreamfire," the colorful, swirling dust that accompanies a dream storm, is that it is beautiful. Storms do not happen very often in Irinah, where Mehr lives, but when one does, she accidentally becomes lost in it as she tries to make her way to Lalita's house. To her surprise, she finds she can compel the dreams to her bidding. Little does Mehr know that this is a rare and coveted talent. Inevitably, the Maha finds out about Mehr and sends a company of his followers, mystics, to retrieve her. The mystics tell Mehr's father that they have brought a suitor for Mehr.

The Ambhan world is far from matriarchal—men, including the mysterious emperor and the Maha, hold all of the power—but Suri gives it one important twist: Ambhan women choose their husbands, not the other way around. Though Mehr feels compelled to accept Amun, her enigmatic suitor, her choice is calculated, and throughout the book she uses her power of choice to her advantage. She fights to keep a modicum of power over the Maha with the help of Amun, who is truly and irrevocably bound to him. Cursing his own plight, Amun does what he can to shield his new wife from suffering the same fate. The Maha is the book's villain, though Suri offers a more nuanced view of those who serve him. The mystics are bound to the Maha in a different way from the enslaved Amrithi. Many of them are orphans who owe their survival to the Maha. Their reverence springs from actual gratitude—though the purity of their feelings does nothing to diminish the evil the Maha compels them to commit.

Amun is introduced well into the novel, but his relationship with Mehr constitutes the story's heart. Their partnership, built on respect, compassion, and understanding rather than fear and coercion, provides the basis for a new world order. The slow evolution of their love, and an important plot point tied to the prospect of their sexual union, make *Empire of Sand* a serviceable romance novel as well as a fantasy. The sensuality described is tame, but Suri's descriptions of Mehr's awakening to her love for Amun enriches the book as a whole.

Throughout the novel, Mehr makes choices to protect and support those closest to her. She begs her father to send Arwa away so that she will not be bound or harmed because of her Amrithi heritage. Later in the book, she finds her mother and lives for a time with her mother's clan, but she leaves that safety, risking her life, to return to the Maha to save Amun and the world from the nightmares of the gods. Suri consistently links Mehr's love—for Arwa, Amun, and Lalita—to sacrifice. A sacrifice, though, is willingly given, and Mehr relishes opportunities to make her own choices, even when they put her in danger. At the beginning of the book, Mehr laments the strictures of her life as a noblewoman. She rarely ever leaves the palace—thus her confusion when she tries to walk to Lalita's house in a dream storm—and must obey the demands of her cruel stepmother. Her early life with Amun and the Maha, though, is a true imprisonment. Like Amun, she is starved, beaten, and forced to dance the rites against her will. It is unsurprising, then, that Mehr would protect what little power she has. By emphasizing Mehr's awareness of this, Suri underscores the relationship between choice and true freedom.

Empire of Sand received enthusiastic reviews when it was published in 2018. It received starred reviews from both *Kirkus* and *Publishers Weekly*. A reviewer for the latter wrote, "Alongside the fantasy setting's courtly intrigue and magic, Suri explores deeper questions of power, love, and the human cost of prosperity and order." The reviewer also praised the world-building and Suri's prose style. The reviewer for *Kirkus* listed some of the common fantasy tropes Suri includes in the novel—an evil villain, a cruel stepmother, a protagonist who discovers her latent magical powers only to "struggle against overwhelming odds"— but concluded that Suri's handling of them "breathes new life into these elements; she even takes a tired and often cloying trope— the triumph of the power of love—and makes it seem genuine, painful, and beautiful."

Tasha Suri is a librarian who lives in London. Empire of Sand *(2018) is the first in a series called the Books of Ambhan and her first novel.*

Liz Bourke, who reviewed *Empire of Sand* for the science fiction and fantasy magazine *Tor*, was deeply moved by the novel. She described it as an "astonishingly accomplished debut . . . about compassion: about the risks, and the rewards, of choosing to be kind." Bourke was particularly drawn to the various female relationships in the novel. Mehr loves Arwa and Lalita, but her antagonists, aside from the Maha, are also female (namely, Maryam and the complex but dangerous mystic Kalini). In an interview included at the end of the book, Suri writes that her research of the Mughal Empire inspired her to write about women on the margins of power. Maryam, for instance, has no hard power—her husband, Mehr's father, rules Irinah—but behind the scenes, in the domestic realm of the palace, she is the absolute ruler. Suri presents a similar dynamic at the Maha's palace, where power is uneasily divided between Kalini and her sister, Hema.

Eric Brown, writing for the *Guardian*, praised Suri's rendering of Mehr. "In Mehr she has created a believable, fully rounded heroine, by turns vulnerable and yet full of guile and agency, who will get readers cheering," he wrote. "*Empire of Sand* marks an impressive debut." Swapna Krishna, for the SyFy Channel blog *SyFy Wire*, compared the book to S. A. Chakraborty's *The City of Brass* (2017), a high fantasy novel set in eighteenth-century Cairo. Krishna concluded: "*Empire of Sand* manages to be entertaining from beginning to end; Suri is never too heavy-handed with the issues or the message she's trying to get across. It's a lush, consuming read that you can devour in one sitting."

Molly Hagan

Review Sources

Bourke, Liz. "Power and Compassion: *Empire of Sand* by Tasha Suri." Review of *Empire of Sand*, by Tasha Suri. *Tor*, 13 Nov. 2018, www.tor.com/2018/11/13/ book-reviews-empire-of-sand-by-tasha-suri. Accessed 11 Feb. 2019.

Brown, Eric. "The Best Recent Science Fiction, Fantasy and Horror—Reviews Roundup." Review of *Girls of Paper and Fire*, by Natasha Ngan; *Empire of Sand*, by Tasha Suri; *Sherlock Holmes and the Sussex Sea-Devils*, by James Lovegrove; *The Subjugate*, by Amanda Bridgeman; and *The Dark Vault*, by V. E. Schwab. *The Guardian*, 9 Nov. 2018, www.theguardian.com/books/2018/nov/09/the-best-recent-science-fiction-fantasy-and-horror-reviews-roundup. Accessed 11 Feb. 2019.

Review of *Empire of Sand*, by Tasha Suri. *Kirkus*, 18 Sept. 2018, www.kirkusreviews.com/book-reviews/tasha-suri/empire-of-sand. Accessed 11 Feb. 2019.

Review of *Empire of Sand*, by Tasha Suri. *Publishers Weekly*, 1 Oct. 2018, www.publishersweekly.com/978-0-316-44971-7. Accessed 11 Feb. 2019.

Krishna, Swapna. "*Empire of Sand* by Tasha Suri Is a Rich Fantasy Novel Based on Indian History." Review of *Empire of Sand*, by Tasha Suri. *SyFy Wire*, SyFy, 13 Nov. 2018, www.syfy.com/syfywire/empire-of-sand-by-tasha-suri-is-a-rich-fantasy-novel-based-on-indian-history. Accessed 11 Feb. 2019.

Endure
Mind, Body, and the Curiously Elastic Limits of Human Performance

Author: Alex Hutchinson
Publisher: William Morrow (New York). 320 pp.
Type of work: Science

Endure *explores the science of athletic stamina. It is journalist Alex Hutchinson's third book.*

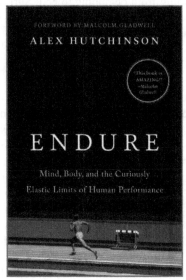

Courtesy of HarperCollins

Principal personages

ELIUD KIPCHOGE, a marathon runner who was hired by Nike to set a new record by running just over twenty-six miles in under two hours

DIANE VAN DEREN, an ultramarathon runner whose brain surgery may, arguably, have improved her ability to endure

TIM NOAKES, a controversial sports scientist who first proposed the "central governor" theory

STÉPHANE MIFSUD, a French diver who set a world record for holding his breath

Alex Hutchinson has long had a fascination with the relationship between the human body and exercise. In interviews, the critically acclaimed contributor to *Outside* magazine (among other publications), who studied physics at the University of Cambridge, has revealed that his interest in the mechanics of the human machine is a personal one—in addition to being a scientist and writer, Hutchinson is also a competitive long-distance runner. He first explored this passion on the page in *Which Comes First, Cardio or Weights?* (2011), a book that provides athletes with tips and techniques to improve their performance. In *Endure: Mind, Body, and the Curiously Elastic Limits of Human Performance* (2018), which is his third book, the author continues his goal to learn more about the forces behind physical excellence.

Unlike its predecessor, *Endure* is not a practical "how-to" guide but rather a work of nonfiction that seamlessly blends exciting sports stories with cutting-edge research. The book's central purpose is to challenge the long-held idea that an individual's capacity for endurance is based exclusively on the size and strength of their heart, lungs, and muscles. Instead, Hutchinson posits, the brain has a much more essential role in determining how far an athlete can go. This is a revolutionary idea—if athletes can control their mind, they can control their performance.

Endure is the result of several years of research. During this time, Hutchinson traveled the world to interview top athletes, adventurers, and scientists. In addition to learning more about how the human body works, he got a front row seat to some incredible sporting events. For example, Hutchinson was able to watch top Olympic marathoner Eliud Kipchoge train for Nike's Breaking2 initiative. As a participant of Breaking2, Kipchoge was assigned the challenge of running just over twenty-six miles in less than two hours. His efforts to set this record provides an overarching narrative framework; Hutchinson introduces Kipchoge's goal in the first few pages and concludes the book with the story of the runner attempting to break the record in Italy in May 2017. Hutchinson dedicates the chapters in between to exploring other relevant topics, such as how athletes' performances are affected by muscles, oxygen, pain, heat, thirst, and food. In turn, he provides readers with a scientific context to better understand Kipchoge's abilities.

Although Hutchinson discusses the accomplishments of athletes and physical extremists from all fields, he focuses primarily on runners. It makes sense—while most other sports involve teammates and myriad skills, running is the simplest, most straightforward use of the human body. To push oneself further in running simply means going faster, harder, or longer. The other reason Hutchinson focuses on running is because he has a long history with the sport. As a student at McGill University in Montreal, Hutchinson qualified for the Canadian Olympic trials. He effectively uses anecdotes from his own competitive running career to illustrate the scientific and physiological phenomena he is trying to explain to readers. For example, when discussing how the mind may factor into endurance, he recalls one of the fastest runs of his life, when a mistake by the lap counter allowed him to relieve himself of expectations as he believed that he was running faster than he actually was.

Hutchinson's first-person perspective and personal anecdotes make *Endure* feel warm and intimate and not like a piece of objective journalism. This approach also provides readers with the exciting sense that they are along with him on an investigative adventure as he tries to crack the code of what makes the human body work. Furthermore, this stylistic choice allows for Hutchinson's passion for athletics to reverberate off the page, especially when he is recalling remarkable endurance stories like the one about a man who survived eight days in the Sonoran Desert without water, or the one about Stéphane Mifsud, a Frenchman who set a world record of holding his breath underwater for eleven minutes and thirty-five seconds. Hutchinson ensures that each one of these stories not only illustrates the important physiological phenomena behind endurance but also contains intriguing details.

A large part of what makes *Endure* such an engaging read is the superhuman characters whom Hutchinson encounters. The book captures some of the most fascinating people in the world of sports. This is especially true of Diane Van Deren, an ultramarathon runner from Colorado who, according to Hutchinson, won the Yukon Arctic Ultra by pulling a forty-five-pound sled over 430 miles of frozen tundra. What makes Van Deren such an interesting and unusual athlete is the fact that her career did not really start until she had a small piece of her brain removed to stop her from having epileptic seizures. She experienced many effects from the seizures and this surgery, including memory loss, poor direction, and a compromised sense of time. However, her stamina also drastically improved. While some doctors have theorized that this is because she no longer feels pain like normal people, Van Deren attributes it to her lack of a sense of time. Unlike other athletes, she does not pace herself or ruminate on how much further she has to go. Instead, she just focuses on the immediate task at hand—moving her body forward.

The interview with Van Deren proves to be the jumping-off point for Hutchinson's exploration into how the mind affects endurance. He discusses this topic with a number of scientists, but none stand out quite as much as the South African sports scientist Tim Noakes. Noakes was the one to first propose the "central governor" theory, which argues that the brain sends signals to the rest of the body to slow down or stop before serious damage is done—but athletes can in fact keep going. All that is required is that they ignore these signals, which is not an easy feat. For example, Mifsud was able to hold his breath for more than eleven minutes because he ignored brain signals like muscle convulsions. Although many scientists disagree with Noakes's central governor theory, readers will find it difficult to dismiss his hypothesis entirely.

© Florence Tsui

Alex Hutchinson began his career as a physicist trained at the University of Cambridge. He eventually began to focus on the science of exercise and endurance, becoming a regular columnist for such publications as Outside *and* Runner's World.

As Hutchison examines all of the physical factors that affect athletic performance, it becomes clear that there is no "winner" in the mind-body debate. Instead, it seems that endurance is the result of a composite of different factors. Still, Hutchinson succeeds in demonstrating that the mind does play a more important role in stamina than most have historically believed. While he is not able to prove the central governor theory, Hutchinson reveals several interesting ways that athletes' performances benefit from mental manipulation. For example, smiling can fuel a runner. In fact, studies have shown that smiling while running can improve performance by about two percent. Similarly, cyclists who were shown images of smiling faces lasted twelve percent longer than those who were shown frowning faces. Inner monologues are another example of the importance of the mind in endurance. Hutchinson found that athletes who challenged negative thoughts of pain and wanting to quit with positive self-talk were able to last longer than those who did not. Ultimately, *Endure* proves that with some careful tweaks to the way they think, people may be able to achieve greater exercise and athletic performances.

Although *Endure* was on the New York Times Best Sellers list, reviews for the book have been somewhat spare, with limited mainstream attention from critics. The press it did receive, however, was predominantly positive. *Kirkus*, in a starred review, called *Endure* "a captivating and often moving book with something to offer readers interested in health, athleticism, neuroscience, and the human condition." It is true that this book is for a specialized audience in many ways, specifically athletic people, in terms of providing inspiration and insight into how their bodies work. Readers who enjoy the work of Malcolm Gladwell will also enjoy *Endure*. Like Gladwell, who wrote the book's foreword, Hutchinson likes to blend science with journalism and storytelling in an effort to better understand how human beings work. While Gladwell once posited that people could master any skill with ten thousand hours of practice, Hutchinson argues that people could improve their athletic performance by learning to control their minds.

Endure is well written and researched, an informative read that is easy to become absorbed in. However, there are qualities that a handful of readers may find to be disappointing. For example, while the book focuses on athletics and exercise, it does not have any step-by-step practical advice for those actively looking for ways to improve their performance. This was noted in the *Publishers Weekly* review, which commented, "Readers seeking simple answers or straightforward workout directives won't find them in Hutchinson's intriguing study, but they will be prompted to think deeply about how human limits can be transcended." However, there are still insights that will inspire athletic readers to try and improve their brain-body connection. Richard Chin wrote for the *Star Tribune*, "'Endure' isn't a how-to training manual for the weekend warrior, but even casual athletes will wonder if they are capable of a faster race if only they could persuade their brains to let them push a little harder."

Endure may not be for everyone, but those who love stories about superhuman athletes and accomplishments will greatly enjoy this book. With the perfect balance of research and storytelling, Hutchinson succeeds in providing readers with the right amount of inspiration to unlock their minds and achieve more with their bodies. Furthermore, the author's scientific background proves to be helpful as he explains complex forces in a way that is easy to understand. With simple language and straightforward examples, most people will finish the book satisfied that they learned a great deal about the science of sports. Ultimately, *Endure* is a highly engaging and worthwhile work of nonfiction.

Emily Turner

Review Sources

Chin, Richard, and Hewitt, Chris. Review of *Endure: Mind, Body, and the Curiously Elastic Limits of Human Performance*, by Alex Hutchinson, and *To Die but Once*, by Jacqueline Winspear. *Star Tribune*, 27 May 2018, www.startribune. com/reviews-endure-by-alex-hutchinson-and-to-die-but-once-by-jacqueline-winspear/483722401/. Accessed 5 Dec. 2018.

Review of *Endure: Mind, Body, and the Curiously Elastic Limits of Human Performance*, by Alex Hutchinson. *Canadian Running*, 14 Feb. 2018, runningmagazine. ca/reviews/review-endure-by-alex-hutchinson. Accessed 5 Dec. 2018.

Review of *Endure: Mind, Body, and the Curiously Elastic Limits of Human Performance*, by Alex Hutchinson. *Kirkus*, 11 Dec. 2017, www.kirkusreviews.com/book-reviews/alex-hutchinson/endure-hutchinson/. Accessed 5 Dec. 2018.

Review of *Endure: Mind, Body, and the Curiously Elastic Limits of Human Performance*, by Alex Hutchinson. *Publishers Weekly*, 9 Apr. 2018, www.publishersweekly.com/978-0-06-249986-8. Accessed 5 Dec. 2018.

Enlightenment Now
The Case for Reason, Science, Humanism, and Progress

Author: Steven Pinker (b. 1954)
Publisher: Viking (New York). Illustrated. 576 pp.
Type of work: History, philosophy

In Enlightenment Now: The Case for Reason, Science, Humanism, and Progress, *Steven Pinker argues that humankind is better off than it was centuries before thanks to the enduring ideals of the Enlightenment.*

For many, the first decades of the twenty-first century were a time of turmoil, as political unrest, war, terrorism, economic instability, climate change, and a multitude of other factors created widespread uncertainty about the future of human society. For linguist and cognitive psychologist Steven Pinker, however, such large-scale concern is unwarranted, as he asserts that human lives are conclusively better in the second decade of the twenty-first century than in previous centuries. Pinker, the Johnstone Family Professor of Psychology at Harvard University, previously argued that violence has decreased worldwide over time in his 2011 book *The Better Angels of Our Nature*, which also delves into the forces behind that global change. He builds upon that argument in 2018's *Enlightenment Now: The Case for Reason, Science, Humanism, and Progress*, in which he suggests that the world has grown better not only in the realms of war and violence but also in terms of health and safety, economic growth, human rights, and overall quality of life. Throughout the book, Pinker credits these improvements to the enduring legacy of the Enlightenment, the eighteenth-century European philosophical movement whose faith in reason and progress Pinker asserts have been essential to the improvement of human lives throughout the subsequent centuries.

Enlightenment Now begins with a preface in which Pinker explains the core mission of his work: to demonstrate that the "bleak assessment of the state of the world" in the twenty-first century presented by individuals on both ends of the political spectrum is incorrect. In addition, Pinker sets forth his ultimate goal of demonstrating the enduring relevance of the Enlightenment ideals of reason, science, humanism, and progress, which he considers to be essential to the improvement of human society. Although he links the bleak assessment he mentions to the era in which his book was published, noting for example that both supporters and opponents of controversial US president Donald Trump expressed such a view during and after the 2016 election campaign, he notes that he began to consider the ideas expressed within the book long before 2016 and that they will remain relevant far into the future. This is an example of a point that Pinker makes repeatedly in the book, that opposition to Enlightenment-inspired forms of progress is a bipartisan phenomenon.

The main text of *Enlightenment Now* begins with "Part I: Enlightenment." This encompasses a trio of chapters that not only define some of the key concepts on which the rest of the text relies but also explore the historical and philosophical context necessary to an understanding of the work. The first chapter, "Dare to Understand!" defines the concept of "enlightenment" in its historical and modern incarnations, as well as the period known as the Enlightenment, which Pinker locates primarily in the mid- and late eighteenth century. He explains the defining ideals of the period and its major thinkers, who focused primarily on the concepts of reason, science, humanism, and progress. Pinker contrasts such ideals with the historical schools of thought in Europe. He notes that the Enlightenment emphasis on science and humanism, for example, represented a significant shift away from the religious superstition and harshness that had characterized previous eras.

After providing the reader with helpful historical context for his work, Pinker goes on to discuss the development of Enlightenment-inspired thought in later centuries. He presents three concepts that became key to later philosophers' understanding of the human condition: entropy, which in Pinker's rendering describes the dissipation of order; evolution; and information. He concludes the first portion of the book with a chapter on what he terms "counter-enlightenments," or forces that contradict or oppose the philosophies elaborated during the Enlightenment. According to Pinker, such forces have included philosophical movements such as Romanticism and nationalism. He also identifies religion, environmentalism, identity politics, and devotion to particular political ideologies as impediments to Enlightenment humanism, noting again that opposition to that philosophy comes from both right-wing and left-wing individuals and groups.

The lengthiest portion of *Enlightenment Now*, "Part II: Progress," deals with a multitude of areas that Pinker identifies as having improved significantly over the more than two centuries since the Enlightenment. He begins by noting that the findings presented in that section conflict directly with the prevailing perception of the world's trajectory among the public and the media. Pinker writes that Americans surveyed consistently claimed that crime was increasing while it was in fact decreasing, among other examples, and the book presents a chart demonstrating that the tone of the news in the *New York Times* trended more negative over the decades between the 1940s and the beginning of the twenty-first century. That chart is the first of many in Part II that provide a striking visual accompaniment to Pinker's assertions that the world is getting better.

Over the next chapters, he presents some of the many areas in which that improvement has manifested, beginning with the area of life itself. In "Life," he notes that humankind's average life expectancy increased significantly beginning in the nineteenth century, in part due to a corresponding dramatic decrease in infant mortality. Although he acknowledges that the average life expectancy in some regions of the world has been affected at times by catastrophic epidemics, including the Spanish

© Rose Lincoln

Steven Pinker is the author of nonfiction works such as The Stuff of Thought *(2007),* The Better Angels of Our Nature *(2011), and* The Sense of Style *(2014). He holds the position of Johnstone Family Professor of Psychology at Harvard University.*

flu pandemic of the early twentieth century and the AIDS crisis that began in the 1980s, such crises represented problems that could be solved through science and reason. Pinker goes on to discuss numerous additional improvements in human well-being that he credits in part to the influence of the Enlightenment, particularly the emphasis on reason-based scientific research that developed out of it. Such improvements include decreases in childhood deaths from infectious diseases, undernourishment, extreme poverty, deforestation, deaths from war and homicide, and nuclear proliferation. He likewise highlights key increases, including increases in available calories, social spending, human rights, literacy, protected natural areas, and leisure time. Based on such data, Pinker argues that life is clearly improving for humankind as a whole, despite individual humans' feelings to the contrary. Pinker's argument may not convince all readers, particularly those who object to minimizing the experiences of individual humans in favor of drawing conclusions about the broader population. However, the data presented in Part II is thought provoking and may raise key questions about the true nature of progress.

Enlightenment Now concludes with "Part III: Reason, Science, and Humanism," which encompasses three chapters in which Pinker seeks to defend such Enlightenment ideals from those who disregard, doubt, or criticize them. He notes that this task is difficult, as many ostensible opponents of Enlightenment ideals do not necessarily disagree with them, yet do not actively promote them either. He notes that his goal is not to persuade the public at large of the importance of concepts such as reason and humanism. Rather, as he writes at the start of Part III, his points are "arguments directed at people who care about arguments." In addition to engaging with the works of other academics and philosophers, Pinker draws upon his earlier strategy of making arguments through the use of data and presents examples of how such ideals have benefited society: in the "Reason" chapter, for instance, he cites several examples of ways in which reason has improved areas of society, including the advent of evidence-based medicine and data-based crime-prevention technology. With such arguments, Pinker hopes to introduce Enlightenment ideals more deeply into twenty-first-century society. The extensive notes and references that follow the conclusion of *Enlightenment Now* further emphasize that point, both supporting Pinker's assertions and providing further avenues of research for readers intrigued by the Enlightenment philosophy of the eighteenth century and its later incarnations.

Upon its publication in 2018, *Enlightenment Now: The Case for Reason, Science, Humanism, and Progress* received mixed reviews from critics. Many praised aspects of Pinker's writing and approach while expressing skepticism about or criticizing others. Much of the critical praise of the work focused on Pinker's engaging and informative prose, with the reviewer for *Kirkus* describing the book as "impeccably written" and noting that it features numerous "interesting tidbits" from a variety of fields. In a review for the *Atlantic*, Alison Gopnik commented on Pinker's eloquence as well as the "compelling" nature of his arguments, which he supports with a large quantity data. Gopnik also praised the ways in which *Enlightenment Now* addresses the potential of science and the Enlightenment ideals that Pinker links to scientific pursuit. However, she went on to critique the book's lack of engagement with human attachments to family and the local community, which often come into conflict with Pinker's more utilitarian arguments.

Indeed, much of the criticism of Pinker's work focused on *Enlightenment Now*'s tendency to focus on the world's population as a whole, at the expense of individuals and of marginalized groups. In a review for the *New York Times*, which also delves briefly into the similarly mixed nature of the critical response to Pinker's earlier *The Better Angels of Our Nature*, Jennifer Szalai noted that some of the "crude utilitarian sentiments" expressed in *Enlightenment Now* make it "a profoundly maddening book." Writing for the *New Statesman*, critic John Gray went so far as to describe the book as "embarrassing" and "a parody of Enlightenment thinking at its crudest," because it does not depict the varieties of Enlightenment thought that conflict with Pinker's conclusions. Gray also argued that Enlightenment concepts like reason and progress do not at all, as Pinker argues, necessarily lead to liberal values, but rather have also played important roles in such excesses as communism and fascism. However, Gray, like other reviewers critical of *Enlightenment Now*, acknowledged that if viewed as a work designed to comfort an audience of readers who already share Pinker's views about the Enlightenment and the state of the world, the book is both "highly topical" and "much needed."

Joy Crelin

Review Sources

Davies, William. "*Enlightenment Now* by Steven Pinker Review—Life Is Getting Better." *The Guardian*, 14 Feb. 2018, www.theguardian.com/books/2018/feb/14/ enlightenment-now-steven-pinker-review. Accessed 30 Sept. 2018.

Review of *Enlightenment Now*, by Steven Pinker. *Kirkus Reviews*, 26 Nov. 2017, www.kirkusreviews.com/book-reviews/steven-pinker/enlightenment-now/. Accessed 30 Sept. 2018.

Gopnik, Alison. "When Truth and Reason Are No Longer Enough." Review of *Enlightenment Now*, by Steven Pinker. *The Atlantic*, Apr. 2018, www.theatlantic. com/magazine/archive/2018/04/steven-pinker-enlightenment-now/554054/. Accessed 30 Sept. 2018.

Gray, John. "Unenlightened Thinking: Steven Pinker's Embarrassing New Book Is a Feeble Sermon for Rattled Liberals." Review of *Enlightenment Now*, by Steven Pinker. *New Statesman*, 22 Feb. 2018, www.newstatesman.com/culture/books/2018/02/unenlightened-thinking-steven-pinker-s-embarrassing-new-book-feeble-sermon. Accessed 30 Sept. 2018.

Szalai, Jennifer. "Steven Pinker Wants You to Know Humanity Is Doing Fine. Just Don't Ask about Individual Humans." Review of *Enlightenment Now*, by Steven Pinker. *The New York Times*, 28 Feb. 2018, www.nytimes.com/2018/02/28/books/review-enlightenment-now-steven-pinker.html. Accessed 30 Sept. 2018.

Winterer, Caroline. "Buck up, Everyone! We Are Riding along the Enlightenment's Long Path of Progress." Review of *Enlightenment Now*, by Steven Pinker. *The Washington Post*, 23 Feb. 2018, www.washingtonpost.com/outlook/buck-up-everyone-we-are-riding-along-the-enlightenments-long-path-of-progress/2018/02/23/5535b602-f24a-11e7-b390-a36dc3fa2842_story.html. Accessed 30 Sept. 2018.

Eternal Life

Author: Dara Horn (b. 1977)
Publisher: W.W. Norton (New York). 256 pp.
Type of work: Novel
Time: First century CE–present day
Locales: New York City, Jerusalem, flashbacks to other places around the world

Eternal Life follows a two-thousand-year-old immortal woman named Rachel on a quest to finally die. Along the way, she strives to settle matters in her latest family in modern-day New York City.

Principal characters
RACHEL AZARIA, an immortal woman who has been alive for two thousand years
YOCHANAN, her first-born son, for whom she sacrificed her mortality; based on the historical figure Yochanan ben Zakkai
ELAZAR, her lover and Yochanan's father, also immortal
ROCKY, her present-day fifty-six-year-old son who lives in her basement
HANNAH, her favorite granddaughter and Rocky's daughter, a DNA researcher

Courtesy of W.W. Norton

In her fifth novel, *Eternal Life*, award-winning author Dara Horn explores the human condition through the character of Rachel Azaria, a two-thousand-year-old woman who cannot die. When the story begins, Rachel is posing as a contemporary grandmother living in New York City. A widow, her children and grandchildren largely dismiss her youthful appearance and offhanded comments about immortality as nothing more than eccentricities. What they do not realize is that she has been burdened with the secret of everlasting life for two millennia.

Despite her supernatural qualities and age, Rachel is a highly relatable and accessible character. In part, this is due to Horn's decision to set a large portion of the novel in the present day. Consequently, the world and culture that surround Rachel feel familiar rather than foreign and readers do not need any context to jump into her world. In turn, the transition into the rest of Rachel's story, which is significantly more complex, is seamless.

In some ways, the premise of *Eternal Life* is quite simple. As a young woman living in ancient Jerusalem under Roman occupation, Rachel fell in love with Elazar, the son of a high priest, despite the fact that their relationship is forbidden. After she is married off to someone else, Rachel's continued affair with Elazar results in a pregnancy. When her son, Yochanan, becomes sick, she believes that it is because he was conceived with a man other than her husband. She goes to a priestess to beg for her son's life, offering her own in exchange. Instead, the priestess saves Yochanan in return for Rachel and Elazar giving up their mortality. While initially it does not seem like a curse, Rachel soon realizes the tragedy of not being able to die. Without death, she learns, life is less precious and therefore less meaningful.

Horn is relatively straightforward in describing how the story's concept of immortality works practically, although she leaves more room for mystery as to how it is actually made possible. After they are cursed, Rachel and Elazar age over time but cannot die. Even if they are burned alive, they will wake up in a new place with a youthful body. And no matter where Rachel ends up in the world, Elazar always finds her. After first becoming immortal, the two lovers try to find a way to continue their affair. However, when Elazar facilitates the death of her husband, Rachel decides that she cannot ever go back to the way it was between them. She instead opts to marry and have children with different men throughout the centuries. Over and over, she falls in love with someone new, starts a family, and then when the time comes, disappears to start a new life elsewhere. Still, she is drawn to Elazar, who continues to love her, because he is the only person in the world who can truly understand her.

Eternal Life is a novel that blends the genre of historical fiction with magical realism. Horn does not have to do any world building, like so many magical realist authors must, because all of Rachel's story line takes place in highly realistic settings—they just happen to be throughout different eras of history. One of the most pleasurable qualities of the book is how well Horn depicts these past times. From first-century Jerusalem to Poland during the Holocaust, she excels at setting the historical scenes with as much elaborate and accurate detail as the present-day sections.

The settings of ancient Jerusalem and the Holocaust hint at another important aspect of the book: Jewish identity. Over her many years, Rachel's identity changes radically in some ways and evolves slowly in others, both through the necessity of living multiple lives and the impact of accumulated experience. The one constant is her identity as a Jewish woman. In this way, *Eternal Life* is a novel that uses its protagonist as a vessel to examine modern Jewishness within the context of its past. Through her two-thousand-year-life, Rachel bears witness to the endless challenges and transformations of her faith.

This theme factors directly into the novel's plot, especially in the historical sections. Born to a scribe, Rachel witnesses the practice of Judaism transition from sacrifices toward the study of sacred texts when she is still a young woman. She is present during the destruction of the Second Temple in 66 CE, a pivotal time in Jewish history. Indeed, the event divides her family; while her husband supports the Zealots in the fight against the Romans, her son sides with the pacifists. It eventually becomes clear that the character of Yochanan is based on the historical figure Yochanan ben Zakkai, a Jewish scholar who had a strong influence on the development of the religion. Ultimately, the character of Rachel symbolizes the rich complexity of Judaism and the capacity of its traditions to endure.

Another of the book's biggest themes is that of motherhood. Over the course of her life, Rachel has hundreds of children and grandchildren. While she likes some more than others, she has great love for all of them. Their presence proves to be both

© Michael B. Priest

Dara Horn was selected as a best young American novelist by Granta *in 2007. Her works have won honors including the National Jewish Book Award and the Harold U. Ribalow Prize, and she has taught Jewish literature and history at several universities.*

a blessing and a curse—they bring meaning into her life, but having to watch them die again and again brings unbearable pain. By having Rachel live forever, Horn captures the never-ending feeling of motherhood. Mothers always worry about their children, no matter how old they grow. This is particularly evident when, by the third act of the novel, Rachel has found a potential way to finally die, thanks to the help of her biologist granddaughter Hannah, but decides to not go through with it until she helps her aimless adult son Rocky get his life together.

Relating to all the other themes throughout the book is the concept of time, something Horn has explored in several of her works. At first glance, it may appear that Rachel has an advantage in having an endless amount of time at her disposal. However, time continues forward at the same pace for her as it does for everyone else, and there is a limited window that she gets to spend with the people she loves along the way.

Along these lines, the concept of change versus stagnation becomes apparent in the characters and the story line. A large part of the tragedy of Rachel stems from the fact that she cannot change—she is stuck in the same body, doomed to repeat the same pattern again and again. Even her feelings for Elazar are static; no matter how much she tries to forget him, her love for him continues. And yet, Rachel wants more. At one point, she and Elazar get married and for a long time she is happy to be with apparently her true love. However, when they discover that they cannot have children together, Rachel leaves him. She wants an element of unpredictability and evolution in her life in whatever way she can get it. Therefore, when she thinks that her granddaughter has found a way for her to die, the prospect of something new and unfamiliar gives her a feeling she has not had in thousands of years: hope.

Critical reception of *Eternal Life* was largely positive, with many reviewers commending its skillful combination of deep, evocative themes with lighter moments. In a review for the *Washington Post*, Ron Charles noted that the book has "moments of broad comedy amid the grief, but it still shimmers with Horn's signature blend of tragedy and spirituality." *Publishers Weekly* called it "funny and compassionate," while *Kirkus* deemed it "a powerful—and occasionally playful—exploration of what it is to be mortal." Indeed, the book successfully blends clever and often humorous social commentary with its central pathos. Whether or not Horn fully succeeds in revealing something insightful about the human condition and life's purpose is perhaps largely subjective, but it is fair to say that most readers will walk away from the novel with something new and interesting to think about.

Critics also generally agreed in praising Horn's talent for writing historical fiction. In his review for the *New York Times*, Joshua Max Feldman particularly lauded the book's "deft and convincing" depiction of ancient Jerusalem. Horn is clearly a passionate student of history and this translates to the page. She is not only highly successful at transporting readers to foreign worlds that existed thousands of years ago, but also at generating story lines that are timelessly compelling. The forbidden love that develops between Rachel and Elazar, for example, feels relevant and exciting despite the fact that it exists amid what could easily feel like a dusty setting.

It should be noted that the novel has its limitations. At times, the way in which *Eternal Life* handles its central premise of immortality feels underwhelming. The *Kirkus* reviewer, for instance, noted that "some readers are likely to feel there's not enough explanation, while others might feel that there's not enough mystery. And there are moments when dialogue, character development, and storytelling are subordinate to the novel's conceit." As the *Kirkus* review itself quickly notes, however, such complaints are common among works of speculative fiction, and here they do not outweigh the work's strengths.

While the way in which Horn explores the idea of immortality may feel too small for some readers, it is still effective in delivering the author's distinct vision. As a whole, *Eternal Life* is a compelling read. Smart, nuanced, and packed with detail, it is a rich story complete with fully fleshed out characters that successfully examines the human condition through a distinctly Jewish perspective. In the context of mainstream contemporary literature, it is both unique and enjoyable.

Emily Turner

Review Sources

Charles, Ron. "Does Living Forever Sound Ideal? These 5 New Books Will Change Your Life." Review of *Eternal Life*, by Dara Horn, et al. *The Washington Post*, 23 Jan. 2018, www.washingtonpost.com/entertainment/books/does-living-forever-sounds-ideal-these-5-new-books-will-change-your-mind/2018/01/23/2adb5460-ff7f-11e7-bb03-722769454f82_story.html?utm_term=.59d37ba4dfd6. Accessed 24 Aug. 2018.

Review of *Eternal Life*, by Dara Horn. *Kirkus*, 15 Oct. 2017, www.kirkusreviews. com/book-reviews/dara-horn/eternal-life/. Accessed 24 Aug. 2018.

Review of *Eternal Life*, by Dara Horn. *Publishers Weekly*, 30 Oct. 2017, www.pub-lishersweekly.com/978-0-393-60853-3. Accessed 24 Aug. 2018.

Feldman, Joshua Max. "The Downside of Immortality." Review of *Eternal Life*, by Dara Horn. *The New York Times*, 9 Mar. 2018, www.nytimes.com/2018/03/09/books/review/eternal-life-dara-horn.html. Accessed 24 Aug. 2018.

Eunice
The Kennedy Who Changed the World

Author: Eileen McNamara (b. 1952)
Publisher: Simon & Schuster (New York).
416 pp.
Type of work: Biography
Time: 1920s through the present day
Locale: United States

Pulitzer Prize–winning journalist Eileen McNamara tells the story of Eunice Kennedy Shriver, a lesser-known but influential figure from one of America's most famous families.

Courtesy of Simon & Schuster

Principal personages
EUNICE KENNEDY SHRIVER, the book's subject, a political lobbyist and founder of the Special Olympics
JOHN FITZGERALD "JACK" KENNEDY, her older brother, the thirty-fifth president of the United States
ROSEMARY KENNEDY, her older sister
JOSEPH KENNEDY, her father
SARGENT SHRIVER, her husband

In *Eunice: The Kennedy Who Changed the World*, Pulitzer Prize–winning journalist Eileen McNamara tells the story—through elucidating details gleaned from the diligent combing of files obtained from organizations she worked with; interviews with friends, family members, and peers; and private papers shared by her children—of Eunice Kennedy Shriver, a generally lesser-known member of one of America's most famous families. Without deifying her subject, McNamara argues that Eunice, the fifth of nine children born to multimillionaire businessman Joseph Kennedy and his wife, Rose, was the most impactful of the Kennedy children, including Jack, who served as the thirty-fifth president of the United States. In McNamara's estimation, Eunice's contributions to the world also trumped those of Bobby, US attorney general and a presidential hopeful, and Ted, who served in the US Senate for nearly fifty years.

Eunice's famous brothers served her causes, though. Spending most of her life working behind the scenes, she pushed her brothers to lobby for and pass laws supporting the needs of children with intellectual disabilities. In the 1960s, with the heft of the charitable Joseph P. Kennedy Jr. Foundation behind her, she shepherded an idea for a citywide athletic event into what would become the international Special Olympics. Her commitment to social justice and disability rights arose from her devotion to the Catholic Church—she had serious intentions of becoming a nun—but also, McNamara successfully argues, a profound grief, and perhaps guilt, over the treatment of her older sister, Rosemary, who was intellectually disabled.

In large part due to the gendered culture in which they were raised, Eunice and her sisters Kathleen "Kick," Pat, and Jean lived their lives largely in service of their brothers' careers; however, Eunice carved out a space for herself to pursue her own philanthropic and public service passions. From an early age, she chartered the course of the Kennedy Foundation, harnessing her family's extraordinary wealth to serve her lofty goals. Her vision for the Special Olympics—which, McNamara writes, was initially at odds with the Games' original founders—is indicative of her boundless ambition. She believed that she could make anything happen, and, mostly, she did. Her talents, and their value in the society in which she lived, can be summed up in a quote from her father, who was reported to have said of Eunice that if she had been born a man, "'she would have been a hell of a politician.'"

The story of the Kennedy family is a genuine American saga. The Kennedys were, and remain, a complex clan, notably stoic in the face of tragedy. The eldest Kennedy, Joe Jr., died as a bomber pilot in World War II. A few years later, after the vivacious Kick had lost her new husband, William Cavendish, Marquess of Hartington, to a sniper in the war, the twenty-eight-year-old died in a plane crash. Two more Kennedy siblings—Jack and Bobby—were assassinated in the 1960s. (One might also include the mysterious car accident, caused by Ted Kennedy, that claimed the life of campaign strategist Mary Jo Kopechne.)

But another, more unusual family tragedy would most shape Eunice's life trajectory, and McNamara fully supplies the familial and social context needed to understand her path. Growing up, she was often paired with her older sister, Rosemary. Rosemary was a pretty, quiet girl described by teachers to her parents as developmentally "delayed." The exact extent of Rosemary's intellectual disability remains unclear—though, for most of her life, she participated in the family alongside her brothers and sisters. In London, where her father served as US ambassador in the lead-up to the war, she "came out" as a debutante alongside Eunice and Kick—though she was always chaperoned, according to McNamara, for the family's sake, due to the stigma around intellectual disabilities and mental illness. Still, after a handful of violent episodes a few years later—McNamara suggests that Rosemary might have been struggling with an undiagnosed mental illness or was merely frustrated with the intensity of her family after some years spent living at a religious school—Joe decided to have Rosemary lobotomized in 1941. The procedure, considered barbaric today, did not go as planned, and Rosemary was left unable to speak or walk.

Joe institutionalized Rosemary but told her siblings that she was working with intellectually disabled children as a teacher in the Midwest. At the time, it was common for intellectually disabled children to be put away as Rosemary was, or even killed. Giving birth to a child with any perceived cognitive disability was considered a great shame. It is unclear when any of the Kennedy siblings were told the truth about their sister, but for the next twenty years, she was entirely excluded from the family's life. Eunice, who revered her father, obeyed his wish to publicly forget Rosemary, but, as McNamara authoritatively chronicles, she ultimately threw herself into work on behalf of intellectually disabled people.

Having spent her childhood playing with Rosemary, Eunice was convinced that children of various abilities could play and learn together. A talented athlete, she was particularly adamant that intellectually disabled children could find fulfillment in playing sports just like any other child. As an adult with her own children, she hosted a camp for children with intellectual disabilities in her own backyard. By then recognizing, as McNamara points out, the power of the federal government to enact change, she also pushed her brother Jack, president of the United States beginning in 1961, to further fund research regarding intellectual disability and brain development with the creation of the National Institute on Child Health and Human Development in 1963. Meanwhile, following her father's stroke and death, she had welcomed her sister back into the family fold. In 1968, her activist efforts were fully realized with the hosting of the first Special Olympics in Chicago, which she had set in motion.

McNamara, a former columnist for the *Boston Globe*, won the 1997 Pulitzer Prize in Commentary. Collected among her winning work is a column recalling a young neighbor who was murdered in the 1970s; the case was never solved. In another column, McNamara tells the story of a widow, suffering from depression after the sudden death of her husband, who had exhausted the number of therapy sessions her insurance would agree to cover. A nod to the for-profit nature of the insurance business, McNamara titled the piece "Crushed under the Bottom Line." She even wrote a column about two intellectually disabled men who had grown up together after they were institutionalized as small children in the 1940s. During the 1980s, McNamara worked as a congressional correspondent and got to know Ted Kennedy, the long-serving Massachusetts senator. "From him I first heard the word most often used to describe his sister: *formidable*," she writes in the book's introduction. McNamara is also the author of a 1994 book titled *Breakdown: Sex, Suicide, and the Harvard Psychiatrist*,

© Roger Pelissier

Eileen McNamara won the Pulitzer Prize in Commentary in 1997. The former journalist for the Boston Globe *was named the best reporter in the city in 1987 by* Boston *magazine. She is also the author of* Breakdown: Sex, Suicide, and the Harvard Psychiatrist *(1994). Additionally, she directs the journalism program at Brandeis University.*

which tells the story of a troubling relationship between a psychiatrist and her patient, who later died by suicide. Along with photographer Eric Roth, she additionally published *The Parting Glass: A Toast to the Traditional Pubs of Ireland* (2006).

In *Publishers Weekly*, an anonymous reviewer wrote of *Eunice*, "While the author clearly admires her subject, this is no hagiography; Shriver can come across as arrogant and entitled, among other flaws. McNamara's book is an exemplary biography: thoroughly researched, beautifully written, and just the right length. It deserves a wide readership." Indeed, the book's primary selling point is McNamara's willingness to interrogate her subject at every turn, from a supposedly charming family anecdote in which Eunice demanded that a stranger surrender her dress to her so that the socialite could present an award to the president, to her views on the feminist movement, which were striking for their lack of self-awareness. Evan Thomas, who reviewed *Eunice* for the *Washington Post*, similarly described it as a "fair-minded, well-reported book" and "a sensitive, nuanced portrait."

In a starred review for *Kirkus*, another reviewer noted the pleasurable asides and myriad anecdotes, stretching from the 1930s to the 2000s, involving "characters from domestic politics, international diplomacy, and high society." For instance, in the late 1940s and early 1950s, Jack and Eunice shared a house in Washington, DC. Among their favorite dinner guests were Senator Joseph McCarthy, a tyrannical politician who accused hundreds of people of being Communist spies for the Soviet government, and future Republican president Richard Nixon. As a teenager in Europe, Eunice crossed paths with film star Marlene Dietrich, writer Somerset Maugham, and the new pope, who had, years earlier, come to tea at the Kennedys' house in New York. "Difficult and driven Eunice Kennedy Shriver certainly was, but she used her prickly personality (and the Kennedy fortune) for the lasting benefit of others," Wendy Smith concluded in her review for the *Boston Globe*. "Famous for her indifference to such social niceties as good grooming and good manners, she would likely have appreciated Eileen McNamara's forthright portrait." While critics and readers may argue over which Kennedy should be deemed the most influential, most will agree that McNamara's well-researched and well-written biography cogently illuminates the significant extent of Eunice Kennedy Shriver's impact on the country in her own right.

Molly Hagan

Review Sources

Review of *Eunice: The Kennedy Who Changed the World*, by Eileen McNamara. *Kirkus*, 10 Jan. 2018, www.kirkusreviews.com/book-reviews/eileen-mcnamara/ eunice. Accessed 27 Oct. 2018.

Review of *Eunice: The Kennedy Who Changed the World*, by Eileen McNamara. *Publishers Weekly*, 19 Feb. 2018, www.publishersweekly.com/978-1-4516-4226-1. Accessed 27 Oct. 2018.

Smith, Wendy. "The Formidable Kennedy Sister." Review of *Eunice: The Kennedy Who Changed the World*, by Eileen McNamara. *The Boston Globe*, 20 Apr. 2018, www.bostonglobe.com/arts/books/2018/04/19/the-formidable-kennedy-sister/ Bpq5PIzCvKsrS6yID09jjM/story.html. Accessed 27 Oct. 2018.

Thomas, Evan. "The Fierce Rebellion and Compassion of Eunice Shriver." Review of *Eunice: The Kennedy Who Changed the World*, by Eileen McNamara. *The Washington Post*, 13 Apr. 2018, www.washingtonpost.com/outlook/the-fierce-rebellion-and-compassion-of-eunice-shriver/2018/04/13/dbbaa1ea-3365-11e8-8abc-22a366b72f2d_story.html. Accessed 27 Oct. 2018.

A False Report
A True Story of Rape in America

Authors: T. Christian Miller and Ken Armstrong
Publisher: Crown (New York). 304 pp.
Type of work: Current affairs
Time: Largely 2008 through the present day
Locales: Washington State, Colorado

Through the case of a serial rapist, A False Report *examines the problematic way that law enforcement handles sexual assault investigations in America. It is written by Pulitzer Prize–winning journalists T. Christian Miller and Ken Armstrong.*

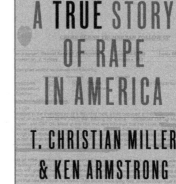

Courtesy of Crown Archetype

Principal personages

MARIE, an eighteen-year-old rape survivor who was charged by the police with falsely reporting a crime
JEFFREY MASON, a Washington State detective who investigated and doubted her claim
JERRY RITTGARN, Mason's partner, another Washington State detective
STACY GALBRAITH, a Colorado detective who investigated a series of sexual assaults in her community
EDNA HENDERSHOT, a Colorado detective in a neighboring town with whom Galbraith teamed up
MARC O'LEARY, a serial rapist who terrorized communities in Washington State and Colorado

In 2015, two journalists by the names of T. Christian Miller and Ken Armstrong realized that they were both working on the same story about a woman who had been criminally charged with falsely reporting a rape. Rather than compete, the two decided to collaborate. Their subsequent article, "An Unbelievable Story of Rape," was published in December of that year by ProPublica in cooperation with the Marshall Project to great critical acclaim. It eventually went on to win a Pulitzer Prize the following year, generating such buzz that the authors decided to expand their article into a full-length book. The result was *A False Report: A True Story of Rape in America* (2018).

A False Report focuses on the same case as "Unbelievable" while simultaneously showcasing how the justice system often fails rape victims. At the center of the book is the story of Marie, a young woman from Lynnwood, Washington, whose entire community turned against her not long after she reported that she had been raped. The book follows Marie's trajectory beat by beat, from when she was sexually assaulted by a masked stranger who broke into her apartment to when she reported the crime to the police and beyond, including the moment when she was declared a liar by authorities and when she acquiesced to police pressure, agreeing that her rape claim was a lie. Marie's journey proves an especially heartbreaking one; prior to the incident, she was a hopeful eighteen-year-old who had recently aged out of the foster care system and was building a new life for herself. In part, it was because she had a troubled childhood that the detectives doubted her claim. Additionally, they felt that she was acting too calm and unfazed to have been raped.

The authors make many conclusions throughout *A False Report*, but perhaps the most resonant is that there is no "right" way for a rape victim to act. This becomes especially clear in the book's secondary story line, which follows two Colorado detectives as they team up to solve a series of connected rape cases. The victims of these crimes were

© Lars Klove

T. Christian Miller is an award-winning journalist who serves as a senior reporter for the news organization ProPublica. *In addition to spending time as a foreign correspondent, he has had his work published in such publications as the* Washington Post *and the* New York Times.

women from a diverse range of ages and backgrounds. However, they had all been assaulted in the same way, with a masked man breaking into their homes, tying them up, violating them for hours, taking photographs, and forcing them to shower to destroy DNA evidence. While they had all experienced the same type of assault, their reactions to these horrendous crimes differed. When talking with the police, some were scared, while others were detached. Importantly, though, the Colorado detectives believed these women and aimed to corroborate their claims no matter how outlandish they may have seemed initially. By maintaining an open, trusting mindset toward the victims, they were able to discover that they were on the hunt for a serial rapist.

A False Report zigzags back and forth between Marie and the Colorado victims for two-thirds of the book before tying the two story lines together. The intention of this format seems to be to compare and contrast the details of Marie's case with those of the Colorado victims. The crime was the same, but the outcomes were vastly different simply because of the detectives' attitudes. Ultimately, the Colorado detectives got enough insight and clues from the victims to identify a man named Marc O'Leary as the rapist. The negligence of the Washington detectives, on the other hand, comes into focus when the Colorado detectives find photos of all of O'Leary's victims on his hard drive. Within this collection is an image of Marie. It is no surprise—from the book's first pages the reader can surmise that the man who assaulted Marie was likely also responsible for the Colorado crimes. However, the true intention of this big "reveal" is to illustrate the fact that the Colorado women might have been spared had the

Steve Ringman

Ken Armstrong is an award-winning journalist who has worked for the Seattle Times *and the* Chicago Tribune, *among other publications. A former staff writer for the* Marshall Project, *he became a senior reporter for* ProPublica *in 2017.*

Washington police simply believed Marie.

Although Miller and Armstrong are journalists, the book does not maintain an objective tone or perspective. In fact, *A False Report* takes a very clear and critical position on the justice system and how it handles rape cases. The primary takeaway is that there is often too much doubt cast on women at a systemic level. To illustrate how this is a national, top-down problem, the authors provide readers with carefully curated research that reaches back into history. At one point, even Thomas Jefferson argued that making a habit of taking women's rape claims seriously and subsequently administering serious punishments to accused rapists could lead to more women making rape accusations as a means of exacting revenge. Miller and Armstrong also affectingly point out that throughout the early twenty-first century, research conducted by entities ranging from news organizations to the White House has discovered up to hundreds of thousands of untested rape kits nationwide. As a result of such attitudes, mixed with improper investigation techniques and processes, a significant percentage of rape cases are dismissed as false in some police districts. The longer the police continue to doubt women, the less likely they are to come forward when they have been attacked. Ultimately, the authors prove that by not being more open minded about rape reports, police may put their communities at risk.

Another effective example of the book's strong perspective is its depiction of the Colorado detectives, Stacy Galbraith and Edna Hendershot. On the page, these two detectives are the undisputed heroes. Their bravery, analytic minds, and tireless police work provide the backbone to the story, and they are rarely, if ever, shown in a critical light. For most people, this somewhat glorifying depiction will not be a problem—after all, these detectives were responsible for identifying O'Leary and ensuring that he spend the rest of his life in prison. At the same time, it is important to note that the authors depict Galbraith and Henderson in this way to emphasize the "right" way to handle rape cases. In turn, they also make the story feel more dramatic and resonant, particularly as the authors fill in details of their backgrounds and thought processes.

For true-crime enthusiasts, *A False Report* will likely be a deeply satisfying read. The authors spend a great deal of attention on the strange patterns and fascinating clues surrounding the crimes. They parse out information about O'Leary slowly over time, building suspense around his identity and motivation. It all snowballs to a dramatic climax when a final piece of information confirms that O'Leary is the serial rapist. Readers will find the scene of O'Leary being confronted by Galbraith and arrested to be especially satisfying. While the subject matter of *A False Report* is grim, the authors notably never fetishize the horror or pain of the victims. Descriptions of O'Leary's crimes are spare in detail and often use clinical language. These efforts to refrain from anything that might be titillating largely succeed. The book is still a page turner simply by focusing on the intelligent police work involved.

Compared to the original article, public reception of *A False Report* has been somewhat mixed. Positive reviews often praise the book's suspenseful storytelling as well as the way it highlights the injustice that many rape victims face. For example, *Kirkus Reviews* called it "a riveting and disturbing true-crime story that reflects the enduring atrocity of rape in America." The "riveting" description can be attributed to the narrative tension that Miller and Armstrong achieve by weaving between Marie's story line and the ones unfolding in Colorado. Additionally, the rich details they provide for each step of the investigation make the book feel as like a police procedural on television. Another quality that makes *A False Report* so engaging is how it explains the inner motivations and logic of excellent detective work in a straightforward way. As described by Emily Bazelon in her review for the *New York Times*, "Miller and Armstrong tell their story plainly, expertly and well. It's gripping and needs no dressing up."

Despite its many positive attributes, *A False Report* is not without flaws. Rosita Boland wrote for the *Irish Times* that "the polemic interrupts the narrative of the women involved in this particular story. The book is trying to be both a true-crime story and a public service piece of reporting: the reporters just couldn't stop being reporters, instead of focusing solely on being writers." While some readers may agree that the book feels too much like a piece of morally instructive journalism at times, others are likely to enjoy this quality. Furthermore, the way in which they present the story is so captivating that the didactic quality never feels heavy handed.

Ultimately, *A False Report* brings much-needed attention to the issue of how rape is handled in America. As several critics pointed out, having been published in 2018, several months into the #MeToo movement, which aims to bring attention to the issue of sexual assault, the book feels especially relevant. Among the biggest aspects of #MeToo has been addressing how women are often not believed when they come forward. *A False Report* is essential reading because it addresses this problem and its cultural underpinnings on a systemic level. Through the humanized story of Marie, Miller and Armstrong demonstrate how perilous it is to dismiss someone just because they do not seem to act like a rape victim or have a story that appears far-fetched.

Emily Turner

Review Sources

Bazelon, Emily. "The Lesson Here Is Listen to the Victim." Review of *A False Report: A True Story of Rape in America*, by T. Christian Miller and Ken Armstrong. *The New York Times*, 6 Mar. 2018, www.nytimes.com/2018/03/06/books/review/a-false-report-t-christian-miller-ken-armstrong.html. Accessed 22 Oct. 2018.

Boland, Rosita. "*A False Report* Review: A Powerful Story about a Serial Rapist That Falls Flat." Review of *A False Report: A True Story of Rape in America*, by T. Christian Miller and Ken Armstrong. *The Irish Times*, 17 Feb. 2018, www.irishtimes.com/culture/books/a-false-report-review-a-powerful-story-about-a-serial-rapist-that-falls-flat-1.3388458. Accessed 22 Oct. 2018.

Review of *A False Report: A True Story of Rape in America*, by T. Christian Miller and Ken Armstrong. *Kirkus*, 22 Nov. 2017, www.kirkusreviews.com/book-reviews/t-christian-miller/a-false-report. Accessed 22 Oct. 2018.

Review of *A False Report: A True Story of Rape in America*, by T. Christian Miller and Ken Armstrong. *Publishers Weekly*, 20 Nov. 2017, www.publishersweekly.com/978-1-5247-5993-3. Accessed 22 Oct. 2018.

Fatal Discord
Erasmus, Luther, and the Fight for the Western Mind

Author: Michael Massing
Publisher: Harper (New York). Illustrated.
 1,008 pp.
Type of work: Biography, religion, history
Time: Fifteenth and sixteenth centuries
Locale: Europe

In Fatal Discord: Erasmus, Luther, and the Fight for the Western Mind, *Michael Massing documents the relationship between European religious reformers Erasmus and Martin Luther, the conflicts between their respective philosophies, and the ways in which those philosophies have influenced the world.*

Courtesy of HarperCollins

Principal personages

DESIDERIUS ERASMUS ROTERODAMUS, a.k.a. Erasmus of Rotterdam, a Dutch Christian
 humanist scholar best known for his 1516 revised and annotated translation of the
 New Testament

MARTIN LUTHER, a German friar whose Ninety-Five Theses, published in 1517, ush-
 ered in the Protestant Reformation

In the second decade of the sixteenth century, two publications altered Christian philosophy in ways that would shape the entire religion for the next several hundred
years. The first was the 1516 publication of a revised edition of the New Testament
of the Bible by Christian humanist scholar Erasmus, which suggested that the Latin
translation long in use was fundamentally flawed in its language and therefore offered
the possibility for flaws in interpretation. The second was friar Martin Luther's 1517
Ninety-Five Theses, a collection of religious arguments initially presented as topics for
debate. Earning Luther the ire of Pope Leo X and sparking a schism among European
Christian thinkers, the publication of the Ninety-Five Theses marked the beginning of
the Protestant Reformation, altering the course of religion, politics, and world history
forever. Luther's Ninety-Five Theses was influenced in part by Erasmus's work, and
the two thinkers engaged with each other in various forms throughout the period.

 In *Fatal Discord: Erasmus, Luther, and the Fight for the Western Mind*, established
journalist Michael Massing documents the intellectual debate between the two philosophers, the conflicts that arose between them and their respective beliefs, and the long-
term effects that their differing approaches had on Christianity. The author of books on
US drug policy and the role played by the US news media prior to the 2003 invasion of
Iraq, Massing diverged significantly from his previous body of work in writing *Fatal*

Discord. He notes that the book arose out of independent research he conducted after traveling to Rome, Italy, in the 1990s. Despite its shift in subject matter and historical scope, *Fatal Discord* benefits significantly from the author's journalistic prowess, reflecting a commitment to presenting the pertinent details of complex events both cohesively and comprehensibly.

Massing begins *Fatal Discord* by introducing Erasmus and Luther and the overarching theses of his work, which include the assertions that Erasmus was a key figure of the Northern Renaissance, that Luther's work was influenced by that of Erasmus, and that the two thinkers' respective humanist and evangelical perspectives helped to shape Western society during the centuries following their deaths. He likewise explains that *Fatal Discord* is unique in its depiction of the relationship and conflicts between the two influential figures, since most biographies of Luther and Erasmus rarely include more than a mention of their rivalry. With his work, Massing sets out to present Erasmus and Luther in relation to each other, delve into the key elements of their philosophies, and demonstrate the modern-day echoes of their intellectual and philosophical conflict.

Following the introduction, *Fatal Discord* is divided into five parts dealing with the lives and careers of the book's key figures. In "Part I: Early Struggles," Massing begins by chronicling the early lives of Erasmus and Luther, providing key biographical details, and demonstrating how the circumstances of their childhoods, entry into the church, and academic study shaped their later worldviews. Born in the Netherlands between 1466 and 1469, Erasmus was the son of unmarried parents, one of whom was a priest. As Massing notes, the illegitimate children of priests faced systemic discrimination under the church, and he writes that the circumstances of Erasmus's birth would be a lifelong cause of distress for the thinker. Despite his social status, Erasmus pursued an education, attending schools in Gouda and Deventer, where he developed a distaste for corporal punishment and an interest in classical Latin literature. Massing then discusses the early life of Martin Luther, who was born in the Holy Roman Empire in 1483. He states that Luther's childhood in a working-class mining region and experiences with a harsh father may have shaped his outlook on authority figures. Luther's schooling in Mansfeld, Magdeburg, and Eisenach introduced him to many of the same classical texts that influenced Erasmus. Luther's experience, however, was significantly shaped by what he called *Anfechtungen*—periods of spiritual and existential despair—which Massing links to Luther's preoccupations with sin and death. Massing also documents Erasmus and Luther's university studies as well as their entry into—and in Erasmus's case, departure from—monasteries, all of which laid the groundwork for their careers to come.

Massing next delves into the duo's separate, yet somewhat complementary, trajectories during the early years of the sixteenth century in "Part II: Discoveries." In 1503, Erasmus published his influential work *Enchiridion Militis Christiani* (*The Handbook of the Christian Soldier*). He then began to consider the most significant project of his career: his revised and annotated edition of the New Testament, which was initially published under the title *Novum Instrumentum*. The project arose out of Erasmus's recognition that the Vulgate New Testament in common use was riddled with errors introduced by scribes and resulting from mistranslations of earlier Greek texts. As Massing emphasizes, revising the Bible based on earlier sources was a particularly risky prospect because changes in wording could result in changes in meaning, thus rendering crucial portions of Christian doctrine invalid. Luther, meanwhile, was ordained as a priest. In 1508, he made his first trip to the town of Wittenberg, to which he relocated permanently in 1511. There, Luther served as a Bible professor and gave lectures on Scripture. He also read the works of Saint Augustine and began to reject humanism. By 1516, following the publication of the *Novum Instrumentum*, Luther and Erasmus began to cross paths philosophically, with Luther referring to Erasmus's work frequently in his lecture notes. The final chapter of part 2 documents the writing of Luther's Ninety-Five Theses, which drew inspiration from Erasmus's annotations on the New Testament as well as Luther's strong opposition to the practice of selling indulgences—documents purchased from the church that supposedly reduced or even eliminated the penalties faced in the afterlife for committing sins on earth. In October 1517, Luther began to distribute his Ninety-Five Theses, publicizing controversial views that soon found numerous adherents in the Holy Roman Empire and elsewhere.

Courtesy of HarperCollins

Michael Massing is a contributor to publications such as the Nation, *the* New York Review of Books, *and the* Columbia Journalism Review. *He is the author of* The Fix *(1998) and* Now They Tell Us: The American Press and Iraq *(2004).*

The remainder of *Fatal Discord* documents the events following the appearance of the Ninety-Five Theses, including Luther's excommunication from the church by Pope Leo X, the church's efforts to suppress growing dissent, Luther's marriage to the former nun Katharina von Bora, and the ideological split between Erasmus and Luther. He highlights how Erasmus and Luther corresponded with each other, both directly and indirectly. Massing also extends his discussion beyond Erasmus and Luther, focusing at times on the rise of additional reformers, such as Huldrych Zwingli and John Calvin, as well as the political significance of the Protestant Reformation in countries like England. The final chapters of "Part V: Rupture" deal in part with Erasmus's death in 1536 and Luther's death a decade later, in 1546. Massing concludes with two epilogues that focus on what he describes as the "afterlife" of Erasmus and Luther's ideas. In addition to mentioning historical events such as the Counter-Reformation and the Council of Trent, Massing links Erasmus's brand of humanism to later efforts such as the formation of the European Union. In contrast, Massing identifies Luther's philosophical perspective as the root of forms of populist evangelical Christianity found in the United States, noting that while some such religious sects could be more directly traced back to the writings of reformers such as Calvin, they could not exist without

Luther and the early stage of the Reformation with which he is closely identified.

With *Fatal Discord*, Massing provides a compelling overview of one of the most influential periods in Western European history. Although his focus is primarily on Erasmus and Luther, he frequently provides information about other historical figures, religious institutions, and locales that are relevant to the narrative. When discussing Erasmus and Luther's early lives, for instance, Massing pauses to consider fourteenth-century poet Francesco Petrarch, who sought to rescue and preserve classical texts that had survived in monastery libraries. Such discussions provide context that locates Erasmus and Luther within their time as well as within their era of literary and biblical scholarship. Massing also makes it clear that without the work of Petrarch and other earlier scholars, many texts would not have survived or been widely disseminated and thus would not have influenced the religious scholars of the Northern Renaissance and Protestant Reformation. Among the most notable elements of *Fatal Discord* is the author's apt demonstration of the ways in which all great thinkers, even those perceived as particularly original, draw from and build upon the work of those who came before. Similarly, the book's epilogues emphasize how sixteenth-century thought continues to influence religious philosophy into the twenty-first century. An entertaining and clearly written work, *Fatal Discord* renders complex religious concepts and a tumultuous era of history easy for general audiences to navigate. It serves as a strong starting place for readers seeking to dig deeper into the works of either, or both, of its key figures. In addition to a useful bibliography and extensive endnotes, *Fatal Discord* includes a selection of illustrations, including contemporary portraits of Erasmus and Luther, drawings and photographs of the environments in which they lived, and images of related figures such as Leo X, Holy Roman Emperor Charles V, and the reformers Philipp Melanchthon and Zwingli. The selected illustrations provide additional historical context for the work and assist in further humanizing Erasmus, Luther, and their contemporaries.

Reviews of *Fatal Discord* were largely positive, with critics praising both its historical and its literary value. An anonymous reviewer for *Kirkus Reviews* described the book as "riveting" and "an impressive, powerful intellectual history," while *New York Times* critic Rebecca Newberger Goldstein characterized Massing's choice to focus on the philosophical relationship between Luther and Erasmus as "inspired." Many reviewers focused on Massing's ability to present a significant amount of information clearly and cohesively. In a review for the *Wall Street Journal*, Jeffrey Collins noted that while the book offers little original research or unique insights on Erasmus or Luther, Massing's strong writing and comprehensive overview render *Fatal Discord* particularly suitable for general audiences. Although reviews of *Fatal Discord* were generally positive, some critics found portions of the narrative to be weaker than others. Collins found Massing's attempt to link the philosophies of Erasmus and Luther to the modern-day European Union and United States to be unconvincing, while *Financial Times* reviewer Ulinka Rublack likewise deemed the arguments made in the book's introduction and epilogues "messy." Nevertheless, most critics, including the reviewer for *Kirkus*, found Massing's argument to be persuasive and a strong contribution to religious and philosophical history.

Joy Crelin

Review Sources

Collins, Jeffrey. "Review: The 'Fatal Discord' of Luther and Erasmus." Review of *Fatal Discord: Erasmus, Luther, and the Fight for the Western Mind*, by Michael Massing. *The Wall Street Journal*, 23 Feb. 2018, www.wsj.com/articles/review-the-fatal-discord-of-luther-and-erasmus-1519419620. Accessed 31 Aug. 2018.

Review of *Fatal Discord: Erasmus, Luther, and the Fight for the Western Mind*, by Michael Massing. *Booklist*, 1 Feb. 2018, www.booklistonline.com/Fatal-Discord-Erasmus-Luther-and-the-Fight-for-the-Western-Mind-Michael-Massing/pid=9244899. Accessed 31 Aug. 2018.

Review of *Fatal Discord: Erasmus, Luther, and the Fight for the Western Mind*, by Michael Massing. *Kirkus Reviews*, 20 Nov. 2017, www.kirkusreviews.com/book-reviews/michael-massing/fatal-discord/. Accessed 31 Aug. 2018.

Review of *Fatal Discord: Erasmus, Luther, and the Fight for the Western Mind*, by Michael Massing. *Publishers Weekly*, 11 Dec. 2017, www.publishersweekly.com/978-0-06-051760-1. Accessed 31 Aug. 2018.

Goldstein, Rebecca Newberger. "Erasmus vs. Luther—a Rift That Defined the Course of Western Civilization." Review of *Fatal Discord: Erasmus, Luther, and the Fight for the Western Mind*, by Michael Massing. *The New York Times*, 29 Mar. 2018, www.nytimes.com/2018/03/29/books/review/fatal-discord-michael-massing.html. Accessed 31 Aug. 2018.

Rublack, Ulinka. "Erasmus and Luther: How a Dispute over Faith Is Still Felt to This Day." Review of *Fatal Discord: Erasmus, Luther, and the Fight for the Western Mind*, by Michael Massing. *Financial Times*, 6 July 2018, www.ft.com/content/e49775f0-7b8f-11e8-af48-190d103e32a4. Accessed 31 Aug. 2018.

The Feather Thief
Beauty, Obsession, and the Natural History Heist of the Century

Author: Kirk Wallace Johnson
Publisher: Viking (New York). Illustrated. 320 pp.
Type of work: Science, natural history
Time: The nineteenth century, 1998–2016
Locales: The United Kingdom, the United States, South America, Southeast Asia, Germany, Norway

In The Feather Thief: Beauty, Obsession, and the Natural History Heist of the Century, *Kirk Wallace Johnson details the 2009 theft of hundreds of priceless specimens from the Natural History Museum in Tring, England, and the complex history underlying the robbery.*

Courtesy of Penguin

Principal personages

EDWIN RIST, a young American flautist and avid flytier studying in England
LONG NGUYEN, his friend, a Norwegian flytier
EDWARD "MUZZY" MUZEROLL, an American flytier who taught him to tie his first salmon fly
LUC COUTURIER, a Canadian flytier who first suggested that he visit the Tring museum
ADELE HOPKIN, the detective sergeant tasked with investigating the theft of valuable specimens from the Tring museum
ALFRED RUSSEL WALLACE, a Welsh-born naturalist who collected many of the specimens found in the Tring museum during his nineteenth-century voyage to Southeast Asia
LIONEL WALTER ROTHSCHILD, a wealthy aristocrat whose private zoological museum in Tring became part of the British Natural History Museum following his death

On June 23, 2009, a burglary occurred in Tring, England, a small town less than an hour from London by train. Unlike in many burglaries, however, the target of the crime was not cash, electronics, or jewelry but dead birds. The former residence of the wealthy banker and zoology aficionado Lionel Walter Rothschild, Tring was home to what in the late nineteenth century had been Rothschild's private zoological museum and since the mid-twentieth century had been part of the British Natural History Museum. In addition to Rothschild's collections and a variety of other specimens, the Natural History Museum at Tring housed the museum organization's collection of preserved bird skins, representing a vast array of species and collected over the course of hundreds of years, some by prominent naturalists such as Charles Darwin and Alfred Russel Wallace. While not on exhibition, the birds in the collection represented a wealth of data for researchers, who used such specimens not only for research concerning birds themselves but also to glean valuable insights into changes in climate and other key areas over time. In June 2009, however, a thief, unknown at the time, broke into the area of the museum where the birds were stored and made off with nearly three hundred of them, including some of the scientifically priceless birds collected by Wallace. In *The Feather Thief: Beauty, Obsession, and the Natural History Heist of the Century*, Kirk Wallace Johnson chronicles the theft and its aftermath as well as the complex ornithological and cultural history that led up to it. In doing so, he not only sheds light on one of the more unusual crimes of the early twenty-first century but also calls attention to the harm humankind has caused to the natural world through its drive to possess rather than to understand.

The Feather Thief begins with a prologue detailing both the events that took place on the night of June 23, 2009, and the author's subsequent introduction to the facts of the case. Johnson recounts that on that night in 2009, a twenty-year-old American named Edwin Rist—a talented flautist and a student at the Royal Academy of Music in London—traveled by train to Tring and made his way on foot to the local Natural History Museum facility. There, he broke a window, entered the building, and made his way to the vault where the museum's collection of preserved birds was stored. He quickly filled a suitcase with colorful male specimens from several species, including the Resplendent Quetzal, several varieties of Cotinga, and the King Birds of Paradise. He then left the museum, having avoided attracting the attention of the facility's security guard. Johnson goes on to explain that he first heard about the theft from a guide while fly-fishing. He had taken up the hobby as a form of escape after years spent working for USAID in Iraq and subsequent running of the nonprofit List Project to Resettle Iraqi Allies, which sought to help Iraqi translators and other professionals who had assisted US efforts in that country flee persecution. As Johnson reports, he was shocked to learn that his peaceful hobby was, in a way, related to the theft of specimens from the museum in Tring, as Rist, a devotee of the hobby of tying elaborate salmon flies, had stolen the bird skins specifically so that their rare feathers could be used to create impressive flies based on "recipes" developed during the Victorian era. The unusual crime and the world of flytiers surrounding it became a new obsession for Johnson, who writes that he felt compelled to solve the mystery of what had happened to the specimens.

Following the prologue, *The Feather Thief* is divided into three parts, each dealing with a portion of the events leading up to or surrounding Rist's 2009 crime. Part 1, "Dead Birds and Rich Men," provides extensive historical context for the theft, delving first into the history of the bird specimens themselves. Johnson chronicles the voyages of Wallace, a contemporary of Darwin and a prominent naturalist in his own right. After an initially successful journey to South America to collect specimens of native birds that ended in a disastrous shipwreck, Wallace set off on a new expedition to the Malay Archipelago, where he collected numerous bird skins, including multiple examples of the impressive King Birds of Paradise. Wallace's specimens would go on to become a key part of the research collection at the museum in Tring, enabling scientific research for decades to come. However, scientific curiosity was not the only force prompting the killing and collection of exotic birds during the nineteenth century, as the subsequent chapters make clear. Johnson credits the fashion industry with causing the mass slaughter of many species as companies collected feathers and even full bird skins for use in apparel such as hats.

Even as public opinion of feathered apparel declined, however, exotic bird feathers continued to be prized by those engaged in the hobby of tying elaborate lures known as salmon ties, which in mid-nineteenth-century Britain began to be considered an art form that required the use of brightly colored feathers, primarily from birds that were not native to the region. Although the hobby became less popular as the Victorian era came to a close, it endured through the twentieth century and gained further popularity late in that period, as a new generation of flytiers formed a thriving community. Their hobby was aided in part by the rise of the internet, which facilitated not only communication between flytiers but also the sale of both feathers dyed to resemble the increasingly rare feathers called for in the Victorian fly recipes and the real thing. While many of the birds whose feathers had been prized by

© Maria Josee Cantin Johnson

Kirk Wallace Johnson is the author of the 2013 work To Be a Friend Is Fatal: The Fight to Save the Iraqis America Left Behind *and the founder of the non-profit List Project to Resettle Iraqi Allies.*

nineteenth-century flytiers could no longer be collected in the wild or shipped internationally due to a variety of environmental regulations and treaties, antique hats and taxidermy were generally considered fair game for flytiers searching for authentic feathers.

Johnson next turns his attention to Edwin Rist, a young American who was introduced to the concept of tying flies as a young child. He soon gravitated to the world of complex and colorful salmon flies, learning to tie his first fly from established flytier Edward "Muzzy" Muzeroll. Rist soon established himself as a prodigy of tying flies, a hobby he maintained alongside extensive studies in flute playing. Although mentors in the flytier community at times gave him small amounts of authentic feathers to use in his craft, he was largely unable to afford many of the feathers he would need to complete the most renowned flies of the Victorian era. As Johnson makes clear in part 2 of *The Feather Thief*, "The Tring Heist," Rist would soon develop a plan to secure a nearly limitless supply of feathers as well as a substantial income that could support his hobby and his aspirations as a flautist. First encouraged to visit the museum in Tring by Canadian flytier Luc Couturier, Rist became obsessed with the idea of accessing the museum's collection of specimens and ultimately carried out the break-in in June 2009. The crime initially went unnoticed, and Rist was able to begin selling off the stolen birds, both whole and in the form of feathers and partial skins that he removed from the specimens.

Following a lengthy investigation led by Detective Sergeant Adele Hopkin, law enforcement managed to track down Rist, who immediately confessed to the crime, and recover a portion of the stolen specimens. However, many of the bird skins remained unaccounted for, and even some of those recovered were missing their collection tags and were thus rendered nearly useless to the scientific community. In the third and final section of the book, "Truth and Consequences," Johnson details his own attempts to track down the missing birds, which led him to reach out to many members of the close-knit community of flytiers, including Rist himself and Norwegian flytier Long Nguyen, whom Johnson suspects may have been an accomplice. *The Feather Thief* takes on a tone similar to that of a mystery novel as Johnson attempts to piece together the fate of the specimens through social media posts, archived forum conversations, and eBay records. Amid his search for the birds, he comes to recognize the extent to which countless bird species and research collections such as that at the Tring museum remain threatened by an array of external forces, including the greed and desire to possess that led to the endangerment or even extinction of many of the world's bird species. In addition to presenting an engrossing narrative and a compelling depiction of a hobbyist community that would likely be unfamiliar to many readers, *The Feather Thief* at heart makes a strong argument in favor of the conservation of the world's threatened avian species as well as the preservation of specimen collections that could prove critical to future research.

Reviews of *The Feather Thief* were largely positive, with many critics praising the book's compelling nonfiction narrative. The anonymous reviewer for *Kirkus* described the book's premise as "captivating" and "storytelling gold," while the *Publishers Weekly* critic called Johnson's work a "page-turner." Critics particularly identified *The Feather Thief* as a strong addition to the true-crime genre, while in a review for NPR, Maureen Corrigan likened the book's subject matter and tone to that of a thriller novel. She went on particularly to praise the author's handling of his dual mission to locate the missing bird skins and to make the public aware of the scientific importance of such specimens and their vulnerability to theft and other threats. Critics likewise appreciated Johnson's depictions of the key individuals involved in the robbery and its aftermath. Writing for the *New York Times*, Joshua Hammer described Johnson's profile of Rist as "fascinating" and also praised the glimpse into the inner workings of the flytier community that the book provided. However, Hammer objected to characteristics of Johnson's prose, which he noted was at times marred by clichés and "self-aggrandizing pronouncements." In addition, multiple reviewers found the ending of the book to be anticlimactic; however, they widely agreed that much of the disappointment sparked by the book's conclusion was due not to flaws in the book itself but to the fact that justice, in the case of the Tring museum robbery, had not truly been served.

Joy Crelin

Review Sources

CORRIGAN, Maureen. "A Weird but True Story Takes Flight in *The Feather Thief.*" Review of *The Feather Thief: Beauty, Obsession, and the Natural History Heist of the Century*, by Kirk Wallace Johnson. *NPR*, 30 Apr. 2018, www.npr. org/2018/04/30/607079309/a-weird-but-true-story-takes-flight-in-the-feather-thief. Accessed 29 Oct. 2018.

REVIEW OF *THE FEATHER THIEF: BEAUTY, Obsession, and the Natural History Heist of the Century*, by Kirk Wallace Johnson. *Kirkus*, 23 Jan. 2018, www.kirkusreviews. com/book-reviews/kirk-wallace-johnson/the-feather-thief/. Accessed 29 Oct. 2018.

REVIEW OF *THE FEATHER THIEF: BEAUTY, Obsession, and the Natural History Heist of the Century*, by Kirk Wallace Johnson. *Publishers Weekly*, 13 Nov. 2017, www. publishersweekly.com/978-1-101-98161-0. Accessed 29 Oct. 2018.

HAMMER, Joshua. "The Man Who Stole Bird Feathers." Review of *The Feather Thief: Beauty, Obsession, and the Natural History Heist of the Century*, by Kirk Wallace Johnson. *The New York Times*, 1 June 2018, www.nytimes. com/2018/06/01/books/review/kirk-wallace-johnson-feather-thief.html. Accessed 29 Oct. 2018.

MILLEN, Robbie. "Review: *The Feather Thief: Beauty, Obsession and the Natural History Heist of the Century* by Kirk Wallace Johnson—a Fowl Tale of Mania." *The Times*, 21 Apr. 2018, www.thetimes.co.uk/article/review-the-feather-thief-beauty-obsession-and-the-natural-history-heist-of-the-century-by-kirk-wallace-johnson-a-fowl-tale-of-mania-gss2m30qw. Accessed 29 Oct. 2018.

NOLAN, Tom. "*The Feather Thief* Review: A Fuss Over Feathers." Review of *The Feather Thief: Beauty, Obsession, and the Natural History Heist of the Century*, by Kirk Wallace Johnson. *The Wall Street Journal*, 20 Apr. 2018, www.wsj.com/ articles/the-feather-thief-review-a-fuss-over-feathers-1524257312. Accessed 29 Oct. 2018.

Feel Free

Author: Zadie Smith (b. 1975)
Publisher: Penguin Press (New York). 464 pp.
Type of work: Essays
Time: Present
Locales: United States, England

Feel Free *is a collection of essays that explores topics ranging from politics to pop culture. It is British writer Zadie Smith's seventh book.*

Zadie Smith feels uneasy about her literary success. She discusses this sense of anxiety in the foreword of her book *Feel Free* (2018), in which she describes an event where one of

Courtesy of Penguin

her friends called her career a "fifteen-year psychodrama." Smith reveals that this statement touched on a fear that she has been grappling with for some time: that she is a fraud who is not actually qualified to write. To many of her fans, this idea might sound ludicrous. The Jamaican British writer made her literary debut to great critical acclaim with her novel *White Teeth* in 2000, when she was only twenty-five years old. Deemed a genius and a prodigy, she went onto to become a best-selling author and an esteemed professor at New York University. And yet, Smith has never felt as though she has deserved any of the awards or accolades. She claims that this is because, unlike her peers, she does not have a master of fine arts degree or a doctorate.

Though she does have an impressive academic background—she earned her undergraduate degree from Cambridge University—whatever Smith may lack in advanced degrees, she makes up for in talent and passion. Indeed, *Feel Free* is a testament to both Smith's voracious appetite for knowledge and her incredible autodidactic mind. The book's collection of thirty-one essays demonstrate the fact that, first and foremost, Smith is a student of life. Exploring myriad, motley topics, *Feel Free* has a tone of curiosity that makes its subjects more interesting. It can be argued that this is one of the qualities that make Smith such an engaging writer—she is genuinely fascinated by and excited to write about topics with which she is unfamiliar. Her enthusiasm radiates off the page in the most contagious way.

The scope of subjects and themes found throughout *Feel Free* is enormous. Smith explores everything from Brexit to the rise of rapper Jay-Z to a billboard near her apartment and how it makes her feel. The essays are organized loosely into five broad sections in an effort to tie the disparate topics into major themes or ideas. For many, the sections will feel somewhat arbitrary, as most pieces are not much more than standalone snapshots of a moment in Smith's life. She has also included editorial pieces that seem as though they were originally written for other projects or publications. As such, *Feel Free* has a kind of meandering quality that would be frustrating if it were written by an author of lesser talent. Fortunately, Smith's ability to transform everyday events and ideas into exceptional pieces of literature is unrivaled.

Take her essay "Some Notes on Attunement," for example. This essay, the eighth installment in *Feel Free*, is ostensibly about how Smith's love for Joni Mitchell developed unexpectedly and seemingly spontaneously one day. The essay begins with Smith describing how, for years, she did not like the folk singer-songwriter—in fact, she spent most of her twenties despising Mitchell's voice, which she likened to piping. And then one day, sometime in her thirties, Mitchell's work began to speak to Smith and regularly bring her to tears. The author spends the rest of the essay exploring the idea of "attunement," or how one can go from not understanding something to having a sublime feeling of connectedness to it. In addition to using biographical storytelling to describe the phenomenon, Smith also looks to philosophy. She uses Søren Kierkegaard's *Fear and Trembling* (1843) as well as the ancient Greek philosopher Seneca's *De Brevitate Vitae* (*On the Shortness of Life*) to try and explain how people's taste changes over time. The essay is a highly academic analysis; however, it feels emotionally authentic and accessible. Ultimately, it is about the universal experience of how someone can be a completely different person than their former selves at different points in life.

Smith's approach to "Some Notes on Attunement" is repeated throughout the rest of *Feel Free*. That is to say, she continues to identify seemingly mundane subjects and then explore what their significance is in the broader context of life. For example, her essay "Generation Why?" ostensibly begins as a review of the 2010 film *The Social Network*. Written by Aaron Sorkin and directed by David Fincher, it recounts the rise of Facebook and the ethically ambiguous actions of its founder Mark Zuckerberg. Smith begins the essay by critiquing certain scenes, the film's dialogue, direction, and action. She marvels at how well Jesse Eisenberg, who plays Zuckerberg, is able to capture the prototypical tech nerd so well. Eventually, however, the essay begins to look at the implications of Facebook on people's lives. Smith argues that, thanks to Facebook, people can no longer be private or a mystery to the world—or themselves. The platform has forever changed human interaction, at a cost.

Feel Free proves that Smith can write about nearly anything and make it interesting. However, some of the book's most compelling essays are profiles on well-known celebrity personalities. This includes "The House That Hova Built," in which Smith interviews rapper Jay-Z. Sitting across from the legendary artist at a SoHo Italian eatery, Smith considers his legacy now that he is in his forties and has become one of the "elder statesmen" of the rap community. She analyzes his style and its evolution from "pyrotechnical" to a slower, more open style. Reflecting on the new wave of hip-hop artists, she concludes that the era he once represented has now passed. It is a fascinating, smart read on the history of hip-hop and one man's role in shaping it. "Brother from Another Mother" is another excellent profile piece that shines a light on the genius of Jordan Peele and Keegan Michael Key. Smith followed the two comedians around on set of their former sketch show *Key and Peele* to learn about who they are as people and performers. The final product is a beautiful, in-depth work of literature about everything from race in America to the nebulous comedic process.

Reviews of *Feel Free* have been overwhelmingly positive. Most critics agree that the essay collection is further proof of Smith's literary genius. In his *Los Angeles Times* review, Walton Muyumba marveled at Smith's "sentence-level precision, the refined elucidation of her insights, the exuberance and humor that sustains readers' attention." These sentiments are not Muyumba's alone. Other critics have extolled the book for its superbly written prose in a similar fashion. A reviewer for *Kirkus Reviews* concluded that *Feel Free* showcases Smith's "formidable intellect" as well as her "imposing command of literary and artistic canons." It is true that most readers will walk away from the book with a newfound appreciation for the author's talent and unique voice.

© Dominique Nabokov

Zadie Smith is a British novelist and essayist, and the award-winning author of White Teeth *(2000). She is a professor of creative writing at New York University.*

What really makes *Feel Free* stand out is the way it explores so many unexpected topics, places, and ideas. Where many essay collections often have a strong uniting theme or purpose, *Feel Free* rejects this approach. Its essays share a similar unpredictable quality, which keeps readers on the edge of their seats. As Amanda Fortini wrote in her review for the *New York Times*, "It is exquisitely pleasurable to observe Smith thinking on the page, not least because we have no idea where she's headed." Without a clear direction, *Feel Free* essentially becomes a journey through Smith's mind. It is both intellectual and deeply personal.

Despite the many enjoyable attributes of *Feel Free*, there are several flaws that can be difficult to overlook. For one, some of the essays feel somewhat stale. While enjoyable, pieces like "Generation Why?" and "Brexit: A Brexit Diary" discuss events and ideas that are no longer as urgent and necessary to discuss as they were when originally published. The points that Smith makes in these essays about social media and the dismantling of Western Europe are sharp, but the world has since moved on and started talking about these issues in new and different ways. Still, it is important to note that the book's essays were written over the eight-year time line of Barack Obama's presidency and as such function as a kind of time capsule. They may no longer be relevant, but they do reveal something about the moment in time they were published. In this way, the collection can be thought of as a kind of cultural companion to Ta-Nehisi Coates's *We Were Eight Years in Power* (2017).

For some, another problematic aspect of *Feel Free* is its size. At times, the book can feel overstuffed and under-curated. In her review for *National Public Radio*, Maureen Corrigan argued that the essay "Meet Justin Bieber" made her feel as though she would have preferred the book to have less content—not more. She wrote that the essay that imagines a meeting between the pop star Justin Bieber and the philosopher Martin Buber "falls into what I think of as the 'empty cereal grain' category of writing: in other words, forgettable filler often used to bulk up collections like this one." It is true that the book might have benefited from some careful pruning. Still, there are so many outstanding pieces within the collection that disregarding anything that comes across as filler seems a worthwhile and easy endeavor.

Feel Free may not be perfect; however, its positive attributes greatly outweigh any flaws. Readers are likely to enjoy it, whether they decide to work their way through all of the collection's pieces or focus on the individual essays that interest them. At the end of the day, Smith is an extraordinary writer whose true gift is providing a fresh perspective onto well-worn topics of conversation. Brimming with sharp insights, humor, and pathos, *Feel Free* is a book that should not be missed.

Emily Turner

Review Sources

Corrigan, Maureen. "Zadie Smith Ruminates on Brexit, Bieber, and Much, Much More in *Feel Free*." Review of *Feel Free*, by Zadie Smith. *NPR*, 20 Feb. 2018, www.npr.org/2018/02/20/585118218/zadie-smith-ruminates-on-brexit-bieber-and-much-much-more-in-feel-free. Accessed 19 Sept. 2018.

Review of *Feel Free*, by Zadie Smith. *Kirkus Reviews*, 15 Dec. 2018, www.kirkusreviews.com/book-reviews/zadie-smith/feel-free/. Accessed 19 Sept. 2018.

Fortini, Amanda. "From Justin Bieber to Martin Buber, Zadie Smith's Essays Showcase Her Exuberance and Range." Review of *Feel Free*, by Zadie Smith. *The New York Times*, 21 Feb. 2018, www.nytimes.com/2018/02/21/books/review/zadie-smith-feel-free.html. Accessed 19 Sept. 2018.

Muyumba, Walton. "Zadie Smith's Brilliance is on Display in *Feel Free*." Review of *Feel Free*, by Zadie Smith. *Los Angeles Times*, 7 Feb. 2018, www.latimes.com/books/jacketcopy/la-ca-jc-zadie-smith-20180207-story.html. Accessed 19 Sept. 2018.

The Female Persuasion

Author: Meg Wolitzer (b. 1959)
Publisher: Riverhead Books (New York).
464 pp.
Type of work: Novel
Time: 1970s–2019
Locales: Massachusetts, Connecticut, New York

Courtesy of Penguin

Written by the best-selling American author Meg Wolitzer, The Female Persuasion *examines the state of contemporary feminism through the experiences of an idealistic young woman and her mentor.*

Principal characters

GREER KADETSKY, a young woman searching for her life's purpose after graduating from college
FAITH FRANK, her mentor, a second-wave feminist icon comparable to Gloria Steinem
CORY PINTO, her high school sweetheart and the son of Portuguese immigrants
ZEE EISENSTAT, her best friend, a young queer woman who wants to help the underprivileged

Meg Wolitzer is an American novelist with a penchant for complex female characters. More often than not, these characters are the kind of women on missions of self-discovery who get caught in the wormy landscape of societal gender expectations. This theme first became evident in Wolitzer's 2008 book *The Ten-Year Nap*, which follows a group of forty-something women who, years earlier, left their high-powered jobs to become mothers. Jobless by the time their children get older and more independent, they must reckon their reality with the feminist dream of "having it all."

Wolitzer explores similar ideas about gender in *The Female Persuasion* (2018), a novel that takes a broader scope to examine the state of American womanhood. In its simplest description, *The Female Persuasion* is about the passing of the torch from one generation of feminists to the next. It begins with the character of Greer Kadetsky, a smart, albeit deeply insecure, first-year college student who is grappling with the aftermath of being sexually assaulted. Greer wants to become the kind of feminist who dismantles the very misogynist culture that enabled the assault, but she lacks the tools and knowledge to do so. It is this desire for justice, however, that leads her to an on-campus lecture by Faith Frank, a second-wave feminist icon generally known as a slightly less famous Gloria Steinem. Greer bumps into Faith in the bathroom after the lecture, and they exchange contact information. It is a small, powerful moment that ultimately transforms Greer's life. Not only does the interaction galvanize the young woman spiritually, but it also provides her with a life-changing professional connection. Once Greer graduates, she reaches out to the famous feminist. The mentor-protégé dynamic that subsequently develops between the two women becomes the beating heart of *The Female Persuasion.*

A large part of what makes Wolitzer's novel so engaging is the author's refrain from idealism. Few works of literature exist about professional women trying to change the world and lift one another up in the process; therefore, it would be tempting for any self-proclaimed feminist novelist to sugarcoat such a narrative to inspire and empower female readers. Yet Wolitzer instead infuses the many story lines that comprise *The Female Persuasion* with a kind of thorny realism. For example, after she graduates, Greer lands what seems like her dream job when she is hired by Faith to work at her new foundation, Loci. According to Faith, Loci will host conferences and fund projects that help women around the world. However, it is eventually revealed that the venture capitalist backing Loci has less-than-ethical motivations, and Faith is in fact willing to bend her morals to achieve her personal goals. Not only does it turn out that Greer's job is not what she had hoped, but her hero is flawed.

Another character who demonstrates Wolitzer's proclivity for realism is Greer's best friend from college, Zee Eisenstat. Zee, like Greer, wants to make a difference in the world. At one point after graduation, she asks Greer to get her a job at Loci, but her friend, uncomfortable with performing such a favor as she is trying to find her place at the organization, lies and says that she had tried with no luck. Zee then moves to Chicago to work as an educator for the underprivileged at an organization called Teach and Reach. Wolitzer depicts Zee's experience there as a dissolution of youthful idealism—the work is challenging, discouraging, and even traumatizing at times. In one especially memorable scene, a student gives birth in Zee's classroom. In the end, Zee fails to make a substantial impact on her students' lives and realizes that her identity as an activist has been a way for her to feel better for herself and is not actually to the benefit of others. She eventually decides the best way to help others directly is to become a trauma counselor. By Wolitzer's careful hand, both characters end up shedding their hopeful, naïve perspectives and learn to see the world for what it is.

There is no real formal structure to *The Female Persuasion*, and yet it never feels chaotic or meandering. Wolitzer expertly shifts between the story lines of Greer, Faith, Zee, and a young man named Cory Pinto. The time line spans between the 1970s, when Faith first has a feminist awakening, to 2019, when Greer is mostly settled into her identity as an adult. Ultimately, Greer is the connective tissue between all four story lines, as she is the only one with a unique relationship to each of the other characters. Cory is her longtime boyfriend and the lone male perspective of *The Female Persuasion*. Raised in a working-class immigrant family, Cory provides readers with a glimpse into a less-privileged world than the other characters. He and Greer were high school sweethearts who bonded over being the "smart kids" of their class and had plans to attend the same Ivy League university together. When Greer's father messes up the financial aid paperwork, however, she is forced to go to a third-tier college in Connecticut while Cory attends Princeton University. This plot development is presented as a fateful twist that sends the two characters on separate, unexpected trajectories.

A large part of what makes Greer and Cory's relationship so interesting is this fact that when the novel begins, they are almost mirror reflections of one another; however, with Wolitzer's carefully crafted plotting, they end up in very different places in life. Though the schism that grows between them is kicked off when they end up at different colleges, what ultimately causes conflict is the disparity among their familial backgrounds. When Cory's younger brother dies in a tragic accident, he is forced to leave his lucrative consulting job in the Philippines to come home and take care of his mother. He takes over his mother's job as a house cleaner and essentially gives up on his dreams in the process. Greer cannot understand his commitment to his family; as Wolitzer depicts her, she may want to make the world a better place but cannot see enough outside herself to empathize with the person she loves the most.

© Nina Subin

Meg Wolitzer is a best-selling American novelist best known for The Ten-Year Nap *(2008),* The Uncoupling *(2011), and* The Interestings *(2013). She teaches creative writing at Stony Brook Southampton.*

The Female Persuasion is an enjoyable and compelling read largely because of the way in which Wolitzer blends the complex, frustrating realities of contemporary feminism with humor. As a writer, she captures both the everyday and the sociopolitical thoughts and aspirations of women in a way that is highly engaging. Wolitzer's prose is at once sharp and warm, accessible and deeply insightful. These qualities are evident in the following passage: "Faith thought that she didn't have to like them all, but she also recognized that they were in it together—'it' being the way it was for them. For women. The way it had been for centuries. The stuck place." The novel is filled with passages just like this that appear conversational in tone but express profound messages. So much of *The Female Persuasion* is about the endless struggle of the feminist movement and how personal and professional obstacles impede women's progress, generation after generation. It is a novel that explores both how far women have come and how far they have yet to go.

Reviews of *The Female Persuasion* have been largely positive, with most critics remarking on its timeliness. Published in April 2018, the novel arrived shortly after the beginning of the #MeToo movement, a time when women across America and the world began to share stories of victimization and demand an end to sexual harassment and assault. Many critics have applauded the way in which Wolitzer captures the paralyzing effects of assault, and also argued that the novel's scope, intent, prose, and general literary prowess are exceptionally executed. Lena Dunham wrote for the *New*

York Times, "The book itself is 456 ambitious pages, tight but inclusive, and deserves to be placed on shelves alongside such ornate modern novels beginning in college as 'A Little Life,' 'The Secret History' and 'The Marriage Plot.'" Back in 2012, in an essay titled "The Second Shelf," Wolitzer argued that novels about relationships written by men were considered to have literary merit whereas novels on the same subject written by women were not. In their reviews, most critics have noted that *The Female Persuasion* has broken through the gendered constraints of the publishing world to earn universally acclaimed status.

Despite this initial wave of positive critical reception, the novel also received a fair amount of backlash. Although *The Female Persuasion* succeeds in depicting many critical issues of modern feminism, many readers considered it myopic in its perspective, specifically in limiting its scope to the middle-class white woman's experience. While *The Female Persuasion* does fails to examine the increasingly intersectional dimensions of contemporary feminism, it remains an important, well-written, captivating work that succeeds in transforming one type of feminist experience into a piece of timeless literature. The anonymous reviewer for *Kirkus Reviews* extolled the novel's "can't-put-it-down plot" and concluded that it is "the perfect feminist blockbuster for our times." This may be its most accurate description—despite its flaws, *The Female Persuasion* is an entertaining powerhouse of a novel that deftly taps into the zeitgeist of the year that it was published.

Emily Turner

Review Sources

Dunham, Lena. "Meg Wolitzer's New Novel Takes on the Politics of Women's Mentorship." Review of *The Female Persuasion*, by Meg Wolitzer. *The New York Times*, 29 Mar. 2018, www.nytimes.com/2018/03/29/books/review/review-female-persuasion-meg-wolitzer-lena-dunham.html. Accessed 24 July 2018.

Review of *The Female Persuasion*, by Meg Wolitzer. *Kirkus Reviews*, 6 Feb. 2018, www.kirkusreviews.com/book-reviews/meg-wolitzer/the-female-persuasion. Accessed 24 July 2018.

Franklin, Ruth. "*The Female Persuasion* Should Be a Literary Breakout. Will It Be?" Review of *The Female Persuasion*, by Meg Wolitzer. *The Atlantic*, May 2018, www.theatlantic.com/magazine/archive/2018/05/the-persuasive-female/556847. Accessed 24 July 2018.

Quinn, Annalisa. "Meg Wolitzer Asks the Big Questions in *The Female Persuasion*." Review of *The Female Persuasion*, by Meg Wolitzer. *NPR Books*, National Public Radio, 3 Apr. 2018, www.npr.org/2018/04/03/598234453/meg-wolitzer-asks-the-big-questions-in-the-female-persuasion. Accessed 24 July 2018.

Schwartz, Alexandra. "Meg Wolitzer Rides the Feminist Waves." Review of *The Female Persuasion*, by Meg Wolitzer. *The New Yorker*, 9 Apr. 2018, www.newyorker.com/magazine/2018/04/09/meg-wolitzer-rides-the-feminist-waves. Accessed 24 July 2018.

Fight No More

Author: Lydia Millet (b. 1968)
Publisher: W. W. Norton (New York). 224 pp.
Type of work: Short fiction
Time: Present day
Locale: Los Angeles

Lydia Millet's darkly comic, insightful, and superbly crafted collection of linked short stories set in Los Angeles, Fight No More, *focuses on characters who are either searching for or fleeing from their homes. Nina, the real estate agent who brokers their transactions, prompts them to contemplate the meaning of home as they struggle with relationships, abuse, and grief, yet rarely give up on the possibility of a brighter future.*

Courtesy of W.W. Norton

Principal characters

NINA, real estate agent employed by many of the other characters
LYNN, teacher and member of a band whom she meets while showing a home
LEXIE, a high school dropout, abused by her stepfather
JEREMY, a.k.a. Jem, Lexie's affluent friend and former client
ALESKA, Jem's grandmother

Lydia Millet's *Fight No More* is a finely crafted and compelling collection of short stories centering on the real estate market in Los Angeles and the ways in which moving, whether forced or voluntary, impacts the characters. Through a series of thirteen linked stories, Millet raises philosophical questions on the meaning of home in the context of "fight or flight" response theory. Millet portrays her characters' attachments to their houses, exploring how they are an anchor for memory and stability. While many characters are forced, due to divorce, aging, or abuse, to leave their homes, their struggle to readjust to a new setting also prompts them to reassess other aspects of their lives and make hard decisions. It is this struggle on which Millet focuses, with some characters fighting to keep their homes and others desperate to flee them in the hope of finding something better. Millet portrays these struggles with depth, complexity, and humor.

Although the book's cover clearly marks it as a collection of short stories, some reviewers, including NPR's Lily Meyer, have referred to the collection as a novel, and the novel label has some merit. There is one character, Nina, the real estate agent, who unifies the stories and helps them cohere. She has a major role in half the stories and a minor role in most of the others. Nina is the catalyst for change, finding homes for those in need or those forced to downsize due to aging and ill health. Thus, Nina could be

©Jade Beall

Lydia Millet is the author of a dozen works of literary fiction, winning the PEN Center USA Award for Fiction for her novel My Happy Life *(2002) and a John Simon Guggenheim Memorial Foundation Fellowship (2012). She has also been a finalist for the Pulitzer Prize and the National Book Critics Circle Award.*

viewed as the lead protagonist. She is a witness to or facilitator for much of the book's action. Despite Nina's presence, however, there is not one clear narrative thread from beginning to end. Nina is a dominant presence in the first half of the book but not the second. The second half of the book focuses more on Lexie, a teenager who left home to escape her stepfather's sexual abuse, and these stories center on Lexie's attempts to remain independent and survive her family's manipulations and efforts to control her. Though many of the stories share characters in addition to Nina, they are linked more through the theme of home and the struggles surrounding it than by any one character or an overriding story arc, making the author's classification of the book a short-story collection more appropriate.

Millet most often explores the theme of home through the lens of the "fight or flight" response, which is also suggested by the book's title. Walter Bradford Cannon (1871–1945), a physiologist at Harvard Medical School, first coined the term "fight or flight" in the early twentieth century. After observing animal behavior, he described how animals responded to stress or a threat to their survival by either fleeing the situation or staying and fighting the threat. Millet's characters make similar decisions, sometimes about the homes they are being forced to leave and sometimes about their complicated relationships. In the first story, "Libertines," for example, told through Nina's point of view, a potential buyer of a house she is showing nearly drowns in the homeowner's pool. After Nina calls for help, she reflects on the situation philosophically:

Fear could turn you into a statue. Some people were statues all their lives. They feared the freedom of others, that others' freedom could end up hurting them. A person might want to be free to do something to you, often. One man's freedom was another man's aggravated assault.

But then, if you stood still like that, you couldn't go anywhere. And was it fair to blame the libertines for moving?

Earlier in the story, Nina reads a brief passage from the Marquis de Sade's *The 120 Days of Sodom* (1904), which she finds in the bathroom of a home she is about to show to a prospective buyer. Sade was a libertine and his novel depicts his characters' debaucheries in graphic detail. After reflection, Nina critiques the inertia that can be an element of the fight or flight syndrome, a moment (or more) of indecision before the impulse toward fight or flight is enacted. Nina suggests that those who stand as statues and are indecisive cannot blame those that do move for their fate, even if those movements are difficult to watch and accept. Like Nina herself, who in later stories takes a chance to connect with both Lynn, a new man in her life, and Marnie, her estranged sister, many of Millet's characters believe that taking some action, even if misguided, is better and offers more hope and potential for success than inertia and indecision.

Another character, Jem, is a teenager who struggles with losing his home due to his parents' divorce and his increasingly difficult relationship with his father, whose desertion made keeping their home impossible. In the second story, "Breakfast at Tiffany's," Jem, also known as Jeremy, has little control over his rage. He is angry about the move to a smaller house and angry at the way his father has treated his mother. While Jem and his mother struggle financially, Jem's father, Paul, continues to live an affluent life with his new, much younger wife and their new baby. Jem chooses to rebel and concocts an elaborate sabotage plan to thwart the sale of his house. He later attempts other "pay back" initiatives against his father, including referring Lexie, whom he met through a pornography chatroom, to become the family's new au pair. Jeremy, who is ultimately a more complex and compassionate character than these examples reveal, fights for himself and his mother. Other characters, such as Delia, flee. In "The Men," Delia, who was suddenly and unexpectedly abandoned by her husband when he ran off with his secretary, deserts her home after men "about the size of dachshunds" appear and take over the running of it, silently planning meals and making repairs. Delia employs Nina to sell her home and refuses to enter it again, especially once these very small men start to grow to normal size and ignore all her preferences for meals and home renovations. Millet strains reality in "The Men" to show Delia's difficulty in coping with the unexpected, yet most of her characters respond to their difficulties by running or fighting. Millet's characters struggle and they make mistakes, and although few of the stories are uplifting in a traditional way, hope, or the possibility of hope, is offered through action.

Millet provides her characters with depth and poignancy through unexpected details and humor. Lexie, for example, who has fled her sexually abusive stepfather, Pete, and taken a job as an au pair in Jem's father's household, is a high school dropout, but she is also working diligently to build a future for herself. She initially started a business in internet pornography to make money so she could leave her abusive household. Although she continues that business when she becomes an au pair, caring for Jem's new sister and his aging grandmother, Aleska, she begins to see a future with more possibilities. Lexie grows to love the baby, Rachel, as well as Aleska and considers staying longer than the six months she had initially intended to work. Lexie is also smarter than she appears, and she proves this on numerous occasions. When Aleska, who was both a Holocaust survivor and a career professor of sociology specializing in World War II propaganda, moved some of her favorite artwork to her new home in the guest house, the pieces upset her family members. One art piece depicted a swastika, and another is a portrait of Stalin. Aleska keeps these works as a reminder of the importance of the past, not to advocate Nazism, and some family members have difficulty understanding the distinction. Most do not know who Stalin was. Lexie, however, when asked, knows exactly who Stalin was, due to her stepfather's incessant chatter about the war at the dinner table. Lexie is an astute listener and retains information, and Aleska understands and admires those qualities and encourages her to go back to school. Through Aleska, Lexie, Jem, and others, Millet creates full, complex characters who should not be underestimated because they never fail to surprise.

Most importantly, Millet offsets death and general despair with dark humor. For example, when Lexie is applying for the au pair position, she tries to make herself more Christian-like so she will be perceived as a good influence on the baby and trustworthy. She knows very little about the Bible, however, and she wants to avoid being a "fake Christian," so she researches quotes from the Psalms and chooses several, such as "Children are a gift from the Lord." Jeremy listens attentively to her practice answers and preparation and then informs her that she should not pronounce the *P* in Psalms, saying it is a "rookie mistake." The notion that an internet porn businesswoman is applying for the au pair position and that she is trying to learn Bible quotes to impress the new parents adds a lighter dimension to the story of a young girl fleeing her sexually abusive stepfather. Lexie wants a new life and she wants to make it work, and she is grateful for Jem's gentle, light-hearted correction. Jem initially attempts to install Lexie in his father's house to spy on him and obtain blackmail material, and while Jem and Lexie each have their own motives for helping each other, their relationship is one of the most thoughtful, humorous, and poignant in the book due to Millet's deft writing.

Together, the stories in *Fight No More* reverberate with struggle and grief, yet Millet's complex exploration of theme; her vivid, surprising characterizations; and her use of dark humor confirm that hope exists in action and the least expected places.

Marybeth Rua-Larsen

Review Sources

Review of *Fight No More*, by Lydia Millet. *Kirkus Reviews*, 20 Mar. 2018, www. kirkusreviews.com/book-reviews/lydia-millet/fight-no-more/. Accessed 21 Sept. 2018.

Lorentzen, Christian. "Lydia Millet Is Not Nearly as Famous as She Should Be. But It's Only a Matter of Time." Review of *Fight No More*, by Lydia Millet. *Vulture*, 14 June 2018, www.vulture.com/2018/06/lydia-millet-is-not-nearly-as-famous-as-she-should-be.html. Accessed 21 Sept. 2018.

Meyer, Lily. "In *Fight No More*, Life Rushes by, but Sometimes There's Beauty." Review of *Fight No More*, by Lydia Millet. *NPR*, 16 June 2018, www.npr. org/2018/06/16/617310305/in-fight-no-more-life-rushes-by-but-sometimes-theres-beauty. Accessed 21 Sept. 2018.

Mirakhor, Leah. "The Fraught Lives of Angelenos and Their Real Estate Are the Focus of Lydia Millet's Superb *Fight No More*." Review of *Fight No More*, by Lydia Millet. *Los Angeles Times*, 8 June 2018, www.latimes.com/books/la-ca-jc-lydia-millet-20180608-story.html. Accessed 21 Sept. 2018.

The Fighters
Americans in Combat in Afghanistan and Iraq

Author: C. J. Chivers (b. 1964)
Publisher: Simon and Schuster (New York).
   400 pp.
Type of work: History, current affairs
Time: 2001–16
Locales: Afghanistan, Iraq

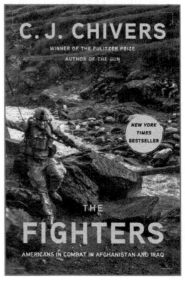

The Fighters offers a view on the ground of the drawn-out US conflicts in Iraq and Afghanistan. Eschewing policy pronouncements from generals and government officials, author C. J. Chivers instead records the experiences of six service members in both countries up close.

Principal personages
LIEUTENANT LAYNE MCDOWELL, Naval
   aviator
SERGEANT FIRST CLASS LEO KRYSZEWSKI, Special Forces soldier
HOSPITAL CORPSMAN DUSTIN E. KIRBY, Navy corpsman serving with the Marines
GAIL KIRBY, Kirby's mother
CHIEF WARRANT OFFICER MICHAEL SLEBODNIK, Army pilot of a Kiowa Warrior scout
   helicopter
SPECIALIST ROBERT SOTO, Army infantryman
LIEUTENANT JARROD NEFF, Marine infantry officer

In *The Fighters*, the Pulitzer Prize–winning journalist C. J. Chivers presents a series of portraits of American service members living on the "sharp end" of the wars in Afghanistan and Iraq. Though Chivers is critical of the US government's direction of these conflicts, he spends little time discussing military and political strategy; instead, he focuses on the experiences of individual troops. The heart of the book is brilliant reportage on soldiers, sailors, and marines before, during, and after combat. This gives Chivers's book a compelling immediacy, and adds to the power of his indictment of the war on terror's military futility.

   C. J. Chivers is eminently qualified to write an account of the soldiers fighting America's wars in Afghanistan and Iraq. He is a respected journalist who has twice won Pulitzer Prizes because of his combination of solid reportorial skills and vivid prose. In addition to this, he is a veteran of the United States military himself, having served as a Marine Corps officer in the 1990–91 Gulf War. As both a serviceman and as a correspondent, Chivers has walked the walk with the men and women engaged in modern combat. Like the service members that he writes about, Chivers found himself caught up in the long war on terror. He was a witness to the al-Qaeda attack on the World Trade Center on September 11, 2001, as a reporter for the *New York Times*. In subsequent years, he was present in the field with military men and women, some of whose stories are chronicled in *The Fighters*. For the book, he took a ride in an F/A-18 Hornet fighter jet flying from the deck of the USS *John C. Stennis* and went out on patrol with soldiers in Afghanistan and Iraq.

This is a personal book in more ways than one. Chivers knows most of the people who appear in its pages. In writing *The Fighters*, he was determined to tell their stories, as much as humanly possible from their perspectives. He is interested in exploring the impact of war on individual human beings rather than adding one more contribution to the long list of journalistic analyses of Washington's conduct of recent military operations in the developing world. This is not to say that Chivers does not have strong opinions on these matters. He makes it quite clear that he believes that the wars in Afghanistan and Iraq have been military and political disasters; as he sees it, these conflicts have failed to produce viable democratic governments in either country, and instead have destabilized South Asia and the Middle East, inadvertently producing new generations of Islamist fighters to replace the many that American forces have killed. Rather than simply denouncing what he perceives to be the follies of the administrations of both George W. Bush and Barack Obama, he wants to tell a more universal tale, an ageless tale, the story of the toll taken on troops by the experience of combat. This keeps his book from becoming a predictable political screed, easily forgotten as events move on and new crises occupy the attention of readers. Wars follow one another in an endless succession, weapons and tactics change and evolve over time, but the existential essentials of war—killing and risking being killed, terror and exultation, suffering and comradeship—remain the same. These are the things that Chivers chooses to describe.

This focus on individual experience makes *The Fighters* both emotionally compelling and intellectually important. It takes its place in a long and honorable tradition of reportorial war writing that stretches back to the origins of mass media and the first war correspondents of the nineteenth century. In modern times, journalists such as Richard Harding Davis, Floyd Gibbons, Ernie Pyle, Bernard Fall, Michael Kelly, and Dexter Filkins have taken on the role of Homer, singing songs of battle, glory, pain, and loss. Chivers does the same while recounting the deeds of warriors ranging from the pilots of fighter bombers and attack helicopters to infantry slogging up and down hills and along booby-trapped roads and fields. While situated in America's most recent overseas military entanglements, Chivers's book is about enduring truths concerning war and human nature.

The wars in Afghanistan and Iraq, though responses to an attack on the homeland of the United States, never demanded the sort of commitment from the American people that was required during the two world wars of the twentieth century. For everyone other than the families of the soldiers, sailors, and airmen serving abroad, the only sacrifices expected were abstractions, such as higher percentages of taxes going into the budgets of these overseas contingencies. If a person wanted to, he or she could avoid newspapers, websites, and the television, and ignore the fact that the United States was at war. There was little enough otherwise to remind one that American troops were locked in combat with tough and resourceful enemies. As a result, it comes as something of a shock when Chivers addresses the statistics concerning the American military conflicts of the early twenty-first century: Some 2.7 million Americans have served in the wars in Afghanistan and Iraq; of these, over 7,000 have been killed, and many thousands more seriously wounded. Despite these numbers, he notes that in the contemporary United States, many Americans may not know anyone who has served in the military.

Chivers is determined to address the gulf of ignorance and incomprehension that separates those who serve in the military from many of their fellow citizens. He sees this as an act of demystification, breaking through any preconceptions that might have arisen about American troops because of political differences or tropes in the popular media.

© Mick Chivers

C. J. Chivers is a correspondent for the New York Times *and a writer-at-large for the* New York Times Magazine. *He has twice won the Pulitzer Prize for his journalism. He is also the author of* The Gun *(2010).*

On one point Chivers is emphatic; he had no interest in recording the experiences and opinions of high-ranking officers. He distrusts the "brass," believing that they are more likely to be self-interested in their accounts, like generals in every war, often more anxious to defend their decisions than to capture the truth of wartime encounters. Fairly or unfairly, Chivers sees these officers as apologists for the strategies employed in Afghanistan and Iraq. He is convinced that the stories told by those lower in rank and hence in the midst of the action are more likely to be honest and closer to the realities of combat. Consequently, *The Fighters* is a grunt's eye view of America's most recent wars.

In an effort to capture something of the full range of the American military experience in Afghanistan and Iraq, both geographically and chronologically, Chivers looks at the wartime experiences of six men. His roster of protagonists includes an elite naval aviator, a Special Forces operator, a Kiowa helicopter pilot, a Navy corpsman serving with the Marines, an Army infantryman, and a Marine lieutenant commanding an infantry platoon. Three of these men fought in Afghanistan and three in Iraq; two fought in both countries. The naval pilot flew in the first missions into Afghanistan in 2001, during the successful invasion that overthrew the Taliban regime sheltering Osama bin Laden and al-Qaeda. He also patrolled the skies over Afghanistan in 2011, as a surge of American forces in the country during the first years of the Obama presidency was drawing to an end. The other stories of battle fall in between these dates. Chivers also describes a 2013 meeting between a veteran, badly wounded physically and spiritually, and former president George W. Bush. The essential honesty of Chivers's reporting is such that, though he clearly has little personal regard for the man who first sent troops into Afghanistan and Iraq, Bush comes across as a warm and compassionate man as he sits down with the troubled veteran and his family.

The heart of *The Fighters* resides in, as the title implies, a series of dramatic and graphic narratives of Americans at war. Here, Chivers demonstrates that he is a worthy successor to the great war correspondents who came before him. Through intensive research and interviews, he is able to place readers inside the heads of his subjects as they ride the roller coaster of life in a war zone. As a denizen of many military trouble spots himself, he understands the stark alternation between military tedium and the heart-stopping, adrenaline-charged ferocity of battle. Because of this, Chivers does not judge the men he writes about when they exult in killing an enemy. He remains faithful to his determination to tell the unvarnished story of men caught up in the altered state of war. The calculus of ordinary feeling shifts when dealing with enemies who use children to lure soldiers into ambushes. One of the most remarkable aspects of Chivers's gritty book is the degree to which, under enormous provocation, the American soldiers he covers resist descending into the bloody-minded savagery attributed to GIs in antiwar literature from the Vietnam War to the present day. None of his subjects abandons his moral compass. American troops in Afghanistan and Iraq operated under strict rules of engagement. All the men in Chivers's book abide by these. Even the men flying planes and helicopters, and killing at a distance with the push of a button, are concerned about mistakenly killing civilians. The naval pilot followed by Chivers is haunted by the possibility that during the air war in Kosovo in the 1990s, he struck a home rather than a military target.

Despite this, collateral damage does occur. On February 14, 2010, during a Marine operation in the small town of Marja, Afghanistan, a US rocket slams into a home, killing most of the family sheltering there. No one could determine who called in the rocket strike. The Marines who sifted through the ruins, pulling out bodies and body parts, were dismayed and angered. This was not the sort of war they signed up to fight. They did soon get the fighting they expected, however. Chivers is especially good at describing combat. His evocations of the back-and-forth fighting at Marja, and an Army ambush in Afghanistan's Korengal Valley, are masterful. He captures the chaos, horror, and wild excitement of battle. His accounts of war remind us that only the military technology has changed since the conflicts recorded by Homer, Herodotus, and Thucydides.

C. J. Chivers's *The Fighters* will take its place on the short shelf of books essential for understanding the American experience of the long war on terror. His book is war reportage at its best. By focusing on the heart of what his subjects endured, rather than polemics, Chivers has crafted a book that will be read long after the wars in Afghanistan and Iraq have receded into history.

Daniel P. Murphy

Review Sources

Ackerman, Elliot. "Two Unfinished Wars in All Their Thrill and Horror." Review of *The Fighters: Americans in Combat in Afghanistan and Iraq*, by C. J. Chivers. *The Washington Post*, 7 Sept. 2018, www.washingtonpost.com/outlook/two-unfinished-wars-in-all-their-thrill-and-horror/2018/09/07/ada869a4-a255-11e8-8e87-c869fe70a721_story.html. Accessed 12 Dec. 2018.

Review of *The Fighters: Americans in Combat in Afghanistan and Iraq*, by C. J. Chivers. *Publishers Weekly*, 21 May 2018, www.publishersweekly.com/978-1-4516-7664-8. Accessed 12 Dec. 2018.

Gallagher, Matt. "An Honest Reckoning." Review of *The Fighters: Americans in Combat in Afghanistan and Iraq*, by C. J. Chivers. *The Wall Street Journal*, 18 Aug. 2018, p. 1.

Kaplan, Robert D. "On the Ground in Afghanistan and Iraq." Review of *The Fighters: Americans in Combat in Afghanistan and Iraq*, by C. J. Chivers. *The New York Times*, 14 Aug. 2018, www.nytimes.com/2018/08/14/books/review/cj-chivers-fighters.html. Accessed 12 Dec. 2018.

Pekoll, James. Review of *The Fighters: Americans in Combat in Afghanistan and Iraq*, by C. J. Chivers. *Booklist*, July 2018, www.booklistonline.com/The-Fighters-Americans-in-Combat-in-Afghanistan-and-Iraq-C-J-Chivers/pid=9529961. Accessed 12 Dec. 2018.

Vick, Karl. "Life during Wartime." Review of *The Fighters: Americans in Combat in Afghanistan and Iraq*, by C. J. Chivers. *Time*, 20 Aug. 2018. *Academic Search Complete*, search.ebscohost.com/login.aspx?direct=true&db=a9h&AN=131153638. Accessed 12 Dec. 2018.

Flights

Author: Olga Tokarczuk (b. 1962)
First published: *Bieguni*, 2007, in Poland
Translated: from the Polish by Jennifer Croft
Publisher: Riverhead Books (New York). 416 pp.
Type of work: Novel
Time: Present, flashbacks to various time periods from the seventeenth century on
Locales: Poland, Croatia, the Netherlands, Germany, France, several other locations

Celebrated Polish novelist Olga Tokarczuk creates a mosaic work in 116 sections, loosely based around the travels of an unnamed narrator, which relate a variety of stories and meditations on travel, grotesquerie, and what it means to be human.

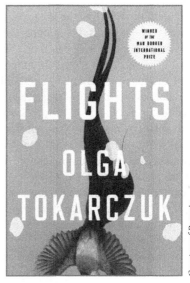

Courtesy of Penguin

Principal characters

THE NARRATOR, an unnamed woman who travels obsessively, seeking out people and their stories, as well as anatomical curiosities
KUNICKI, a man whose wife and child mysteriously disappear on a Croatian island
DR. BLAU, an anatomist obsessed with preserving body parts
PHILIP VERHEYEN, seventeenth-century Flemish anatomist, based on the historical figure of the same name
LUDWIKA, sister of legendary composer Frederick Chopin who is transporting his heart back to his native Poland after his death; based on the historical figure Ludwika Jędrzejewicz

During her extensive journeys in Europe and Asia, Polish novelist Olga Tokarczuk experienced an epiphany of sorts when she conceptualized modern travel as more like fragmented jumping from place to place than the relatively linear motion of the past. This revelation caused her to rethink her writing process, spawning an idea for a new work that would be informed by her subjective experience of her own travels. Returning home, she began working on a book made up a series of seemingly disparate fragments that nonetheless would have certain thematic and narrative connections.

The result was her 2007 novel *Bieguni*, published in English translation a decade or so later as *Flights*. Made up of 116 different sections, each with its own heading, *Flights* jumps freely across geographic settings as well as time periods, mimicking the disorientating and thrilling sense that often results from long travel. The book is built around a handful of longer pieces that tell more extended stories, but the bulk of the sections are much shorter segments, often no more than a paragraph, that allow the book's unnamed narrator (and its author) to muse on different aspects of travel, writing, and the often-fraught experience of contemporary living. The result is a rich and varied text that skillfully captures the disorientating nature of the twenty-first century.

The narrator, loosely based on Tokarczuk herself, ties all the threads together somewhat. The reader is meant to understand that the stories that unfold throughout the book are in some way tied to her, either belonging to people she meets in her travels or related to her in more tangential ways. She is, she explains, not a "real writer," but a collector of other's stories, a "gargantuan ear that listened to murmurs and echoes and whispers, far-off voices that filtered through the walls." The first few sections of the novel provide what scant background is offered about the narrator. In first-person narration she reveals her inveterate need to travel—in contrast to the rooted existence of her parents, who took her as a child only on safe, controlled journeys defined by the return home—her education in psychology, and her obsession with the grotesque.

This last quality often comes to dictate the people the narrator associates with and the places that she visits. As she tells the reader early on, she suffers from a condition she calls Recurrent Detoxification Syndrome, an affliction that draws her to the same images over and over. In her case she is a connoisseur of the imperfect, "drawn to all things spoiled, flawed, defective, broken." This causes her to constantly haunt anatomical museums and public displays of oddities and to pore over the narratives of those who traffic in the further recesses of medicine and anatomy. As she puts it, "my weakness is for teratology and for freaks. I believe, unswervingly, agonizingly, that it is in freaks that Being breaks through to the surface and reveals its true nature." Because as a novelist Tokarczuk is, like her narrator, interested in exploring the true nature of existence, she smartly chooses to dwell on the imperfect, the grotesque, as a way of looking beneath the surface of ordinary life and finding something that brings with it a greater truth.

But for all her philosophical searching, Tokarczuk is also a highly skilled storyteller, and what makes *Flights* such a gripping read is the quality of the half dozen or so longer stories, which the narrator relates in the third person. These stories deal with anatomists both benevolent (the real-life Flemish scientist Philip Verheyen) and sinister (the fictional Dr. Blau), with people who meet with mysterious disappearances, and with individuals driven by circumstances to flee their everyday lives. As such, these stories teem with mystery and possibility, opening up the reader's understanding of the world. Here, there is always more to life than is initially apparent.

One of the most extended sections partakes of just this sense of mystery. Kunicki, a Polish man on vacation on a Croatian island with his wife and child, looks for them after they unaccountably disappear. They ask him to stop his car on one of the island's roads, then get out and simply do not return. Kunicki enlists the aid of the authorities, all of whom insist that they could not have gone far since they are on a small island, and yet the two missing persons do not turn up. As in the other narratives that she includes in the book, Tokarczuk does not bring this story to a tidy conclusion but leaves Kunicki hanging. This is the way that travelers interact with the world. They get glimpses of places, of people's lives and stories, and then they move on to the next location.

The Kunicki narrative is unique, though, in that Tokarczuk does pick it up again, several hundred pages later. This is not a courtesy extended to any of the book's other narratives. It is almost as if something about Kunicki's story proved too tantalizing and so Tokarczuk jumps forward in time, situating the reader at a later moment in the life of the hapless protagonist. When Kunicki reappears, he is back at home in Poland, his wife and child returned. His wife insists that there was nothing mysterious about the disappearance, that they simply wandered off, got lost, and then found their way back. Kunicki, though, cannot accept this explanation, and becomes obsessed with finding out what really happened. At the end of the section, he sets off again for the Croatian isle, determined to get to the bottom of the mystery, another inveterate traveler in *Flights'* constellation of wanderers, in this case journeying to relieve (or fuel) his neurotic obsession.

Alongside the longer narrative sections, the shorter fragments give little glimpses of the narrator's journeys or offer various insights into her twin obsessions: travel and human grotesquerie. Sometimes these fragments take on moments of unexpected beauty, as in one short anecdote the narrator relates about an airsickness bag she found on one of her endless series of flights. Flying from Warsaw to Amsterdam, she picks up the bag in front of her, only to discover the following inscription written on the bottom: "10/12/2006: Striking out for Ireland. Final destination Belfast. Students of the Rzeszów Institute of Technology."

Olga Tokarczuk is a critically acclaimed and best-selling Polish author of novels and short stories. She won Poland's top literary prize, the Nike Award, in 2008 and 2015, and received the Man Booker International Prize in 2018. Her work has been translated into many languages.

These simple words betray a hopefulness and an anxiety that take on strong poetic resonances, a sort of haiku of travel, and they move the narrator. She muses on this act of witness, wondering if the writer expected to find a reader for the metaphorical message in the bottle. The situation conjured up by those few simple words haunts the narrator, and she wonders about the fate of the students. But, she realizes that, even setting aside the logistics of the thing, she is unlikely to ever find out. "I know that writing on bags," she concludes, "is something people do only out of anxiety and uncertainty. Neither defeat nor the greatest success is conducive to writing."

And so, caught in between, suffering neither defeat nor any particular success, the narrator keeps traveling and keeps recording. Although she accepts her role as a witness and recounter, it is one that she occasionally questions. Halfway thought the book, she wonders whether the controlled, linear format of a lecture or scientific paper would be more effective in getting clear points across. And yet, she determines that what she is doing is the only thing she can be doing, that it is important to record these lives in flux. Furthermore, she knows she is temperamentally suited to this task. "Tales have a kind of inherent inertia that it is never possible to fully control," she writes. "They require people like me—insecure, indecisive, easily led astray. Naive."

Ultimately, Tokarczuk and her narrator conflate the act of writing, of telling people's tales, with the goals of several of the anatomists whose narratives she has recounted. In particular, she aligns her goals with that of the most sinister character in the book, Dr. Blau. Blau, who also enjoys taking close-up photographs of women's genitals, aims to preserve the human body in all its forms by a method he is working with called plastination, in which the water and fat in dead bodies are replaced by plastic, leading to perfect preservation. At the end of the book, the narrator is waiting at the airport and sees a man writing down his observations in a notebook. She then takes out her notebook and does the same, inwardly calling on everyone else around them to follow suit. "We will simply write each other down, which is the safest form of communication and of transit; we will reciprocally transform each other into letters and initials, immortalize each other, plastinate each other, submerge each other in formaldehyde phrases and pages."

In this call for people to take up their pens, then, Tokarczuk gets at the excitement of the narrative impulse, but also at the guilt that inevitably comes from writing about other people. In her massive novel—which partakes of numerous nonfiction elements—this conflicted attitude toward the nature of truth, the ethics of independent existence, and the project of writing itself create a productive tension that is deeply stirring. Critics around the world responded enthusiastically to *Flights*, which in its original Polish version won Poland's prestigious Nike Award in 2008 and was a major commercial success. After its English publication, the book earned the 2018 Man Booker International Prize and was a finalist for the National Book Award for works in translation, among other honors, bringing Tokarczuk a new level of recognition in the English-speaking world.

Andrew Schenker

Review Sources
Kassabova, Kapka. "Flights by Olga Tokarczuk Review – The Ways of Wanderers." Review of *Flights*, by Olga Tokarczuk. *The Guardian*, 3 June 2017, www.theguardian.com/books/2017/jun/03/flights-by-olga-tokarczuk-review. Accessed 5 Dec. 2018.
Ramji, Shazia Hafiz. "A Soaring Novel in 116 'Flights'." Review of *Flights*, by Olga Tokarczuk. *Chicago Review of Books*, 31 Aug. 2018, chireviewofbooks.com/2018/08/31/flights-olga-tokarczuk-review/. Accessed 5 Dec. 2018.
Sehgal, Parul. "Fables Leap Back and Forth Through Time in 'Flights'." Review of *Flights*, by Olga Tokarczuk. *The New York Times*, 14 Aug. 2018, www.nytimes.com/2018/08/14/books/review-flights-olga-tokarczuk.html. Accessed 5 Dec. 2018.

Florida

Author: Lauren Groff (b. 1978)
Publisher: Riverhead Books (New York).
288 pp.
Type of work: Short fiction
Time: Present day
Locale: Florida

Florida, author Lauren Groff's newest collection of short stories, explores dread and time through the lens of the state of Florida.

Courtesy of Penguin

Lauren Groff is best known for her bestselling novel *Fates and Furies* (2015), which was a finalist for the National Book Award for Fiction and the National Book Critics Circle Award. President Barack Obama named it his favorite book of 2015. The book follows the story of Lotto and Mathilde, a couple whose marriage is told in the manner of a Greek tragedy. The first half of the novel tells Lotto's story, with parenthetical interjections from the "fates." The second half, wildly divergent in tone, is told from the perspective of Mathilde. Florida figures into that book as well. Overall, *Fates and Furies* is emblematic of Groff's style: unruly narratives built by precise and vivid sentences.

Groff published her first book, a novel titled *The Monsters of Templeton*, in 2008. It is a fantastical, generational tale about her hometown, Cooperstown, New York, and is inspired by the nineteenth-century writer James Fenimore Cooper. The novel won praise from Stephen King and award-winning short-story writer Lorrie Moore. Groff next published a collection of short stories titled *Delicate Edible Birds* in 2009, which was followed by a novel about a girl growing up on a commune in the 1960s titled *Arcadia* in 2011.

In her 2018 story collection, *Florida*, Groff explores the sweltering backwater of her adopted state, a place she evocatively describes as an "Eden of dangerous things." Most of the eleven stories in the collection take place in Florida, and all of them are gravitationally centered there. In "For the God of Love, For the Love of God" and "Salvador," characters travel the world on borrowed time, knowing that they must soon return. Groff's Florida is beautiful but unkind. It is elemental, a wild and deadly place. Her characters do not so much live there as they are locked in a constant battle with Florida's oppressive heat, sinkholes, alligators and frequent, obliterating storms.

In "Dogs Go Wolf," two young sisters are abandoned on a fishing island. In "At the Round Earth's Imagined Corners," a boy named Jude grows up in Central Florida, in a swamp house teeming with snakes. But for an unnamed mother, the central character of five of the stories, the danger is more difficult to quantify. The character is a lot like Groff herself, a novelist with two young boys. In "Ghosts and Empties," the first story in the collection, the woman takes long, nightly walks to stave off her anxiety. "I have somehow become a woman who yells," she says. Passing the variety of twilit life on the street, she worries about poverty, racism, climate change, and raising good sons. Those fears are so intense in "Flower Hunters" that she burrows into herself, at the expense of her friends and family, only finding solace in a book by a long-dead naturalist. In "The Midnight Zone," an unseen panther prowls her holiday cabin, as she lies, incapacitated, in bed with a concussion: the personification of dread. In "Yport," the collection's last and longest story, Groff writes of the mother: "She can't stop the thought that children born now will be the last generation of humans. . . . She feels it nearing, the midnight of humanity. Their world is so full of beauty, the last terrible flash of beauty before the long darkness."

Katy Waldman, who reviewed the book for the *New Yorker*, described it as "a psychogeography of Florida, exploring both a state in the union and a state of mind." Each individual story represents the wilderness of a character's mind, and their realization of the ultimate fragility of human beings in an ancient, hostile place. But the totality of *Florida* is Groff's most impressive achievement. The stories, even the ones that feature the same unnamed mother character, do not cohere narratively, but rather come together in images—storms, injuries—and form. As Sophie Gilbert wrote in her review for the *Atlantic*, *Florida* "isn't a short story collection so much as an ecosystem."

Groff finds unity in her displacement of time. "Time is impassive, more animal than human," she writes in "The Midnight Zone." "Time would not care if you fell out of it. It would continue on without you. It cannot see you; it has always been blind to the human and the things we do to stave it off." In "Ghosts and Empties" she writes of the moon, "we lonely humans, who are far too small and our lives far too fleeting for it to give us any notice at all." With the immensity of time as her guiding principle, Groff plays fast and loose with human-scale time in her stories. In "Dogs Go Wolf," her authorial voice enters at a climactic moment—will the sisters starve to death on the island or will be they be rescued?—to offer a glimpse of the sisters years in the future. She employs a similar sleight of hand in the transcendent conclusion to "Above and Below," perhaps the collection's best stand-alone story, about a graduate student who becomes homeless.

Awareness of time is at the heart of the stories, from "At the Round Earth's Imagined Corners," which describes, in overview, a man's entire life, to "Eyewall," in which a woman is visited by ghosts from her past during a hurricane. In "The Midnight Zone," two days become a hellish drip of eternity. The anxious unnamed mother alternatively struggles with and embraces time; in two stories, she can only face the present by focusing on a distant past.

The concluding story of the collection, "Yport," follows the unnamed mother and her two young boys—ages four and seven—to France. The mother professes to be working on a story about the nineteenth-century writer Guy de Maupassant, but her true purpose is escape from her overworked husband. The story is unusual in the context of Groff's larger oeuvre, but also in the context of *Florida*. It lacks the fecund surrealism of her other stories but it feels brisk and refreshing set against the lushness of the Floridian world. The mother and her boys travel to Yport, a small town in Normandy. They eat pastries and admire the towering white cliffs, sculpted by glaciers millions of years ago. But the mother is unsettled. Each night, instead of writing, she knocks back two bottles of good, cheap French wine.

There is no real plot to the story. It radiates with warmth, though—Groff has a knack for finding humor in the children's individual voices—and in it, she begins to zero in on her theme. A lot of the mother's anxiety stems from the worry that she is a bad mother—is she too inattentive? Is she untruthful? Should she have let the boys play near that church when it was so close to the cliffs? At one point, she bristles when a smug British couple suggest that her youngest son is anxious. But in a more visceral sense, the mother struggles between two poles of reasoning— how much danger should she let the boys encounter on their own? How much danger can she reasonably protect them from? There are

Lauren Groff is a best-selling novelist and short story writer who has won many awards for her fiction. Her novel Fates and Furies *(2015) was a finalist for the National Book Award for Fiction and the National Book Critics Circle Award.* Florida *was a finalist for the National Book Award for Fiction in 2018.*

no answers to these questions. The only question that is answered in the story regards Maupassant: the mother and sons agree, finally, that they hate him. Given the evidence, the reader might agree. It would not be a spoiler to share the story's enigmatic and powerful final image, in which the youngest boy holds a rock in his hand above his head, aimed at a snail. Like a distant and merciful god, he chooses not to throw it.

Florida, published in June 2018, was a finalist for the National Book Award for Fiction and was met with almost universal praise. *Kirkus* named it one of their best books of the year. In a starred review, a reviewer described it as a "literary tour de force." A reviewer for *Publishers Weekly* wrote that while "pessimism threatens to sink a few" of the stories, "Groff's skillful prose, self-awareness, and dark humor leaven the bleakness, making this a consistently rewarding collection." Waldman offered an illuminating and positive critique in her review for the *New Yorker*. "Despite its departures from Groff's earlier work"—by which she meant a bolder surrealism— "the collection still conjures that feeling of when the floor falls out from under you; as in *Fates and Furies*, familiar, everyday life dangles by a thin string." She even went as far as to describe the book as autobiography by way of a Salvador Dali painting. The "emotional disclosures," she wrote, "are encrypted in phantasmagoria." Gilbert, writing for the *Atlantic*, also noted that the book, at times, feels "intensely personal." As a collection, she wrote, "*Florida* is as eerie and ominous as it's exquisite." She compared *Florida* to other writers who have explored their own psychogeography through the state, including playwright Tarell Alvin McCraney, who wrote the film

Moonlight (2016). Author Christine Schutt, who reviewed the book for the *New York Times*, wrote that Groff was "a great storyteller," and described the "11 dramatic tales" as "full of event and surprise, instruction and comfort." She concluded: "*Florida* is restorative fiction for these urgent times."

Molly Hagan

Review Sources

Elkin, Lauren. "*Florida* by Lauren Groff Review—Rage and Refusal as Earth Reaps the Whirlwind." Review of *Florida*, by Lauren Groff. *The Guardian*, 14 June 2018, www.theguardian.com/books/2018/jun/14/florida-lauren-groff-review-women-fury-eco-apocalypse. Accessed 17 Jan. 2019.

Review of *Florida*, by Lauren Groff. *Kirkus Reviews*, 15 Apr. 2018, p. 1. *Literary Reference Center Plus*, search.ebscohost.com/login.aspx?direct=true&db=lkh&AN=129042834&site=lrc-plus. Accessed 17 Jan. 2019.

Review of *Florida*, by Lauren Groff. *Publishers Weekly*, 9 Apr. 2018, p. 49. *Literary Reference Center Plus*, search.ebscohost.com/login.aspx?direct=true&db=lkh&AN=128972421&site=lrc-plus. Accessed 17 Jan. 2019.

Gilbert, Sophie. "*Florida*, Full of Dread." Review of *Florida*, by Lauren Groff. *The Atlantic*, 14 June 2018, www.theatlantic.com/entertainment/archive/2018/06/florida-full-of-dread/562712/. Accessed 17 Jan. 2019.

Schutt, Christine. "Lauren Groff Reveals the Stormy Side of the Sunshine State." Review of *Florida*, by Lauren Groff. *The New York Times*, 17 July 2018, www.nytimes.com/2018/07/17/books/review/florida-lauren-groff.html. Accessed 17 Jan. 2019.

Waldman, Katy. "Lauren Groff's Stunning New Collection, 'Florida,' Unfolds 'in an Eden of Dangerous Things.'" Review of *Florida*, by Lauren Groff. *The New Yorker*, 4 June 2018, www.newyorker.com/books/page-turner/lauren-groffs-stunning-new-collection-florida-unfolds-in-an-eden-of-dangerous-things. Accessed 17 Jan. 2019.

Flunk. Start.
Reclaiming My Decade Lost in Scientology

Author: Sands Hall (b. 1952)
Publisher: Counterpoint Press (Berkeley, CA). 416 pp.
Type of work: Memoir
Time: 1950s–present day
Locales: Squaw Valley, California; Los Angeles, California

Reclaiming My Decade Lost in Scientology

Sands Hall

Courtesy of Counterpoint Press

In Flunk. Start., *Sands Hall describes the ten years of her life during which she was influenced by Scientology. While under the group's influence, she struggled with many of its philosophies, but she was drawn to the commitment of the individual members. Though she often thought of leaving, she was also running away from family issues that her involvement both complicated and soothed.*

Principal personages

SANDS HALL, writer, singer, actor, former Scientologist
OAKLEY "TAD" HALL III, her older brother
OAKLEY HALL, her father
JAMIE FAUNT, her first husband, a Scientologist
SKYE STRYDER, her lover, a Scientologist
L. RON HUBBARD, founder of Scientology

Questions about Scientology began rising to public consciousness in the 2010s, as celebrities like actor Leah Remini started speaking out about problems with the religious group. In 2018, Sands Hall's voice joined those who are attempting to broaden the understanding of a religion where she found both peace and confusion. One main difference between Hall's memoir, *Funk. Start.: Reclaiming My Decade Lost in Scientology*, and many of those expressing discontent with Scientology is that Hall does not focus solely on the negative aspects of Scientology, but also suggests that the religion also has some positive elements. In addition, *Flunk. Start.* not only explores the seven years she spent in Scientology and three years it took to leave the religion, but it follows her life from early childhood to the 2010s.

The book is organized into three major sections as well as a foreword and afterword. In the foreword, Hall shares the meaning of the title and the purpose for the book: "Scientologists, to learn a particular skill, practice or 'drill' that skill with a partner. If one does the drill incorrectly, the partner says, 'Flunk.' And immediately,

© Graham Hayes

Sands Hall is a writer, musician, teacher, and student of words. She has also written a novel, Catching Heaven, *which was a Willa Award Finalist for Best Contemporary Fiction; a book about writing,* Tools of the Writer's Craft; *and multiple plays. She teaches writing at Franklin & Marshall College in Pennsylvania.*

'Start.' Harsh as 'flunk' may sound, there's no intended animosity; it's just a way of communicating that you're doing it wrong." Hall continued, explaining that she related that practice to her time in Scientology, initially viewing her seven years with the religion as a "flunk." As she continued to work on the memoir, however, Hall realized she had gained something, a "start," from those years as well. The first section of the book, titled "Nothing Better to Be," contains seventeen chapters. This section, alternates back and forth between a time when Hall had been a member of the church for five years and her early childhood. The chapters about the church establish the doubt that she had always felt regarding certain aspects of the religion, while the chapters about her family establish an early desire for the kind of certainty that religion could provide. The second section, "The Whole Agonized Future of This Planet," contains twenty-two chapters that trace the years immediately before an accident that left her brother, playwright Oakley "Tad" Hall III, with a brain injury, as well as the ensuing years as Hall was drawn to Scientology. The final eight-chapter section, "After Such a Storm," relates the years following her separation from Scientology.

The memoir begins with a flashback to a time when, in her thirties, Hall was working as a course supervisor, helping new Scientologists study the religious literature required by Scientology founder L. Ron Hubbard. Hall establishes some of the basic understandings of Scientology as well as her ongoing doubts about the religion. While the memoir focuses on explaining the manipulation tactics and strict rules of Scientology, Hall also shares bits of humor and reminders of the attractions of the religion. For instance, she quotes an auditor (counselors in Scientology) who says, "You know that phrase 'Life's a bitch, and then you die'? Well, for us, it's 'Life's a bitch, and then you live forever!'" When she struggled with personal doubts, her former husband, Jamie Faunt, told her, "You talk about the chaos, Sands, it ends the chaos," highlighting the religion's ability to help Hall escape the uncertainty of life. She continues to share her journey into the religion throughout the memoir, as well as the questions she raised about the religion, even while she was immersed in it. After Hubbard's death, she hoped the church "would, just, well, close," but it did not, and among other things, the changes by its new leadership helped her eventually make the decision to leave.

Scientology, however, was not the only connection to religion in Hall's life. In numerous flashback chapters, she takes readers back to her childhood with artistic, literary parents who eschewed formal religion in any manner. She shares a story of her father's retelling of an event when she was two: "'To our horror,' Dad said, 'and remember, she's just two years old, she starts shuffling on her knees toward the altar. Well, I'll tell you, I jerked her to her feet so hard and fast I dislocated her shoulder.'" An eight-year-old child at the time she relates the story, Hall recalls knowing that from her father's perspective, "I'd been jerked to my senses, as well as jerked to my feet." Regardless of their disagreement with established religion, Hall's parents had a strange attraction to religious symbols and filled their home with iconic religious pieces, art, and music, something that often confused her as a child. Despite her parents' attitudes, Hall was drawn to the idea of religion throughout her youth and into her adulthood. So, when she began a romantic relationship with Faunt, a Scientologist, she clung to the security of the ideas of both a husband and a religion. She did not, however, retain the security she searched for in either. She and Jamie divorced after less than two years of marriage, and she constantly questioned her decision to become and remain a Scientologist. Her parents also continued to argue with her about religion, acting as what Scientology calls suppressive persons by asking her to leave the church.

Hall remained a Scientologist for another five years after her divorce from Faunt, until she could no longer stand certain aspects of the religion. The third part of the book reflects on this departure and the way members of Scientology cut off those who leave the religion from their former lives. Hall writes, "Being *in* Scientology hadn't felt particularly traumatic, but leaving it certainly did." Her religious experiences were not all negative, however. The majority of members Hall interacted with were good people, and aspects of the religion helped Hall transition to other faiths, like Buddhism, later in life.

Though Scientology is one of the main focuses of the book, another main theme is family. Hall's family comes to life as she tells of a childhood traveling the world with artistic parents who encouraged free thinking as long as it was not about religion. Her older brother Tad was a larger than life figure throughout her childhood and early years. However, when he fell from a bridge, Hall found it difficult to accept the changing situation. She told herself, "Nothing was irretrievably broken. Except his brain. But I didn't know that yet." As Tad changed, however, Tad's wife told Hall that her presence was hurting her brother's recovery. This idea, coupled with the inability to accept that Tad was no longer the same man, led Hall to move from New York to Los Angeles. This flight from reality, combined with depression over a lack of mission in her own life, left her open to the temptations of Scientology, a religion that encouraged her to separate from the family she loved. After she left Scientology, Hall recognized that she had worsened Tad's condition and noted what she had lost in staying away from him. Years later, after reconnecting with her brother, she was able to reconcile the person she had known with the person Tad was now. She writes, "For the first time since the accident, I was able to see him as he now was. And I loved that person. He was witty, incredibly droll, wise and compassionate." She ends the book with a reflection on their journeys: "My brother and I both flunked. His version was awful; mine, in the end, fairly mundane. He fell off a bridge, damaging his brain; I clambered along one that, for a while, torqued my mind."

Hall's family's artistic expression inspired her fascination with words, which provided an unexpected tie to Scientology. She says, "I was so attracted to the study of the religion that even the understanding that I was, thus, binding myself to it, more and more tightly did not deter me. Delving into words in this intimate way made me feel as if I was doing with my life exactly what I should be doing." She loved the study of language that she found in Scientology. Once she left, she turned that love to writing, getting a master's degree, completing a novel and multiple plays, and becoming a teacher. Even at the end of the memoir, however, she gives credit to Scientology for helping her move in this direction: "What I acquired, in that seven-year dance with the Church, is an awareness of spirit that permeates my days, and a way to interact with words that is deeply satisfying."

Her skill with language can be seen throughout *Flunk. Start.* and the memoir received generally positive reviews from critics. *Kirkus Reviews* (1 Feb. 2018) highlights Hall's ability to create a balance between her opinions and experiences with Scientology and explaining the religion itself, stating, "The author is sincere and open about why Scientology appealed to her, and she effectively uses Hubbard's work to show the complexity and strangeness of thinking. Using the terminology of the Scientologists, she discusses the tactics of "auditing," or counseling, the training routines. . . . All of these tactics are used to drill into the minds of believers that Hubbard's version of reality is the absolute truth." The memoir is a contemplative work that provides insight not only into a controversial religion but into the heart and mind of a person who dared to step away from a philosophy that contained too many ideas that just did not add up.

Theresa L. Stowell, PhD

Review Sources

Dryer, Rachael and Derek Sanderson. "Memoirs of Merit." Review of *Coffee House*, by Myriam Mean Gurba, *Flunk. Start.: Reclaiming My Decade Lost in Scientology*, by Sands Hall, *The Milk Lady of Bangalore: An Unexpected Adventure*, by Shoba Narayan, *I Am, I Am, I Am: Seventeen Brushes with Death*, by Maggie O'Farrell, and *First Time Ever*, by Peggy Seeger. *Library Journal*, 1 Mar. 2018. *Literary Reference Center Plus*, search.ebscohost.com/login.aspx?direct=true&db=lkh&AN=128234132&site=lrc-plus. Accessed 28 Nov. 2018.

Engel, Christine. Review of *Flunk. Start.: Reclaiming My Decade Lost in Scientology*, by Sands Hall. *Booklist*, 1 Feb. 2018. *Literary Reference Center Plus*, search.ebscohost.com/login.aspx?direct=true&db=lkh&AN=127808195&site=lrc-plus. Accessed 28 Nov. 2018.

Review of *Flunk. Start.: Reclaiming My Decade Lost in Scientology*, by Sands Hall. *Kirkus Reviews*, 1 Feb. 2018. *Literary Reference Center Plus*, search.ebscohost.com/login.aspx?direct=true&db=lkh&AN=127646345&site=lrc-plus. Accessed 28 Nov. 2018.

Review of *Flunk. Start.: Reclaiming My Decade Lost in Scientology*, by Sands Hall. *Publishers Weekly*, 8 Jan. 2018. *Literary Reference Center Plus*, search.ebscohost. com/login.aspx?direct=true&db=lkh&AN=127171336&site=lrc-plus. Accessed 28 Nov. 2018.

Ralphs, Camille. "Clear Because They're Clear: Life inside a 'Cult.'" *TLS*, 2 Oct. 2018, www.the-tls.co.uk/articles/private/scientology-dianetics-hubbard/. Accessed 28 Nov. 2018.

The Flying Mountain

Author: Christoph Ransmayr (b. 1954)
First published: *Der fliegende Berg*, 2006, in Germany
Translated: from the German by Simon Pare
Publisher: Seagull Books (New York). 336 pp.
Type of work: Novel, poetry
Time: Early twenty-first century
Locales: Horse Island in southwest Ireland, the Kham region of Tibet

In this English translation of Austrian author Christoph Ransmayr's 2006 German-language blank verse novel, two Irish brothers embark on an epic journey to the land of Kham in eastern Tibet, where they seek to find and conquer a mythical unmapped mountain.

THE FLYING MOUNTAIN
Christoph Ransmayr

TRANSLATED BY SIMON PARE

Courtesy of Seagull Books

Principal characters

PADRAIC, the narrator, an Irish merchant seaman
LIAM, his older brother, a computer programmer and cyber-cartographer
NYEMA DOLMA, a young, widowed Tibetan nomad who becomes Padraic's lover
FERGUS, Padraic and Liam's father
SHONA, their mother

In Austrian author Christoph Ransmayr's blank verse novel *The Flying Mountain* (2018), Horse Island, lying at the southwestern edge of Ireland, is a mystical place of windswept ruins and rugged beauty. For the novel's protagonist and narrator, Padraic, a merchant navy seaman, the island offers refuge from the sea, satisfying a longing for peace and quietude in "an *immovable place* beneath / an *immovable sky*." After spending years abroad, he is lured there by his older brother, Liam, an accomplished computer programmer who is the island's only year-round inhabitant. It is on this remote, primeval expanse of black rock cliffs and overgrown pastures that these two adventure-seeking Irish brothers lay the seeds for the epic journey at the center of the novel, one to the historical Kham region of eastern Tibet. There, in the forbidden Chinese Himalayas, the two seek to find and conquer a mythical hidden peak known as Phur-Ri, or "the flying mountain," which is believed to be higher than Mount Everest.

Whether or not the brothers fulfill their mission is revealed in the novel's opening pages. Still, Ransmayr retains an air of mystery, as Padraic begins to narrate his and his brother's tale in a seemingly postmortem state. (Padraic's name is not revealed until near the end of the novel.) Lost in a hallucinatory, high-altitude-induced haze,

Padraic describes the scene of his "deathplace," which lies somewhere high above the clouds—6,840 meters, to be exact—on Phur-Ri. Surrounded by blinding pillars of ice, he sees constellations speckled across the sky and hears foaming waves crashing on a beach. His mind conjures up the images of a woman (later understood to be his Tibetan lover Nyema Dolma) as he distantly hears Liam commanding him to get up, determinedly talking him out of his delirium. The two brothers, it turns out, have successfully summitted Phur-Ri but became separated from each other during the blizzard-plagued descent from the mountain. Their reunion, however, is short-lived, as Liam, in a cruel twist of fate, dies in an avalanche after saving Padraic.

This powerful, standout opening section acclimates readers to the novel's unconventional style. In an introductory aside, Ransmayr explains that the book consists of what he calls "floating" or "flying" lines, which have replaced meter and verse as the common building blocks of poetry. Such writing does not adhere to a specific meter and rhyme scheme, with free-flowing lines arranged in stanzas of varying length. Yet, although the work resembles poetry, Ransmayr notes it is meant to be read as prose. *The Flying Mountain* thus reads like a classic heroic narrative, containing, from its outset, scenes of sweeping beauty and grandeur. It also features elements of the surreal, such as when Padraic, after being rescued by Liam, experiences the phenomenon of black snow, which comes in the form of swarms of dead butterflies that fall from the sky "like charred, / shredded paper from an invisible fire."

As hinted at early on, Ransmayr's novel does indeed include a love story, but at its heart, it is an epic adventure tale that chronicles the complicated relationship between two brothers. Following his account of Liam's death, Padraic shifts focus to the events leading up to their journey, beginning with his arrival on Horse Island. Liam has transformed a house there that had been abandoned during Ireland's nineteenth-century famines into a twenty-first century retreat. It serves as the headquarters for his endeavors, professional and otherwise. He has parlayed his computer programming skills into a lucrative trade as a cyber-cartographer, creating high-tech digital atlases and globes for clients all over the world. In his spare time, Liam scours the internet for geographical and topographical oddities. He eventually discovers an old black-and-white photograph, taken by a Chinese bomber pilot, that suggests the existence of an unknown mountain in Tibet's Kham region.

It is this discovery that sets in motion Liam's plans of summiting a mountain that may be the tallest in the world. Liam convinces his brother to travel with him to Tibet, though Padraic has reservations. Most notably, the alleged mountain is situated in an area of China that is forbidden to foreigners. Unlike Liam, Padraic is indifferent to technology, but he does share his brother's passion for climbing, which was cultivated by their father, Fergus. Throughout his narration, Padraic delves into his and his brother's upbringing and family history. The brothers were raised at the foot of the Caha Mountains, located in Ireland's southwest County Cork, and took hiking and camping trips there with their father as youths. Strict and demanding, Fergus, a diehard supporter of the Irish Republican Army, used such trips to toughen up his sons. However, Liam, hungrier than Padraic for toil and physical challenges, was the one who won their father's affections, prompting an intense rivalry between the brothers.

As Padraic relates, it was these early climbing expeditions that initially led him to hate "life under the open sky." It is only after Padraic moves in with Liam on Horse Island decades later that he begins to enjoy climbing. By this time, their father is long deceased, having died from a combination of lung disease and grief, the latter caused by their bitter and resentful mother, Shona, returning to her native Belfast to take up with a more kind-hearted electrician. Family difficulties notwithstanding, Liam and Padraic's trip to the highlands of Kham takes two years to realize, largely due to bureaucratic roadblocks. After sending out overtures to various officials, Liam eventually secures them passage to the region under the ruse that they will be traveling there as surveyors on an officially endorsed trip.

Once they escape into Kham (through the help of an itinerant trader), however, Liam and Padraic's goals diverge. Blinded by his single-minded obsession of scaling Phur-Ri, Liam refuses to let any obstacles stand in his way. Padraic, on the other hand, reassesses his priorities after he meets Nyema, the woman he imagines in the opening section. Nyema, a young widow, is a member of a nomadic tribe that the brothers travel with, one that has endured inexplicable suffering at the hands of the Chinese. Ransmayr's vivid descriptions of the landscapes and human scenes the brothers encounter offer readers glimpses of such suffering.

Christoph Ransmayr is an acclaimed Austrian author of novels, nonfiction, and drama whose works have been translated into more than thirty different languages. He has received numerous prestigious literary honors and awards.

Despite these unsettling images, Liam remains unfazed, concerned only with the task he has set out to accomplish. This puts him at odds with Padraic, who soon develops strong romantic feelings for Nyema. A love affair between them ensues, leading Padraic to question whether he should even continue with the journey. As this dilemma unfolds, Padraic accompanies his brother on an ascent of a mountain called Cha-Ri ("bird mountain"), an expedition that almost ends in disaster. Liam is then unsuccessful in persuading Padraic to go with him on a trial ascent of another mountain, Te-Ri ("cloud mountain"), and his solo trip results in a second close brush with death. Padraic and Liam, nevertheless, restore their brotherly bond during their final climb of Phur-Ri. The novel inevitably ends where it starts, but prior to Liam's death, the two brothers ultimately reach a respectful understanding with one another.

The climbing passages are among the novel's highlights, as Ransmayr, drawing from his real-life experiences as a globe-trotting mountaineer and travel writer, vividly recreates the fury of elements at play in unforgiving high-altitude mountain environments. Furthermore, the novel evokes the story of Ransmayr's close friend, Reinhold

Messner, a legendary Italian mountaineer noted for being the first climber to summit all fourteen of the world's 8,000-meter peaks. In 1970, Messner and his younger brother, Günther, successfully summitted Nanga Parbat, an extremely dangerous mountain situated in the western Himalayas of Pakistan. However, Günther died during their descent from the mountain, presumably killed in an avalanche like Liam in *The Flying Mountain*. The event had a lasting effect on Messner's life. Ransmayr has, for the most, part reworked the story for his own artistic purposes, but this central similarity unavoidably invites comparison between fiction and reality.

Ransmayr likened the novel's structure to that of a song, taking inspiration from the oral storytelling tradition of Tibet's nomadic peoples. Helping to render this unique, harmonious quality of the writing in the English version is translator Simon Pare, who does an admirable job of retaining the spirit of the original German (the novel was also previously published in a number of other languages). Ransmayr and Pare's collaboration received significant positive critical recognition. Most notably, *The Flying Mountain* was long-listed for the 2018 Man Booker International Prize, a prestigious UK literary award that is given out annually to a single book in English translation.

In a review for the Swansea, Wales, magazine *The Bay*, Sarla Langdon lamented the novel being passed over for the Man Booker short list, commenting that its "timeless beauty" was reminiscent of Homer's *The Odyssey* (ca. eighth century BCE) and Seamus Heaney's 1999 translation of *Beowulf* (ca. 1000 CE). "It is an outstanding work of great sophistication," she concluded, "ultra-modern in its technology theme and as ancient as time in the tragic inevitability of the denouement." This accessible English translation will likely serve as a gateway for readers to Ransmayr's other works. Among his other novels in English translation are the similarly experimental *The Terrors of Ice and Darkness* (1991), which is based on the 1870s Austro-Hungarian North Pole expedition, and *The Dog King* (1997), an alternative history that focuses on the reconstruction of a fictitious Germany after World War II.

Chris Cullen

Review Sources

Duvernoy, Sophie. "Climbing Flying Mountain." Review of *The Flying Mountain*, by Christoph Ransmayr, and *The Naked Mountain*, by Reinhold Messner. *The Harvard Advocate*, 2018, theharvardadvocate.com/content/climbing-flying-mountain/. Accessed 1 Nov. 2018.

Hewitt, Séan. "Stories of Brotherly Love, the Fractures of Marriage and Bell's Palsy." Review of *The Flying Mountain*, by Christoph Ransmayr, et al. *The Irish Times*, 1 Nov. 2018, www.irishtimes.com/culture/books/stories-of-brotherly-love-the-fractures-of-marriage-and-bell-s-palsy-1.3608233. Accessed 1 Nov. 2018.

Langdon, Sarla. "Booker International 2018 Longlist." Review of *The Flying Mountain*, by Christoph Ransmayr, et al. *The Bay*, May 2018, www.theswanseabay.co.uk/2018/04/27/booker-international-2018-longlist/. Accessed 1 Nov. 2018.

Force of Nature

Author: Jane Harper (b. ca. 1980)
Publisher: Flatiron Books (New York). 336 pp.
Type of work: Novel
Time: Present day
Locales: Melbourne, Australia, and the Giralang Ranges

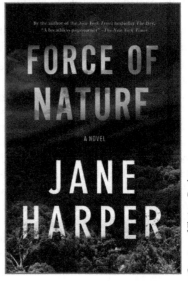

Alice Russell is sharing information with federal agents Aaron Falk and Carmen Cooper regarding fraud at BaileyTennants. However, her disappearance during a company team-building exercise in the wilderness leads to a mystery: Did she leave of her own accord or did someone make her disappear? Since Falk was the last person she attempted to contact, he and his partner set off to help find the missing woman.

Principal characters
AARON FALK, a federal investigator
CARMEN COOPER, his new partner
ALICE RUSSELL, their informant
JILL BAILEY, a partner in BaileyTennants
BREANNA "BREE" MCKENZIE, Alice's administrative assistant
BETHANY "BETH" MCKENZIE, Bree's identical twin sister, a recovering alcoholic and drug addict
LAUREN SHAW, the strategic head of forward planning for BaileyTennants
DANIEL BAILEY, a partner in BaileyTennants, Jill's brother

Jane Harper's award-winning debut novel, *The Dry*, introduced Federal Agent Aaron Falk. Aaron investigates financial matters, but his investigations often lead to dangerous situations. In *The Dry*, the mother of Aaron's high school best friend informally hires him to clear her son's name after that son had been accused of the alleged murder-suicide that killed himself, his wife, and their son. Aaron solves the case, but he is badly injured in a fire at the end of the novel, and that injury continues to plague him through the new book, providing one of several connections between the stories.

    Force of Nature starts just a few months after the first novel ends. Aaron is back in Melbourne, working with a new partner, Carmen Cooper, in the financial crimes investigation unit. Their current case involves money laundering by a "boutique accountancy firm" called BaileyTennants. Carmen and Aaron have approached Alice Russell, a member of upper management, to provide contracts and other information as evidence

© Eugene Hyland

Jane Harper's Force of Nature *is the second book in her Aaron Falk series. Her debut novel and series starter,* The Dry *(2016), was an international best seller and won several awards, including the British Book Awards Crime and Thriller Book of the Year and the ABIA Australian Book of the Year.*

of the company's illegal activities.

The novel follows various plots and subplots. The main plot, revealed in four days of flashbacks, revolves around the women's team-building group from BaileyTennants. Five women have been sent on an outdoors expedition with the goal of improving communications. Jill Bailey, one of the company's partners, is also using the adventure as an opportunity to observe employees who have either had performed effectively or questionably, to see if they should be promoted or let go. Twins Bree and Beth McKenzie have been selected for the trip, but for different reasons. Bree is an ideal employee who is up for promotion, while Beth's work in the mailroom and data-storage area has been less than stellar, and her gloomy attitude has brought her to the attention of the upper management. Lauren Shaw's performance during her two-year tenure with the company was solid until personal problems started to undermine her ability to put her full effort into her job. Alice's ambitious attitude and hard work, in contrast, has pushed her into the spotlight. After the first day of the expedition, the five women get lost without food, water, or contact with the outside world, and their secrets and interpersonal conflicts eventually explode into a violent argument about how best to survive and return to civilization. When only four of the women walk out of the wilderness, a search-and-rescue team forms to look for Alice, who had threatened to strike out on her own and whom each surviving woman has had a reason to dislike.

The secondary, present-day plot follows Aaron and Carmen as they become involved in the search for Alice, worried that her efforts as an informant may have made her a target. A mysterious call from Alice's cell phone early in the morning that she allegedly walked away from the other women, taking their only cell phone and working flashlight, adds to their concern when the only discernable words are "hurt her." Going back and forth between their home base in Melbourne and the national park area of the fictional Giralang Ranges, the two agents search for evidence of Alice's whereabouts as part of their ongoing pursuit of the files they need for their fraud investigation.

Additional subplots include the relationship between estranged twins Bree and Beth, an old high school rivalry between Alice and Lauren, current problems involving Alice's and Lauren's teenage daughters, and a twenty-five-year-old mystery concerning Martin Kovac, a serial killer who had used the Giralang Ranges as his hunting grounds a quarter century earlier. Kovac had killed four young women before he was caught, but his final victim has never been found and there are ongoing rumors that his son may be hiding out somewhere in the area.

Varied thematic ideas are explored as the multiple plots are laid out. One of the strongest themes involves familial relationships. Aaron carries the emotional baggage of his estrangement from his father, who had died prior to events in *The Dry*. During the search for Alice, Carmen challenges Aaron to reconsider the interactions that he had with his father during his teen years. By the end of the novel, he has come to an understanding that his father had been trying to reach out to him for a long time, but their similar solitary personalities had limited their ability to connect. The parent-child relationship is also briefly seen in the twins, whose mother has multiple sclerosis. Their shared desire to protect their mother from further pain leads to some reconciliation between the sisters despite deep-seated resentments. Jill's love for her father is brought up as a motivating factor behind her decision to give up her dream of being a humanities teacher and join in the family's illegal activities. At the same time, she is proud of her children, both teachers themselves, for following their own paths.

Old feuds surface between two pairs of women in the wilderness group. Beth is overweight, angry, and insecure, while Bree is the picture of health; they are so physically different that it is almost impossible to see that they are identical twins. Tensions in their relationship date back to when they were in college, even before Beth's addiction issues led to jail time. Lauren and Alice are also a focus. As classmates at a private high school, the two have shared experiences that almost crippled one with insecurity while meaning very little to the other. Now, their daughters attend the same private school but face a much more treacherous social milieu. Both girls have been negatively exposed on social media—Lauren's daughter for eating problems and Alice's daughter for sexual activities with Daniel Bailey's son. The haunting words "it's a family matter," and the secret shames elided by the phrase, have repercussions for all the characters.

Harper has chosen an apt title for the novel, one with several possible meanings. The most obvious meaning alludes to the wilderness that swallows the five women during their corporate team-building adventure. They have been sent into the wild Giralang Ranges in late autumn with only basic camping supplies, limited food and water, one map, and one contraband mobile phone. When they go off course after their first night of camping, they become hopelessly lost. Nature is not kind. Kangaroo trails look like hiking paths, leading the group to take a wrong turn. After one woman slips and drops her water canteen, another falls into a raging river, trying to rescue it. Further essential equipment is lost as she is pulled from the water. Cold temperatures and lack of shelter cause additional problems for the group. Hungry, cold, and frightened, the women turn on each other, with Alice at the heart of most of the disagreements. Beth dislikes Alice's attitude and the way Alice takes advantage of Bree. Bree is learning that she means less to Alice than she had thought and remembers times that her boss has taken advantage of her. Lauren remembers childhood taunting from her more popular high school classmate while believing that Alice's daughter Margot has continued in her mother's path by torturing Lauren's daughter, who already struggles with emotional issues. Jill's antagonism toward Alice is more a result of the other woman's selfish demands that the group work harder to find their way back to civilization, ostensibly so that she can go to Margot's awards ceremony. Though it is unclear whether Jill knows about Alice's involvement with the federal financial crimes unit, there is the suggestion that this could be the basis of further problems between Jill and Alice.

These disagreements suggest that the title may also refer to Alice herself. Alice is an attractive but hard woman who has fought for her high position in BaileyTennants' corporate hierarchy. Those who know her see her as overly ambitious and mean, out only for herself. Having turned informant to save her own reputation reinforces this image, even for Aaron and Carmen. Alice's cruelty toward her colleagues and self-centeredness raise several troubling questions for those investigating her disappearance. Did she leave the group to return to civilization on her own, was she harmed by Martin Kovac's son, or was she attacked by a member of her own group for a more personal reason?

To a lesser extent, Aaron could also be interpreted as a force of nature. Readers familiar with *The Dry* will recognize that he was injured when a fire swept the drought-stricken landscape of Kiewarra, his fictional hometown, and that his survival was nothing short of a miracle. In *Force of Nature*, he finds a series of his father's maps with notations regarding several popular hiking areas, including the Giralang Ranges. These maps give him extra insight into the natural dangers the missing woman might face. Finally, his compassionate personality leads him to jump into the waters of a treacherous waterfall to save another character's life without regard for his own.

Critical reception of the second work in the series has been largely positive. Dan Forrest, writing for the *Library Journal*, compliments the "realistically complex personalities" and the "satisfying yet not gratuitous conclusion." Jane Murphy's *Booklist* review touts that Harper "manages to match her debut's intensity with another riveting, tension-driven thriller." The *Kirkus* reviewer comments on the novel's "crackerjack plotting" and "hidden depths." Although the *Publishers Weekly* review states that "certain plot strands seem contrived," it praises Harper, saying that she "once again shows herself to be a storytelling force to be reckoned with." The novel has been short-listed as a fiction finalist for the Australian Independent Booksellers' 2018 Indie Book Awards.

Theresa L. Stowell, PhD

Review Sources

Review of *Force of Nature*, by Jane Harper. *Kirkus Reviews*, 1 Dec. 2017, p. 1. *Literary Reference Center Plus*, search.ebscohost.com/login.aspx?direct=true&db=lkh&AN=127742550&site=lrc-plus. Accessed 9 Oct. 2018.

Review of *Force of Nature*, by Jane Harper. *Publishers Weekly*, 23 Oct. 2017, p. 63. *Literary Reference Center Plus*, search.ebscohost.com/login.aspx?direct=true&db=lkh&AN=125843331&site=lrc-plus. Accessed 9 Oct. 2018.

Forrest, Dan. Review of *Force of Nature*, by Jane Harper. *Library Journal*, 15 Oct. 2017, p. 71. *Literary Reference Center Plus*, search.ebscohost.com/login.aspx?direct=true&db=lkh&AN=125690910&site=lrc-plus. Accessed 9 Oct. 2018.

Murphy, Jane. Review of *Force of Nature*, by Jane Harper. *Booklist*, 15 Nov. 2017, p. 26. *Literary Reference Center Plus*, search.ebscohost.com/login.aspx?direct=true&db=lkh&AN=126411000&site=lrc-plus. Accessed 9 Oct. 2018.

Stasio, Marilyn. "Taking One for the Team." Review of *Force of Nature*, by Jane Harper. *The New York Times Book Review*, 4 Mar. 2018, p. 11.

Frankenstein in Baghdad

Author: Ahmed Saadawi (b. 1973)
First published: *Frānkištāyn fī Baġdād,* 2013, in Iraq
Translated: from the Arabic by Jonathan Wright
Publisher: Penguin Books (New York). 288 pp.
Type of work: Novel
Time: 2005–6
Locale: Baghdad, Iraq

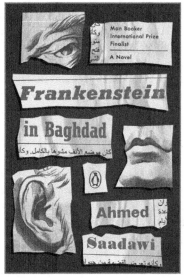

Courtesy of Penguin

Frankenstein in Baghdad *is a loose retelling of Mary Shelley's classic horror novel. Set in Iraq's capital during the city's occupation by American forces, it offers insight into the terrible effects of pervasive violence on society.*

Principal characters
HADI, a junk dealer
WHATSITSNAME, a monster he creates from various body parts
MAHMOUD AL-SAWADI, a young journalist who covers the monster's exploits
ELISHVA, an elderly widow who believes the monster is her missing son

Iraqi author Ahmed Saadawi first published his third novel, *Frankenstein in Baghdad,* in Arabic in 2013. It quickly won much acclaim, winning the 2014 International Prize for Arabic Fiction (making Saadawi the first Iraqi to win the prestigious award). The book was then translated into English by British translator and journalist Jonathan Wright in 2018, and more accolades soon followed. Later in 2018 the translation was named a finalist for the Man Booker International Prize, signaling the work's great reception by the global literary community.

Saadawi, a trained journalist, first published a book of poetry called *Anniversary of Bad Songs* in 2000. His other novels include *The Beautiful Country* (2004), *Indeed He Dreams or Plays or Dies* (2008) and *The Chalk Door* (2017). In 2010, he was named one of the thirty-nine best Arab writers under age forty by the Hay Festival's Beirut39 competition. Saadawi was born and raised in Baghdad, Iraq, and the tumultuous, violent experience of his country would significantly influence his writing. Indeed, *Frankenstein in Baghdad* was written as a reaction to his home city's occupation by American forces during the Iraq War (2003–11).

As the title suggests, the novel is a loose retelling of Mary Shelley's 1818 classic *Frankenstein; Or, The Modern Prometheus.* In Shelley's foundational horror novel, a young scientist named Victor Frankenstein is driven to create a living man stitched together from various corpses. The story provides incisive social commentary, both through the misunderstood monster himself and through Frankenstein, who is almost immediately horrified by what he has done. Similarly, in *Frankenstein in Baghdad* a man assembles parts from multiple dead bodies into a single body, only for the creation to take on a life of its own and initiate a bizarre chain of events. While from there the plot details of Saadawi's novel largely depart from those of its inspiration, the book continues the tradition of using horror to comment on very real social issues.

Like the original *Frankenstein, Frankenstein in Baghdad* has a frame story structure. In Shelley's version, the story of the monster is told in a series of letters from a ship captain, who describes meeting Dr. Frankenstein and hearing the tale second-hand; the section of the book ostensibly narrated by the monster is understood as coming from Frankenstein's memory. This classic literary device suggests that the story being told is not a work of fiction devised by the author, but a true story that the author discovered and was compelled to share. It is a particularly fruitful device for stories that involve some element that cannot be explained in the natural world. Continuing this tradition, *Frankenstein in Baghdad* is presented as the contents of a top-secret government file. A character called the writer, ostensibly Saadawi, has written the story after meeting the journalist Mahmoud al-Sawadi. Mahmoud conducted interviews with all of the characters involved, and even gave a voice recorder to the monster, accounting for the sections from its perspective. The author's written account, it is suggested, is being suppressed by the government because, contrary to the official narrative, the monster has never been caught.

© Safa Alwan

Ahmed Saadawi is an award-winning Iraqi novelist. His novel Frankenstein in Baghdad *won the International Prize for Arabic Fiction and was a finalist for the Man Booker International Prize. His other works include* The Beautiful Country *(2004),* Indeed He Dreams or Plays or Dies *(2008), and* The Chalk Door *(2017).*

Central to both Shelley and Saadawi's narratives is the creation of the monster. However, Saadawi replaces his predecessor's archetypal mad scientist with a junk dealer named Hadi. A poor drunk, Hadi is happy enough telling tall tales to the patrons of his favorite coffee shop, but after the death of his roommate and close friend, a young man named Nahem, he feels compelled to embark on a strange mission. Nahem was killed in a suicide bombing—an all-too common occurrence in Baghdad circa 2005, as the city is rife with violence from the American occupation and longstanding sectarian conflict. When Hadi goes to the morgue to retrieve his friend's body, he discovers there is no intact body to retrieve. Only fragments of Nahem will be buried. When Hadi complains, an exhausted technician implores him to take miscellaneous parts from other fragmented corpses and create a whole body himself. After the funeral, Hadi is compelled to do exactly this, raiding recent bombing sites for arms, ears, and noses. He fashions a single corpse in his junk shop, intending to bury it in honor of people like Nahem who were robbed of a proper burial. But before he can, the body is inhabited by the spirit of yet another bombing victim and sets off on its own. The story then becomes not only a gripping portrait of war-torn Iraq, but also a complex, surrealist exploration of violence and atonement.

While Hadi and the monster, eventually dubbed Whatsitsname, are the central figures, several other prominent characters quickly become involved. In fact, much of the first chapter takes the perspective of an elderly Christian woman named Elishva, who lives in a crumbling but still beautiful large house in the Bataween neighborhood of Baghdad. Her daughters and grandchildren have left the country and her husband is dead, but Elishva insists on staying in the old house despite the war. A mangy cat and a painted portrait of Saint George are her only company. She believes the portrait speaks to her. It promises her that her son Daniel, who disappeared twenty years before after being forced to fight in a previous war, will soon return to her. So, Elishva waits.

Saadawi's story shifts perspective abruptly, and early in the book, after the reader has met Hadi, a young security guard named Hasib Mohamed Jaafar is introduced. Hasib is killed in a suicide bombing, though he does not realize it right away. He is a soul without a body—a terrible condition, as the ghost of a teenage boy warns him. He must find a body right away or risk a terrible fate. Hasib, grief-stricken by the loss of his life, pours himself into the first body he sees, slumped in an alleyway. The body, of course, is Hadi's monstrous creation. The first person the newly animated monster encounters is Elishva, who mistakes him for her long-lost son and welcomes him in despite his grotesque appearance.

The monster cannot stay with the old woman; he is compelled to avenge his own death and the deaths of those whose parts make up his body. There is a horrific, poetic logic to it all. As Whatsitsname kills, his limbs putrefy and fall off, compelling him to find more victims to replace those limbs. This, of course, means he has more parts of himself to avenge, creating an escalating cycle of violence with rich metaphorical implications. Eventually, the monster moves beyond killing direct perpetrators and murders almost anyone to refresh his decaying parts. He justifies his actions by reflecting that everyone is guilty of something, a thought-provoking idea in light of wartime tragedy.

Contingencies and twists of fate continue to shape the plot, emphasizing the randomness of war and violence. "Isn't life a blend of things that are plausible and others that are hard to believe?" says the journalist Mahmoud, who comes to document Whatsitsname's activities. And the way the killings—and the monster's very existence—are received by the press, the public, and the authorities is as meaningful as the action itself. Whatsitsname eventually garners enough attention to have three separate cults formed in his name. The disagreements among these cults become another metaphor for sectarian conflict and how fruitless it is to make any sense of it.

Even as it develops in its own unique way, *Frankenstein in Baghdad* includes several parallels to Shelley's masterpiece. In each, the monster haunts its creator, ruing him for giving it life in the first place. The monsters both prefer to kill people by strangling them, but perhaps more importantly, believe that they are deeply misunderstood. Whatsitsname sees itself as a force of justice and a literal embodiment of a diverse Iraq, even as to others he is a representation of fear itself. These tensions come to a head as things spiral further and further from initial intentions. Toward the novel's end, another person is charged with the monster's crimes, but like the violence that continues to consume parts of Iraq, the insatiable Whatsitsname will never be satisfied.

Saadawi's novel was critically praised upon its original 2013 publication, and Wright's translation likewise received positive reviews. Dwight Garner of the *New York Times* praised it as a "complex allegory" combining horror and humor, noting that the author's "tone can be sly, but his intentions are deadly serious." In a review for the *Guardian*, Sarah Perry called the book "a remarkable achievement, and one that, regrettably, is unlikely ever to lose its urgent relevancy." She also detected the influence of Franz Kafka, the nineteenth-century master of existential dread and surrealism, in addition to Shelley. Sam Metz of the *Los Angeles Review of Books* categorized the book's world as a dystopia for dystopian times, particularly considering the social and political climate in which the English translation appeared. Some critics did note weaknesses: Rayyan Al-Shawaf of the *Chicago Tribune* suggested many of the supporting characters were less than captivating, and *Publishers Weekly* felt the connection to the original Frankenstein failed to fully sustain itself. However, even more mixed reviews acknowledged the novel's strength in portraying an Iraq so wrought by violence that a murdering monster seems hardly fictional.

Molly Hagan

Review Sources

Al-Shawaf, Rayyan. "'Frankenstein in Baghdad' by Ahmed Saadawi Offers Powerful Allegory." Review of *Frankenstein in Baghdad*, by Ahmed Saadawi. *Chicago Tribune*, 24 Jan. 2018, www.chicagotribune.com/lifestyles/books/sc-books-frankenstein-baghdad-ahmed-saadawi-0124-story.html. Accessed 8 Oct. 2018.

Garner, Dwight. "In 'Frankenstein in Baghdad,' a Fantastical Manifestation of War's Cruelties." Review of *Frankenstein in Baghdad*, by Ahmed Saadawi. *The New York Times*, 22 Jan. 2018, www.nytimes.com/2018/01/22/books/review-frankenstein-in-baghdad-ahmed-saadawi.html. 8 Oct. 2018.

Metz, Sam. "Fiction of Dystopian Times: Ahmed Saadawi's 'Frankenstein in Baghdad.'" Review of *Frankenstein in Baghdad*, by Ahmed Saadawi. *Los Angeles Review of Books*, 5 Jun. 2018, lareviewofbooks.org/article/fiction-dystopian-times-ahmed-saadawis-frankenstein-baghdad/#!. 8 Oct. 2018.

Perry, Sarah. "Frankenstein in Baghdad by Ahmed Saadawi Review—Strange, Violent and Wickedly Funny." Review of *Frankenstein in Baghdad*, by Ahmed Saadawi. *The Guardian*, 16 Feb. 2018, www.theguardian.com/books/2018/feb/16/frankenstein-in-baghdad-by-ahmed-saadawi-review. 8 Oct. 2018.

Scranton, Roy. "A Surreal Story from Baghdad." Review of *Frankenstein in Baghdad*, by Ahmed Saadawi. *The New Republic*, 2 Mar. 2018, newrepublic.com/article/147263/surreal-story-baghdad. 8 Oct. 2018.

The Friend

Author: Sigrid Nunez (b. ca. 1950)
Publisher: Riverhead Books (New York).
  224 pp.
Type of work: Novel
Time: Present day with flashbacks
Locales: New York City, the Hamptons

Courtesy of Penguin

Sigrid Nunez's seventh novel, The Friend, *explores grief and companionship through a woman's relationship with a Great Dane following its owner's suicide. Told through a series of flashbacks to the narrator's inter-actions with her mentor—the dog owner in question—and her present-day attempts to make sense of the loss and wrangle a giant dog in the cramped spaces of New York City,* The Friend *is as much a meditation on art, connection, and mortality as it is a tale of loss and recovery.*

Principal characters

NARRATOR, a professor and writer who lives in New York City
THE LOST FRIEND, her mentor, who killed himself and who is referred to as "you"
    throughout the book
APOLLO, a large, stubborn Great Dane who comes to live with her after her friend's
    death

Sigrid Nunez's National Book Award–winning novel *The Friend* opens with a series of epigraphs from Natalia Ginzburg, Hans Christian Andersen, and Nicholson Baker. Each speaks to a specific aspect of the story that follows. Ginzburg's touches upon grief and writing, while Andersen's introduces the image of a large, but gentle, dog. But the Baker quote, which comes from an interview with the *Paris Review*, cuts to the quick of the story. He states, "The question any novel is really trying to answer is, Is life worth living?"

    Following this epigraph, the novel begins rather abstractly, telling a story about a group of Cambodian women living in California in the 1980s. They women are war refugees who have lost their sense of sight. However, doctors cannot find a cause for the affliction. The prognosis is psychosomatic blindness brought on by years of violence, trauma, and loss.

    The unnamed narrator uses this anecdote to begin her story about her lost friend. "This was the last thing you and I talked about while you were still alive," the narrator says. She then notes that her friend's obituary contained two mistakes: the date he moved from London to New York and the spelling of the maiden name of his first wife.

Following the memorial service of her friend, the narrator slips back into her every-day life but often experiences periods of sobbing that leave her bedridden. After some time has passed, she receives an invitation from her friend's third wife, requesting that they meet at a café near the deceased man's brownstone.

The reason for the visit? The man's third wife is requesting the narrator take his Great Dane. The narrator describes her reaction to the surprising request as "equally relieved and annoyed" and tells the other woman that she cannot do this favor: her apartment building does not allow dogs. Ultimately, though, she does take in the Great Dane, Apollo, making room for his gigantic frame in her tiny apartment. Unable to leave the dog alone, she tells her family she cannot visit them for Christmas and soon comes to enjoy taking Apollo for long, solitary walks in the cold weather.

The premise—the death of a close friend, the adoption of his dog—has the poten-tial to devolve into a clichéd tale; however, what Nunez weaves from the relationship between the two is original and poignant. Nunez's narrator must rearrange her life—letting the dog have her bed and finding a more dog-friendly place to live—just as the dog must rearrange his. Told by a neighbor that the dog has been howling during the day, the narrator thinks, "He has to forget you. He has to forget you and fall in love with me. That's what has to happen."

As the narrator works through her own feelings of sadness, she comes to under-stand Apollo, considering a pet therapist and music and massage to help quell his depression. By taking care of another being, the narrator is able to navigate her own grief. "The only animal that commits suicide is also the only animal that weeps," writes Nunez. True, Apollo does not exhibit the same signs of grief as a human; how-ever, the two beings find solace in each other.

The Friend drifts between time periods and locations in a dreamlike manner, giving the prose the disconnected feeling someone in mourning experiences. However, what makes *The Friend* stand apart from other novels about death and grief is its unique approach to exploring loss through works of literature, art, and philosophy. For example, in part 8, the narrator comments that one piece of advice often given to writers is to read their work out loud to find moments of awkward prose, lulls in rhythm, and general typos. The narrator is preparing to do this as Apollo wakes from a nap across the apartment. As he approaches the desk, the two are eye to eye—the narrator sitting and Apollo standing. The narrator discovers that Apollo loves to be read to as she goes through the draft of her prose. Following this discovery, she begins to read aloud to the dog, which she finds soothing as well. The first book she shares with him is Rainer Maria Rilke's *Letters to a Young Poet*.

The introduction of her reading the book is followed by a meditation on both the book and Rilke, his body of work, and the philosophical teachings of her writing. This is soon followed by further reminiscence of the lost friend. "I think about how there

Sigrid Nunez is the author of seven nov-els, including A Feather on the Breath of God *(1995),* For Rouenna *(2001),* The Last of Her Kind *(2006), and* Salvation City *(2010). She is also the author of a memoir about Susan Sontag,* Sempre Susan *(2011). A recipient of the Whiting Award, Rome Prize in Literature, and the Berlin Prize, she teaches in undergradu-ate and MFA programs throughout the East Coast.*

was a time when you and I believed that writing was the best thing we could ever hope to do with our lives," she says. "I think about how you had started telling your students that if there was anything else they could do with their lives instead of becoming writers, any other profession, they should do it."

The narrator also meditates on Flannery O'Connor; J. R. Ackerley, who wrote a memoir about his German shepherd dog, Queenie, called *My Dog Tulip*; and countless films, among many other references. In his review for the *Los Angeles Review of Books*, Charles Taylor said of Nunez's use of literature in novel, "At times *The Friend* reads like a writer's notebook—diary entries sharing space with literary anecdotes, themes pursued for a few pages before another train of thought takes over."

The Friend's tone is nearly as important to the novel's overall effectiveness as its plotline. Nunez's narrator creates a specter from the memory of her lost friend, continuously addressing him throughout the entirety of the book. Apollo acts as a bridge between the two, as their relationship deepens. That specter is also created through the narrator's passive movement through her thoughts. Her actions tend to be overcome by her mind, delightfully so. A simple walk with the dog turns to page upon page of philosophical meditation, taking the reader on a trip through the narrator's highly intellectual mind as well as down a New York City street.

In 2018, *The Friend* won the National Book Award after being widely hailed by critics and readers alike. In her review for the *New York Review of Books*, where Nunez worked as a young writer and editor, Laura Kipnis wrote, "*The Friend* is a delicious read, but also a wrenching one. All perfect friendships eventually come to an end, and less-than-perfect ones too: this is a book about two deaths." Dwight Garner, in his review for the *New York Times*, wrote that the novel's tone "is mournful and resonant. It sheds rosin, like the bow of a cello."

The Friend marks a brilliant new release from an underrated writer, recalling the haunting, subtle prose of Nunez's other works, such as her first novel, *A Feather on the Breath of God* (1995), and the widely praised *The Last of Her Kind* (2006).

Melynda Fuller

Review Sources

Review of *The Friend*, by Sigrid Nunez. *Kirkus*, 1 Oct. 2017, www.kirkusreviews. com/book-reviews/sigrid-nunez/the-friend-nunez. Accessed 11 Feb. 2019.

Review of *The Friend*, by Sigrid Nunez. *Publishers Weekly*, 4 Dec. 2017, www. publishersweekly.com/978-0-7352-1944-1. Accessed 11 Feb. 2019.

Garner, Dwight. "Mourning with the Help of a Great Dane." Review of *The Friend*, by Sigrid Nunez. *The New York Times*, 5 Feb. 2018, www.nytimes. com/2018/02/05/books/review-friend-sigrid-nunez.html. Accessed 8 Feb. 2018.

Kipnis, Laura. "You Old Dog!" Review of *The Friend*, by Sigrid Nunez. *The New York Review of Books*, 28 June 2018, www.nybooks.com/articles/2018/06/28/you-old-dog-sigrid-nunez. Accessed 8 Feb. 2018.

McAlpin, Heller. "'The Friend' Is No Shaggy Dog Story." Review of *The Friend*, by Sigrid Nunez. *NPR*, 23 Jan. 2018, www.npr.org/2018/01/23/579233885/the-friend-is-no-shaggy-dog-story. Accessed 8 Feb. 2018.
Taylor, Charles. "Melancholy Dane: Sigrid Nunez's 'The Friend.'" Review of *The Friend*, by Sigrid Nunez. *Los Angeles Review of Books*, 21 Mar. 2018, lareviewofbooks.org/article/melancholy-dane-sigrid-nunezs-the-friend. Accessed 8 Feb. 2018.

From Cold War to Hot Peace
An American Ambassador in Putin's Russia

Author: Michael McFaul (b. 1963)
Publisher: Houghton Mifflin Harcourt (New York). 528 pp.
Type of work: Memoir
Time: 1990s–2010s
Locale: Russia

In former ambassador Michael McFaul's memoir From Cold War to Hot Peace: An American Ambassador in Putin's Russia, *the author recalls his career as a policymaker and diplomat in Russia.*

Principal personages
MICHAEL MCFAUL, the author
VLADIMIR PUTIN, president of Russia
PRESIDENT BARACK OBAMA, forty-fourth president of the United States

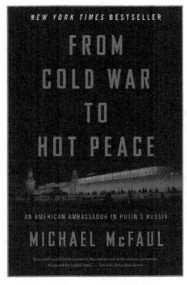

Courtesy of Houghton Mifflin Harcourt

Michael McFaul's memoir, *From Cold War to Hot Peace: An American Ambassador in Putin's Russia* chronicles the author's professional career as a policymaker, diplomat, and ambassador, and his dogged pursuit of improved relations with Russia, ultimately as the US ambassador to that country. McFaul writes that he first became interested in Russia—at the time the Soviet Union—as a high school student in Montana. During college, he traveled to the country for the first time, and in the early 1990s, as the Soviet Union was crumbling, he joined pro-democracy activists in the streets of Moscow demanding change. The end of the Cold War—the decades-long standoff between the United States and the Soviet Union, the two most heavily armed countries on the planet—was certainly cause for celebration, but people at that time could not have foretold the later period of US-Russian tensions that McFaul aptly describes as a "hot peace." In about 500 pages of history, policy, and personal anecdotes, McFaul attempts to understand how the two countries got into such a situation, but his narrative keeps returning to one particular answer—or rather, one particular man: the corrupt, autocratic Russian president Vladimir Putin. In the book's introduction, Mc-Faul recalls a meeting with Putin in 2012, shortly after he became US ambassador to Russia under US president Barack Obama. McFaul was shocked in the meeting when Putin accused him of seeking to ruin US-Russia relations. That vitriol would characterize McFaul's interactions with Putin throughout his tenure as ambassador. More broadly, the anecdote serves as a chilling example of Putin's dangerous and vengeful calculus when it comes to foreign relations. McFaul resigned his post in 2014, just before Russia invaded Ukraine. Years later, in July 2018, Putin asked US president

Donald Trump to make McFaul available to the Russian government for questioning in its blatantly political case against American British businessman Bill Browder. Alarmingly, Trump expressed openness to the idea.

Putin, a former agent with the KGB, the Soviet secret police force, came to power after Boris Yeltsin's resignation in 1999. He served as president from 2000 until 2008, when he became prime minister (the second-most powerful position in the Russian government) and Dmitri Medvedev became president. The Medvedev years, in McFaul's view, were extraordinarily fruitful for US–Russia relations, but in 2011, Putin announced that he would seek another term as president. The announcement triggered street protests by Russians alarmed at rising authoritarianism, but Putin handily won the 2012 election, judged flawed by international observers; he was reelected in 2016. Putin's second ascension to power upended the fragile relationship with the United States, and McFaul's term as ambassador lasted only two years before he stepped down. Readers

Michael McFaul is a political science professor at Stanford University. He served as the senior director for Russian affairs on the National Security Council from 2008 to 2011, and as US ambassador to Russia from 2012 to 2014. He is also the author of several previous books, including Russia's Unfinished Revolution: Political Change from Gorbachev to Putin *(2001).*

looking for McFaul's analysis of Russian meddling in the 2016 election will be disappointed (though he does touch on it briefly in the book's epilogue). Instead, McFaul's story, concerning the interim years of tentative friendship between the US and Russia, provides context for the current state of affairs.

McFaul is a political science professor at Stanford University. He has authored a number of books about Russia, including *Russia's Unfinished Revolution: Political Change from Gorbachev to Putin* (2001). He has also written numerous articles and essays about Russia and foreign policy for major newspapers including the *Washington Post*. McFaul joined Obama's campaign as a Russia advisor in 2008. After the election, he was appointed senior director for Russian affairs on the National Security Council. In the book, McFaul writes about the challenge of transitioning from dreaming up big ideas as a professor, to implementing tangible policies as a bureaucrat. But McFaul was eager to succeed in his new post. His crowning achievement was an overarching policy directive known as the "Reset" of US relations with Russia. Deployed during Obama's first term, the Reset (McFaul consistently capitalizes it) sought to pursue a positive relationship with Russia while still holding the country accountable for autocratic behavior and human rights abuses. It was a delicate diplomatic dance, but Obama and then-president Medvedev made progress on a number of issues regarding arms control, Iran's nuclear program, and the war in Afghanistan. A significant chunk of McFaul's book explores the intricacies of the Reset and McFaul's experiences working closely with Obama. (McFaul writes that he attended nearly every meeting and listened in on every phone call between Obama and Medvedev.) If the iconic image of Obama and Medvedev sharing burgers at a famous diner in Virginia is the emblem of the Reset's success, then the assassination of Libyan dictator Muammar Gaddafi is the emblem of the policy's ultimate failure, McFaul argues. Putin was outraged by Medvedev's decision—at the behest of Obama—to abstain from rather than veto a UN Security Council resolution approving NATO airstrikes in Libya. Medvedev risked precious political capital with Putin on the understanding that the attacks would not precipitate regime change. Of course, after Gaddafi's death in the melee, that equation was fundamentally changed.

Where Medvedev often showed willingness to support the US and embrace American culture—McFaul recalls how the president traveled to Silicon Valley and opened a Twitter account—Putin views the US with pointed suspicion. When McFaul assumed his post as ambassador, moving into the ornate Spaso House in Moscow, he immediately felt the chill of Putin's Russia. In the lead-up to the 2012 election, Putin cast the US as Russia's international foe. More specifically, Putin singled out McFaul as an interlocutor intent on fomenting revolution in Russia. As McFaul puts it, "I was not Mr. Reset, but Mr. Revolutionary. . . . For the rest of my time in Russia as ambassador, I battled nearly every day to dispel that myth, and never really succeeded." The state-controlled media released "documentaries" about McFaul's secret mission, and pro-Putin groups kept constant vigil outside of Spaso House. Worse, government agents harassed McFaul's family and staff—a serious breach of diplomatic convention. For his part, McFaul tried to appear unruffled. He fought for greater transparency, actively maintaining a Twitter account and holding literally thousands of public events and lectures at Spaso House. Ordinary Russians were charmed by McFaul's obvious love for Russian culture and his facility with the language; their praise enraged Putin. But as McFaul writes, the worst was yet to come. After McFaul resigned his post—flying home on the high of a reasonably successful Olympic Games in Sochi in early 2014—Russia invaded Ukraine and subsequently annexed Crimea. It was a shocking violation of the post–World War II order. Not long after, according to the assessment of the US intelligence community, Russian intelligence began working to influence the results of the 2016 US presidential election. As for McFaul, he discovered that he had been banned from the country in 2016. The last US ambassador to be declared persona non grata in Russia was George Kennan, who was ousted by Joseph Stalin in 1952.

Reviewers offered tempered praise for McFaul's book, but also critically engaged with its various premises. A reviewer for *Kirkus* described the book as a "gimlet-eyed view of the new Cold War," lamenting alongside McFaul how Trump's rise—with his accusations of "fake news" and preoccupation with a "deep state"—has "played straight into Putin's conspiracy theories" about the US. A reviewer for *Publishers Weekly* described *From Cold War to Hot Peace* as a "smart, personable mix of memoir and political analysis," concluding, "The author's privileged perspective as both an academic and policy maker makes this an essential volume for those trying to understand one of the US's most significant current rivals." Archie Brown, an author and professor at Oxford who reviewed the book for the *Washington Post*, described it as a "vigorously argued political memoir," though he was unconvinced by McFaul's assertion that the "new ideological struggle . . . between Russia and the West, [is] not between communism and capitalism but between democracy and autocracy." Democratic socialist countries, allied with the US during the Cold War, did not consider themselves defenders of capitalism, Brown wrote. By the same token, the US has allied itself with more brutal autocrats. A more nuanced analysis in this regard, Brown argued, is needed. Brown engages McFaul on other points as well. "How did we get from the relative amity of the negotiated end of the Cold War to the mutual distrust and dangerous tensions of today?" he wrote. "McFaul takes that issue seriously, and his contribution to the debate is significant, based on his experience as a political practitioner as well as an academic analyst. But I find it only partly convincing." Brown's review in full serves as a smart counter-text to McFaul's book. Daniel Beer, an author and historian who reviewed the book for the *New York Times*, similarly challenged McFaul, questioning the author's focus on Putin at the expense of other hard-liners in the Kremlin. Blaming Putin for deteriorating relations, Beer wrote, "holds out the promise that Kremlin policy toward the West might pivot once again when Putin finally retires or is pushed out. Maybe so, but the more pessimistic view is that Putin represents a now-entrenched nationalism that sees the liberal international order as a mere smokescreen for the advancement of Western political agendas. Deep-rooted antagonism toward the United States might well endure long after Putin has gone."

Molly Hagan

Review Sources

Beer, Daniel. "Does Vladimir Putin Speak for the Russian People?" Review of *From Cold War to Hot Peace: An American Ambassador in Putin's Russia*, by Michael McFaul. *The New York Times*, 6 July 2018, www.nytimes.com/2018/07/06/books/review/michael-mcfaul-from-cold-war-to-hot-peace.html. Accessed 17 Dec. 2018.

Brown, Archie. "How Did the End of the Cold War Become Today's Dangerous Tensions with Russia?" Review of *From Cold War to Hot Peace: An American Ambassador in Putin's Russia*, by Michael McFaul. *The Washington Post*, 4 May 2018, www.washingtonpost.com/outlook/how-did-the-end-of-the-cold-war-become-todays-dangerous-tensions-with-russia/2018/05/04/d54d527e-3d03-11e8-8d53-eba0ed2371cc_story.html. Accessed 17 Dec. 2018.

Review of *From Cold War to Hot Peace: An American Ambassador in Putin's Russia*, by Michael McFaul. *Kirkus*, 3 Mar. 2018, www.kirkusreviews.com/book-reviews/michael-mcfaul/from-cold-war-to-hot-peace/. Accessed 17 Dec. 2018.

Review of *From Cold War to Hot Peace: An American Ambassador in Putin's Russia*, by Michael McFaul. *Publishers Weekly*, 5 Mar. 2018, www.publishersweekly.com/978-0-544-71624-7. Accessed 17 Dec. 2018.

Green, Lloyd. "From Cold War to Hot Peace Review: Obama Ambassador Charts Path to Trump and Russia." Review of *From Cold War to Hot Peace: An American Ambassador in Putin's Russia*, by Michael McFaul. *The Guardian*, 9 May 2018, www.theguardian.com/books/2018/may/09/from-cold-war-hot-peace-book-review-trump-russia. Accessed 17 Dec. 2018.

Fruit of the Drunken Tree

Author: Ingrid Rojas Contreras
Publisher: Doubleday (New York). 320 pp.
Type of work: Novel
Time: Early 1990s
Locales: Bogotá, Colombia; East Los Angeles, California

Ingrid Rojas Contreras's debut novel, Fruit of the Drunken Tree, *is a fictionalized account of her family's difficulties in violence-wracked Bogotá, Colombia. Set during the reign of drug king Pablo Escobar, the story is narrated by characters from vastly different backgrounds who are both simply trying to survive.*

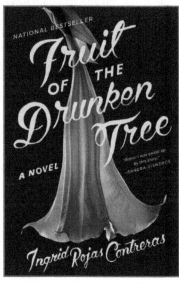

Courtesy of Knopf Doubleday

Principal characters

CHULA SANTIAGO, the main narrator, a young girl from a middle-class family
PETRONA SÁNCHEZ, her family's preteen maid and housekeeper
CASSANDRA SANTIAGO, her older sister
ALMA SANTIAGO, her mother, who comes from a poor background
ANTONIO SANTIAGO, her often-absent father, an oil worker
GORRIÓN, Petrona's boyfriend

Slums exist around the world, characterized by the poverty and marginalization of their inhabitants. Indeed, the negative connotations of the word "slum" begin to hint at the challenges people living in such conditions face. In the Caribbean, Central America, and South America, where many sprawling informal communities have grown up around urban centers, the variety of colorful words and phrases referring to these places even more clearly illustrates the depth of the issue. In Argentina, they are called *villas de emergencia* ("emergency villages") or *villas miséria* ("misery villages"), while Mexico has the similar term *cinturón de miséria* ("belt of misery") as well as *cartolandia* ("cardboard-land"). In the Dominican Republic, they are bluntly called *barrio malo* ("bad neighborhood"). Another common term, used in Colombia among other nations, is *invasión*, a designation that captures the negative public perception of slum dwellers—many of whom come from rural areas in search of work—as unwanted invaders. Whatever the name, these are communities of abject poverty—often without electricity, running water, or sewage lines—created and shaped by complex social, economic, and political forces.

The invasiónes of Bogotá, Colombia, figure prominently in Ingrid Rojas Contreras's debut novel, *Fruit of the Drunken Tree* (2018). In fact, the first character described in the opening lines, Petrona Sánchez, is a resident of a Bogotá invasión called simply the

Hills, a squalid tangle of makeshift shacks on steep terrain with a tendency to collapse and wash away in heavy downpours. This initial introduction comes through the eyes of the book's primary narrator, Chula Santiago, who is reflecting on an old photograph of Petrona in her midteens, shown holding her newborn son. The novel uses a classic frame structure, as fifteen-year-old Chula, living in Los Angeles, California, recounts her earlier life in Bogotá in the early 1990s, when Petrona served as her family's maid. Chula's narration is interspersed with short chapters from Petrona's point of view, giving readers two quite different perspectives on life in and out of the slums.

The main arc of the story begins when Chula, at seven years old, meets Petrona, thirteen. Chula's beautiful, fiery mother, Alma, an occasional tarot-card reader who grew up in an invasión herself, often hires poor young women to help as maids and caregivers for her two young daughters, because her husband, Antonio, a worker in an

© Jeremiah Barber

Ingrid Rojas Contreras's stories and essays have been published in numerous periodicals. The recipient of fellowships and awards from the National Association of Latino Arts and Culture, the Bread Loaf Writer's Conference, and others, she has taught at the University of San Francisco and worked in public radio.

oil field, is often away from home for long periods of time. (Alma is sometimes also gone from home while her husband is away, fooling around with other men in retaliation for her husband's suspected unfaithfulness.) Petrona is the latest such worker. Chula is particularly taken with Petrona because she seldom speaks more than a few syllables, is capable of walking with cat-like silence, and seems mysterious.

The Santiago family lives in a three-story house with barred windows within a gated, guarded community of similar dwellings. In the front yard grows a distinctive example of the Drunken Tree—which becomes both a plot device and a symbol of nightmarish conditions prevailing in Colombia during the story. Also called Devil Tree, the plant is *Brugmansia arbore alba*. Though attractive, it is toxic. In ancient times, tribes used leaves, flowers, and fruit to create a drug that made people tame and zombie-like, so intoxicated servants could be buried alive alongside deceased chieftains to accompany them into the afterlife. In modern times, the tree has become the source of memory-erasing date-rape drugs.

Petrona's background is quite different from that of the Santiagos. Part of a large family descended from fair-skinned, dark-haired Spanish ancestors, she grew up on a self-sufficient rural farm. Then the guerrillas came. Their home and land were burned, and her father and several older siblings disappeared, never to be seen again. Surviving members of the Sánchez family—Petrona, her mother, and several younger siblings—migrated to Bogotá. They live in a tumbledown hovel in the Hills, constructed of used, broken, and discarded items. Petrona is breadwinner and by default head of the family. She tries to look after her younger brothers and her sister, Aurora, but cannot protect everyone. Her brother Ramón, just twelve, hangs out with a local guerrilla group that feeds him, and is eventually found dead, his small body riddled with bullets. He was probably murdered by government troops, or possibly by a rival paramilitary group. The identity of the perpetrators hardly matters: it cannot change the fact that Ramón is dead and his family has no money to bury him.

Though the Santiagos are middle-class citizens, to deprived Petrona they seem fabulously wealthy. Chula and her sister Cassandra get to attend Catholic school and church. The Santiago home, unlike the jury-rigged, dirt-floored Sánchez shelter, has actual rooms, windows, and doors. There is hot water for showering. They enjoy a varied diet, unlike Bogotá's poor, who, at every meal, eat *pan con gaseosa*, crude bread made with flavored carbonated drinks. It is because of this huge disparity in relative comfort that Petrona, persuaded by her young boyfriend, Gorrión, becomes caught up in a plot to kidnap the Santiago children and hold them for ransom. Overcome by remorse for agreeing to betray people who have treated her well—Alma, for example, makes her a dress so she can experience communion for the first time—Petrona swallows seeds from the Drunken Tree and falls ill. This only delays the inevitable for a few days, however. Once she recovers, Petrona is again forced to participate in the abduction. She ultimately assists Chula in escaping the clutches of the kidnappers, but it is an action that will cost her dearly.

The urban backdrop of *Fruit of the Drunken Tree* adds extra layers of interest and increased tension to the story. Due to drought compounded by governmental incompetence and widespread corruption, there are occasional water shortages that make the Santiago family scramble to collect what is necessary to drink or launder or bathe. There are frequent blackouts in the city, which children like Chula and Cassandra treat like a game: carrying flashlights, they play mischievous versions of hide-and-seek with a pair of impish neighborhood twins, Isa and Lala. During the time of much of the action, a civil war is under way. More than one hundred guerrilla, narco-terrorist, and paramilitary groups—including the Begrimed, Black Eagle, Alfa 83, the Crickets, Menudo, M-19, Rambo—some with vicious death squads, roam the countryside. Newspaper articles and television news broadcasts report daily about massacres, mutilations, mass graves, kidnappings, and disappearances.

One real historical figure looms large in the background throughout the story: Pablo Escobar. Engaged in various criminal activities from his teens, Escobar grew up in Medellín, about two hundred miles northwest of Bogotá. In the 1980s, as head of the Medellín cartel, he became a drug kingpin, growing fabulously wealthy while distributing tons of cocaine to the United States and elsewhere. Escobar was ruthless in protecting his ill-gotten fortune, bribing officials, killing judges and policemen, assassinating politicians, kidnapping the influential, and otherwise terrorizing ordinary citizens as a warning to never cross him. In the two years before his sudden death in 1993, Escobar contributed to the escalation of violence among competing drug cartels that made Colombia's murder rate the highest in the world. Yet despite his depredations, Escobar was considered heroic among many poor Colombians, for whom he often built schools and otherwise assisted financially. After he was killed during a shootout with government troops (described in the novel), his funeral was attended by tens of thousands of mourners.

The climate of violence and fear that Escobar created is apparent in several incidents that affect young Chula Santiago. The girl and her family see a television report on a car bomb blamed on the drug lord, with the aftermath including a little girl's leg, still wearing its shoe, lying in the middle of the street. Alma is inspired to tell her daughters what happens to a body after death, and Chula is afterward haunted by images of worms eating her skin but leaving behind bones, teeth, and hair. Chula also accompanies her mother to hear presidential candidate Luis Carlos Galán speak at a political rally, and witnesses his assassination, later attributed to Escobar. Chula is even cut by flying glass when her bedroom window is blown out by a car bomb detonated ominously close to the Santiago home.

Scenes throughout the novel, subtly playing off the opening image of a photograph, have the starkness of black-and-white snapshots taken with flashbulbs in the dark of night. Here are Chula and Cassandra, making up stories of war or accident to explain their Barbie dolls' mutilation (Cassandra compulsively chewed off the arms and legs), and Petrona bringing a new level of imagination to their play: her doll, she says, was born deformed because the mother smoked and drank while pregnant. There is Chula, making an entry in her diary about the suspicious people and vehicles she has observed passing on the next street over. Here is Cassandra, checking her backpack full of emergency supplies in case she has to flee home. There is the sorry corpse of Ramón stinking in its cheap coffin outside the Sánchez shack, Gorrión offering his meager savings to bury the young victim, and finally the body interred the only affordable way: laid to rest atop the coffin of a woman buried years earlier.

For a debut novel, *Fruit of the Drunken Tree* is mature autobiographical fiction. The two strong first-person female narrators, Chula and Petrona, are especially well drawn, but secondary and minor characters are also given considerable substance. The language used is smooth and deceptively simple, with Spanish expressions slipped here and there into passages where they naturally belong. Rojas Contreras is also skilled at using structural elements to reinforce the themes and atmosphere of the story. For example, the chapters that Chula narrates bear numbers, but Petrona's chapters are unnumbered, as if reflecting that, to the world at large, she is not important enough to count.

The critical reception to Rojas Contreras's first book was largely positive. While a few reviewers, such as that for *Kirkus*, noted some flaws, the general consensus was that the author is an emerging talent to watch. Writing for the *New York Times*, Julianne Pachico praised the "memorable prose and absorbing story line" and especially appreciated the way Petrona is given a voice of her own. In a review for the *San Francisco Chronicle*, Elizabeth Rosner called it "one of the most dazzling and devastating novels I've read in a long time."

Jack Ewing

Review Sources

Review of *Fruit of the Drunken Tree*, by Ingrid Rojas Contreras. *Kirkus*, 16 Apr. 2018, www.kirkusreviews.com/book-reviews/ingrid-rojas-contreras/fruit-of-the-drunken-tree/. Accessed 4 Feb. 2019.

Review of *Fruit of the Drunken Tree*, by Ingrid Rojas Contreras. *Publishers Weekly*, 21 May 2018, www.publishersweekly.com/978-0-385-54272-2. Accessed 4 Feb. 2019.

Pachico, Julianne. "A Novel about Growing Up in the Middle of Death." Review of *Fruit of the Drunken Tree*, by Ingrid Rojas Contreras. *The New York Times*, 25 July 2018, www.nytimes.com/2018/07/25/books/review/ingrid-rojas-contreras-fruit-of-the-drunken-tree.html. Accessed 4 Feb. 2019.

Read, Katherine. "'Drunken Tree' a Powerful Novel about Growing Up In Violent Bogotá." Review of *Fruit of the Drunken Tree*, by Ingrid Rojas Contreras. *San Francisco Examiner*, 9 Sept. 2018, www.sfexaminer.com/drunken-tree-powerful-novel-growing-violent-bogota/. Accessed 4 Feb. 2019.

Rosner, Elizabeth. Review of *Fruit of the Drunken Tree*, by Ingrid Rojas Contreras. *San Francisco Chronicle*, 26 July 2018, www.sfchronicle.com/books/article/Fruit-of-the-Drunken-Tree-by-Ingrid-Rojas-13105767.php. Accessed 4 Feb. 2019.

Fryderyk Chopin
A Life and Times

Author: Alan Walker (b. 1930)
Publisher: Farrar, Straus and Giroux (New York). 727 pp.
Type of work: Biography, history
Time: 1810–49
Locales: Poland, France, Spain, and Great Britain

With Fryderyk Chopin, *the distinguished musicologist Alan Walker presents a comprehensive biography of the great composer of piano music. Walker painstakingly sifts fact from fiction in Chopin's life, illuminating the many facets of the composer's life, including his famous and complicated relationship with the novelist George Sand. He also provides insightful commentary on Chopin's extensive catalogue of works.*

Principal personages

FRYDERYK CHOPIN, a celebrated Polish composer and pianist
MIKOLAJ CHOPIN, his father
TEKLA JUSTYNA CHOPIN, his mother
LUDWIKA CHOPIN, his sister
MARIA WODZINSKA, his fiancée until her family allowed the engagement to lapse
GEORGE SAND, a novelist, his lover for several years
FRANZ LISZT, his friend and rival, a famous composer and virtuoso pianist
JANE STIRLING, a Scottish student and supporter of his

The music of Fryderyk Chopin remains a treasured part of the classical repertory, a challenge and delight for pianists ever since the composer himself enthralled audiences with his playing. While many of Chopin's nocturnes, mazurkas, and polonaises are familiar favorites, the man himself has disappeared behind the clichéd category of Romantic composer. It is all too easy to assume him to be a Sturm und Drang artist, emoting violently through his music. Chopin's case is not helped by the fact that aside from his Polish nationality, the most remembered element of his life is his liaison with the notorious writer George Sand, who shocked her contemporaries by dressing as a man and smoking cigars. Yet, while the Romantic designation for Chopin is correct up to a point, certainly chronologically, it is wholly inadequate to fully measure the Polish composer's musical achievement. The real Chopin was an artist who revered J. S. Bach and never warmed to Ludwig van Beethoven. He was a far cry from the flamboyant Romantic pianists who stirred rapt audiences with their thunderous musical theatrics, and whenever possible shunned performing at public concerts. Chopin as a man and as a composer defies any easy categorization.

The distinguished musical scholar Alan Walker is eminently suited to recover Chopin from the historical fog of myth and indifference. He is best known as the definitive biographer of Franz Liszt, a contemporary of Chopin who fully lived up to the image of Romantic provocateur. In this work, Walker has done for Chopin what he earlier did for Liszt and provided readers with a meticulously researched and comprehensive biography. Running to 671 pages of text, this is a substantial study of a man who lived only thirty-nine years. Walker as a biographer has never shied away from length; his study of the longer-lived Liszt ran to three hefty volumes. But in Walker's hands bulk does not lead to tedium. He is an engaging writer who holds his reader's interest whether he is describing love affairs or offering sophisticated analyses of musical compositions. When nearing the end of this volume many readers will be saddened both by the premature passing of Chopin and the imminent end of Walker's narrative.

Fryderyk Chopin was born on the first day of March 1810, in a village a few miles west of Warsaw. His father was a native of France but moved to Poland and fully embraced a Polish identity, changing his name from Nicolas to Mikolaj. He worked as a tutor and, not long after his son Fryderyk's birth, took a position as instructor in French at the prestigious Warsaw Lyceum. To bolster his income, Mikolaj and his wife, Justyna, ran a small boarding school for boys. Through his parents' efforts, Fryderyk and his three sisters were raised in an atmosphere of comfortable gentility. As he grew up in the shadow of some of Poland's leading educational institutions, Fryderyk mixed with boys from upper class and aristocratic backgrounds and made a number of lasting friendships. The great shadow over Fryderyk Chopin's youth was the decline and death of his sister Emilia at the age of fourteen due to tuberculosis. This disease would eventually claim Chopin's own life. He long wrestled with ill health. His prodigious creative output was at least in part an outlet for a man limited in many ways by the weakness of his body.

Chopin began playing the piano early. It soon became obvious that he was a musical prodigy. He gave his first public concert before he turned eight and began composing at around the same time. The Warsaw press proudly proclaimed him "a Polish Mozart." While Chopin benefited from the assistance of devoted teachers, it is evident from his precocity and his original and idiosyncratic style of playing that he was largely self-taught. From the start, Chopin was a genius whose creativity could not be channeled or contained. His parents had the wisdom to nurture his gifts without trying to control or profit by them. The chief reaction of his family, friends, and fellow citizens was to celebrate Chopin's gifts. The young pianist was even called upon to perform a useful public service by being available to play for the temperamentally erratic Grand Duke Constantine, the head of the Russian occupation forces in Poland; those around the grand duke believed that Chopin's music soothed their royal master's violent passions.

Chopin received his formal education at the Warsaw Lyceum and at the Warsaw Conservatory. Throughout his student days, he worked hard on honing his talent as

© Tom Horbett

Alan Walker is a professor emeritus at McMaster University in Hamilton, Ontario. He is the author of the prize-winning three-volume biography Franz Liszt (1983–96).

a composer. Some of his productions were inspired by the peasant songs that he heard while on vacation in the Polish countryside. Chopin's talent broadened his world. It became obvious that he needed to travel and take part in Europe's cosmopolitan musical scene. In 1829, he performed two successful concerts before a demanding public in music-saturated Vienna. A career as a concert soloist beckoned. At the same time, he was playing frequently before select gatherings in aristocratic salons, such as that of Prince Antoni Radziwill, a leading magnate in Poland. Such intimate performances would be Chopin's favored form of musical expression for the remainder of his life.

Early in November 1830, Chopin set out on a European trip that was intended to be the launch of his musical career. He hoped to arrange concerts and meet fellow musicians as he visited the metropolises of Western Europe. A few weeks after Chopin left Warsaw, a bloody insurrection against Russian domination broke out in Poland. After some initial military successes, the Polish revolutionary forces were bloodily suppressed by Russian armies. Although Chopin did not return to participate in the fighting, he ardently supported the Polish revolutionaries. Once the Russians reestablished their control, Chopin considered himself an exile from his homeland. In future years he refused honors from the Russian government and supported Polish émigré organizations.

Chopin traveled to Paris. The French capital would be his home for most of the rest of his life. Here he made his way in a vibrant musical environment where a number of dynamic piano virtuosos competed for public acclaim. Chopin rejected the overwrought theatrics of his musical rivals. His playing style was notably softer, taking advantage of his supple fingerwork and fluttering of the piano's pedal to give a distinctive tone to his music. He did not go in for the bravura dramatic effects that rival pianists used to thrill audiences in the Romantic era. The German poet Heinrich Heine lived in Paris and acted as an acidulous music critic who damned much of what he heard, comparing most of the great piano virtuosos of the day to "a plague of locusts." But Heine greatly admired Chopin's style of playing, and called him "the Raphael of the piano." Chopin rarely performed public concerts, which he disliked. He was better known for his playing in the homes of aristocratic friends and patrons. He supported himself by giving piano lessons to affluent students. Another source of income came from the royalties from his published music.

In 1836, Chopin became engaged to Maria Wodzinska, the teenage daughter of Polish aristocrats. Much to Chopin's chagrin, the Wodzinski family saw to it that the engagement lapsed because of their misgivings about a sickly musician as a son-in-law. In the aftermath of his unsuccessful betrothal to Maria Wodzinska, Chopin began an extended relationship with the novelist George Sand. Born Amantine-Lucile-Aurore Dupin, Sand was a prolific writer famed for her deliberately unconventional life, assuming the prerogatives of a man, from dress to a succession of lovers. The comparatively prim Chopin was shocked and unimpressed when he first met her, but Sand was smitten by the young composer and launched a successful campaign for his affections. In late 1838, the lovers undertook what would ultimately prove to be a disastrous getaway trip to the Spanish island of Majorca. Both local opinion and the weather turned against the unmarried couple. Chopin's health suffered as surprisingly cold winds buffeted their lodgings in a hilltop monastery. A retreat to France brought relief and a new pattern to their lives. The two resided near each other in Paris, and Chopin spent much of his summers in Sand's house at Nohant. The passion of the relationship eventually ebbed away, especially for Sand, and they stayed together as friends. Sand found herself increasingly acting as the caregiver for the ailing composer, a role she grew to resent. The final break between Chopin and Sand came in 1847 after a series of quarrels. Sand even lampooned a caricature of her former lover in a novel.

By this time Chopin's brief life was nearing its crisis. The accumulating ravages of his tuberculosis cut into his productivity. The political instability in France following the Revolution of 1848 dried up his income from teaching. His pupil Jane Stirling arranged a tour of Great Britain. Her attentions were kindly meant, but the schedule she devised was too strenuous for a man who was by then gravely ill. He returned to Paris and attempted to resume his routine. Late in the summer of 1849, he moved to a new apartment, where he immediately took to his bed and never left it. He died on October 17.

Walker never forgets that Chopin is remembered because of his transcendent music. One of the greatest strengths of his book is his analysis of Chopin's work. Walker fills many of his pages with bars of Chopin's music, expertly explaining the ways in which the composer crafted his original and beautiful compositions. Largely self-taught, and unmoved by fad and fashion, Chopin was a bold innovator who blended genres to capture the musical effects he sought. The crowning achievement of Walker's *Fryderyk Chopin* is that he provides readers a compelling portrait of genius in action.

Daniel P. Murphy

Review Sources

Cone, Edward B. Review of *Fryderyk Chopin: A Life and Times*, by Alan Walker. *Library Journal*, 1 July 2018, 72–75. *Literary Reference Center*, search.ebscohost.com/login.aspx?direct=true&db=lfh&AN=130388547. Accessed 1 Feb. 2019.

Da Fonseca-Wollheim, Corinna. "An Ingenious Frédéric Chopin." Review of *Fryderyk Chopin: A Life and Times*, by Alan Walker. *The New York Times*, 25 Nov. 2018, www.nytimes.com/2018/11/19/books/review/fyderyk-chopin-alan-walker-frederic-chopin-biography.html. Accessed 1 Feb. 2019.

Review of *Fryderyk Chopin: A Life and Times*, by Alan Walker. *Kirkus Reviews*, 13 Aug. 2018, www.kirkusreviews.com/book-reviews/alan-walker/fryderyk-chopin-walker. Accessed 1 Feb. 2018.

Review of *Fryderyk Chopin: A Life and Times*, by Alan Walker. *Publishers Weekly*, 30 Apr. 2018, www.publishersweekly.com/978-0-3741-5906-1. Accessed 1 Feb. 2018.

Moravcsik, Andrew. Review of *Fryderyk Chopin: A Life and Times*, by Alan Walker. *Foreign Affairs*, 18 Oct. 2018, www.foreignaffairs.com/reviews/capsule-review/2018-10-18/fryderyk-chopin-life-and-times. Accessed 1 Feb. 2019.

"Piano Forte: A Magisterial Account of Chopin's Life and Times." Review of *Fryderyk Chopin: A Life and Times*, by Alan Walker. *The Economist*, 8 Nov. 2018, www.economist.com/books-and-arts/2018/11/08/a-magisterial-account-of-chopins-life-and-times. Accessed 1 Feb. 2019.

The Future of Humanity
Terraforming Mars, Interstellar Travel, Immortality, and Our Destiny beyond Earth

Author: Michio Kaku (b. 1947)
Publisher: Doubleday (New York). 368 pp.
Type of work: Science

In The Future of Humanity: Terraforming Mars, Interstellar Travel, Immortality, and Our Destiny beyond Earth, *Michio Kaku explores the ways in which evolving technology may enable humans to leave Earth, their own physical bodies, or even the universe itself.*

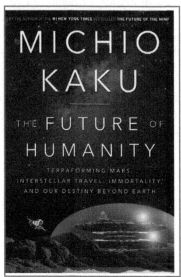

Courtesy of Knopf Doubleday

The planet Earth, Michio Kaku writes in the prologue to the 2018 book *The Future of Humanity*, is perpetually at risk of a cataclysm. In addition to human-created threats such as nuclear warfare, bioterrorism, and climate change, the planet and its occupants face a vast range of dangers completely outside of human control, from the eventual eruption of the Yellowstone supervolcano to a meteor impact similar to the one that resulted in the extinction of most dinosaurs. Any such threat would render the planet inhospitable to human life and could potentially spell the end of humanity. Furthermore, even if such disasters could be avoided, the eventual death of Earth's sun billions of years in the future is inevitable. How, then, can humankind ensure its survival? The answer, Kaku proposes, lies in creating a backup plan of sorts in which humanity is no longer tied solely to its planet of origin. In *The Future of Humanity: Terraforming Mars, Interstellar Travel, Immortality, and Our Destiny beyond Earth*, he explores potential means of escaping humankind's seemingly inevitable fate, including terraforming and colonizing nearby planets, traveling far from Earth's solar system, and perhaps even moving beyond the limitations of the human body. The Henry Semat Professor of Physics at the City College of New York and the author of multiple books exploring potential future scientific developments, including *Physics of the Future* (2011) and *The Future of the Mind* (2014), Kaku is particularly dedicated to speculating about humanity's future while linking that future to the scientific and pop-cultural developments of the late twentieth and early twenty-first centuries, a mission he carries out in a manner that is both entertaining and thought provoking.

Following the prologue and introduction, in which Kaku sets forth his book's core premise and introduces the reader to the key areas he plans to discuss, *The Future of Humanity* is divided into three parts, each focusing on a different area of humankind's potential future trajectory. The first part, "Leaving the Earth," encompasses chapters speculating on humanity's efforts to leave Earth and seek out natural resources and, potentially, a new home. Kaku begins by chronicling the history of space flight, including the development of liquid-fueled rockets by Robert Goddard in the early decades of the twentieth century. Such early developments were followed by expansions in the US and Soviet space programs, and Kaku goes on to note that the US space program in particular declined in the late twentieth and early twenty-first centuries due to both the end of the Cold War rivalry between the two countries and the US government's increasing unwillingness to pay to send people or technology into orbit, which Kaku notes costs $10,000 per pound. Although Kaku makes his disappointment about the fate of the US space program apparent, he expresses optimism about the potential for new developments by private companies and entrepreneurs working in conjunction with the federal government. He delves into some of those developments in the following chapter, particularly highlighting the work of entrepreneurs such as Jeff Bezos, Elon Musk, and Richard Branson in the fields of space exploration. He notes that Bezos, in particular, expressed hopes of returning astronauts to the moon and goes on to explore what might go into creating a permanent base on the moon as well as the natural resources, such as rare Earth elements widely used in electronics, that might be mined from that body. He delves further into the idea of mining bodies such as asteroids in the following chapter and goes on to consider another body that humans might consider traveling to in addition to the moon: the planet Mars. To sustain human life on that planet, scientists would need to master the process known as terraforming, which has the goal of creating planetary conditions hospitable to human life. Part 1 concludes with a chapter detailing additional potential new areas for human exploration and colonization, including moons of the planets Jupiter and Saturn and the comets found in areas of the solar system known as the Kuiper Belt and the Oort Cloud.

In the second part, "Voyage to the Stars," Kaku expands his discussion of space travel beyond Earth's own solar system, delving into interstellar travel and the technologies that could facilitate it, among them nanotechnology and artificial intelligence. He particularly stresses the importance of robots that are autonomous rather than remote controlled. Kaku notes that while robots have already proven useful in fields such as manufacturing, as well as in space exploration in the form of remote-controlled landers and probes, the key next step is to develop robots capable of completing tasks and making decisions with little input from humans. He argues that such robots would prove essential to the creation of colonies on bodies such as Mars or the moon, as they are capable of performing "the 'three D's'—jobs that are dangerous, dull, or dirty," which would be plentiful in such environments. Kaku likewise devotes extensive time to discussing the considerations necessary in designing a vessel capable of carrying out interstellar voyages, including the need to power such a ship. As he points out, traditional rockets cannot carry the amount of fuel necessary to reach the nearest star system and even if one could, the journey would take as much as seventy thousand years. However, tiny ships known as nanoships powered by laser beams could potentially be used as probes to investigate planets and other bodies far from Earth. Kaku also discusses the potential of rockets powered by nuclear energy, fusion, or antimatter, and he assesses the viability of so-called space elevators—a cable fixed

© AsianBoston/Rob Klein

Michio Kaku is the author of numerous books, including Einstein's Cosmos *(2004),* Physics of the Impossible *(2008),* Physics of the Future *(2011), and* The Future of the Mind *(2014). He is the Henry Semat Professor of Physics at the City College of New York.*

to Earth at one end and extending into orbit with a counterweight at the far end; vehicles would climb the cable to reach outer space, rather than using rockets. Space elevators have been a fixture in science fiction, but Kaku argues they could be realized late in the twenty-first century. He goes on to engage with other topics well known to fans of science fiction, including faster-than-light travel and wormholes, and discusses the science behind the ongoing search for Earth-like planets outside of Earth's solar system.

The third and final section of *The Future of Humanity*, "Life in the Universe," moves into even more speculative territory, beginning with a chapter in which Kaku presents some of the ways in which humans could potentially achieve immortality of a sort. He notes that potential processes such as cloning could solve some of the problems associated with lengthy space voyages, but they could also raise serious ethical questions, particularly in regard to identity. Kaku also explores ongoing research into the physical mechanisms of aging, which may one day help scientists determine how to slow or stop aging's effects. In subsequent chapters, he highlights efforts to attain digital immortality through the recording of memories as well as the promise of innovations such as clustered regularly interspaced short palindromic repeats (CRISPR) technology, which can be used to edit genomes. As the reader might expect from a work that focuses heavily on the subject of space exploration, *The Future of Humanity* also considers the possibility of extraterrestrial life. Kaku takes a cautious approach to the idea of making contact with extraterrestrial beings, noting that on Earth, interactions between cultures with disparate levels of technology have often ended poorly for the less technologically advanced group. The book concludes by acknowledging that even if humankind succeeds in leaving Earth to travel throughout the solar system and beyond, the universe itself will one day die. In response to such an inevitability, Kaku speculates, humankind could perhaps travel through a wormhole to a younger universe, where the progress of humanity could continue further.

Although concerned primarily with humankind's future, *The Future of Humanity* is deeply rooted in the era of its publication, offering a broad overview of cutting-edge technology being developed and scientific research being carried out in the second decade of the twenty-first century. Kaku, as an established physicist and science writer, is well suited to discuss such topics and provides both clear explanations of the scientific concepts at hand and ample historical context for existing and potential future advancements. In addition to sharing historical anecdotes surrounding the development of certain technologies, he makes frequent references to works of science fiction, including books such as Isaac Asimov's Foundation series and films such as *Iron Man* (2008), *Total Recall* (2012), *The Martian* (2015), and others. While some readers might prefer to read about the hard science rather than pop-cultural references, others may find that such references help render complex concepts and potential technologies easier to visualize and comprehend. Following the end of the book's main text, *The Future of Humanity* concludes with extensive notes documenting Kaku's sources and providing additional information as well as a suggested reading list featuring more than thirty fact-based and fictional books that delve further into relevant areas of science and potential forms of future technological and scientific advancement. Such resources will likely prove useful for readers who, having gained a broad understanding of the topics at hand through *The Future of Humanity*, might want to learn more about specific concepts explored to a limited extent in the book, such as asteroid mining or transhumanism. Above all, *The Future of Humanity* is a thought-provoking work that introduces its readers to a wide range of proposed solutions—some more viable than others—to the problems facing humanity as a whole.

Prior to and following its publication, *The Future of Humanity* received a mixed response from critics, who highlighted both strengths and flaws in Kaku's work. Critics generally agreed with the book's core premise, particularly Kaku's assessment that humankind and Earth itself face a variety of threats, both in terms of Earth-based threats such as climate change and volcanoes as well as in terms of external threats such as meteors. In positive reviews of the book, the anonymous critic for *Kirkus* called *The Future of Humanity* "an exhilarating look at the future," while the reviewer for *Publishers Weekly* praised Kaku's ability to present complex scientific topics in a manner that is easy for a general audience to understand. Writing for the *New York Times*, astrophysics professor Adam Frank echoed the latter view, commenting positively on Kaku's use of pop-cultural references and ability to connect with readers. However, Frank also noted that the book does not delve much into the ethical ramifications of many of the potential technological advances Kaku proposes. In a review for *The Times*, Oliver Moody further criticized portions of the book's premise, describing the idea of colonizing Mars as "mad" and characterizing terraformed planets as "dodgy refurb jobs." Moody likewise found the work as a whole to be "weary, clunkily written and incoherent" and argued that it contained a number of factual errors, including apocryphal historical trivia and quotes. Some critics, including Steve Donoghue for the *Christian Science Monitor*, argued that Kaku was speculating about the future of fields in which he had little academic authority. Despite such objections, Donoghue noted that Kaku was "unfailingly interesting" and praised his skill as a writer and his "smooth, perfect control" over the book's key arguments and vision of the future.

Joy Crelin

Review Sources

Donoghue, Steve. "*The Future of Humanity* Recommends Evacuating Earth in Order to Save the Species." Review of *The Future of Humanity: Terraforming Mars, Interstellar Travel, Immortality, and Our Destiny beyond Earth*, by Michio Kaku. *Christian Science Monitor*, 21 Feb. 2018, www.csmonitor.com/Books/Book-Reviews/2018/0221/The-Future-of-Humanity-recommends-evacuating-Earth-in-order-to-save-the-species. Accessed 31 Oct. 2018.

Frank, Adam. "Downloadable Neurons, Life on Mars: A Physicist's View of Where We're Headed." Review of *The Future of Humanity: Terraforming Mars, Interstellar Travel, Immortality, and Our Destiny beyond Earth*, by Michio Kaku. *The New York Times*, 25 May 2018, www.nytimes.com/2018/05/25/books/review/the-future-of-humanity-michio-kaku.html. Accessed 31 Oct. 2018.

Review of *The Future of Humanity: Terraforming Mars, Interstellar Travel, Immortality, and Our Destiny beyond Earth*, by Michio Kaku. *Kirkus*, 24 Dec. 2017, www.kirkusreviews.com/book-reviews/michio-kaku/the-future-of-humanity/. Accessed 31 Oct. 2018.

Review of *The Future of Humanity: Terraforming Mars, Interstellar Travel, Immortality, and Our Destiny beyond Earth*, by Michio Kaku. *Publishers Weekly*, 12 Feb. 2018, www.publishersweekly.com/978-0-385-54276-0. Accessed 31 Oct. 2018.

Moody, Oliver. "Review: *The Future of Humanity* by Michio Kaku—Should We Colonise Mars?" *The Times*, 17 Feb. 2018, www.thetimes.co.uk/article/review-the-future-of-humanity-by-michio-kaku-should-we-colonise-mars-07ltcp695. Accessed 31 Oct. 2018.

Poole, Steven. "Review: Onward, Upwards and 'The Future of Humanity.'" Review of *The Future of Humanity: Terraforming Mars, Interstellar Travel, Immortality, and Our Destiny beyond Earth*, by Michio Kaku. *The Wall Street Journal*, 22 Feb. 2018, www.wsj.com/articles/review-onward-upward-and-the-future-of-humanity-1519343797. Accessed 31 Oct. 2018.

The Girl Who Smiled Beads
A Story of War and What Comes After

Author: Clemantine Wamariya (b. 1988)
with Elizabeth Weil
Publisher: Crown (New York). Illustrated.
288 pp.
Type of work: Nonfiction, memoir
Time: 1994 to present day
Locales: Kigali, Rwanda; Kigoma Refugee
Camp, Burundi; Dzaleka Refugee Camp,
Malawi; Durban, South Africa; Chicago,
Illinois

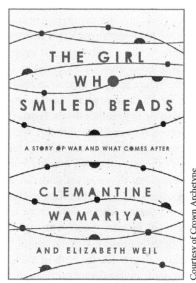

Courtesy of Crown Archetype

*A survivor of the Rwandan genocide, Clem-
antine Wamariya reckons with her experiences as a child refugee, offering a rare,
first-person glimpse of a child's experience
of atrocity. Moving back and forth between
past and present,* The Girl Who Smiled
Beads *explores her long road toward stability in a new, American life.*

Principal personages

CLEMANTINE WAMARIYA, the author, a Rwandan refugee
CLAIRE WAMARIYA, her elder sister
MRS. THOMAS, her American foster mother
ROB, husband of Claire
MARIETTE, daughter of Claire and Rob
FREDDY, son of Claire and Rob

Until the age of six, Clemantine Wamariya enjoyed a middle-class childhood in Kigali,
Rwanda. She was the first of the three children in her family to attend kindergarten—
her parents had just achieved sufficient financial stability to afford this luxury—and
she recognized the privilege, considering herself "the most special child there, maybe
the most special child in all Rwanda." But, this stable life quickly unraveled with the
outbreak of the *intambara* ("the conflict"). *The Girl Who Smiled Beads* is Wamariya's
account of her experience as a child refugee from the 1994 Rwandan genocide and
of her eventual struggles to wrestle with her trauma and to build a stable life in the
United States after her resettlement in Chicago, Illinois, at age twelve. *The Girl Who
Smiled Beads* offers a powerful, devastating view into the experiences of a child in the
face of exceptional human atrocity and a window into a lifelong search for healing, a
quest the book's young author (around age thirty at the time of its publication) has only
begun to pursue. Beyond sharing Wamariya's individual experiences, the book also
seeks to undercut the "clinical, overly general, bloodless, and dehumanizing" concept

of genocide, as it has entered (or failed to enter) popular consciousness. Critiquing policy makers, intellectuals, and others who believe they have "completed the moral project of remembering," Wamariya reminds readers that each such event is composed of myriad "one-person experience[s]." She challenges readers to consider more complex, less universalized ways of remembering, and to beware of grand narratives that purport to allow individuals to wrap their head around such tragedies.

Wamariya and her elder sister Claire, who is fifteen at the outset of the *intambara*, endure six years living as refugees, uncertain about the survival of their parents, brother Pudi, or any of their extended family. At first, their mother sends the two girls to their grandmother's farm, close to the southern border near Burundi. Soon, however, they are forced to flee for their survival—two young girls making their way through a dangerous and shifting landscape of mass killing. From a familiar, middle-class existence, the two quickly become wanderers buffeted by forces of hatred and violence that they cannot understand. Reflecting on her sudden and shocking transition from loved child to refugee, Wamariya comments, "It's strange, how you go from being a person who is away from home to a person with no home at all. . . . You are unwanted, by everyone." Although the sisters are physically inseparable, they are not emotionally close. Claire is distant, and often harsh, with Clemantine, though always working to provide for both of them. Though Clemantine is only six when she arrives at Ngozi Refugee Camp in Burundi, only the first of several camps in which the sisters eventually find themselves, she sheds her childhood quickly, replacing games with the daily menial tasks necessary for survival. While Clemantine cooks, cleans, and washes laundry, Claire works at the camp and pursues entrepreneurial schemes that help the two to stave off starvation. They are entrapped in the "horrible groove" of life in a refugee camp, in which "there is no path for improvement," but extreme effort is needed just for survival. Wamariya begins to lose sight of herself, her history, her identity, her name—and, even at her young age, to feel extreme exhaustion and disconnection from her own body.

A major turning point for the girls comes when Claire accedes to the courtship of an aid worker from Zaire. Rob is handsome and persistent and follows through on his promise to get the girls legal paperwork. They briefly leave the camp and find fleeting stability living with Rob's family. But the situation soon deteriorates as conflict spreads to the region, and Rob the aid worker becomes a refugee himself. Bitter and impoverished, he lashes out at those around him, turning to alcohol, domestic violence, and extramarital affairs. Heightening their instability, Claire and Rob have one child, Mariette, shortly after their marriage, for whom Wamariya becomes a fierce caretaker. After several more relocations, the group finds stability, if continued severe poverty, in South Africa. This is soon disrupted by Rob, who insists that Claire and the children head north and attempt to return to Rwanda, which plunges them back into terrifying conflict zones and refugee camps. During these travels, Claire gives birth to Rob's second child. Eventually, they settle in Lusaka, Zambia, first with other Rwandan refugees and later reunited with Rob. While Wamariya tends to the younger children, Claire ensures the family's survival, working in an array of transient jobs. Eventually, she also secures a coveted relocation for all, including Rob, to enter the

United States as refugees. They settle in Chicago.

The memoir's narrative progresses in alternating chapters that advance the story of Wamariya's life as a refugee and of her life after emigration to the United States. This format is integral to the structure of the book, because it allows for moments of memory rather than a continuous, authoritative narrative. It also integrates both of these periods of time as pertaining to the same life, so that the homeless child in Africa cannot be separated from the more privileged persona of her later life. The format also allows the reader to experience Wamariya's childhood traumas as memories that continue to have an impact on her life in the present. Her troubled relationships with her family and other relationships, and her excessive or obsessive attachment to certain *katundu* (possessions) that connect to

Clemantine Wamariya holds a BA from Yale University in comparative literature. The Girl Who Smiled Beads *is her first book.*

the years in which she had nothing, are examples of the types of continuous reminders of past trauma that pull the two narrative sequences of the book together.

In the United States, Wamariya's life separates from that of Claire and her children. A wealthy family takes Wamariya informally under their wing, gaining her admission to an elite high school, feeding her, clothing her, and offering her access to every facet of upper-class success. While they cannot erase the traumas of her past and her deep psychological damages, the family allows Wamariya to enter into an elite world, eventually gaining entry to Yale University. Claire, meanwhile, fends for herself and her family, sustaining a small apartment in public housing and building a close-knit community in a working-poor inner-city neighborhood.

For both sisters, a turning point of their lives in the United States was their appearance on *Oprah* in 2006, an incident with which the memoir opens. They found themselves in the national spotlight because Wamariya had been one of fifty winners in an essay competition concerning Elie Wiesel's memoir *Night*, which recounts his experiences of the Holocaust in World War II Germany. In the two-part episode, the sisters met Wiesel, but they also became the center of the spectacle, because host Oprah Winfrey surprised them with an unexpected reunion on stage with their parents and younger siblings. Although they had known that their parents survived the war, this was the first meeting the daughters had with them since being spirited to their grandmother's house in 1994. Followed by a brief two-day visit before their family was flown back to Rwanda, this encounter forced Wamariya into a charged emotional reckoning with the attachments she remembered having with her parents and her current feelings of disconnection and abandonment. Later in the memoir, Wamariya describes the first telephone conversation Claire arranged with her parents as "surreal and awful" as the severed worlds of daughters and parents collided. They sought to recreate the relationships, but would have to do so from scratch: "None of us were the same people who'd lived together in that house in Kigali. Those people had died. We had all died."

Wamariya's struggle to rebuild the bonds with her family, in particular with her mother, becomes a significant theme of the American narrative within the book. The parents and younger siblings also move to the United States, enabled by a financial infusion from one of Wamariya's wealthy supporters, but they live with Claire and tension abounds. Wamariya finds it impossible to rekindle feelings of deep connection to her parents. A possible turning point in this dynamic comes when Wamariya takes her mother on a mother-daughter trip to Europe. While she had planned an impressive itinerary, the unexpected becomes the most significant. In the Basilica of Saint Paul in Rome, her mother seeks out the chapel of Saint Brigid, patron saint of babies. There, she celebrates her reunion with her daughters in front of the saint to whom she prayed during the years in which they were lost to one another. Although Wamariya does not share her mother's faith or her sense of resolution, in this moment she feels happiness and basks in the warmth of her mother's enduring affection.

The Girl Who Smiled Beads is a significant work that brings a human and individual face to the horrors of the Rwandan genocide. Importantly, it also links the worlds of Africa and the United States, making evident the importance of the international community in the face of such unspeakable human horrors. Had Wamariya and her family not been granted asylum in the United States, for example, this story would remain untold and the world would have lost a window into understanding this set of historical events. Wamariya's memoir contains many horrific memories, but also countless acts of generosity from strangers in both Africa and the United States. It is a story of unspeakable violence and inhumanity, but also of the persistence of the human spirit, often at the hands of those who have the least to offer. Ultimately, through the story of her own survival and resilience, Wamariya also counters colonial ideas of self and other. Throughout, both she and Claire are agents working to continue advancing their own stories. Like "the girl who smiled beads," protagonist of a story that Wamariya used to enjoy hearing from her nanny Mukamama, Wamariya follows the individual drive to forge a path, even through extreme uncertainty.

Julia A. Sienkewicz

Review Sources

Hertzel, Laurie. Review of *The Girl Who Smiled Beads: A Story of War and What Comes After*, by Clemantine Wamariya with Elizabeth Weil. *Star Tribune*, 6 July 2018, www.startribune.com/review-the-girl-who-smiled-beads-by-clemantine-wamariya-and-elizabeth-weil/487435831. Accessed 26 Dec. 2018.

Hulbert, Ann. "*The Girl Who Smiled Beads* Defies Easy Uplift." Review of *The Girl Who Smiled Beads: A Story of War and What Comes After*, by Clemantine Wamariya with Elizabeth Weil. *The Atlantic*, May 2018, www.theatlantic.com/magazine/archive/2018/05/cover-to-cover-the-girl-who-smiled-beads/556898. Accessed 26 Dec. 2018.

Krug, Nora. "A Moment on 'Oprah' Made Her a Human Rights Symbol. She Wants to Be More Than That." Review of *The Girl Who Smiled Beads: A Story of War and What Comes After*, by Clemantine Wamariya with Elizabeth Weil. *The Washington Post*, 19 Apr. 2018, www.washingtonpost.com/entertainment/books/a-moment-on-oprah-made-her-a-human-rights-symbol-she-wants-to-be-more-than-that/2018/04/18/f394dd0c-3d98-11e8-a7d1-e4efec6389f0_story.html. Accessed 26 Dec. 2018.

Okeowo, Alexis. "From the Rwandan Genocide to Chicago: A Young Author Survived to Tell Her Story." Review of *The Girl Who Smiled Beads: A Story of War and What Comes After*, by Clemantine Wamariya with Elizabeth Weil. *The New York Times*, 7 May 2018, www.nytimes.com/2018/05/07/books/review/clemantine-wamariya-girl-who-smiled-beads.html. Accessed 26 Dec. 2018

Girls Burn Brighter

Author: Shobha Rao (b. 1973)
Publisher: Flatiron Books (New York). 320 pp.
Type of work: Novel
Time: 2001–ca. 2005
Locales: Indravalli Konda, Namburu, and Vijayawada, India; Seattle, Washington; South Dakota

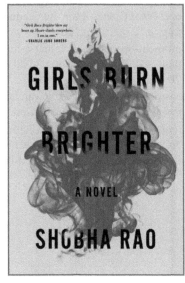

Courtesy of Flatiron Books

With Girls Burn Brighter, *debut novelist Shobha Rao tells the harrowing story of two young people from a poor village in India who become fast friends. They are traumatically separated, endure a series of hardships, undergo horrific ordeals, and survive by clinging to the hope of an eventual reunion.*

Principal characters

POORNIMA, a.k.a. Poori, a teenager from a poor weaving family
SAVITHA, her friend from an even poorer family
RAMAYYA, a marriage broker
KISHORE, her husband by arranged marriage
GURU, the operator of a chain of brothels, a human trafficker
MOHAN, the sensitive son of a human trafficker

The protagonists of *Girls Burn Brighter*, teenagers Poornima and Savitha, have major obstacles—poverty, gender, tradition—to overcome in the course of their fractured friendship. They live in Indravalli, Karnataka, India, a poor rural village of several hundred individuals. Both come from families of weavers. Poornima's mother has just died of cancer, and her family barely scrapes by with the extra rupees Poornima, as eldest of five children, earns spinning thread to supplement her father's meager income weaving cotton saris. Savitha's family, with her father disabled by alcoholism and arthritis and with a broken *charkha* (spinning wheel), is even worse off. Savitha has to fight feral dogs and pigs while picking over the town dump for scraps of paper and plastic to sell. Both young women operate at a disadvantage in a patriarchal society where women do not count, literally or figuratively: the village only records the births of male children. Poornima's father, in fact, when his daughter was a toddler and ran into a river, nearly let her drown because she was "just a girl."

Now that she is of age, Poornima's father wants to marry her off as soon as possible. First, however, he will have to raise the money for his daughter's dowry. In local custom—despite laws against dowries in India—this is a combination of money and property. The amount and a payment plan will be negotiated between marriage broker

Ramayya and the groom's family. The price must be of sufficient value that they will consent to take Poornima off his hands, yet low enough to be affordable to a man of modest means. Poornima is resigned to her fate: "Everything is already written in the stars."

But the stars did not reckon on the influence of Savitha. Poornima's father hires the young woman to help complete orders for saris. Savitha will work twelve hours per day on the second loom Poornima's late mother once used, and be given lunch daily and a portion of the profits. Though Savitha is just a year or two older than Poornima, she seems much more mature. She has large, strong hands, perfect for gripping a loom picking-stick. She has confidence: Savitha was born during a solar eclipse, a bad omen among the superstitious villagers, but does not care. She has attitude, characterized by her favorite meal: rice, yogurt, and banana, all mashed together. Poornima and Savitha hit it off, especially after Savitha protects her friend from the catcalls of village lay-abouts who accost them as they hike from the town well with their water.

The friendship between Poornima and Savitha grows and becomes more complicated as a heat wave and drought hit the region. Savitha is a tireless worker and produces well-woven saris; she promises to make a special sari for Poornima's wedding—if she ever gets married. A potential mate, a farmer, thinks Poornima too dark-skinned for his liking and looks for someone else to wed. A meeting with a second possible suitor, an apprentice weaver, is arranged, but some of Savitha's personality has rubbed off on Poornima, for she fails a crucial test. When the prospective groom asks if she can sing (a question that concerns obedience more than musical ability), she says she cannot. The family demands a higher dowry that Poornima's father cannot afford, and the wedding is called off. Worse, word gets around about Poornima's less-than-submissive behavior. Her father abuses her for her failure, and Savitha comforts her.

Finally, a match is made with Kishore, an accountant whom she has never met. Poornima's father has, by this time, come to hate her, and he does not know how he will raise the high dowry. Before the wedding, however, something occurs that splits Poornima and Savitha apart: Savitha is traumatized by a sexual assault, after which Poornima comforts her. The community is scandalized by the event, and village elders declare the attacker must marry Savitha as punishment for his actions. The thought of marrying her rapist is repugnant, so Savitha takes Poornima's half-finished sari and flees.

From this point, at about the one-quarter mark in the novel, *Girls Burn Brighter* divides into the separate and alternating narratives of Poornima and Savitha. Neither story is cheery, though both illustrate the protagonists' resilience, their willingness to do whatever it takes to survive, and their common bond: in times of strife, each gains strength by thinking of the other.

There is plenty of strife ahead. Poornima eventually marries Kishore and discovers his secret. At first, everything seems fine, however. The groom and his family live in a two-story house made of concrete. With her husband and his sisters, Poornima eats at her first restaurant and sees her first movie. When she examines her husband's accounting work, she realizes it is simple mathematics and teaches herself to do some of that. But storm clouds soon gather. The in-laws question Poornima about missing

Shobha Rao won the 2014 Katherine Anne Porter Prize for Fiction and previously published a story in The Best American Short Stories 2015 *as well as her own collection,* An Unrestored Woman*, in 2016. Her work has also been nominated for a Pushcart Prize.* Girls Burn Brighter *is her first novel.*

jewelry and accuse her of purposely staining an expensive sari while doing laundry. When her father has difficulty paying off the dowry, the in-laws blame her for his failure. After Poornima does not become pregnant following six months of nightly rough sex, she is called barren but has the temerity to suggest her husband might be sterile, for which she is punished and threatened. After eighteen months of marriage, the family's hostility toward the perceived interloper culminates in a vicious, coordinated attack on Poornima, who then does steal and escape, intending to find Savitha. As she travels, people look at her disfigurement and wonder about which method was used. This is a sad commentary on the fact that violence associated with dowries is not uncommon in India. It also suggests a sinister possibility: that her father may have intentionally withheld dowry payments, anticipating she would be harmed.

Poornima makes it as far as the train station a large northern city before she runs into a major obstacle. Through a convoluted set of circumstances, she ends up working as a bookkeeper for Guru, the owner of several brothels in the city. Nine months later, she learns that Savitha was one of Guru's working girls—but it is too late to reunite with her, as Savitha has left for what at first appears to be a better situation in the United States. Nevertheless, Poornima painstakingly plans and prepares to reconnect with her in America. To earn money, she carries out assignments for Guru, escorting young women to be sold to wealthy men abroad. Finally, her chance comes: Guru asks Poornima to deliver a girl to Seattle and she eagerly sets out, prepared to follow her missing friend across America, if necessary.

Upon publication, *Girls Burn Brighter* met with mixed reviews. Though punctuated by strong lyric scenes, and peppered with Indian terms that add to the flavor, the novel is unrelenting in its depiction of the many ways in which men take advantage of or abuse women, to such an extent that some readers may feel it becomes gratuitous. As several reviewers noted, the story relies heavily on coincidence, though some of that can be excused by the intuitive relationship between two individuals who probably never had a friend before they met. The narrative is one of contrasts: Poornima is demure and Savitha independent; small-town values come into conflict with the callousness of big cities; and the girls' poverty is magnified by the wealth accumulated by the men who exploit them. Along with its use of foils and lyricism, the novel is to be commended on its steady pacing and, as an anonymous reviewer for *Kirkus Reviews* noted, its "resplendent prose" that "captures the nuances and intensity of two best friends on the brink of an uncertain and precarious adulthood."

In the end, Rao's novel—part character study, part adventure tale, part East-versus-West parable, part polemic against the traffic in human sex slaves—leaves several questions unanswered. Regardless, it is ultimately both a fascinating and insightfully disturbing read.

Jack Ewing

Review Sources

Basu, Diksha. "A Devastating Friendship Forged in India's Underbelly." Review of *Girls Burn Brighter*, by Shobha Rao. *The New York Times*, 26 May 2018, www.nytimes.com/2018/05/26/books/review/girls-burn-brighter-shobha-rao.html. Accessed 15 Feb. 2019.

Beckerman, Hannah. "'Girls Burn Brighter' by Shobha Rao Review—Teenage Trial by Misogyny." *The Guardian*, 13 May 2018, www.theguardian.com/books/2018/may/13/girls-burn-brighter-shobha-rao-review. Accessed 15 Feb. 2019.

Felicelli, Anita. Review of *Girls Burn Brighter*, by Shobha Rao. *San Francisco Chronicle*, 21 Mar. 2018, www.sfchronicle.com/books/article/Girls-Burn-Brighter-by-Shobha-Rao-12771665.php. Accessed 15 Feb. 2019.

Review of *Girls Burn Brighter*, by Shobha Rao. *Kirkus Reviews*, 7 Dec. 2017, www.kirkusreviews.com/book-reviews/shobha-rao/girls-burn-brighter/. Accessed 15 Feb. 2019.

Levin, Ann. "'Girls' Burns with Intensity as Two Teen Friends in India Face Abuse." Review of *Girls Burn Brighter*, by Shobha Rao. *USA Today*, 13 Mar. 2018, www.usatoday.com/story/life/books/2018/03/13/girls-burn-brighter-novel-burns-intensity-teen-friends-india-face-abuse/386294002. Accessed 15 Feb. 2019.

Patrick, Bethanne. "Women Tend the Flames of Their Ambition in Shobha Rao's 'Girls Burn Brighter.'" Review of *Girls Burn Brighter*, by Shobha Rao. *Los Angeles Times*, 9 Mar. 2018, www.latimes.com/books/la-ca-jc-girls-burn-brighter-20180309-story.html. Accessed 15 Feb. 2019.

Give Me Your Hand

Author: Megan Abbott (b. 1971)
Publisher: Little, Brown (New York). 352 pp.
Type of work: Novel
Time: Present day
Locale: Unnamed university town

Megan Abbott's noir thriller Give Me Your Hand *follows the intertwining lives of two ambitious scientists.*

Principal characters
KIT OWENS, a hard worker from a working-class background
DIANE FLEMING, a brilliant scientist with a terrible secret
DR. LENA SEVERIN, an elegant, widely respected researcher

Megan Abbott's thriller *Give Me Your Hand* follows the intertwining lives of two chemists. The novel flips backward and forward in time, alternating between Kit Owen's narration as a teenager in high school, just starting to figure out her potential, and her life as a postdoc, doing her best to shine in the lab of Dr. Lena Severin. Severin is a brilliant scientist spearheading research in premenstrual dysphoric disorder (PMDD), a severe form of premenstrual disorder in which common symptoms like anger, depression, hunger, and pain are experienced to a debilitating and sometimes dangerous degree. A woman from one of Severin's case studies on the disorder recalled an act of blind rage, stating, "I don't even remember throwing the frying pan at him. His head is like collapsed in the center. And his skin is, like, sizzling."

Severin has just won a career-making grant to continue her research on PMDD; Kit is hoping to land a coveted spot on her research team when she is confronted by a ghost from her past. Diane Fleming, a strange girl with whom Kit was once friends in high school, joins Severin's staff. Diane, effortlessly brilliant, is a shoe-in for the research team. The number of spots available dwindles from three to two. Kit is jealous of Diane, but she also fears her. As a teenager, Kit describes Diane as resembling a knobby-kneed deer, or a similarly fragile, skittish animal; as an adult, she is tall, impossibly thin, and almost transparently white. She speaks softly and precisely. As Kit observes, "It felt like you could hurt her just by looking at her, or you could never hurt her at all."

As teenagers, Kit and Diane pushed each other to excel, both at cross-country running and at academics. Shortly into their friendship, however, Diane told Kit a secret that drove Kit away. Now, in a drunken tumble with Alex, a flirtatious researcher in her lab, Kit lets the secret (which had strategically and bluntly been revealed to the reader in an earlier flashback to create a sense of suspense and add to the tension that effectively hangs over the rest of the novel) slip. Abbott toggles back and forth, shuffling Diane's secret alongside, inevitably, a pivotal and deadly choice for Kit. Soon—or perhaps, Abbott suggests, it was always the case—the women are bound by more than ambition; they are bound by blood.

Abbott is a crime writer known for her explorations of the female psyche. Rage, assault, and the discreet horrors of a developing adolescent body are the dark underpinnings of Abbott's traditionally female protagonists. Like her previous novels—including *You Will Know Me* (2016), in which a teenage superstar gymnast is caught in the morass surrounding a young man's death, and *Dare Me* (2012), about another man's death at the hands of an elite cheerleading squad—the inciting incident in *Give Me Your Hand* is the murder of a man. Katy Waldman, writing for the *New Yorker* on July 18, 2018, described *Give Me Your Hand* as "feminine gothic." In the same article, Waldman discussed how Abbott works to subvert the trope of the femme fatale, a character who personifies, as Abbott writes in *Give Me Your Hand*, the "fear all men have that there's something inside us that shifts, and turns. A living thing, once dormant, stirring now, and filled with rage."

Abbott, a student of classic noir, wrote the book *The Street Was Mine: White Masculinity in Hardboiled Detective Fiction and Film Noir* (2002), on the construction of white masculinity in the works of crime novelists like Raymond Chandler and James M. Cain. She uses this background, and her understanding of the femme fatale trope as a personification of male anxiety about the unknowable power of women, in the creation of her female characters. In *Give Me Your Hand*, Kit and Diane are unwitting femme fatales, at least at first. Their actions spring from their own ambition and desires. They do not use sex as a lure, a common element of the femme fatale; rather, Diane deflects suspicion by projecting a virginal innocence. Other characters, however, specifically Severin, do portray the otherworldly elegance and sexual power typically given to a femme fatale, without fulfilling the rest of the role.

While Abbott subverts a Victorian trope of women driven to madness and blood lust by their hysterical womb, she draws on other tropes more commonly associated with noir. Kit's narration, much of which is told in flashback, brims with regret for her adolescent acquaintance with Diane, a mysterious character with a dark past. In the prologue, an older, wiser Kit ruefully jokes to herself, in a spin on the line from the classic film *Casablanca* (1942), "Of all the labs in all the world, she had to walk into mine." Diane's revelation of her secret sends teenage Kit into an existential crisis that alters the way she sees the world. She soon discovers, though, that she and Diane are inextricably linked, and in noir, one can never escape one's fate. Furthermore, the world of the lab, separate from the outside world, is morally ambiguous, a place where the distinction between right and wrong is blurred. Finally, and crucially, both Diane and Kit set out with the best of intentions, but it all goes terribly awry.

Abbott returns to other favorite themes in *Give Me Your Hand*. As with *You Will Know Me* and *Dare Me*, Abbott is interested in young women awakening to their own power. Her characters are often good at physically painful and demanding athletics.

© Drew Reilly

Give Me Your Hand *is Megan Abbott's ninth novel. Previous novels include* Dare Me *(2012) and* You Will Know Me *(2016). Her 2014 thriller* The Fever *was optioned for television. Abbott is also a writer for the HBO television series* The Deuce.

Kit and Diane are scientists, but as teenagers, they are also devoted cross-country runners. The relentlessness of that sport is mirrored in Kit and Diane's marathon study sessions in high school. Having each seen Severin speak at science camps, they both hope to win a full-ride scholarship awarded by Severin herself, vowing to one day work for her. "The Severin," as they call the scholarship, "gave everything we were doing a center, a unifying force. It wasn't about the grades, but what the grades could get you."

As Kit ascends the academic ranks, she becomes euphoric with the realization of her own power and its limitless possibility. For a girl who grew up poor in a grey town suffused in a chemical fog, even the concept of possibility is new. A line from scientist Marie Curie appears multiple times throughout the novel: "My head is so full of plans that it seems aflame." No obstacle seems too great. Events that might fell others only serve as fuel to the flame of her power. Early in the novel, a young Kit tells Diane about an adult man who once assaulted her. Afterward, he gave her a pair of expensive of running shoes that she continued to wear through high school. Crucially, though, the rage created by the violation remains. As Hillary Kelly wrote in her review for *Slate*, Abbott "digs into the gravitas of adolescent emotional wounds," explaining that she draws from the life-altering experiences of the teenage years to create suspense.

Give Me Your Hand received mostly positive reviews, and Abbott was widely praised for her ability to craft complex villains. A starred review for *Publishers Weekly* explained, "No writer can touch Abbott in the realm of twisted desire and relationships between women, both intimate and feral." Another reviewer, in a starred review for *Kirkus Reviews*, wrote, "In Abbott's deft hands, friendship is fused to rivalry, and ambition to fear, with an unsettling level of believability." Invoking Abbott's previous novels, Waldman wrote of *Give Me Your Hand*, "Just as success at élite levels is impossible without sacrifice, Abbott slyly hints, the sweetness, the impossible innocence, of femininity entails a dark seam."

While the novel does have similarities to the majority of Abbott's work, Kelly pointed out that in *Give Me Your Hand*, the crimes and the perpetrators are known to the reader early on. The novel is less a "whodunit," she wrote, than "a caustic nightmare about our youthful bad decisions. Even if you have committed no crimes and harbor no weighty secrets, this book will leave you nauseous with the memories of your own manic, pulsing teenage nature, the emotions you barely kept in check and the ones that overflowed." British crime novelist Ruth Ware, in a review of the novel for the *New York Times*, also gave her appreciation to Abbott for the complexity of the dynamics between the two women, as well as with the setting. She wrote that "the mazelike network of loyalties in the lab, the complicated truth of Kit's own past with Diane, their statuses as women in a male-dominated field—all are masterfully portrayed." She did, however have some complaints about the plot, stating that "the motivations of Kit and Diane" sometimes seem as "opaque" as the nature of the strange affliction they are studying. Despite some flaws, *Give Me Your Hand*, which includes the hallmarks of Abbott's writing that have made her work in the crime genre popular, also provides an engaging, well-executed exploration of ambition, female relationships, and the long-term psychological effects of secrets—particularly traumatic ones—making for an affecting read.

Molly Hagan

Review Sources

Corrigan, Maureen. "Cliques, Obsessive Moms and Now PhDs: Megan Abbott Sets Female Rivalries Afire." Review of *Give Me Your Hand*, by Megan Abbott. *The Washington Post*, 17 July 2018, www.washingtonpost.com/entertainment/books/cliques-obsessive-moms-and-now-phds-megan-abbott-sets-female-rivalries-afire/2018/07/16/9c6af570-86cc-11e8-8f6c-46cb43e3f306_story.html. Accessed 21 Feb. 2019.

Review of *Give Me Your Hand*, by Megan Abbott. *Kirkus Reviews*, 15 May 2018, p. 1. *Literary Reference Center Plus*, search.ebscohost.com/login.aspx?direct=true&db=lkh&AN=129583187&site=lrc-plus. Accessed 21 Feb. 2019.

Review of *Give Me Your Hand*, by Megan Abbott. *Publishers Weekly*, 21 May 2018, p. 50. *Literary Reference Center Plus*, search.ebscohost.com/login.aspx?direct=true&db=lkh&AN=129761541&site=lrc-plus. Accessed 21 Feb. 2019.

Kelly, Hillary. "In the Blood." Review of *Give Me Your Hand*, by Megan Abbott. *Slate*, 25 July 2018, slate.com/culture/2018/07/megan-abbotts-give-me-your-hand-reviewed.html. Accessed 21 Feb. 2019.

Scholes, Lucy. "Give Me Your Hand by Megan Abbott, Book Review: An Engrossing Literary Thriller. *Independent*, 2 Aug. 2018, www.independent.co.uk/arts-entertainment/books/give-me-your-hand-megan-abbott-book-review-a8472836.html. Accessed 21 Feb. 2019.

Ware, Ruth. "Competing Scientists Plus a High-Stakes University Lab Equals Murder." Review of *Give Me Your Hand*, by Megan Abbott. *The New York Times*, 16 July 2018, www.nytimes.com/2018/07/16/books/review/megan-abbott-give-me-your-hand.html. Accessed 21 Feb. 2019.

God Save Texas
A Journey into the Soul of the Lone Star State

Author: Lawrence Wright (b. 1947)
Publisher: Alfred A. Knopf (New York).
366 pp.
Type of work: Sociology, history, memoir
Time: Largely nineteenth century through
the present day
Locale: Texas

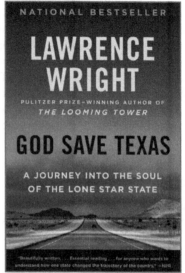

*Pulitzer Prize–winning author, journalist,
and longtime Texan Lawrence Wright explores the mythology of his home state in*
God Save Texas: A Journey into the Soul of
the Lone Star State.

Principal personages
LAWRENCE WRIGHT, author and Texan
STEPHEN "STEVE" HARRIGAN, novelist and
Texan, a friend of Wright

Pulitzer Prize–winning author and journalist Lawrence Wright explores the mythology of the state that he has long called home in *God Save Texas: A Journey into the
Soul of the Lone Star State*. Wright was born in Oklahoma, but spent the majority of
his formative years in Texas. After leaving following his high school graduation, he
returned to the state as an adult and raised his own children there. He describes his
love for Texas as begrudging, writing, "Many times I've considered moving to New
York, where most of my colleagues live, or Washington, which is Lotus Land for political journalists." However, Wright, a longtime staff writer for the urbane *New Yorker*
magazine and a respected authority on international terrorism, concludes, "I've never
felt at home in either spot."

In *God Save Texas*, Wright wrestles with the state's history, politics, and culture,
while mixing in elements of his personal experience living and working in the state,
as if he were, as Andrew R. Graybill put it for *Texas Monthly* in April 2018, "a spouse
reporting from inside a troubled marriage." Wright's feelings about Texas are representative of his feelings about contemporary life in the United States. Early in the
book, Wright and his longtime friend, Texas novelist Steve Harrigan, discuss the idea
of Texas as a bellwether state. He goes on to write, "Because Texas is a part of almost
everything in modern America—the South, the West, the Plains, Hispanic and immigrant communities, the border, the divide between the rural areas and the cities—what
happens here tends to disproportionately affect the rest of the nation."

Wright is a political journalist best known for his Pulitzer Prize–winning book *The
Looming Tower: Al-Qaeda and the Road to 9/11*, published in 2006. The book, which

© Kenny Braun

Lawrence Wright is a Pulitzer Prize–winning author and journalist. His best-known books include The Looming Tower: Al-Qaeda and the Road to 9/11 *(2006) and* Going Clear: Scientology and the Prison of Belief *(2013). He is also a playwright and screenwriter.*

was adapted into a television series in 2018 and is based on over five hundred interviews, explores the rise of the terrorist organization al-Qaeda in addition to describing the series of events that led to the attack on New York's World Trade Center towers on September 11, 2001. Another nonfiction work, *The Terror Years: From al-Qaeda to the Islamic State* (2016), focuses on various jihadist movements in the Middle East. Wright's other books include *Going Clear: Scientology and the Prison of Belief* (2013), which was a finalist for the 2013 National Book Award for Nonfiction and was made into a documentary film for HBO in 2015, and *Thirteen Days in September: Carter, Begin, and Sadat at Camp David* (2014). Wright, who initially wrote for *Texas Monthly* upon his return to the state, is also a playwright and screenwriter; he wrote the script for the 1998 film *The Siege*, starring Denzel Washington and Annette Bening, about counterterrorism operatives in New York City.

As a few reviewers additionally noted, Wright has written about Texas once before, in his 1987 memoir *In the New World: Growing Up with America from the Sixties to the Eighties*. In that book, he describes coming of age in Dallas. He was a teenager when President John F. Kennedy was assassinated there in 1963, and he writes about the trajectory of Dallas in the years that followed. That book examines Texas and America through such lenses as Kennedy's Camelot, the Vietnam War, and the Watergate scandal. *God Save Texas*, while also grounded in Wright's personal connections and stories, provides an examination of the contemporary state that includes a consideration of its history as well as the impact of such current affairs as the 2016 election of Donald Trump.

While Wright does offer some criticism of certain aspects of his state, to characterize *God Save Texas* as an anti-Texas book would be inaccurate. Early in his narration, Wright describes the night he was convinced to move back to the state. He was writing an article about astronauts for *Look* magazine in 1979. The restaurant critic for *Texas Monthly* took him on a wild tour of Hill Country, culminating in a trip to Greune Hall, the oldest dance hall in Texas. Future country music superstar George Strait was the opening act. "Dancers were two-stepping; the boys had longnecks in the rear pockets of their jeans and the girls wore aerodynamic skirts," he writes. "There was something suspiciously beguiling about the scene, verging on being staged for my benefit." Wright writes lovingly about this Texas, embodied in the diverse culture of the growing, more liberal city of Austin, the friendliness and resiliency of Houston after

Hurricane Harvey, and the music of artists like Willie Nelson and Roy Orbison. He writes about the beauty of Big Bend, a sprawling national park straddling the United States' border with Mexico, and the allure of the state's countless tiny towns, like a semi-inhabited ghost town just outside of Big Bend called Terlingua that is arranged around an abandoned quicksilver mine. In fact, it is easy to talk about the state's virtues, but Wright cannot enjoy those virtues without grappling with Texas's history and how that history continues to shape its future. He writes about Texas's fierce allegiance to slavery—at the expense of its own independence—its segregation and racism, and its slavering devotion to the oil industry. He also delves into how these legacies have contributed to a political culture bent on preserving a mythologized ideal of Texas, defined only—and almost humorously—by its direct opposition to a mythologized ideal of California.

Wright devotes discussion within more than one chapter in the book to the political jockeying over the 2017 "bathroom bill" that sought to ban transgender people from using public restrooms that correspond with their gender identity. A similar law had been a failure when it was enacted in North Carolina the year before, yet Lieutenant Governor Dan Patrick made the "bathroom bill" the center of an unusually dogged, personal crusade. Wright uses this story, and the resulting standoff between two key Republican figures, to illustrate what he views as the divide between the reasonable and the rogue elements of Texas politics. In a discussion of the condition of health care in the state, particularly in the context of the rights of men versus women, Wright points out that after Governor Rick Perry slashed funding for family planning, maternal deaths in Texas doubled between 2010 and 2014. Wright further notes that the 2014 number—35.8 per 100,000 live births—rated Texas the worst in the nation in terms of maternal deaths, and beyond that, worse than countries such as Egypt, Armenia, and Romania. Wright writes bitterly about this and other human rights issues in Texas, such as the abysmally underfunded, chaotic, and poorly managed foster care program.

God Save Texas tackles a lot of material, but there is an organization to the topics discussed by chapter that, combined with Wright's poignant personal anecdotes, keeps the reader engaged and able to follow along. Wright talks about everything from the state's border with Mexico to the gun culture and gun laws, the boom and bust cycles of Texas oil, and fracking. He also further examines the state's cultural landscape through discussions of specific prominent political and celebrity figures, some of whom, such as George W. Bush and his family and conspiracy theorist radio host Alex Jones, he has at least some personal familiarity with. He was also neighbors for a time with actor Matthew McConaughey and was once invited by Willie Nelson's harmonica player to go on one of the musician's tour buses and hold his guitar. At the same time, he touches on his own upbringing in Dallas, his early writing career, and his work covering the civil rights movement. All of these individual topics are interesting, but ultimately, some readers may feel that Texas is too loose of a glue to hold them all together. Jennifer Szalai, who reviewed the book for the *New York Times*, described it, positively, as an "illuminating primer for outsiders," though from the meticulous Wright, one might have hoped for something with a little more depth.

Other reviewers, including Jacob Sherman, writing for *Library Journal*, noted Wright's effort to write about such a convoluted subject in a largely "balanced tone." Graybill summed up the likely varied impact that such a book will have on readers: "One suspects that the intended audience for *God Save Texas* is coastal cosmopolitans . . . who will probably have a bifurcated reaction to the book." Fellow Texan Cecile Richards, the former head of Planned Parenthood and the daughter of former Texas governor Ann Richards, struck a more hopeful note in her review for the *Washington Post*. She described the book as "more of a plea than a prophecy." Continuing, she wrote, "Economically and demographically, there is little doubt that, as Wright has written, 'America's future is Texas.' Whether that declaration is hopeful or ominous depends on whether Texas itself will embrace the future, including a growing, young, multicultural population." Her point of view illuminates an important aspect of Wright's insightful and timely book: there is an elasticity and increasingly influential evolution to Texan culture that the nation's powerful would do well to embrace.

Molly Hagan

Review Sources

Markovits, Benjamin. "*God Save Texas* by Lawrence Wright Review—The Future of America?" *The Guardian*, 2 June 2018, www.theguardian.com/books/2018/jun/02/god-save-texas-journey-america-lawrence-wright-review. Accessed 20 Aug. 2018.

Richards, Cecile. "The Political Contradictions of the Lone Star State." Review of *God Save Texas: A Journey into the Soul of the Lone Star State*, by Lawrence Wright. *The Washington Post*, 20 Apr. 2018, www.washingtonpost.com/outlook/the-political-contradictions-of-the-lone-star-state/2018/04/20/fdfc8018-27a1-11e8-bc72-077aa4dab9ef_story.html. Accessed 20 Aug. 2018.

Schaub, Michael. "'God Save Texas' Is Essential Reading for Everyone—Even Non-Texans." Review of *God Save Texas: A Journey into the Soul of the Lone Star State*, by Lawrence Wright. *NPR*, 19 Apr. 2018, www.npr.org/2018/04/19/600902732/god-save-texas-is-essential-reading-for-everyone-even-non-texans. Accessed 20 Aug. 2018.

Sherman, Jacob. Review of *God Save Texas: A Journey into the Soul of the Lone Star State*, by Lawrence Wright. *Library Journal*, 1 Mar. 2018, p. 92. *Literary Reference Center Plus*, search.ebscohost.com/login.aspx?direct=true&db=lkh&AN=128234130&site=lrc-plus. Accessed 20 Aug. 2018.

Szalai, Jennifer. "In *God Save Texas*, Lawrence Wright Ranges Far and Wide." Review of *God Save Texas: A Journey into the Soul of the Lone Star State*, by Lawrence Wright. *The New York Times*, 18 Apr. 2018, www.nytimes.com/2018/04/18/books/review-god-save-texas-lawrence-wright.html. Accessed 20 Aug. 2018.

The Great Alone

Author: Kristin Hannah (b. 1960)
Publisher: St. Martin's Press (New York).
448 pp.
Type of work: Novel
Time: 1974–2009
Locales: Seattle, Washington; Kaneq, Alaska

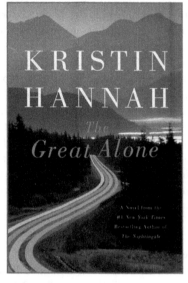

Courtesy of St. Martin's Press

In this follow-up to her blockbuster The Nightingale *(2015), Kristin Hannah follows a family of three as they move from Seattle to Alaska hoping to leave behind the demons the father brought back with him from Vietnam.*

Principal characters

LENORA "LENI" ALLBRIGHT, a teenage girl whose family moves to Alaska
ERNT ALLBRIGHT, her father, a Vietnam veteran with post-traumatic stress disorder (PTSD)
CORA ALLBRIGHT, her mother
MATTHEW WALKER, her best friend/boyfriend
MARGE "LARGE MARGE" BIRDSALL, the Allbrights' neighbor, a store owner
TOM WALKER, a wealthy local resident, Matthew's father
"MAD" EARL HARLAN, an alcoholic friend of Ernt's

War changes people—at least that is what Cora Allbright tells her daughter Leni when Ernt Allbright loses another job or comes up with another crazy idea. Change becomes both an excuse and reason for almost everything Ernt Allbright does. Thirteen-year-old Leni tries to understand, but she is tired of moving around, always being the new girl at school and never making real friends. When Ernt receives a letter from Earl Harlan, the father of a lost Vietnam friend, their lives move in yet another direction: Harlan's letter informs Ernt that his son Bo has left his property in Alaska to Ernt. Ernt's eager acceptance of this bequest, his wife's hesitant agreement, and his daughter's skepticism foreshadow the difficulties the Allbright family will face; Leni is compliant despite her misgivings, "Because that was what love was."

The novel is broken into three sections that follow vital changes in Leni's life. The first section, "1974," follows the Allbright family to Kaneq, Alaska. Though the move shows some promise for the family, the long winters drive Ernt to a dark place, and by the end of their first year, some of the locals prevail on Ernt to leave his family to take a well-paying job on an oil pipeline under construction on Alaska's North Slope. The second section of the novel returns to the family in 1978. For four years, there has been peace in the Allbright house, at least during the winter months, when Ernt is away working on the pipeline; however, he is eventually fired from his job and returns home angrier than before. At seventeen, Leni has grown up and begins to challenge her father's authority, resulting in a loss that almost cripples her ability to function and forces her mother to stand up to Ernt's abuse. The novel moves to a close with a final section that takes place almost eight years later in 1986. Life has changed again, and as a grown woman, Leni must deal with loss once more.

The novel is primarily character driven, with the Allbrights as the main focus. The story is told in a limited omniscient point of view with Leni as the main character. Crafted as a bildungsroman, the narrative follows Leni from an insecure thirteen-year-old afraid of facing one more drastic change in her life to a twenty-five-year old woman who willfully chooses to embrace her life's desires. The move to Alaska teaches the young Leni how to work hard, how to be a friend even when she did not want to reveal all of the dirty aspects of her life, and how to cover up for her father. She believes that she can "never tell the truth, never that Dad had trouble keeping a job and staying in one place, and *never* that he drank too much and liked to yell"—even to her friend Matthew, the only local boy her age.

By the middle of their first year in Alaska, Leni is tired of facing her father's illness: "It was exhausting to worry all the time, to study Dad's every movement and the tone of his voice." She is, however, still a child, fearful of losing her parents after Matthew's mother dies. Within four years, which hold some months of peace while her father is away working on the pipeline, Leni is more matter-of-fact about her father; she knows that "Dad wasn't one to let things go." Despite this knowledge, she is still a teen, and when Matthew returns to Kaneq after spending four years away while grieving the loss of his mother, Leni falls in love with him, even knowing that the relationship is dangerous because of her father's hatred of Matthew's father. Her love for Matthew makes her see her life differently, and Hannah skillfully paints a picture of the fragmentation in her life: "Leni had gotten used to seeing

© Kevin Lynch

Kristin Hannah is an award-winning novelist with over twenty books to her credit. Formerly an attorney, Hannah has been writing for approximately thirty years.

herself in shards of glass. Herself in pieces." After she and Matthew almost die in a fall, she defies her father at home, declaring that she is pregnant with Matthew's child. Ernt's reaction is to turn on her, and she becomes an adult in an instant when Cora finally stands up against her husband's fury.

Cora's strength at that moment comes in a revelation of love for her daughter that breaks the bonds that have tied her in a twisted and broken way to a man who could never truly return to the personality that she had loved "before" the war. In the years he was gone to Vietnam, Cora had flitted around, trying a variety of lifestyles for herself and her daughter. When he returned, she fell into her old habits of allowing him to make choices and of living mostly for his whims. She was frightened and over-whelmed by the Alaskan landscape and experience, but she put up with it and with the darkness that took over his mind because she loved him, and "she had chosen to dig for treasure through the dirt of Dad's toxic, porous love." She has one moment of strength when Ernt attacks Leni. That moment of strength finally shows Leni the unbreakable bond between mother and child and leads to another, better change in their lives. Only with Ernt truly gone can Cora learn to lean on her own parents and find forgiveness.

Leni and Cora grow and change throughout a number of thematic issues, most of which involve Ernt. For instance, one of the major thematic ideas in the novel is Ernt's post-traumatic stress disorder (PTSD) after Vietnam. The years prior to his service are referenced as "Before": "before" he loved his family, he was gentle and giving, he was fun to be around, and he could hold down a job. The novel, however, follows him after his return from being held as a prisoner of war. At this point in his life, he is too often unable to function. Nightmares and flashbacks are exacerbated by alcohol. As a result, he emotionally and physically abuses Cora, retreats into bizarre conspiracy theories regarding the government, and falls into rages of jealousy. Through the development of Ernt's character, Hannah sheds a light on the tragic repercussions of war on the broken soldiers who are sent home without appropriate care and on the families who cling to a hope that their loved ones will be able to return to the lives they had before. Change, for Ernt, means destruction: of his marriage, of his sanity, of his life. So, he rebels against it with his whole being, not understanding or perhaps not caring that he is dragging his wife and daughter into the abyss with him.

Another point illustrated through the development of the female characters re-volves around women—their powerlessness and their strength. This strength is needed partly because of problematic issues in the 1970s, such as women's lack of voice, even outside of their homes. For example, when Cora goes to the bank to get a credit card, she tells Leni that "they won't give me a credit card unless your father or *my* father cosigns. . . . Sweet Jesus, it's 1974. I have a job. I make money. And a woman can't get a credit card without a man's signature. It's a man's world, baby girl." Soon after ar-riving in Alaska, Cora is warned that the land is also unforgiving, when Thelma, Earl's daughter, warns her, "A woman has to be tough as steel up here, Cora. You can't count on anyone to save you and your children. You have to be willing to save yourselves. And you have to learn fast." Leni understands the powerlessness even more strongly as she watches her family fall apart while spousal abuse is heaped on her mother at her father's hands. Though there are many times when their friends and neighbors offer to help Cora and Leni escape Ernt's abuse, the police will not step in to change the situation unless Cora will press charges, and Leni knows her mother will never be able to do that.

Women are presented positively in the novel as well. After they arrive in Alaska, Cora and Leni learn that the women around them hold a power that can carry them through the long winters. On their first day in Kaneq, Large Marge, who runs the local grocery store, warns, "Well. You'll need to be tough up here, Cora Allbright. For you and your daughter. You can't just count on your man. You need to be able to save yourself and this beautiful girl of yours." Marge and two other women come to their new property the next day, showing the Allbrights how to begin building their homestead into something that will sustain them throughout the long, hard Alaska winter. Later, after Earl's death, his daughter Thelma stands up to Ernt's wild raving, effectively shutting him down and casting him out of the Harlan compound. After the tragedy with Matthew and Ernt's attack on Leni, Cora and Leni both find a strength that holds them up through the rest of their lives. Themes of mother-child love, loneliness, fear, hope, and tragedy further illustrate the lives of the women in the novel.

Perhaps the most striking aspect of the novel centers on Hannah's presentation of the Alaskan frontier of the 1970s. Known as "The Great Alone," a line from a Robert Service poem, the land itself is set apart. People live "off the grid," without electricity or running water. They adapt to the harsh conditions, learning to preserve food, build what they need, and take care of themselves and their neighbors. Regardless of the harsh conditions, Hannah paints a picture of the beauty of a land that makes it "home" for those who are strong enough to "become your best self and flourish."

Critical reception of the novel has been primarily positive, if a bit less enthusiastic than commentary on *The Nightingale* (2015), Hannah's previous novel. Reviewers for *Booklist* (Kristine Huntley), *School Library Journal* (Tara Kehoe), and *Kirkus Reviews* pointed to, respectively, the author's ability to "vividly [evoke] the natural beauty and danger of Alaska" (Huntley), to use "vivid description" (Kehoe), and to re-create "in magical detail the lives of Alaska's homesteaders in both of the state's seasons (they really only have two)" (*Kirkus*). Other prominent notes pointed to the "compelling portrait of a family in crisis" (Huntley), the "incongruous violence" (Kehoe), and the "specific and authentic . . . depiction of the spiritual wounds of post-Vietnam America" (*Kirkus*). Reviewing the novel for *Library Journal*, Bette-Lee Fox highlighted "the astuteness of the story and the unbreakable connection between mother and child." The combination of setting, characterization, and troubling thematic ideas will hold a reader's attention throughout the novel.

Theresa L. Stowell, PhD

Review Sources

Fox, Bette-Lee. Review of *The Great Alone*, by Kristin Hannah. *Library Journal*, 1 Oct. 2017, p. 65. *Academic Search Complete*, search.ebscohost.com/login.aspx?direct=true&db=a9h&AN=125401603. Accessed 17 July 2018.

Review of *The Great Alone*, by Kristin Hannah. *Kirkus Reviews*, 31 Oct. 2018, www.kirkusreviews.com/book-reviews/kristin-hannah/the-great-alone/. Accessed 17 July 2018.

Review of *The Great Alone*, by Kristin Hannah. *Publishers Weekly*, 9 Oct. 2018, www.publishersweekly.com/978-0-312-57723-0. Accessed 17 July 2018.

Huntley, Kristine. Review of *The Great Alone*, by Kristin Hannah. *Booklist*, 1 Nov. 2017, www.booklistonline.com/The-Great-Alone-Kristin-Hannah/pid=9087847.

Accessed 17 July 2018.

Kehoe, Tara. Review of *The Great Alone*, by Kristin Hannah. *School Library Journal*, Mar. 2018, p. 128. *Academic Search Complete*, search.ebscohost.com/login.aspx?direct=true&db=a9h&AN=128357532. Accessed 17 July 2018.

Maslin, Janet. "A Troubled Dad Takes His Family into the Wild." Review of *The Great Alone*, by Kristin Hannah. *The New York Times*, 1 Feb. 2018, www.nytimes.com/2018/02/01/books/review-great-alone-kristin-hannah.html. Accessed 17 July 2018.

Grist Mill Road

Author: Christopher J. Yates
Publisher: Picador (New York). 352 pp.
Type of work: Novel
Time: 1982; 2008
Locales: Upstate New York, New York City

Christopher J. Yates' second novel, Grist Mill Road, *examines the hidden causes behind a traumatic incident and focuses on its effects on the lives of three people, both at the time of the event and more than quarter-century afterward when their paths intersect again.*

Courtesy of Picador

Principal characters

PATRICK "PATCH" MCCONNELL, a.k.a.,
    Tricky, an unemployed food blogger
DON TREVINO, his former boss at a financial institution
HANNAH JENSEN, his wife, a newspaper crime reporter
MATTHEW WEAVER, a.k.a. Matthew Denby, a food supplier
DETECTIVE MIKE MCCLUSKEY, a member of the New York Police Department
    (NYPD)

Grist Mill Road begins with a horrific act. On August 18, 1982, in the small town of Roseborn near New Paltz, New York, a thirteen-year-old girl named Hannah Jensen is tied to a tree. Her school classmate, fourteen-year-old Matthew Weaver, begins shooting her with a BB gun. Another classmate, twelve-year-old Patrick "Patch" McConnell, stands nearby watching, saying and doing nothing to interfere, even after Hannah is struck in the eye and appears to be dead.

The incident serves as the driving force of the novel, which unwinds in triangular fashion, allowing each of the participants to give a unique perspective on what happened. In telling a compelling story, *Grist Mill Road* deals with a multitude of issues, including community status, small-town prejudices, sins of omission, misunderstandings, long-held secrets, and guilt. Layers are peeled away like the skin of an onion, revealing a series of conditions and events that led to the crime and directly or indirectly influenced a number of unforeseen repercussions.

After the opening scenario the story moves forward twenty-six years, to 2008. Patrick is now living in New York City. He has been married to Hannah—who was not killed, after all—for four years. Patrick, unemployed, has been unsuccessful in trying to land a new job. Hannah, meanwhile, works out of the New York City's police headquarters building as a crime reporter for a tabloid. She is often given tips about gory crime scenes by Mike McCluskey, a tough detective with the NYPD.

After establishing the reference points in 1982 and 2008, the novel bifurcates into alternating narratives. Flashbacks to 1982 illustrate the three main characters' upbringings, experiences, and attitudes to show how a series of fateful circumstances brought them together at the precise moment when Hannah is shot. Chapters set in 2008 carry the plot forward, showing each character's current existence and what happens after they reconnect. The twenty-first century material moves the plot inevitably towards what has been hinted throughout: a shocking conclusion.

The novel is divided into three parts. The first part belongs to Patrick. From vignettes that jump back and forth between past and present readers learn that Patrick is the son of the county's chief assistant district attorney, a man with political aspirations. In 1982, Patrick is a small, frightened boy. He unwittingly acquires the larger, tougher Matthew (who calls Patrick "Tricky") as a protector, when he jumps into to save Patrick from a group of middle school bullies. The two young men form a kind of bond, with Patrick playing a passive role to the aggressive Matthew. They spend a great deal of time prowling nearby mountains and caves, inventing games with names such as Rifle Range, Deer Patrol, and Houdini.

After the opening scenario, Patrick feels a sense of guilt that never goes away. He thinks he is a coward, though his actions prove to be life-saving. He suggests to Matthew that they should tell the authorities about Hannah, then has to run from his enraged friend. He falls hard and bloodies his head. By himself, he returns to the scene of the crime to find Hannah still alive and calling for help. He cuts her loose and despite his own serious injury (in falling, he fractured his skull) bicycles her back to civilization so she can receive medical attention. When Patrick himself awakes from a blackout, he is in the hospital. He learns that Matthew has fled the area (he will be caught, convicted, and sentenced for his crime). Hannah, blinded in one eye, insists Patrick was not present when Matthew shot her, and he is too scared to correct her story. Regardless of Hannah's claim, the people of Roseborn figure Patrick must have been involved, given his known friendship with Matthew, and the McConnell family is shunned. They subsequently move to Maine, where his parents divorce. When his mother has to take odd jobs to subsist, Patrick learns to cook to help the fractured family stretch their meager finances.

Even after reaching adulthood and moving to New York City, Patrick cannot rid himself of guilt. He suffers bouts of depression and attempts suicide several times. Following his reconnection with Hannah, who wears an eyepatch like a pirate (he encounters her by accident, tracks her down, courts her, and they marry) his guilt continues to eat at him. He treats his new wife like royalty, creating culinary feasts and comforting her tenderly when she suddenly awakens from one of her nightmares. But he still cannot bring himself to admit to her that he was present the day she was shot. He reserves the truth for a journal intended eventually for his psychotherapist, which he keeps in a computer file. Patrick, self-flagellating, goes so far as to sabotage his own position at a financial investment firm. As compensation for his troubled emotions, and anticipating a time when his repressed feelings will suddenly burst forth, he periodically stalks his former boss, Don Trevino, whom he blames for the loss of his job.

Between periodic excursions into the employment market (he dooms interviews with a downbeat and distracted attitude), Patrick spends his days working on a food blog, lovingly creating a menu for a restaurant he hopes to open one day, to be called the Red Moose Barn. His blog attracts fans, chief among them someone using the name TribecaM. Over time, the unknown person proposes meeting in an exclusive restaurant to discuss a possible business investment. When Patrick attends the meeting, he is astonished to find that TribecaM is his old friend Matthew, now known as Matthew Denby. Handsome Matthew has become a wealthy, Mercedes-driving supplier of exotic foodstuffs to the best restaurants. He has a fleet of trucks. He owns a plush apartment. He knows influential people including a famous French chef, who can connect people with opportunity. Patrick, paranoid about his former friend's motivations, dashes off without hearing what Matthew has in mind.

Part two of the novel is mainly Hannah's. Her story is told in memoir-like excerpts, written in response to an offer of a literary agent specializing in true crime to produce a full-length true crime book for publication. Of all the gruesome stories Hannah has covered, her own is the one she knows best.

Hannah, as it happens, is a member of the richest family in Roseborn. They live in a large house in a landscaped, estate-like setting on an extensive property. The Jensens have been involved for generations in a profitable enterprise producing especially strong, long-lasting cement made from material extracted from a large limestone deposit on family land. Despite her privileged upbringing, Hannah's home life is not especially happy. Her beloved, encouraging father Walt is always busy running the cement factory. Her tactless mother Laura—who broke her leg a few weeks before Hannah became a target for metal pellets—constantly whines for her daughter's attention because her siblings Bobby (twelve years older, an alcoholic) and Pauley (ten years older, a drug abuser) are usually too incapacitated to do anything. It was while living at home that Hannah became interested in true crime: Truman Capote's *In Cold Blood* (1966) became her favorite book.

In the twenty-first century, Hannah enjoys her job as a crime reporter, though she does not need to work. When she was in her early twenties, her whole family perished in the crash of a chartered plane. As the sole living Jensen, Hannah inherited a fortune, the true scope of which she has concealed from her husband. She sold everything—family home, land, factory—and she and Patrick live comfortably, but not ostentatiously. Hannah is so involved in her job that she is oblivious to Patrick's unraveling psyche. She refuses to talk about the past, especially about the shooting incident. Until Patrick accidentally stabs himself with a knife he stuck in a pants pocket, she is not aware of his regular Don Trevino stalking expeditions or the dark current that runs through his veins.

Part three is left for Matthew, and completes the third leg of the tripodal plotline; the individual testimonials collectively produce a complete picture of what happened in 1982, and why. Matthew's story, told in the style of a confessional letter written to an initially unrevealed recipient, is quite different from Patrick's or Hannah's. Unlike the other two, he was not originally from Roseborn, but born in New York City. While Patrick represents the middle class, and Hannah the upper class, the Weavers are strictly lower class. Matthew's mother is a hard-working diner waitress. His father, however, cannot hold a job. Mr. Weaver is a brutal drunk who frequently beats his older son with a belt or his fists, and taunts his younger son, born with Down syndrome. That is just the beginning of his father's malfeasance: he has done much worse and has gotten away with it. Matthew fears he has inherited his father's penchant for violence. He has been in trouble before: he was held back a year, and thus is older than others in the same grade in Roseborn. He fears nothing, because as a youngster, he has nothing to lose. He seems headed toward disaster until he is taken under the wing of nature enthusiast Pete.

© Circe

British-born Christopher J. Yates worked as a magazine puzzle editor before turning to writing. His first novel, the psychological thriller Black Chalk, *was released in 2013 to strong reviews.*

While Patrick is a study in deterioration and Hannah embraces the status quo, Matthew's is a story of redemption. Despite his genetics and his criminal record, he seems genuinely sorry for what he did. In the later portions of the story he has made himself into a new person, one who is successful and who tries to be helpful to those he wronged.

Critical reception of *Grist Mill Road* was largely positive. Many reviewers discussed the work in relation to Yates's previous novel, *Black Chalk*, with most considering it even better than that well-reviewed debut or at least a worthy follow up. In a review for the *New York Times* Sarah Lyall praised "the fully realized stories the characters are awarded in the service of an elegant narrative." Writing for *NPR*, Jason Sheehan felt the finale was not as inventive as that of *Black Chalk*, but appreciated that the later novel "packs a slow-burn punch,"

Stylistically, *Grist Mill Road* may bother linguistic purists. Yates, following in the footsteps of authors such as James Joyce, William Faulkner, Cormac McCarthy, and Louise Erdrich, has eliminated quotation marks. However, readers should have no problem distinguishing dialogue from description. The plot is suspenseful enough that even punctuation traditionalists should soon become fully absorbed in a story that, as Hannah notes, is as much a small-town tragedy as that depicted in her favorite book.

Jack Ewing

Review Sources

Drabelle, Dennis. "Three Lives Forever Linked by an Act of Violence in Their Shared Past." Review of *Grist Mill Road*, by Christopher J. Yates. *The Washington Post*, 12 Jan. 2018, www.washingtonpost.com/entertainment/books/three-lives-forever-linked-by-an-act-of-violence-in-their-shared-past/2018/01/11/66e3f 228-f566-11e7-b34a-b85626af34ef_story.html. Accessed 8 Oct. 2018.

Review of *Grist Mill Road*, by Christopher J. Yates. *Kirkus*, 28 Sept. 2017, www. kirkusreviews.com/book-reviews/christopher-j-yates/grist-mill-road/. Accessed 8 Oct. 2018.

Lyall, Sarah. "In This Thriller, a Cold Case Turns Hot 26 Years Later." Review of *Grist Mill Road*, by Christopher J. Yates. *The New York Times*, 16 Jan. 2018, www.nytimes.com/2018/01/16/books/review-grist-mill-road-christopher-yates. html. Accessed 8 Oct. 2018.

Sheehan, Jason. "'Grist Mill Road' Bears Witness to Horror—And Its Aftermath." Review of *Grist Mill Road*, by Christopher J. Yates. *NPR*, 13 Jan. 2018, www. npr.org/2018/01/13/575489089/grist-mill-road-bears-witness-to-horror-and-its-aftermath. Accessed 8 Oct. 2018.

Heads of the Colored People

Author: Nafissa Thompson-Spires (b. ca.
1984)
Publisher: Atria (New York). 224 pp.
Type of work: Short fiction
Time: Present
Locales: California; Saint Louis, Missouri;
Chicago, Illinois

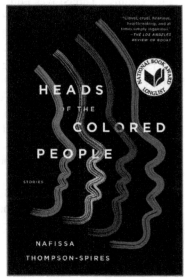

*Short story writer Nafissa Thompson-Spires's
debut collection offers a series of sharply
drawn sketches that illustrate the range of
complex issues facing young, middle-class
African Americans making their way in the
world.*

Principal characters
RILEY, a student and cosplay enthusiast who
is killed by police
BROTHER MAN, a young man with whom Riley has an altercation
DR. RANDOLPH GREEN, an assistant professor at the fictional Wilma Rudolph Univer-
sity
FATIMA, a girl growing up in the Inland Empire region of California, a recurring
figure
BRIAN, a graduate student in anthropology at the University of California, Riverside
ALMA, a nurse who is in demand as a singer at funerals

Between 1852 and 1854, the prominent African American doctor, abolitionist, and
writer James McCune Smith published a series of ten articles in *Frederick Douglass'
Paper*, the abolitionist publication headed by Frederick Douglass. These sketches,
written under the pseudonym Communipaw and titled "Heads of the Colored People,
Done with a Whitewash Brush," depict the lives of a series of free black workers—
bootblacks, grave diggers, washerwomen—mostly living in New York City. The articles, appearing after the passage of the Fugitive Slave Law and during a tough period
for African American workers in the North who were rapidly losing their jobs to European immigrants, aimed to celebrate the dignity of free workers at a precarious time
in their existence.

Taking inspiration from Smith's sketches, Nafissa Thompson-Spires has given the
name *Heads of the Colored People* to both her first collection of stories and to the
lead story in the collection, inviting the reader to see her work as an updated version
of Smith's work. But, as Thompson-Spires explains in an author's note, her collection "departs in most ways from the original content of the nineteenth-century black
writers' sketches." The most notable departure is that Thompson-Spires's pieces are

not simply sketches, but fully developed short stories. Then, too, the characters would seem to be vastly different. Thompson-Spires writes about solidly middle-class African Americans who are, at least on the surface, much more accepted by society than their working-class counterparts in Smith's sketches. But, as Thompson-Spires suggests throughout her collection, her characters are still subject to many of the same restrictions and dangers as Smith's, even if these restrictions are more de facto than de jure.

"Like the original sketches," Thompson-Spires writes, "these stories maintain an interest in black US citizenship, the black middle class, and the future of black American life during pivotal sociopolitical moments." In this similarity lies the usefulness of the gesture, looking back on a little-known historical work as a way to comment on the current state of African American existence in the United States, the ways in which things both have changed and have refused to alter. Throughout the twelve expertly crafted stories in her collection, Thompson-Spires addresses these issues and many more, dealing with serious themes with an often light, ironic touch. In keeping with her interest in continuities, several characters appear throughout the collection, popping up in different stories and allowing the reader to see their lives from different angles.

In the next-to-last story in the collection, "A Conversation about Bread," two black anthropology students debate the proper way to construct an ethnographic sketch for a class assignment. When one student, Brian, criticizes the whole rationale behind another student's efforts, the student, Eldwin, responds that his work is "a good story about cultural differences, interracial differences, class differences. It's more about how many different kinds of black people there are." This explanation would seem to be a tidy summary of what Thompson-Spires is up to in her own collection, expressing the complexities and diversity of African American life. But Brian remains unimpressed by Eldwin's explanation, and the reader too is forced to question its validity. Even in outlining her own project, then, Thompson-Spires is drawn to the consideration of multiple viewpoints. If she is committed to seeing issues from a variety of perspectives, then she invites the reader to view her work in the same way.

This complexity is introduced in the first sentence of the first story. "Heads of the Colored People: Four Fancy Sketches, Two Chalk Outlines, and an Apology" alludes directly to Smith's work, living up to its title by providing the stated number of sketches of a series of black characters living in Los Angeles and St. Louis. The story begins by introducing us to one of these characters: "Riley wore blue contact lenses and bleached his hair . . . and he was black," the narrator says, before informing the reader that "this wasn't any kind of self-hatred thing." Instantly, the story plays with expectations about African American self-presentation, introducing a character who would seem to be trying to make himself less black, a character who inhabits the largely white world of cosplaying but who is nonetheless secure in his black identity.

The next character Thompson-Spires introduces, a man known as Brother Man, certainly sees Riley as compromised in his identity, even if Brother Man himself is also interested in such "white" pursuits as comic books. As Riley heads toward a comics convention, he passes Brother Man, trying to sell his own comics on the street and

© Adrianne Mathiowetz Photography

Nafissa Thompson-Spires is an author and an English professor at the University of Illinois at Urbana-Champaign. Her work has appeared in a wide variety of publications, including The White Review, *the* Los Angeles Review of Books Quarterly Journal, *and* StoryQuarterly. Heads of the Colored People *is her first book.*

attempts to ignore him, a gesture that infuriates Brother Man and leads to a tragic fate for both young men. The rivalry between the two men is born from both their similarities and their differences. Because both Riley and Brother Man are young, educated black men who are both interested in traditionally white pursuits, they are each self-conscious about their identity. Riley, for example, is "irked . . . that he might be mistaken for a self-hating Uncle Tom because he enjoyed cosplay and anime and comic book conventions." For the more bitter Brother Man, who is more of an outsider to this culture than Riley, Riley represents both what he wants to be and what he fears, and so when Riley refuses to acknowledge his presence, he becomes antagonistic.

This exploration of the ways that black people inhabit predominantly white spaces is one that continues throughout the book and is often explored through the same doubling technique that Thompson-Spires used in the opening story. For example, the story "Belles Lettres" takes a comic approach by presenting the antagonistic relationship between the mothers of the two black students in a grade-school class. Consisting entirely of the series of letters that Dr. Lucinda Johnston and Dr. Monica Willis exchange about their daughters, the ironically titled story reveals a latent hostility beneath a polite, well-mannered surface. The letters begin in a highly formal manner, full of passive-aggressive anger. "It sounds—and I say this respectfully, so I hope you won't be offended—like Fatima has had a very hard time getting acclimated here," writes one of the mothers. At issue here is the role that the two girls, Fatima and Christinia, occupy in the school. Whereas Christinia is accustomed to being the only black girl in the class, the arrival of Fatima threatens her role, as well as that of her mother, who also loses the status of the only black class mother. In this way, Thompson-Spires makes clear, with a light comic touch, the complexity of the situation. Both mothers want to fit in in the white world, but they still want the specialness that comes from having a unique African American identity.

Another thread that runs through *Heads of the Colored People* is a barely suppressed anger that is felt by many of the characters and that threatens to break out at any moment. For Professor Randolph Green in "The Necessary Changes Have Been Made," who went from teaching at a largely white school to a historically black college where he is still in the minority as an African American professor, this suppressed anger at having to perform a specific role expresses itself in a petty spat with his officemate Isabela. While Randolph wants the lights turned off because of his migraine headaches, Isabela insists on turning them on. Thompson-Spires makes clear the cause of Randolph's anger when she has Reggie, his former mentor at the white college and who is also black, tell Randolph that his migraines "will go away once you stop feeling like you have to be some kind of standard, once you just let it all out. The problem is once you do that, you won't have a job." This encapsulates the difficult situation that Randolph finds himself in. Reggie confesses that he himself suffers nosebleeds because of being in a similar situation. "The pressure has to come out some kind of way," he explains.

This anger extends to other characters in the book, most memorably to Marjorie, a woman who works at the bursar's office at a university, and who Thompson-Spires follows through an anger-inducing trip to the DMV in one of the best stories in the collection, "Not Today, Marjorie." In documenting this simmering black anger, Thompson-Spires shows that it is an inevitable response to the threat of violence that African Americans face at disproportionate rates. To this end, she begins and ends the collection with stories that deal directly with this sort of violence. In the opening, eponymous story, Riley and Brother Man get in an altercation that the police respond to with outsized force. In the final story, "Wash Clean the Bones," Thompson-Spires delves into the sad situation of African Americans in Chicago subject to violence both within their communities and at the hands of police. The main character, Alma, gets plenty of work singing at funerals as a result, but cannot get over the death of her brother, Terry, who was killed by the cops and who haunts her dreams. In this sobering final story, Thompson-Spires abandons some of the comic levity that she had brought to her previous pieces and lays bare, at last, the sorrow that exists in various ways for all the characters in her book.

Andrew Schenker

Review Sources

Bellot, Gabrielle. "Twenty-First-Century Word Paintings: Nafissa Thompson-Spires's 'Heads of the Colored People.'" *Los Angeles Review of Books*, 30 Apr. 2018, lareviewofbooks.org/article/twenty-first-century-word-paintings-nafissa-thompson-spiress-heads-of-the-colored-people. Accessed 5 Feb. 2019.

Grant, Colin. "*Heads of the Colored People* by Nafissa Thompson-Spires Review—Coolly Ironic Stories." *The Guardian*, 27 Sept. 2018, www.theguardian.com/books/2018/sep/27/heads-colored-people-nafissa-thompson-spires-review. Accessed 5 Feb. 2019.

Lohier, Patrick. Review of *Heads of the Colored People*, by Nafissa Thompson-Spires. *Harvard Review Online*, 19 June 2018, www.harvardreview.org/?q=features/book-review/heads-colored-people. Accessed 5 Feb. 2019.

Williams, John. "Tell Us 5 Things about Your Book: Disarming Humor in 'Heads of the Colored People.'" *The New York Times*, 15 Apr. 2018, www.nytimes.com/2018/04/15/books/heads-of-the-colored-people-nafissa-thompson-spires-interview.html. Accessed 5 Feb. 2019.

A History of Judaism

Author: Martin Goodman (b. 1953)
Publisher: Princeton University Press (Princeton, NJ). 656 pp.
Type of work: History, religion
Time: ca. 2000 BCE–present
Locales: Ancient Judea, Israel, and Palestine; Europe; United States; State of Israel

Courtesy of Princeton University Press

In A History of Judaism, *the distinguished British historian Martin Goodman provides a sweeping survey of Jewish religious beliefs and practices from antiquity to the present day. While demonstrating the extraordinary continuity of Jewish traditions over the two thousand years since the Roman destruction of the Second Temple in Jerusalem, Goodman also highlights the persistent doctrinal and liturgical diversity in Judaism.*

Principal personages

MOSES, leader of the Exodus and lawgiver to the Hebrew people
FLAVIUS JOSEPHUS, Jewish historian of the first century CE
PHILO OF ALEXANDRIA, Jewish philosopher and theologian of the first century CE
SHLOMO YITZHAKI (RASHI), eleventh-century rabbi who wrote an extensive and influential commentary on the Talmud
MAIMONIDES, twelfth-century Sephardic Jewish philosopher and theologian
ELIJAH BEN SOLOMON ZALMAN (VILNA GAON), influential eighteenth-century rabbi and Talmudic scholar who opposed the rise of Hasidic Judaism

Martin Goodman, professor of Jewish studies at the University of Oxford, undertakes a daunting task in *A History of Judaism*: he endeavors to trace the religious history of the Jews, with all its astonishing variety, over the course of more than two thousand years. That he succeeds in crafting a compelling narrative out of the complex interplay of doctrine and custom over such an extended period of time is a tribute to both his erudition and his literary skill. In doing so, Goodman makes no easy concessions to his readers. Though *A History of Judaism* is completely accessible to nonacademic readers, it is not a "popular" history. It is also very much what the title implies, a history of the Jewish religion, rather than the story of the Jewish people. Goodman offers intellectual history and for the most part eschews a record of social or political events. Readers looking for a detailed account of the Jewish War with the Romans in the first century CE that resulted in the devastation of Jerusalem and the mass suicide at Masada; the European persecutions of Jews during the Middle Ages and early modern periods; the Jewish immigrant experience in the United States; the Holocaust; or the foundation of the state of Israel will have to look elsewhere. Goodman briefly alludes to these and other developments, but his focus is on the evolution of the beliefs and practices that embody Jewishness in the world.

The book is a story about faith. Again and again during the course of the long text, Goodman returns to the question: What does it mean to be a Jew? At any given period in history, he is consistently astonished at the multiplicity of responses to that question. The theme of his book is that Judaism has been able to accommodate a wide range of religious conviction and liturgical observances. From the days of the Bible, when the New Testament Gospels record members of various religious factions questioning Jesus of Nazareth, to the present day when Jewish congregations group themselves as Reform, Conservative, Orthodox, and beyond, Judaism has never been a monolithic religious tradition. Yet despite this, over more than two millennia, Jews have managed to accept the differences among themselves without the fratricidal wars that have at times rent Christianity and Islam. A recognition of a common Jewish identity has persevered through wrenching persecution and successive epochs of revolutionary change.

Goodman begins his history in the first century CE with Yosef ben Matityahu, better known as Josephus. A member of the Jewish priestly class, Josephus recorded for posterity a transformative event in the history of Judaism, the destruction of the Second Temple. The future historian rose to prominence as a leader of the Jewish revolt against Roman rule in Judea that ran from 66 to 73 CE. Sensing the direction of events, he surrendered to the Romans. In captivity, he predicted that the Roman general Titus Flavius Vespasian would become emperor, a shrewd and politic observation that came true. His loyalty to Vespasian won him his freedom, and he adopted the Romanized name of Titus Flavius Josephus.

Useful as a translator and advisor, Josephus served in the retinue of Vespasian's son Titus, as the imperial prince in 70 CE supervised the siege and bloody sack of Jerusalem, during which the Temple caught fire and was destroyed. Josephus returned to Rome with his patron and forged a new career as a historian and an apologist for the Jewish religion. He wrote voluminously; his surviving works include *The Jewish War*, an account of the disastrous rebellion against the Romans, *Jewish Antiquities*, a history of the Jews from biblical times through the reign of Herod the Great and the establishment of direct Roman rule in Judea in the early first century, and *Against Apion*, a spirited defense of Judaism against the criticisms of a contemporary orator and philosopher. Taken together, the writings of Josephus provide essential insights into a Jewish world on the brink of dramatic change. Along with the books of the Jewish Bible, they are key sources for helping us understand the political and religious milieu out of which both Christianity and rabbinic Judaism would emerge.

Josephus is not only important for Goodman because he was a witness to profound events; he also enables the modern historian to avoid delicate and intractable issues. Goodman makes no effort to systematically cover the events of the Old Testament, and most importantly the crucial books of the Torah. Stories such as that of Abraham's covenant with God, the epic of Moses and the Exodus from Egypt, the reception of the Ten

Commandments at Mount Sinai, the wandering of the people of Israel for forty years in the desert, the invasion of Canaan, and David's duel with the giant Goliath and subsequent rise to kingship are all central to the popular memory and self-understanding of the Jewish people, but these Biblical episodes are not backed up by any historical or archaeological evidence. Goodman avoids a great deal of complicated and contentious historical argumentation by foregoing his own narrative of these events; instead he simply summarizes Josephus's first-century historical account, which largely tracks with the extant books of the Bible but adds a few interesting details from other sources. Doing this allows Goodman to summarize what Jews thought about their past in the first century CE. Carefully following Josephus's narration of events of the more historically documented times following his people's return from the Babylonian exile and the building of the Second Temple permits Goodman to describe Judaism at a time when the books of the Jewish Bible had been written and this first monotheistic religion had taken mature form. By this point not only had Judaism attained great theological and liturgical richness, but as a result of a growing diaspora of Jewish believers throughout the Roman and Parthian empires, it had become a true world religion.

In his acknowledgements, Goodman notes that his larger history of Judaism grew out of what was originally going to be a monograph on the Jewish religion during the period of the Second Temple. This material takes up fully a third of *A History of Judaism*. Goodman describes in great detail the sacrificial rituals at the temple, which at this time were the biblically ordained heart of Jewish religious practice. The loss of the Temple, and the priestly rites centered there, would be traumatic for Jews. Fortunately, already in the final days of Temple worship there were religious developments taking place that would allow Judaism to survive this catastrophe. Doctrinal pluralism would be the salvation of the Jewish religion.

Both Josephus and the books of the New Testament describe different sects within Judaism. The Sadducees were a group associated with the priestly elite, who rejected the belief in the resurrection of the dead. The Pharisees advocated a strict devotion to religious laws and believed in an afterlife. The Essenes strove to achieve religious purity by living a communal existence. The Zealots sought to overthrow Roman rule and establish a genuinely Jewish state. Despite their differences, all these groups managed to peacefully share the common space of the Temple. Out of their contentions and the piety of the people, practices were taking root that would allow Judaism to weather the coming storm. Groups of Jews gathered in local meeting places for communal prayers and the reading of the Torah. Rabbis, or teachers, were beginning to build up a body of interpretations of the law. Once the Temple was destroyed and the priests dispersed, the synagogues and rabbis would take on an increasingly central role in Judaism.

Following the successive failed revolts against Imperial Rome, Jews would not succeed in reclaiming control over part of their biblically promised homeland until the establishment of the state of Israel in 1948. Once again they saw themselves as a people in exile. Increasingly dispersed, they demonstrated a remarkable ability to adapt to changing circumstances, absorbing influences from the newly ascendant religions of Christianity and then Islam, while retaining their distinctive identity. Judaism's post-Temple history is a dialectical record of challenge and renewal. In the first five centuries CE, rabbis researched and debated the Jewish law; their commentary on this was compiled in the Talmud, which ever since has remained a core text for Judaism. Such was the continuing diversity within Judaism, however, that not all Jews embraced the teachings of the rabbis and the Talmud. The Karaites, possibly under lingering influences from the Sadducees, recognized only the biblical texts themselves as an authoritative source of Jewish law. For a time in the early Middle Ages, Karaism was a significant rival to Rabbinic Judaism; a remnant community of Karaites still exists in the twenty-first century.

Courtesy of Princeton University Press

Martin Goodman is a professor of Jewish studies and president of the Centre for Hebrew and Jewish Studies at the University of Oxford. He is the editor of The Oxford Handbook of Jewish Studies *(2002) and the author of* Rome and Jerusalem: The Clash of Ancient Civilizations *(2007), among many other books.*

Great teachers and philosophers appeared in the Jewish world at regular intervals. During the eleventh century, Rabbi Shlomo Yitzhaki, known by the acronym Rashi, wrote commentaries on the Jewish scriptures and the Talmud that are still read and studied. In the twelfth century, Maimonides was a Jewish philosopher from North Africa who was honored for both his theological and scientific works. New modes of religious devotion also emerged. An enduring and influential form of mysticism known as Kabbalah spread from medieval Spain. Kabbalists sought deeper esoteric meanings in traditional Jewish texts. In the eighteenth century, Hasidic Judaism emerged in Eastern Europe. A pietistic movement that mirrored religious revivals taking place within contemporary Christianity, Hasidism stressed an intense spiritual devotion amongst ordinary Jews. It remains a potent force in Judaism today, associated with traditionalist values. The Enlightenment took some Jews in a different direction. In the nineteenth century a group of well-educated Jews in Germany launched Reform Judaism, shedding aspects of ritual and doctrine that they regarded as out of step with modernity, emphasizing instead the progressive revelation of God's will in the world.

Today, Goodman notes, Judaism remains as vibrantly diverse as Josephus described it in the first century. Given the extraordinary variety of religious expression chronicled in his book, Goodman is disinclined to make any predictions about the future of Judaism, other than that it is likely to survive for the foreseeable future. His *A History of Judaism*, which was met with much critical acclaim, will itself remain an essential guide for anyone interested in Jewish religious history for many years to come.

Daniel P. Murphy

Review Sources

Green, Dominic. Review of *A History of Judaism*, by Martin Goodman. *The Wall Street Journal*, 31 March 2018, www.wsj.com/articles/a-history-of-judaism-review-the-book-of-books-1522440885. Accessed 15 Nov. 2018.

Heller, Margaret. Review of *A History of Judaism*, by Martin Goodman. *Library Journal*, 1 Feb. 2018, pp. 104–5.

Review of *A History of Judaism*, by Martin Goodman. *Kirkus Reviews*, 15 Jan. 2018, www.kirkusreviews.com/book-reviews/martin-goodman/a-history-of-judaism/. Accessed 15 Nov. 2018.

Review of *A History of Judaism*, by Martin Goodman. *Publishers Weekly*, 5 Feb. 2018, www.publishersweekly.com/978-0-691-18127-1. Accessed 15 Nov. 2018.

Kirsch, Adam. "Why Jewish History Is So Hard to Write." Review of *A History of Judaism*, by Martin Goodman, and *The Story of the Jews: Volume Two: Belonging, 1492–1900*, by Simon Schama. *The New Yorker*, 26 March 2018, www.newyorker.com/magazine/2018/03/26/why-jewish-history-is-so-hard-to-write. Accessed 15 Nov. 2018.

Home after Dark

Author: David Small (b. 1945)
Publisher: Liveright (New York). Illustrated. 416 pp.
Type of work: Graphic novel
Time: 1950s
Locale: Primarily Marshfield, California

Courtesy of Liveright

After Russell Pruitt's parents separate, he and his father set off across country to find a new start. Russell's new life is fraught with complications as he struggles to fit into the new community; to deal with being abandoned, first by his mother and then by his father; and to understand that he does not have to be alone in the world.

Principal characters
RUSSELL PRUITT, a shy thirteen-year-old
MIKE PRUITT, his father
WEN MAH, a friendly landlady
KURT, a local bully
WILLIE, a friend of Kurt's
WARREN, a classmate who befriends Russell

David Small's reputation as an author and illustrator was established with his first picture book, *Eulalie and the Hopping Head* (1982), which became a Library of Congress Children's Book of the Year. His artwork in that first book, as well as in several editorial cartoons, attracted enough attention that he was asked to illustrate books by children's authors such as Nathan Zimelman, Eve Merriman, and Beverly Cleary, among others. As a writer or illustrator, he has over forty children's books to his credit. His work on graphic novels started with the autobiographical *Stitches, a Memoir* (2009), which was listed as a New York Times Best Seller, named a National Book Award finalist, and awarded the American Library Association's Alex Award. *Home after Dark* is his second graphic novel.

The story begins with a prologue set in Youngstown, Ohio. This short section is primarily driven by images and contains only three pages with text to clarify the meaning. The following story is broken into seventeen untitled chapters; each chapter is distinguished by an opening two-page spread of artwork that indicates the major setting and often foreshadows the action of the chapter. For instance, chapter 3 begins with a sketch of the Golden Gate Bridge and the next page tells readers that San Francisco is not full of jobs as promised, so "We kept going north and farther inland. To a little town called Marshfield." The rest of the chapter shows Russell and his father settling into life in Marshfield. A later chapter, in contrast, shows the kitchen of the home where Russell and his father have been living. The room is presented as a mess with dirty dishes and trash strewn over every surface, including the floor. This chaotic image is followed by the simple statement "Dad stopped coming home." The following pages tell of Russell's abandonment and struggle to adapt to life on his own.

The artwork uses a cartoon style with simple pen-and-ink lines. A watercolor wash adds shades of gray tones to the otherwise black-and-white images. Outside of the two-page spreads that mark the beginning of new chapters, the structure within the chapters vary in the number of panels provided. Small often uses one large panel to establish a particular mood or idea, such as a single image showing the inside of a tree to depict Russell's battle with feeling inconsequential. A diminished Russell sits in a knothole with his arms crossed on his knees and his head tilted upward, looking at an opening at the top of the page. A much larger version of the bully Kurt points down at Russell with a mocking expression. Later, there is a two-page spread with three panels on one side and five on the other. This larger number of frames allows the author to create a fast-paced action scene where Kurt is picking on Warren, a scene that ultimately leads to a fight in which Kurt attacks the other boy.

Though the actual dialogue and narrative are limited, with some pages containing no words at all, the story confronts a surprising number of important themes. Two of the most prevalent ideas illustrated in the graphic novel are abandonment and rejection. The opening pages show Russell's mother leaving her son and husband. Among the only words in the prologue are "That summer, Mom ran away with Ollie Jackson (known on the football field as 'Action Jackson'), Dad's best friend." This is only the first of many rejections Russell will experience. Russell's father packs him up, and they head to California, where Russell's aunt June smugly says, "This is Southern California. Real estate is going nuts, Mike, let's face it, you can't afford to live here. You need to go north. Around San Francisco. That's where all the jobs are." Even Russell's father rejects and then eventually abandons the boy. Although Russell attempts to make sure their home is clean and meals are ready for his father, the older man often mocks the boy's attempts. At one point, he yells, "I can warm up my own supper. The last thing I need is my son becoming a hausfrau." That chapter ends after Russell has a dream of being fed to a ravenous lion, the final image showing the boy huddled wide-eyed in his bed with an

© Gordon Trice

Author-illustrator David Small's work primarily targets young audiences. He has a master's degree in fine arts from Yale University. He has won numerous awards, including a Caldecott Medal for So, You Want To Be President?, *a collaboration with Judith St. George, and two Caldecott Honors.*

overlapping image of an open-jawed lion. Eventually, his father gives up and leaves without notice. Small's sparse prose presents this shocking rejection with the simple sentence, "Dad stopped coming home." Abandoned by both of his parents, Russell is left to fend for himself.

Home is not the only place where Russell struggles to fit in, and neither is he the only character who experiences rejection. When Russell begins school in Marshfield, he is mocked by a group of boys who push him around and tear his clothing. Another boy, Warren McCaw, attempts to befriend Russell. He cautions Russell that the way to avoid the bullying is to disappear from notice. When Russell asks Warren how the other boy escaped notice, he replies, "I became invisible." Though Russell is intrigued by the idea of a friend, his relationship with Warren is complicated. Warren's pet rat and a necklace of amulets make him appear strange, and the other boys often accuse him of being gay. When Warren asks Russell to "take off our clothes and hug one another," Russell complies with the request but ends the friendship.

Shortly after Russell's friendship with Warren ends, Russell befriends two other boys from his neighborhood, Kurt and Willie. While Willie is kind, Kurt is boastful and rude. Despite that, Russell respects Kurt, believing that "Kurt was the man. He knew all the forms, the brands, and the mystery lingo that maleness seemed to ask of us." Kurt's friendship, however, is unhealthy. He does things that endanger Willie and Russell, and he attacks Warren, accusing him publicly of killing local animals. Russell struggles with the fact that Willie is kind enough to step in and help Warren while he stands back. Eventually, Warren kills himself due to the bullying. Feeling guilty, Russell attempts to make amends with Warren's grandmother, but his naïveté leads him to get beaten up in a strange town where he has no one to help him.

Adults are also the target of hate in the novel. Jian and Wen Mah, a Chinese couple who rent Mike and Russell a room when they first arrive in Marshfield, experience vitriolic racism. For instance, one day while Russell is out riding his bike, an elderly man says to the boy that he should tell them they are unwanted in town, employing a then-common ethnic slur for Japanese people. When Russell corrects the man about the couple's ethnicity, he responds angrily with another slur and says to tell them they should "get back to the laundry. Where they belong." Despite how they are treated by others, the couple welcome Russell and his father into their home. Russell realizes throughout the graphic novel that the only true friends he has are the Mahs. Wen checks up on him when his father disappears, and she takes him in, even forgiving him after he steals from her husband. The older couple accepts him, but Russell is so broken by rejection that he does not know how to accept their welcome until Wen tells him how much he and Jian have in common: "You feel alone? He feels very much alone. You cannot go back to Ohio? He can never go back to China. Your family is lost? His family are all dead. Mr. Mah works very hard but the neighbors see only a 'Chinaman' who belongs in a laundry. They are blind to who he really is." These compassionate words teach Russell a lesson in understanding, and he finally learns to find a sense of peace.

In addition to the novel's strong themes, several literary devices add depth to the story. For instance, on the way to California, Russell finds a puppy in a hotel parking lot. His father refuses to take the dog with them, and Small shows the puppy sitting in the middle of the road starring forlornly after the father and son. In an illustration of the ruthlessness of the world, a semitrailer then hits the dog, leaving it lying dead in the middle of the road. This episode foreshadows the rejection Russell will experience throughout the rest of the story.

The critical reviews glow with praise for *Home after Dark*. Tom Batten for *Library Journal* comments, "Small is a masterful illustrator, with an incredible ability to establish his characters' inner lives through physical gestures or facial expressions, conveying a kaleidoscopic style of storytelling." A review of the graphic novel in *Publishers Weekly* notes, "The story traffics in archetypes—the mean kid who frames the weirdo; the festering cruelty beneath the idyllic small-town facade—but never tips over into trite." *Kirkus Reviews* lauds the artwork as "emotive, kinetic, with a striking balance of realism and cartoon and particularly arresting facial expression." Finally, Colette Bancroft for the *Tampa Bay Times* points to its universality: "Russell's story may be set some 50 years ago, but it's all too contemporary in its concerns—a story that might be even more urgent now."

Theresa L. Stowell, PhD

Review Sources

Bancroft, Colette. "David Small's 'Home after Dark' a Powerful Graphic Novel about Adolescence." Review of *Home after Dark*, by David Small. *Tampa Bay Times*, 15 Oct. 2018, www.tampabay.com/features/books/david-smalls-home-after-dark-a-powerful-graphic-novel-about-adolescence-20181015. Accessed 1 Nov. 2018.

Batten, Tom. Review of *Home after Dark*, by David Small. *Library Journal*, vol. 143, no. 10, 1 June 2018, p. 69. *Literary Reference Center Plus*, search.ebscohost.com/login.aspx?direct=true&db=lkh&AN=129811126&site=lrc-plus. Accessed 1 Nov. 2018.

Hayes, Summer. Review of *Home after Dark*, by David Small. *Booklist*, vol. 11, nos. 19–20, 1 June 2018, p. 57. *Literary Reference Center Plus*, search.ebscohost.com/login.aspx?direct=true&db=lkh&AN=130254890&site=lrc-plus. Accessed 1 Nov. 2018.

Review of *Home after Dark*, by David Small. *Kirkus Reviews*, vol. 86, no. 13, 1 July 2018, p. 1. *Literary Reference Center Plus*, search.ebscohost.com/login.aspx?direct=true&db=lkh&AN=130385971&site=lrc-plus. Accessed 1 Nov. 2018.

Review of *Home after Dark*, by David Small. *Publishers Weekly*, vol. 265, no. 22, 28 May 2018, p. 81. *Literary Reference Center Plus*, search.ebscohost.com/login.aspx?direct=true&db=lkh&AN=129819840&site=lrc-plus. Accessed 1 Nov. 2018.

How Hard Can It Be?

Author: Allison Pearson (b. 1960)
First published: How Hard Can It Be?,
2017, in the United Kingdom
Publisher: St. Martin's Press (New York).
384 pp.
Type of work: Novel
Time: ca. 2015
Locale: United Kingdom

In How Hard Can It Be?*, the sequel to her
2002 novel* I Don't Know How She Does It*,
Allison Pearson documents protagonist Kate
Reddy's struggles with work, marriage, perimenopause, and caring for both her teenage
children and her aging relatives.*

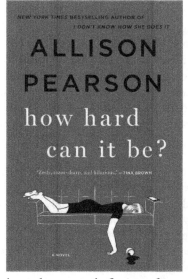

Courtesy of St. Martin's Press

Principal characters

KATE REDDY, a forty-nine-year-old woman returning to her career in finance after a
    seven-year absence
RICHARD SHATTOCK, her husband
EMILY SHATTOCK, their sixteen-year-old daughter
BEN SHATTOCK, their fourteen-year-old son
JEAN REDDY, her mother
DONALD SHATTOCK, her father-in-law
BARBARA SHATTOCK, her mother-in-law
JACK ABELHAMMER, an American former client of Kate's firm

Welsh novelist Allison Pearson's debut novel, *I Don't Know How She Does It*, was a
best seller following its release in 2002 and earned both critical praise and widespread
popularity. The novel's candid depiction of the life of a working mother and focus on
the challenges faced by many women in the male-dominated workplace resonated
with readers. The novel was later adapted into the 2011 film of the same name. With
How Hard Can It Be?, a sequel set more than a decade later, Pearson returns to the
world of protagonist Kate Reddy, whose life has changed significantly in the years
since her first appearance. Now on the edge of turning fifty, Kate attempts to return
to work after a seven-year absence while supporting her household, keeping up with
the lives of her teenage children and unemployed husband, and helping to care for
several aging relatives, all the while confronting the aging process herself as she goes
through perimenopause. Published in the United Kingdom in 2017 and the United
States in 2018, *How Hard Can It Be?* earned a largely positive response that focused
in particular on Pearson's revealing and often feminist take on the pressures placed on
many women in middle age.

At the start of the novel, Kate's life has changed significantly from her life in *I Don't Know How She Does It*. In that book she was a busy, high-paid finance professional in her mid-thirties. Now, having left her job seven years earlier to focus on caring for her family and moved to northern England, she has returned to the suburbs of London in an attempt to reenter the workforce. Her husband, Richard, has been laid off from his architecture job and is likewise seeking a new career, pursuing training as a counselor. However, he will spend two years without an income while undergoing training, and his own costly therapy sessions and serious bicycling habit have become a drain on the family finances. Their lifestyle has been further upended by Kate's insistence that they purchase and live in a fixer-upper home.

Kate and Richard's daughter and son, last seen as small children in *I Don't Know How She Does It*, are now teenagers who encounter many of the challenges typical for their age. Fourteen-year-old Ben spends the majority of his time playing video games, while sixteen-year-old Emily struggles to fit in with a clique of popular girls at her school. At the start of the novel, Kate wakes in the middle of the night to a tearful Emily, who sent a "belfie"—what Emily defines as "a selfie of your bum"—to a female frenemy who in turn posted the photograph on Facebook, ostensibly by accident. The incident begins the novel on a humorous yet thought-provoking note, emphasizing the gulf between Kate's teen years and her daughter's. The episode highlights the often harmful role that social media plays in Emily's life, a topic that Kate considers throughout the novel.

Needing to support her family, Kate prepares to reenter the workforce. This proves to be a challenging task for a forty-nine-year-old whose recent work experience has encompassed volunteer efforts, part-time work, and childcare rather than the forms of work deemed legitimate by society at large. When she visits a recruiter, the recruiter comments negatively on her age and status as a mother, implying that because Kate is nearly fifty years old, she is essentially un-hirable. Indeed, she is far from the only woman facing that challenge: as a member of a Women Returners group that also includes new friend Sally Carter, Kate observes that the difficulties facing older women in the workplace are systemic. However, she desperately needs a job and therefore resolves to play along with the unfair system by lying about her age and altering her body to appear younger and more socially acceptable through procedures such as liposuction.

Amid her efforts to find a job, Kate also becomes the de facto point of contact for Richard's parents, Donald and Barbara, who have been struggling since Barbara began to succumb to Alzheimer's disease. She also spends a significant portion of time worrying about her own mother, Jean, whose behavior has grown increasingly erratic, though Kate is not the adult child primarily responsible for caring for her. As multiple characters point out, Kate is a member of the so-called Sandwich Generation of adults who must deal with both growing children and aging parents. Meanwhile, Kate likewise struggles with the changes taking place within her own body as perimenopause causes a host of physical symptoms that she attempts to manage medically. Her hormonal shifts also contribute to problems with her memory, once a "fabulous, state-of-the-art retrieval system" that has now become "a dusty provincial library."

© Graham Jepson

Allison Pearson is the author of the novels I Don't Know How She Does It *(2002) and* I Think I Love You *(2010). She also wrote as a columnist for newspapers such as the* Daily Telegraph *and the* Daily Mail.

She personifies her compromised recall ability as a character named Roy.

With the help of a heavily doctored CV, Kate, now claiming to be forty-two rather than forty-nine, succeeds in finding a low-level temporary job. In fact, the position is at a new iteration of the same investment company that she had previously founded. However, almost no one still working for the company remembers her, and her deception is successful. At her new job, Kate befriends a younger colleague named Alice and endures disrespect—and at times direct attempts at sabotage—from a colleague named Troy. Despite such challenges, Kate remains a skilled financial professional and is talented at customer relations, and she soon finds success. She wins over new clients and prevents wealthy ones from ending their relationship with the firm, earning respect in the workplace.

However, Kate's return to the financial sector also brings up the past in the form of Jack Abelhammer, an American former client of the company. She fell passionately in love with him in *I Don't Know How She Does It*, but ultimately remained loyal to Richard. As Kate agonizes over the extent of her relationship with Jack, the many other challenges in her life—including her daughter's emotional distress, her husband's suspicious closeness to one of his counseling colleagues, and her parent's and parents-in-law's health—come to a head, forcing Kate to do her best to manage her tumultuous life. By the end of the novel, however, Pearson makes it clear that despite the challenges Kate has and will continue to face, she is deserving of happiness, and she begins to build a new life that is far more satisfying.

An entertaining and lively novel, *How Hard Can It Be?* is perhaps most notable for its forthright discussion of the multitude of pressures placed on women in twenty-first-century society. While many of the points Pearson makes about topics such as ageism, emotional labor, and social media are hardly new and will likely be familiar to many readers, their inclusion in a mainstream novel is refreshing. In addition, Kate's first-person account of her complicated life makes those insights feel particularly personal. At times, the reader may see some of the novel's reveals coming, but that dramatic irony serves to underscore Kate's perimenopause-induced memory problems as well as the sheer number of responsibilities she is expected to stay on top of at all times.

Indeed, the novel is perhaps at its strongest when it is pointing out the unfair expectations placed on women in many families. Kate points out the double standard at hand on multiple occasions, at one point commenting, "Don't you hate the way families assume it's always the women who should take care of the elderly parents, even if a son lives nearer? That may just be connected to the fact that we always do." Kate's commentary and actions throughout the novel reinforce the idea that women often take on essential responsibilities in part because if they do not, no one else will. The novel's devotion to realism likewise extends to its discussion of Kate's experiences with perimenopause, a normal stage of life that nevertheless is dramatically underrepresented in media and literature. Pearson does not shy away from sharing the messy but realistic details of Kate's physical experiences, among them the onset of a severe menstrual period during a client meeting that, in a show of ingenuity, Kate handles with the aid of a hand towel and an orchid leaf. The measures Kate takes to address her symptoms and her body's perceived flaws, including the use of banned hormone patches and a lunch-break session of liposuction, are presented humorously yet in knowing detail, making for a simultaneously entertaining and informative read. In the acknowledgements following the novel, Pearson expresses the desire to make the discussion of perimenopause and menopause no longer taboo in society, and *How Hard Can It Be?* represents a strong step in that direction.

Upon its publication in the United Kingdom and the United States, *How Hard Can It Be?* received a largely positive response from critics. Many focused particular praise on the book's observations on ageism in the workplace, perimenopause, and Kate's numerous and often conflicting responsibilities. The anonymous reviewer for *Publishers Weekly* particularly highlighted Pearson's success in depicting the "cluelessness and powerlessness" felt by parents of teenagers in the digital age. While reviews were generally positive, some critics identified weak areas in Pearson's storytelling and the novel's overarching plot. Although Karin Tanabe for the *Washington Post* found *How Hard Can It Be?* to be relatable and funny, she described the overall story as predictable. Writing for the *New York Times*, Alex Witchel was somewhat more critical, calling the novel "decidedly overlong" and finding aspects such as Kate's asides to Roy, her personified memory, to be "more tedious than amusing." However, even Witchel praised the book's handling of the mother-daughter relationship as well as its commentary on aging, family, and work.

In addition to winning praise from critics, *How Hard Can It Be?* was optioned for television by the production company Made Up Stories in April 2018.

Joy Crelin

Review Sources

Review of *How Hard Can It Be?*, by Allison Pearson. *Kirkus*, 20 Mar. 2018, www.kirkusreviews.com/book-reviews/allison-pearson/how-hard-can-it-be/. Accessed 31 Aug. 2018.

Review of *How Hard Can It Be?*, by Allison Pearson. *Publishers Weekly*, 23 Apr. 2018, www.publishersweekly.com/978-1-250-08608-2. Accessed 31 Aug. 2018.

Pelling, Rowan. "A Rollicking Return for a Funny, Feminist Heroine—*How Hard Can It Be?* by Allison Pearson Review." *The Telegraph*, 4 Sept. 2017, www.telegraph.co.uk/books/what-to-read/rollicking-return-funny-feminist-heroine-hard-can-allison/. Accessed 31 Aug. 2018.

Rhule, Patty. "'How Hard Can It Be?' Just Ask Kate, Who's Turning 50 in Hilarious, Timely New Novel." Review of *How Hard Can It Be?*, by Allison Pearson. *USA Today*, 4 June 2018, www.usatoday.com/story/life/books/2018/06/04/book-review-how-hard-can-allison-pearson/661889002/. Accessed 31 Aug. 2018.

Tanabe, Karin. "The Heroine from *I Don't Know How She Does It* Is Back with a New Juggling Act." Review of *How Hard Can It Be?*, by Allison Pearson. *The Washington Post*, 11 July 2018, www.washingtonpost.com/entertainment/books/the-heroine-from-i-dont-know-how-she-does-it-is-back-with-a-new-juggling-act/2018/07/11/8fcb14d6-851d-11e8-8553-a3ce89036c78_story.html?noredirect=on&utm_term=.4c7a03ec990f. Accessed 31 Aug. 2018.

Witchel, Alex. "Allison Pearson 'Does It' Again." Review of *How Hard Can It Be?*, by Allison Pearson. *The New York Times*, 1 June 2018, www.nytimes.com/2018/06/01/books/review/allison-pearson-how-hard-can-it-be.html. Accessed 31 Aug. 2018.

How Long 'til Black Future Month?

Author: N. K. Jemisin (b. ca. 1972)
Publisher: Orbit (New York). 416 pp.
Type of work: Short fiction

How Long 'til Black Future Month? is award-winning novelist N. K. Jemisin's first collection of short stories. It compiles fascinating, varied tales from throughout her career to date.

How Long 'til Black Future Month? is a short-story collection by award-winning science-fiction and fantasy novelist N. K. Jemisin. She published her first novel, *The Hundred Thousand Kingdoms*, the first volume of her Inheritance trilogy, in 2010. Jemisin is the first author ever to win the Hugo Award for Best Novel, the genre's most prestigious prize, three years in a row (2016–18). She received the award for each installment of her Broken Earth trilogy, including *The Fifth Season* (2015), *The Obelisk Gate* (2016), and *The Stone Sky* (2017). Those books explore a fantastical world in which people called "orogenes" can control the plates of the earth by instinct. The Broken Earth books are apocalyptic fiction, exploring the uncertainties of an earth on the verge of total destruction, but they also offer a nuanced commentary on power and oppression. The orogenes' magical powers keep the world safe, yet orogenes themselves are brutally repressed.

In her August 6, 2015, review of *The Fifth Season* for the *New York Times*, fantasy novelist Naomi Novik wrote that fantasy novels often provide a degree of escape, albeit with oversimplified challenges and individual heroism. In contrast, she noted: "Jemisin's intricate and extraordinary world-building starts with oppression: Her universes begin by asking who is oppressing whom, what they are gaining, what they fear. . . . When escape comes in her novels, it is not a merely personal victory, or the restoration of a sketchy and soft-lit status quo. Her heroes achieve escape velocity, smashing through oppressive systems and leaving them behind like shed skins." This observation seems an appropriate introduction to Jemisin's collection, which spans the length of her career. The stories in *How Long 'til Black Future Month?*—the title is taken from an essay Jemisin wrote about Afrofuturism in 2013—thrillingly explore resistance, revolution, and the upending of old ways.

In the book's introduction, Jemisin recalls that she once thought she could not write short stories. Science-fiction and fantasy writing require copious exposition, which are not easy to package in the short form, but Jemisin had other reasons to be wary. At the time, about fifteen years ago, the genre was dominated by heteronormative white male writers writing about universes dominated by white male characters. "Science fiction claimed to be the fiction of the future," Jemisin writes in her introduction, "but it still mostly celebrated the faces and voices and stories of the past." Much has been written—by Jemisin and many others—about the obscene level of resistance to diverse voices in the genre, best illustrated by an intolerant reactionary movement called the

Sad Puppies in 2013. Regardless, years before that and with some trepidation, Jemisin, devoted herself to learning the craft of short stories.

The twenty-two stories contained in *Black Future Month* offer twenty-two fully realized fantastical worlds, from an alternate nineteenth-century New Orleans in "The Effluent Engine" to the computer code universe of "The Trojan Girl." Stories like "Stone Hunger" and "The Narcomancer" offer a fascinating glimpse of the seeds of Jemisin's longer works, the Broken Earth trilogy and the Dreamblood duology, while two other stories serve as Jemisin's reactions to classic sci-fi and fantasy stories. "Walking Awake" takes place in a world in which people are enslaved by parasitic aliens. In it, one woman makes a revolutionary choice. The story is inspired by Robert A. Heinlein's 1951 novel *The Puppet Masters*. Influenced by the Red Scare, Heinlein imagined the alien parasites as communists; Jemisin offers a different take. Jemisin's "The Ones Who Stay and Fight" is a response to, or in dialogue with, Ursula K. Le Guin's "The Ones Who Walk Away from Omelas." While Le Guin's story examines the human cost of capitalism and suggests that one must abandon the existing, flawed society to create another, better one, Jemisin argues that one must shape the society one has. Still, Jemisin told Abigail Bereola in a December 2018 interview for the *Paris Review*, she struggled to imagine a true utopia "stemming from our [society] that was truly inclusive, truly egalitarian, and truly good for all people."

Not every story in the collection will capture every reader, but each is told with incredible economy and skill. Jemisin is a master at hooking a reader from a story's first sentence, a difficult task in any genre, but all the more impressive when it necessarily involves explaining a totally unknown universe. Jemisin is also a fabulous experimenter with form. She has said that short stories serve as sketchpads for larger ideas, but her offerings are more polished than that might suggest. *Black Future Month* contains fables, allegories, erotica, steampunk, science fiction, High Fantasy (in the mode of witches and wizards), magical realism, and alternative history. One story is written in a series of archived, fragmented emails and instant messages; another is narrated by a bit of code. There is an immediacy to Jemisin's writing that is hard to describe. One can imagine her as the narrator of "The Storyteller's Replacement," who seduces her listener into magical submission.

Several of the stories in *Black Future Month* take place in a fantastical version of New York City or New Orleans. In "The City Born Great," she imagines New York personified, embodied in a queer black man, and in "On the Banks of the River Lex," a personified Death haunts a postapocalyptic New York, meandering from Union Square to the rundown Coney Island aquarium. In "Non-Zero Probabilities," a 2009 story that was nominated for Hugo and Nebula Awards for Best Short Story, Jemisin imagines the city plagued by unlikely events; so many New Yorkers win the lottery that it has to be shut down, but the city also suffers from equally unlikely events such as train derailments. Helping the victims of one such accident, the narrator, Adele, shakes her head: "They should have known better. The probability of a train derailment was infinitesimal. That meant it was only a matter of time."

In the steampunk tale "The Effluent Engine," a cunning heroine named Jessaline Dumonde explores the streets of early nineteenth-century New Orleans. Jessaline is a black Haitian spy, tasked with convincing a Creole scientist to help her create an engine to help the cause of Haitian revolutionaries. The scientist balks, but his younger sister, a chemist, jumps at the chance to work. This swashbuckling tale also chronicles the budding romance between the two women. The captivating "Cuisines des Mémoires" takes place in a fantastical, present-day New Orleans. In it, a cynical New Yorker named Harold visits a restaurant called Maison Laveau. (The name is a reference to Marie Laveau, the nineteenth-century Vodoun queen of New Orleans.) The restaurant creates exact replicas of dishes throughout history, from Marie Antoinette's last meal to a memorable early dinner Harold once enjoyed with his former wife. Jemisin beautifully captures how taste and smell can evoke memories. Another story, "Red Dirt Witch," set in segregated Birmingham, Alabama, turns on the power of herbs. Jemisin has a truly unique ability to write about food the way other fantasy writers write about magic. Finally, the last story in the collection "Sinners, Saints, Dragons, and Haints, in the City beneath the Still Waters," is set in the Ninth Ward during Hurricane Katrina.

N. K. Jemisin is the author of the Inheritance trilogy, the Dreamblood duology, and the Broken Earth series. She is the first author to win the Hugo Award for Best Novel three years in a row. How Long 'til Black Future Month? is her first collection of short stories.

Upon publication, *Black Future Month* received well-deserved critical acclaim. In a starred review for *Publishers Weekly*, one reviewer wrote that *Black Future Month* serves as "an excellent introduction" to Jemisin's work. "Jemisin's versatility is on full display, giving her diverse protagonists numerous chances to shine," they wrote. The book also received a starred review from *Kirkus*. The stories in *Black Future Month* "demonstrate both the growth and active flourishing of one of speculative fiction's most thoughtful and exciting writers," that reviewer wrote.

Slate critic Laura Miller, who reviewed the book for the *New York Times*, criticized what she considered the frustrating didacticism of some of the stories, like the book's opener, "The Ones Who Stay and Fight." Similarly, the "near-perfect" "Sinners, Saints," she wrote, is spoiled by some heavy-handedness near the end. Nevertheless, Miller wrote, there is "much more to love." She offered praise for "Valedictorian," a story about a black girl ostracized for her intelligence. Thanks to her incredible smarts, she must be offered as tribute to the AI that rule a futuristic America. An encounter with one of her supposed overlords, though, fundamentally changes the way she sees the world. Liz Hand pointed out in the *Los Angeles Times* that "The Trojan Girl" cannily draws on elements of Isaac Asimov's "Three Laws of Robotics," a set of rules about how AI should behave in stories, and praised the lush prose of the ancient Egypt–inspired "Narcomancer." *Black Future Month*, Hand wrote, offers "boundlessly imaginative and diverse renditions of worlds to come." In an effusive review for the speculative-fiction website *Tor.com*, Martin Cahill praised the book's incredible diversity and variety. "Jemisin's vision is limitless," he wrote, "and in every story, in every world, you get the sense that she is testing the waters, tasting the air, getting a sense of how this genre works, and how she can best use it to her strengths."

Molly Hagan

Review Sources

Cahill, Martin. "Community, Revolution, and Power: *How Long 'til Black Future Month?* by N. K. Jemisin." Review of *How Long 'til Black Future Month?*, by N. K. Jemisin. *Tor.com*, 27 Nov. 2018, www.tor.com/2018/11/27/book-reviews-how-long-til-black-future-month-by-n-k-jemisin. Accessed 19 Feb. 2019.

El-Mohtar, Amal. "Gorgeous 'Black Future Month' Tracks A Writer's Development." Review of *How Long 'til Black Future Month?*, by N. K. Jemisin. *NPR*, 29 Nov. 2018, www.npr.org/2018/11/29/671583610/gorgeous-black-future-month-tracks-a-writers-development. Accessed 19 Feb. 2019.

Hand, Liz. "'How Long 'Til Black Future Month?' Collects the Marvelous Short Fiction of N.K. Jemisin." Review of *How Long 'til Black Future Month?*, by N. K. Jemisin. *Los Angeles Times*, 28 Nov. 2018, www.latimes.com/books/la-ca-jc-n-k-jemisin-20181128-story.html. Accessed 19 Feb. 2019.

Review of *How Long 'til Black Future Month?*, by N. K. Jemisin. *Kirkus*, 15 Oct. 2018, www.kirkusreviews.com/book-reviews/nk-jemisin/how-long-til-black-future-month. Accessed 19 Feb. 2019.

Review of *How Long 'til Black Future Month?*, by N. K. Jemisin. *Publishers Weekly*, 5 Nov. 2018, www.publishersweekly.com/978-0-316-49134-1. Accessed 19 Feb. 2019.

Miller, Laura. "The Fantasy Master N.K. Jemisin Turns to Short Stories." Review of *How Long 'til Black Future Month?*, by N. K. Jemisin. *The New York Times*, 30 Nov. 2018, www.nytimes.com/2018/11/30/books/review/nk-jemisin-how-long-til-black-future-month.html. Accessed 19 Feb. 2019.

How to Be Safe

Author: Tom McAllister
Publisher: Liveright Publishing (New York). 240 pp.
Type of work: Novel
Time: Present day
Locale: Seldom Falls, Pennsylvania

Courtesy of Liveright

Anna Crawford's life is turned upside down after a teenage boy goes on a rampage at the local high school where she used to work. A report that points to her as a suspect results in an FBI raid of her home, a frightening interrogation, and long-term post-traumatic stress disorder that disrupts her ability to live normally.

Principal characters
ANNA CRAWFORD, a former teacher accused of involvement in a school shooting
CALVIN CRAWFORD, her brother
ROBBIE, her boyfriend
RENEE, her best friend
SYLVIA, the mother of the school shooter

The thought-provoking themes of Tom McAllister's second novel, *How to Be Safe*, reflect issues that pervade the present-day atmosphere of the United States. The novel opens with a prologue that follows a teenage boy who is on his way to the local high school in Seldom Falls, Pennsylvania, where he plans to massacre as many students and school employees as he can. This section tells what he is doing at a single moment and what will happen during and after the massacre. An example of this time shift establishes the amount of damage he will do: "It is eleven o'clock. By noon, he will have killed nineteen people, wounded forty-five. He is armed extensively, enough to take out more than that, but his gun will jam and one of his homemade bombs will not detonate."

The time shift continues even after the shooting, when the story switches focus to Anna Crawford as the main character. While the prologue is told with present and future tense verbs, however, Anna's portions of the novel all use past tense verbs. Despite the past tense style, readers will feel like they are following Anna as the events, including memories from her childhood or teen years, unfold. The sporadic nature of her memories serves to reinforce the causes of her post-traumatic stress disorder (PTSD) and relationship issues. There is a suggestion of chronology as Anna's chapters begin in April, the month of the shooting, and continue to the following April. These chapters tell Anna's story in snapshots, short sections that move fluidly through

Anna's timeline, sharing stories about her relationships, her childhood, her family, and her own angst after her life is turned upside down. In between, there are three chapters that describe the victims of the shooting and three chapters that provide a stream of consciousness litany on "how to be safe."

Despite its comparatively short length, the novel covers several significant issues, starting with the school shooting. Even though it is not described in detail and does not take up much space in the story, McAllister uses the incident as the basis for other events, especially those related to Anna. In the aftermath of the tragedy, the police look for someone to blame and Anna, a teacher who has recently been suspended for insubordination, has unwisely posted online "I should've burned the place down when I had the chance" followed by "hashtag bitter hashtag spite, hashtag f—— that place." This is enough for television news chyrons to scream "FORMER TEACHER HAD MOTIVE." Within moments of the report that pointed to her as a suspect, Anna's home is raided by the FBI, and she is shuffled off to be interrogated. Her life changes, and when she is finally released, she recognizes that she will no longer be able to find privacy or a secure place in her world: "During the few days they held me prisoner, my entire life had been shared with the world. I had become public property."

Within the issue of the school shooting, McAllister also explores the topics of responsibility, violence, and gun control. In respect to responsibility, the author points out the inappropriate placement of blame when an event like this happens. The first hint of blame comes from the shooter himself, who in the prologue, suggests he wants to be stopped. He delays going to the school by stopping for a slice of pizza. On the way to the restaurant, he sees a receptionist in the window of a neighboring business and fantasizes briefly, thinking, "If she would just look up from her phone she would see him and they could make eye contact and have something like a human connection," but she does not and he thinks, "She will see him on the news later and not even know how close he'd been to her, how she could have saved everyone if only she'd taken the time." Later, Anna, the killer's mother, his music, his video games, and even the victims all become scapegoats.

Violence itself becomes another focal point, and Anna pays close attention to other school shootings and different kinds of violent attacks that take place around the world in the months after the Seldom Falls tragedy. One example is provided at the end of August, when we see passages listing this kind of situation: "Three airplanes had gone missing in one week. . . . But then nine people were killed in one night in Chicago, and six in St. Louis, and fourteen in Lansing. . . . Every now and then someone from a forgotten country will plant a homemade bomb somewhere and remind everyone they exist."

Guns become another focus throughout the novel. For instance, a month after the shooting, the issue of gun control is raised, "There were people who said guns were dangerous, that the national obsession with guns is the reason people keep getting killed, that two centuries of gun worship had poisoned our culture, that if we just, once and for all, made a decision to eliminate as many guns as possible then we would all be safer." McAllister deftly handles the complexity of the gun control debate, providing a range of perspectives rather than clearly moralizing for one side or the other.

© LauraBeth McAllister

Tom McAllister is the author of a memoir, short stories, and the novel The Young Widower's Handbook *(2017). He served as the nonfiction editor of* Barrelhouse *magazine and taught at Temple University.*

Another issue that McAllister presents in an almost hyperbolic way is toxic masculinity. After Anna's arrest and five minutes of fame, she is bombarded by messages, threats, and suggestions from men. These are mostly violent and hateful. In June, Anna gets "an email from a man who called himself Patriot Paul and who said, 'I'm going to show up at your house one night when you're not expecting it and I'm going to cut your whore mouth open with my bowie knife and fill it up with dicks. I'm going to cover you in dicks and smother you with them and when you're dead I'll hang you over my mantel like a trophy.'" Later, she comments, "Men do not have a language for loneliness, so they turn to violence and sports, in that order. They cannot cry, so they blow things up instead." Anna's on-and-off boyfriend, Robbie, and her brother, Calvin, are exceptions to this mindset. Both of these men want to take care of Anna, but their nurturing becomes almost suffocating to her, and she avoids them when she becomes overwhelmed.

Anna's PTSD is another effect of the shooting that McAllister highlights in the novel. What happens to those who are only indirectly involved in such a tragedy, those who know the perpetrator or the victims? These are questions readers will find answered at least in some way through Anna and the people she interacts with throughout the novel. Anna's history reveals a deeper set of reasons behind her PTSD, shown through snapshots of her childhood, parents, and brother.

There are a number of additional literary techniques spread throughout to showcase the tragedy of the situation as well as to provide a dark sense of humor. For instance, it is noted that the town of Seldom Falls had once been touted as "America's friendliest city." McAllister often combines irony and dark humor with hyperbole, and more than one example relates to the theme of guns. Early in the book, Anna reveals, "Gun sales had risen 300 percent since the shooting. Everyone had guns, even people who didn't have guns." Later, she says, "Ban everything besides guns. Ban public space. Ban buildings. Ban trigger fingers. Ban anger. Ban flesh and organs and blood loss. Ban women and children who are easy targets and ban men who like to shoot at targets. Ban physics, and ban velocity. Ban human interaction." Additional examples of this sarcastic tone come in the form of seemingly casual advice offered throughout, such as "If you want to make people feel safe, the best thing to do is to ban nature, to arrest nature and put it in jail where it can't bother us anymore," or "Self-medicate whenever possible. Whatever drug is helping you to cope is one that will kill you but at least you're maintaining some control over how and when you go." Meanwhile, the feeling of disorder and depression that comes over the town after the shooting is metaphorically represented by the absence of the sun. Anna notes, "After, the sun turned gray and descended into the lake like a spider dropping from the ceiling. I saw it hit the water, I saw the steam rising up, and I felt the tremors when it crashed against the lake floor. I saw the displaced water splashing over the banks and rushing toward our houses."

Reviews of *How to Be Safe* were primarily positive. A critic for *Kirkus Reviews* wrote, "This novel is an indictment of gun culture, hot-take journalism, and social media, and if that sounds like a miserable premise for a novel, fear not: **McAllister** is a brave and stylish writer." *Booklist* reviewer Annie Bostrom argued that the novel is a "well-voiced and remarkably observed page-turner [that] is in almost all ways an anti-thriller—itself a comment on the current, terrifying mundanity of similar events." Patrick Sullivan, writing for *Library Journal*, also gave a glowing verdict: "A blistering, Swiftian portrait of a nation that has lost its moral center, this book is a compelling from start to finish. Enthusiastically recommended for fans of literary fiction, psychological drama, and dystopian fiction." One negative note came from *Publishers Weekly*, whose reviewer suggested, "Though Anna's voice is strong, the novel falters in its depiction of the tragedy's fallout, often electing to skim the surface instead of going deep."

Theresa L. Stowell, PhD

Review Sources

Bostrom, Annie. Review of *How to Be Safe*, by Tom McAllister. *Booklist*, 15 March 2018, p. 18. *Literary Reference Center Plus*, search.ebscohost.com/login.aspx?direct=true&db=lkh&AN=128581079&site=lrc-plus. Accessed 12 Feb. 2019.

Review of *How to Be Safe*, by Tom McAllister. *Kirkus Reviews*, 1 February 2018, pp. 409. *Literary Reference Center Plus*, search.ebscohost.com/login.aspx?direct=true&db=lkh&AN=127646724&site=lrc-plus. Accessed 12 Feb. 2019.

Review of *How to Be Safe*, by Tom McAllister. *Publishers Weekly*, 26 February 2018, pp. 62. *Literary Reference Center Plus*, search.ebscohost.com/login.aspx?direct=true&db=lkh&AN=128207734&site=lrc-plus. Accessed 12 February 2019.

Sullivan, Patrick. Review of *How to Be Safe*, by Tom McAllister. *Library Journal*, 1 March 2018, pp. 76. *Literary Reference Center Plus*, search.ebscohost.com/login.aspx?direct=true&db=lkh&AN=128234074&site=lrc-plus. Accessed 12 February 2019.

How to Change Your Mind
What the New Science of Psychedelics Teaches Us about Consciousness, Dying, Addiction, Depression, and Transcendence

Author: Michael Pollan (b. 1955)
Publisher: Penguin Press (New York). 480 pp.
Type of work: Medicine, memoir, philosophy
Time: 1930s–present

In How to Change Your Mind, Michael Pollan explores the history of psychedelic compounds such as LSD and psilocybin, their medical and philosophical significance, and his own personal experiences with them.

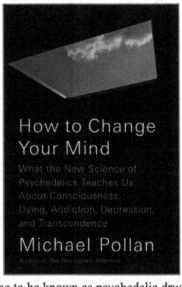

How to Change Your Mind

What the New Science of Psychedelics Teaches Us About Consciousness, Dying, Addiction, Depression, and Transcendence

Michael Pollan

Author of The Omnivore's Dilemma

Courtesy of Penguin

In the 1950s and 1960s, researchers in the United States, Canada, the United Kingdom, and elsewhere carried out numerous studies on the medical use of substances that would come to be known as psychedelic drugs. Testing such drugs on a host of subjects, researchers found that specific substances such as psilocybin—a compound found in certain mushrooms—and LSD (or lysergic acid diethylamide) had the potential to improve the outlooks of individuals struggling with mental-health conditions such as depression and alcohol addiction. For a time, LSD and psilocybin were the subjects of compelling research that not only won the backing of prestigious research institutions and the US government but also proved highly productive, resulting in the publication of more than one thousand papers prior to the year 1965. However, as drugs such as LSD became closely associated with the youth counterculture of the 1960s, a moral panic and subsequent government response put an end to open research into psychedelic substances, and both LSD and psilocybin were classified as schedule-one drugs and banned in the United States by the 1970s. Yet despite that devastating setback, research into both the medical and spiritual sides of psychedelics continued in secret throughout the remainder of the twentieth century, and in the beginning of the twenty-first, a new generation of researchers openly began to pick up where their predecessors had left off.

In *How to Change Your Mind: What the New Science of Psychedelics Teaches Us about Consciousness, Dying, Addiction, Depression, and Transcendence*, science and food writer Michael Pollan chronicles the history of psychedelics following their introduction into the United States in the mid-twentieth century, explores the brief yet productive period of sanctioned research into such substances, and delves into the societal factors that eventually forced the use and study of psychedelics underground. Originating in Pollan's 2015 *New Yorker* article "The Trip Treatment," about ongoing

© Jeannette Montgomery Barron

Michael Pollan is the author of The Botany of Desire *(2001),* The Omnivore's Dilemma *(2006),* In Defense of Food *(2008),* Food Rules *(2010), and* Cooked *(2013). His journalism has been published in venues such as the* New York Times Magazine *and the* New Yorker.

research into treating cancer patients with psilocybin to relieve anxiety about death, *How to Change Your Mind* expands significantly upon the topics discussed in that article, ultimately presenting a nuanced, and at times highly personal, view of some of the twentieth century's most misunderstood substances.

Following a prologue in which Pollan provides a brief overview and recounts his own introduction to the topic of psychedelics, *How to Change Your Mind* is divided into six chapters, each of which covers a particular facet of Pollan's exploration of the history, functions, and significance of those substances. Like many of the researchers he discusses, he focuses primarily on two substances: LSD, accidentally discovered by Swiss chemist Albert Hofmann in 1938, and psilocybin, one of two major compounds found within mushrooms colloquially known as "magic mushrooms," which had been traditionally used by the indigenous cultures of Mexico and Central America for centuries before being introduced to the United States in a 1957 article in *Life* magazine.

In the book's first chapter, "A Renaissance," Pollan documents the ongoing renewal of interest in psychedelic research, which he traces back to the year 2006. During that year, which saw Hofmann's hundredth birthday, the US Supreme Court ruled that the religious group União do Vegetal could import the otherwise-banned hallucinogenic tea ayahuasca into the country for religious purposes, and the journal *Psychopharmacology* published a groundbreaking paper titled "Psilocybin Can Occasion Mystical-Type Experiences Having Substantial and Sustained Personal Meaning and Spiritual Significance." For Pollan, who identifies 2006 as "the start of the modern renaissance of psychedelic research," the period signaled a shift in attitudes toward psychedelics as both researchers and government bodies began to reconsider the personal benefits of substances that since the 1970s had been officially regarded solely as drugs of abuse. Throughout the first chapter of *How to Change Your Mind*, Pollan delves into the research carried out in the first decades of the twenty-first century by scholars such as Johns Hopkins psychopharmacology researcher Roland Griffiths as well as individuals such as Bob Jesse and Rick Dobin, who worked largely outside of the scientific establishment to promote the study of psychedelics' therapeutic and spiritual benefits. He likewise highlights some of the institutions, among them California's Esalen Institute, that sought to keep knowledge of psychedelics' potential alive after official scientific efforts to study such substances ceased. "A Renaissance" provides a valuable overview of many of the individuals and organizations that made Pollan's investigation possible and aptly sets the stage for his deeper dives into the workings of psychedelics.

Over the next chapters, Pollan explores the natural roots of LSD and psilocybin, each of which originated in a fungus—LSD in the grain fungus ergot—prior to being synthesized in laboratories. Much of the second chapter, titled "Natural History," focuses on Pollan's search for psilocybin mushrooms in the wild, a quest in which he was aided by mycologist Paul Stamets. An independent expert on psilocybin mushrooms, Stamets is one of the many fascinating figures Pollan profiles in the book, all of whom share an interest in psychedelics but differ greatly in their scientific approach to, personal engagement with, and philosophical view of such substances. Intriguing personalities likewise abound in chapter 3, "History," which documents the controversial rise and fall of psychedelics in both the scientific world and American society. As appropriate for a history of psychedelics in the United States, the chapter focuses in part on former Harvard University researcher Timothy Leary, who became one of the primary faces of the psychedelic movement in the mid-1960s and is known for encouraging young Americans to "turn on, tune in, [and] drop out." However, throughout the book, Pollan limits his discussion of Leary, whom he suggests "looms a little *too* large in [the history of psychedelics], or at least in our popular understanding of it." Alongside discussion of the notorious Harvard Psilocybin Project, led by Leary and Richard Alpert (later known as Ram Dass), Pollan highlights the contributions of individuals such as Canadian-based researchers Humphrey Osmond and Abram Hoffer, who in the 1950s used LSD to treat alcoholism, and psychotherapists such as Sidney Cohen, Betty Eisner, and Oscar Janiger, who popularized the practice of LSD therapy in California. As the chapter concludes, he documents the events that led to the end of officially sanctioned psychedelic research in the United States but notes that exploration of LSD and psilocybin did not end but was instead forced underground—where, as Pollan learned firsthand, it remained into the twenty-first century.

Among the most striking sections of *How to Change Your Mind* are the portions in which Pollan documents his own personal experiences trying the psychedelic substances on which the book focuses, in addition to others. While he describes experiences with psilocybin mushrooms and ayahuasca at various points in the book, the bulk of Pollan's personal experiences with psychedelics are chronicled in chapter 4, "Travelogue," which describes his cautious attempts to find underground "guides" whom he trusts to supervise his experiences with the drugs as well as his subsequent hallucinatory experiences. The inclusion of such deeply personal experiences in *How to Change Your Mind* underscores Pollan's commitment to his craft, as his well-rounded take on psychedelics would be somewhat incomplete without that firsthand reporting. While capturing any rarefied mental state—be it a dream, mystical experience, or hallucination—in words is a daunting task, Pollan aptly conveys the deeply significant nature of his experiences sampling psilocybin, LSD, and 5-MeO-DMT, the latter a powerful substance produced by certain South American plants and in the venom of the Sonoran desert toad. He follows that chapter, perhaps the most personal segment of a work that blends memoir with medical and philosophical history, with a chapter on the neuroscience underlying the effects he and others who have taken psychedelic substances have experienced. While Pollan makes it clear that research in that area is ongoing, he highlights the work of researchers such as neuroscientist Robin Carhart-Harris, who has found that psilocybin reduces the level of activity in areas of the brain known as the default mode network and that a sharp decrease in activity in those areas correlates with the loss of a sense of self characteristic of many psilocybin experiences.

The book's sixth and final chapter, "The Trip Treatment," shares a title with and draws extensively from Pollan's 2015 *New Yorker* article, focusing on trials at New York University in which researchers gave psilocybin to volunteers who had been diagnosed with cancer. During the trials, the researchers—like others before them—found that the volunteers' experiences while under the influence of the drug significantly alleviated their fears about their diagnoses and their own mortality. Pollan goes on to address experiments in using psychedelics to treat addiction and depression, which, much like the similar trials of the 1950s, have shown significant promise. Indeed, both "The Trip Treatment" and *How to Change Your Mind* present exciting prospects for the future of mental-health treatment, particularly regarding challenging disorders such as alcoholism and treatment-resistant depression. Nevertheless, Pollan takes a measured approach to the subject, emphasizing in the book's epilogue that the state of psychedelic research and its legal status remain in flux. Just as the flourishing field of psychedelic research was unceremoniously shut down in the 1960s, so too could the twenty-first-century renaissance fall to a new wave of moral panic, overzealous drug policy, or even the potential unprofitability of psychedelic treatments. In spite of such risks, *How to Change Your Mind* ultimately provides an optimistic view of the potential of psychedelics and could change numerous minds itself.

How to Change Your Mind won extensive acclaim from critics, who widely praised Pollan's deft and informative handling of a topic with a substantial amount of what Pollan refers to as "countercultural baggage." In a review for the *New York Times*, critic John Williams identifies Pollan as particularly suitable to write about the topic, noting that the author's "initial skepticism and general lack of hipness work wonders for the material." Critics likewise appreciated what the anonymous reviewer for *Kirkus* described as Pollan's "evenhanded but generally positive approach," which leaves room to acknowledge the potential risks of using psychedelic substances—Pollan's fear that taking psychedelics might worsen his existing atrial fibrillation is a recurring concern in the book's fourth chapter—while dispelling urban legends about and highlighting the potential benefits of LSD and psilocybin. *How to Change Your Mind* likewise met with a positive response among reviewers for more science-focused publications: in a review for *Massive Science*, neuroscientist Benjamin Bell notes that Pollan succeeds in rendering the complex scientific concepts at hand accessible for a general audience, "walk[ing readers] through some very high-minded publications." In addition to recognizing the strength of Pollan's work, the positive reception of *How to Change Your Mind* may signal a greater public willingness to reassess substances such as LSD and psilocybin based on their potential benefits rather than on the long-standing stigma surrounding them.

Joy Crelin

Review Sources

Bell, Benjamin. "A Neuroscientist Reviews Michael Pollan's 'How to Change Your Mind.'" Review of *How to Change Your Mind: The New Science of Psychedelics*, by Michael Pollan. *Massive Science*, 21 May 2018, massivesci.com/articles/pollan-lsd-psychedelics-review. Accessed 31 Aug. 2018.

Burkeman, Oliver. Review of *How to Change Your Mind: The New Science of Psychedelics*, by Michael Pollan. *The Guardian*, 22 May 2018, www.theguardian.com/books/2018/may/22/how-to-change-mind-new-science-psychedelics-michael-pollan-review. Accessed 31 Aug. 2018.

Review of *How to Change Your Mind*, by Michael Pollan. *Kirkus Reviews*, 20 Feb. 2018, www.kirkusreviews.com/book-reviews/michael-pollan/how-to-change-your-mind. Accessed 31 Aug. 2018.

Review of *How to Change Your Mind*, by Michael Pollan. *Publishers Weekly*, 12 Mar. 2018, www.publishersweekly.com/978-1-59420-422-7. Accessed 31 Aug. 2018.

Thring, Oliver. "Review: *How to Change Your Mind: The New Science of Psychedelics* by Michael Pollan—the Positive Effects of LSD." Review of *How to Change Your Mind*, by Michael Pollan. *The Times*, 27 May 2018, www.thetimes.co.uk/article/review-how-to-change-your-mind-the-new-science-of-psychedelics-by-michael-pollan-resetting-our-minds-mpvfq7kdc. Accessed 31 Aug. 2018.

Williams, John. "A Strait-Laced Writer Explores Psychedelics, and Leaves the Door of Perception Ajar." Review of *How to Change Your Mind*, by Michael Pollan. *The New York Times*, 14 May 2018, www.nytimes.com/2018/05/14/books/review-how-to-change-your-mind-psychedelics-science-michael-pollan.html. Accessed 31 Aug. 2018.

How to Write an Autobiographical Novel

Author: Alexander Chee (b. ca. 1967)
Publisher: Houghton Mifflin Harcourt (New York). 288 pp.
Type of work: Essays

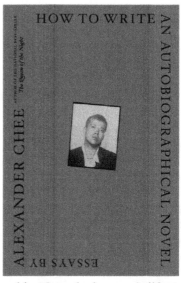

Courtesy of Houghton Mifflin Harcourt

Award-winning novelist Alexander Chee's first collection of essays reflects on his life, his relationships with family, friends, and lovers, and the path that he took to becoming a writer.

For a writer, a person who has devoted his or her life to literature, it is difficult to look back at that life and not see it in terms of the journey undertaken to arrive at that vocation. This is because for a writer, life and literature are so completely intertwined as to appear inseparable. Not only does one's life consist of a path taken toward writerly success, but the author often takes the materials of his or her life and recasts them into fiction, altering the literal truth to get at greater symbolic truths.

Such is the case for Alexander Chee, the American novelist who published his first novel, *Edinburgh*, to much critical acclaim and several awards in 2001, but did not complete his next book until a decade and a half later. When *The Queen of the Night* finally appeared in 2016, it was widely lauded too, and the time seemed right for Chee to follow up with a collection of essays, exploring the hugely difficult and highly unpredictable process of writing and literary success.

Because for Chee, the private life and the writing life are so intimately entwined, the book begins with an essay detailing the foreign exchange program he was in when he was fifteen, an essay that only has a tangential relationship to his later career. In that essay, "The Curse," the teenaged Alexander spends a summer in Mexico with a well-to-do family. Because of the nature of the program, he has little to do except learn the language, which he does readily, and hang out with his handsome seventeen-year-old host brother, Miguel, and his friends. Two of the tensions animating Chee's young life come to the fore in these interactions: his status as a mixed-race American, with a Korean father and white mother, and his budding homosexuality. When the boys hang out, a certain sensual, homoerotic languor hangs over the proceedings, which the young Alexander picks up on, although nothing ever comes of it. Meanwhile, because of Alexander's ambiguous appearance and fluency in Spanish, Miguel and his friend Javier bet on Alexander's ability to "pass" for Mexican, telling some friends who do not know him that he is from their country. The friends believe the ruse, and Alexander is left with an odd sense of his own racial identity. These anxieties over race and sexuality are threads throughout the book, continual concerns of both Chee himself and the books he would come to write, and are established powerfully in the book's first essay.

If the book's title, which is also the title of one of the essays, leads the reader to expect a how-to writing manual, then those expectations are largely thwarted. (Although Chee does provide great, useful insight into the writing process.) But the book itself stands as something of an autobiographical work in its own right—if not a novel, obviously, then something like a memoir in essays. The pieces are arranged roughly in the chronology of Chee's life, proceeding from childhood, to his early education as a writer, to his efforts to write his first novel, and ending with him firmly established as a successful writer with a regular teaching job.

It is a long path, though, and Chee takes us through each step with a retrospective understanding that things were never going to be as easy as he thought they would be. In an early essay, "The Writing Life," Chee discusses his time studying with the legendary writer Annie Dillard (who herself published a book with the same title as the essay) while an undergraduate at Wesleyan University. Upending conventional expectations about the writing process, Dillard taught Chee and his classmates some hard truths about writing, but also provided plenty of affirmation. "You are the only one of you," she tells the class. "Your unique perspective, at this time, in our age, whether it's on Tunis or the trees outside your window, is what matters." Perhaps the most important bit of insight she provides into the writing life is in her conception of writing as "the job," as she puts it. It is a long, arduous process of putting words down on a page day after day and those who succeed are not necessarily those with enormous talent, but those who continue to do the hard work without giving up. This is a lesson that Chee learns well and keeps in mind throughout the book.

"The Writing Life" is clearly well-written and engaging, but it will probably be of most interest to other writers. Many of the other essays, while tying in thematically with his portrait of his literary career, are less explicitly writerly and more of general interest. The essay "Girl," for example, which was selected for *The Best American Essays of 2016*, deals with identity in a way that mirrors the concerns of Chee's writing but is less explicitly about the literary enterprise. In this essay, which deals with the question of identity, Chee begins by recalling Halloween night of 1990 when he dressed as a woman. When his boyfriend first sees him in drag that night, he is entranced and kisses him. Chee realizes that he is playing out a classic scene where the "beautiful girl receives her man's adoration"—a scene he never thought he would get to act out.

All at once, the tensions of Chee's life, those he first outlined in "The Curse," are erased. "In this moment, the confusion of my whole life has receded. No one will ask me if I am white or Asian. No one will ask me if I am a man or a woman. No one will ask me why I love men." This newfound sense of freedom is one that proves intoxicating to him, but it is one that he knows cannot last. He will not dress as a woman every day, and it will not always be Halloween in the gay-friendly Castro district of San Francisco. Ultimately, he must learn to live as himself and internally reconcile his conflicting feelings. Nonetheless, this moment allows him to move forward and find out who he really is. "Sometimes you don't know who you are until you put on a mask," he concludes in a moment of wisdom.

Having lived in San Francisco and New York in the late 1980s and the 1990s, the AIDS crisis was a big part of Chee's life, with many in his community affected. Several of the earlier essays in the book deal with that time in his life, specifically focusing on Chee's activism and the deaths of friends, the latter most notably in a moving tribute to a deceased mentor and lover entitled "After Peter." The most powerful moment of any of these essays, though, occurs at the end of a short piece entitled "1989." The piece details young Alexander's participation in a protest in San Francisco against government inaction on AIDS and ends in a brutal police crackdown. After his friend is leveled by a police baton, a news crew comes to interview him and he describes what he has seen. Chee then ends the essays with a startling moment of realization that registers as a real coming-of-age moment: "After [the news crew] leave, I think about how, up to now, I have thought that I lived in a different country from this. But this is the country I live in, I tell myself, feeling the metal against my fingers. This is the country I live in."

As the book proceeds, Chee's attention does turn more to the writing life, because as he gets older and more established, it becomes the professional milieu in which he finds himself. One of the book's centerpiece essays, "The Autobiography of My Novel," which tells the story of how he came to write and publish *Edinburgh*, brings all the strands of the book skillfully together. Because it was such a long journey—he begins work on the book in 1994—the essay covers much of the same time frame as the rest of the book, switching focus while touching on many of the same events and concerns. The essay also offers the most insight into the novel writing process of any piece, not just in terms of its exhaustive detailing of the steps needed to do it, but in terms of larger realizations. To write the novel, Chee has to come to an understanding about autobiographical fiction and he finally does. "The story of your life, described, will not describe how you came to think about your life or yourself, nor de-

Alexander Chee has written two novels, the award-winning Edinburgh *(2001) and* The Queen of the Night *(2016). He contributes to the* New Republic, *the* Virginia Quarterly Review, *and the* Los Angeles Times, *and teaches creative writing at Dartmouth College.*

Courtesy of Houghton Mifflin Harcourt

scribe any of what you learned," he writes. "This is what fiction can do." In other words, a person cannot simply write down what happened and expect it to be great literature. Instead, the writer must refract that experience get at larger truths and to spin a narrative that reads compellingly for the reader.

Coming up with the proper way of telling his story is especially fraught for Chee because *Edinburgh* deals with child sexual abuse and Chee himself experienced abuse as a boy. For years, he was unable to face the memory of what happened and only by writing about it, first as fiction, was he able to eventually face it. But the process of doing so, and the relationship between what happened to him and the way he wrote about it was incredibly tangled. In a moving essay entitled "The Guardians," Chee details this complicated relationship and finally faces his abuse head-on for the first time in writing. It is a powerful gesture for Chee and one that illustrates the different roles of fiction and nonfiction. In adapting this experience for his novel, Chee was able to address the abuse while keeping his distance. Here, in the essay, he has nowhere to hide and must speak about what happened to him in his own highly recognizable voice.

Andrew Schenker

Review Sources

Kim, Crystal Hana. "The Trailblazing Writing Life of Alexander Chee." Review of *How to Write an Autobiographical Novel*, by Alexander Chee. *The Washington Post*, 20 Apr. 2018, www.washingtonpost.com/entertainment/books/the-trailblazing-writing-life-of-an-openly-gay-korean-american-writer/2018/04/20/401a80f0-434d-11e8-bba2-0976a82b05a2_story.html. Accessed 5 Nov. 2018.

McCormack, J. W. "Writing as Drag: Alexander Chee's Essays Consider the Novelist's Craft." Review of *How to Write an Autobiographical Novel*, by Alexander Chee. *The New York Times*, 27 June 2018, www.nytimes.com/2018/06/27/books/review/alexander-chee-how-to-write-an-autobiographical-novel.html. Accessed 5 Nov. 2018.

McIntosh, Fergus. "How Fiction Helped Alexander Chee Face Reality." Review of *How to Write an Autobiographical Novel*, by Alexander Chee. *The New Yorker*, 9 May 2018, www.newyorker.com/books/page-turner/how-fiction-helped-alexander-chee-face-reality. Accessed 5 Nov. 2018.

Stockton, William. Review of *How to Write an Autobiographical Novel*, by Alexander Chee. *Lambda Literary*, 8 Apr. 2018, www.lambdaliterary.org/reviews/04/08/how-to-write-an-autobiographical-novel. Accessed 5 Nov. 2018.

I'll Be Gone in the Dark
One Woman's Obsessive Search for the Golden State Killer

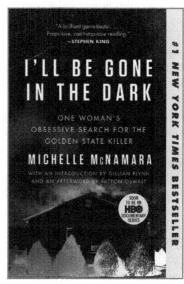

Courtesy of HarperCollins

Author: Michelle McNamara (1970–2016)
Introduction: by Gillian Flynn
Afterword: by Patton Oswalt
Publisher: Harper (New York). Illustrated. 352 pp.
Type of work: History, current affairs
Time: 1976–present
Locale: California

Part memoir, part true crime story, Michelle McNamara's gripping posthumous best seller, I'll Be Gone in the Dark *(2018), connects a series of violent crimes committed between 1974 and 1986 in central California. The result is a chilling portrait of the notorious Golden State Killer, who may have been brought to justice in 2018.*

Principal personages
MICHELLE MCNAMARA, the author
PATTON OSWALT, her widower, an actor and comedian
GOLDEN STATE KILLER, an unknown serial rapist and murderer who terrorized central California for a decade
LARRY POOL, an unsolved crimes investigator for the Orange County Sheriff's Department
PAUL HOLES, a former criminalist with the Contra Costa County Sheriff's Office
MARY HONG, a criminalist with the Orange County Crime Lab

I'll Be Gone in the Dark (2018) is a compelling story for a number of reasons. Its author, Michelle McNamara, did not live to witness its publication. In 2016, she died unexpectedly at age forty-five. A journalist and true-crime blogger, McNamara meticulously researched and wrote about a violent serial rapist and murderer who operated between San Francisco and Los Angeles, California, from the mid-1970s to the mid-1980s. It was McNamara who dubbed the unknown male the Golden State Killer, after he was linked by DNA evidence to numerous, previously unconnected brutal acts, including fifty rapes and several multiple murders.

Michelle's widower is stand-up comedian and actor Patton Oswalt, who was a regular on the television series *The King of Queens* from 1998 to 2007 and performed in such films as *Ratatouille* (2007) and *Big Fan* (2009). Oswalt worked with true-crime writer and researcher Paul Haynes and crime journalist Billy Jensen to finalize the manuscript for publication. In April 2018, shortly after *I'll Be Gone in the Dark* shot onto the New York Times Best Seller List and HBO began filming an adaptation of the book as a documentary series, a viable suspect for the Golden State killings was named. California law enforcement officials arrested a man who was subsequently charged with numerous counts of first-degree murder and other crimes.

I'll Be Gone in the Dark, the title of which is taken from something the killer whispered to a victim, pieces together the movements of the Golden State Killer and follows the investigations into the unknown man. The Golden State Killer escaped detection for many years because he committed a variety of crimes—including prowling, burglary, window peeping, rape, and murder—across a wide range of California law enforcement jurisdictions. Because of the different types of criminal activities committed in numerous locations, the sheriff's offices involved in the respective investigations initially believed it was several perpetrators, rather than a single individual, committing the multitude of crimes.

The Golden State Killer first surfaced in the spring of 1974, in Visalia, California. Known locally as the Visalia Ransacker, he committed dozens of brazen, bizarre burglaries. The intruder was especially noteworthy for casing targets in advance, anonymously phoning to check if anyone was at home, and leaving distinctive patterned footprints in backyards or under bedroom windows when prowling in person. He was infamous for setting makeshift alarms and planning escape routes in case he was interrupted during his crimes. He became known for cruel vandalism (such as ripping up family photos), stealing small, personal items (like one earring from a pair), and for his penchant for fondling women's underwear. The man's activities in the Visalia area culminated in late 1975, when, wearing ski mask and gloves, he attempted to abduct a teenaged girl. Her father thwarted the would-be kidnapping but was shot dead by the unknown intruder. Soon afterward, the burglaries ceased. Investigators figured the perpetrator had left the area because residents had grown more vigilant.

© Robin von Swank

Crime writer Michelle McNamara authored the blog True Crime Diary. *She frequently wrote about the prolific serial rapist and murderer known as the Golden State Killer. Her articles served as the basis for the posthumously published* I'll Be Gone in the Dark, *which has been credited with renewing interest in discovering his identity.*

In mid-1976, a new series of crimes began in communities east of San Francisco with the sexual assault of a young woman. It was the first of more than fifty rapes committed over the next three years in cities across seven counties by a perpetrator dubbed the East Area Rapist (EAR). Victims of the crimes all described a man resembling a person occasionally spotted in the vicinity of some of the burglaries in Visalia. The rapist was young, white, ordinary in appearance, and about five-feet-nine-inches tall, with dirty blond hair, a large nose, and a swimmer's build. The intruder was bold enough to be undeterred by the presence of a man in the home. He typically disoriented sleeping victims with a bright flashlight and sometimes carried a gun. He wore a ski mask and gloves. His opening line was always a variation of the phrase "Do what I say, or I'll kill you." He ordered each female victim to tie the hands of her male partner, then stacked dishes on the helpless man's back so he would be alerted to movement while he was violating the bound woman. The rapist took small, inexpensive items as trophies, such as a driver's license, personalized jewelry, or a photograph. He sometimes taunted victims or the local police by phone. Then, in mid-1979, the assaults ceased as suddenly as they had begun. Law enforcement authorities speculated—and hoped—that the perpetrator had died, been incarcerated, or relocated.

In October 1979, a fresh spate of brutal attacks began in Southern California. Nearly three months after a failed home invasion, Dr. Robert Offerman and his girlfriend, Debra Manning, were found shot to death in Offerman's condominium in Goleta. Eight more rape-murders were enacted in the area between 1980 and 1986 in what was called the Night Stalker Rampage. Each victim was beaten to death with objects of opportunity—such as a piece of firewood, a metal lamp, or a wrench. The media later renamed the perpetrator of the serial attacks the Original Night Stalker (ONS) to distinguish the unknown perpetrator from Richard Ramirez, whom the media also named the Night Stalker, after he committed a series of similar crimes between 1984 and 1985. After the murder of Janelle Cruz in Irvine, the final victim, the ONS apparently stopped. This in itself was unusual, since sexual criminals usually follow their compulsions until they are caught or killed.

Though the Golden State Killer may have ceased activity, law enforcement never stopped investigating his crimes. They were greatly aided by a new forensic technique: the 1984 discovery of profiling via DNA found in blood, saliva, semen, and other human bodily fluids. While early DNA profiling was primitive, within a decade the technology had improved, following the DNA Identification Act of 1994, which established the Combined DNA Index System (CODIS), a DNA database of convicted felons. It was through CODIS that DNA links were made between the Golden State Killer's multiple crimes. However, there were no DNA matches to perpetrators included in CODIS or in the California penal system database.

McNamara, who first became interested in crime when a young woman was murdered in the Oak Park, Illinois, neighborhood where she grew up, launched the blog *True Crime Diary* in 2006. The blog was a forum for amateur sleuths to discuss cold-case murders. McNamara grew fascinated with the Golden State Killer and contributed numerous articles about the case, some of which served as the basis for *I'll Be Gone in the Dark*. In conducting research for the book, she worked closely with many investigators involved in various aspects of the case, particularly criminalist Paul Holes (since retired from law enforcement and a member of Oxygen Media network), with whom she toured crime sites. McNamara personally scanned hundreds of pages of EARS and ONS case files, created digital files, and built indexes of the people, places, and items named in the reports. She was also included in updates of law enforcement's efforts to find the killer using familial DNA obtained via large public genealogy databases, such as 23andMe and Ancestry.com. It was the killer's unique phosphoglucomutase (PGM) marker in his DNA that produced lists of common ancestors connected genetically with the suspect, which ultimately led to his capture, two years after McNamara's death. The alleged perpetrator, Joseph James DeAngelo, a former policeman, was arrested in April 2018 and, shortly after, was charged with thirteen counts of first-degree murder and thirteen kidnapping or abduction attempts.

I'll Be Gone in the Dark provides a close-up look at the behavior of an audacious, ruthless predator who escaped justice during a ten-year reign of terror and for decades afterward. The Golden State Killer's story is told in nonlinear fashion, with forward and backward glimpses highlighting specific incidents from his sordid career of crime. The vignettes, incorporating comments from survivors and members of various law enforcement agencies, illustrate how and what the perpetrator did, without attempting to explain why he began his nefarious activities or why he stopped voluntarily.

The book illustrates the commitment of both professional and amateur crime-fighters in working toward a common cause. It also demonstrates the power of modern technology to assist in the solution of crimes. The Golden State Killer operated in a time period prior to the existence of the internet, personal computers, scanners, or DNA fingerprinting—all elements that ultimately contributed in pinpointing the individual now accused of committing the multitude of offenses.

I'll Be Gone in the Dark is occasionally forced to remind readers of Michelle McNamara's untimely death; several chapters are prefaced by brief statements noting that the information was compiled from the author's notes or excerpted from article drafts. Though the book is slightly weakened by the use of pseudonyms during interviews with survivors, the device is unfortunately necessary. People who have experienced firsthand the horrors of sexual assault are understandably reticent to relive their fear. Receiving positive reviews from critics, McNamara's book brings fresh hope to the possible solution of other cold cases and provides information that may prove valuable in capturing serial offenders in future.

Jack Ewing

Review Sources

Della Cava, Marco. "How Michelle McNamara's Book Renewed Interest in the Golden State Killer: Review." Review of *I'll Be Gone in the Dark: One Woman's Obsessive Search for the Golden State Killer*, by Michelle McNamara. *USA Today*, 25 Apr. 2018, www.usatoday.com/story/life/books/2018/02/26/how-patton-oswalt-friends-brought-his-late-wifes-book-serial-killer-fruition/332963002. Accessed 5 Oct. 2018.

Haigney, Sophie. Review of *I'll Be Gone in the Dark: One Woman's Obsessive Search for the Golden State Killer*, by Michelle McNamara. *San Francisco Chronicle*, 2 May 2018, www.sfchronicle.com/books/article/I-ll-Be-Gone-in-the-Dark-by-Michelle-12883001.php. Accessed 5 Oct. 2018.

Lybarger, Jeremy. "'I'll Be Gone in the Dark' by Michelle McNamara Review—In Search of a Serial Killer." Review of *I'll Be Gone in the Dark: One Woman's Obsessive Search for the Golden State Killer*, by Michelle McNamara. *The Guardian*, 23 Mar. 2018, www.theguardian.com/books/2018/mar/21/ill-be-gone-dark-michelle-mcnamara-golden-state-killer-quest. Accessed 5 Oct. 2018.

Raymond, Ken. Review of *I'll Be Gone in the Dark: One Woman's Obsessive Search for the Golden State Killer*, by Michelle McNamara. *The Oklahoman*, 17 June 2018, newsok.com/article/5597997/oklahoman-book-review-ill-be-gone-in-the-dark-by-michelle-mcnamara. Accessed 5 Oct. 2018.

Tuttle, Kate. "Michelle McNamara's Terrific, Obsessive 'I'll Be Gone in the Dark.'" Review of *I'll Be Gone in the Dark: One Woman's Obsessive Search for the Golden State Killer*, by Michelle McNamara. *Los Angeles Times*, 19 Apr. 2018, www.latimes.com/books/la-ca-jc-gone-in-the-dark-20180419-story.html. Accessed 5 Oct. 2018.

The Immortalists

Author: Chloe Benjamin (b. 1988)
Publisher: G.P. Putnam's Sons (New York).
  352 pp.
Type of work: Novel
Time: 1969–2010
Locales: New York City, Kingston, and Albany, New York; San Francisco and Marin County, California; Las Vegas, Nevada; West Milton, Ohio

Courtesy of Penguin

A Jewish family saga with supernatural undertones, The Immortalists *follows the lives of four siblings who, as children, visit a fortune-teller in New York City. Upon request, the woman tells the children the exact date they will die, and the novel illustrates their different reactions to the information.*

Principal characters
VARYA GOLD, the oldest Gold sibling, a longevity researcher
DANIEL GOLD, the second-oldest Gold sibling, a military physician
KLARA GOLD, the second-youngest Gold sibling, a stage magician and aerial feat performer
SIMON GOLD, the youngest Gold sibling, a dancer at a gay nightclub and a ballet member
EDDIE O'DONOGHUE, a policeman, later an FBI agent
BRUNA COSTELLO, a fortune-teller

The prologue of *The Immortalists* (2018) presents an irresistible storytelling premise. On a hot summer day in volatile 1969, the four Gold siblings of New York City—Varya, thirteen, Daniel eleven, Klara, nine, and Simon, seven—collect their allowance savings and set off to see a woman on nearby Hester Street, on the Lower East Side of Manhattan, New York City. Daniel has heard about an old fortune-teller who can predict the date of someone's death and persuades his brother and sisters to help him find her. They locate where the old woman lives, and one by one enter her apartment to hear her prophecies. Afterward, only Varya, who has been given a death date of January 21, 2044, when she will be eighty-eight years old, reveals what the woman said. The others will not tell what was forecast, except for Simon, who says he was told he will die young.

    The novel is subsequently divided into four parts and the narration unfolds in third-person present tense, which lends an immediacy to passages set in the past. The different sections cover the years and events that lead up to the fateful dates predicted for each of the four siblings. Each part follows one of the siblings—arranged from youngest to oldest child and in predicted order of death—and illustrates the degree of credence the siblings give the supposedly otherworldly knowledge. Introspective Varya, the oldest child, is most skeptical about the clairvoyant's abilities: she thinks they were told what they wanted to hear. However, impressionable Simon, the youngest, accepts his fate: he has always felt that he would not be alive for long and takes the fortune-teller's message to heart. Each character's story is inextricably linked to the other characters, and the sections are interrelated through memories, flashbacks, and references to physical objects that recall specific events (photos, paperweights, cards and letters).

The first part, which takes place between 1978 and 1982, spotlights Simon while also incorporating key elements of Klara's character development. At the beginning of the period, patriarch Saul Gold suddenly dies. As the only available son—as Daniel is in college studying to be a physician—Simon is expected to take over management of the family's tailor and dressmaking business. The idea is repugnant to Simon, then sixteen, who has no interest in women's fashion. Instead, Simon wants to embrace his newly discovered sexuality. At the end of the school year, Simon begs Klara, who has just graduated, to let him accompany her to the West Coast. Since Simon is Klara's favorite sibling, she agrees. Upon their arrival in San Francisco, the siblings stay briefly with a former classmate, before using the last of their scant funds to rent an apartment in the Castro district. To help earn money, Simon secures a job as a go-go dancer at a gay nightclub. Because he is not particularly graceful, Simon takes ballet classes to improve his dancing techniques. There, he meets the handsome ballet dancer Robert. The two men are drawn to one another and become lovers, roommates, and performance partners. Despite comfortable, secure living arrangements, Simon frequently goes nightclubbing and is unfaithful to Robert.

In addition to the main story line, Benjamin introduces a subplot that threads throughout the novel, following city policeman Eddie O'Donoghue as he meets and interacts with the different Gold siblings. Eddie first meets Simon, whom he takes into custody as an underage runaway. The cop forces Simon to call his family, and his mother, Gertie, pleads with him to come home. When Simon refuses, however, Gertie tells him she never wants to see him again. Always supportive, Klara, who is now working as a temp and drinking to excess, comes to pick up Simon from the police station. Eddie is immediately smitten with her, though she feels nothing for him.

In the early 1980s Simon contracts an unknown and often lethal disease (later known as acquired immunodeficiency syndrome, or AIDS) that is having a disproportionate impact on the gay community. On his deathbed, Simon calls home, briefly conversing with his disinterested brother. Just before he dies—on the exact day predicted for his death—Simon tells vigil-keepers Klara and Robert that without having been told his fate, he would never have had the courage to leave home or to pursue the amount of pleasure and experiences he had during his brief life.

Simon's untimely death sends shockwaves through the family. Gertie feels guilty for rejecting her youngest child. Simon's surviving siblings are each struck in different ways by the fact and timing of his passing. Klara believes in the truth of the fortune-teller's words more than ever; Daniel is torn between doubt and belief; and Varya, concentrating on science, needs further proof to determine if there was a correlation between prediction and outcome.

Part 2, covering 1982 to 1991, showcases Klara's development from amateur magician to professional performer, as well as her budding romance with Rajanikant "Raj" Chapal, an Indian immigrant with mechanical skills. Trained in sleight-of-hand while a teenaged employee at an old vaudevillian's magic shop, Klara has created a special show called "the Immortalist." She combines prestidigitation with a circus-type feat. Inspired by photos of her namesake grandmother, Klara performs the "Jaws of Life": a stunt achieved by clinging by her teeth while suspended at a height from a rope. Her grandmother died in a fall while performing the act over Times Square in 1941. Klara's aspirations are initially modest: she is content to travel nomadically, performing at small venues and trying

© Nathan Jandl

Chloe Benjamin's debut novel, The Anatomy of Dreams *(2014), won the Edna Ferber Fiction Book Award from the Council for Wisconsin Writers. The television rights for her second novel,* The Immortalists, *were sold before the book was published.*

to contact Simon in the spirit world. Klara hopes that her act will remind her audiences to believe in magic, something she accomplishes when, after seeing her show several times, Eddie O'Donoghue tells her that she has reminded him that impossible is possible. Raj, however, is more ambitious: he wants the fame and fortune he was denied when born into extreme poverty in India. After he and Klara marry, and she gives birth to their daughter Ruby, Raj slowly assumes greater control of the act. He convinces a reluctant Klara that their future lies in Las Vegas, and she finally agrees to give it a try. Through persistence and charm, Raj manages to secure a contract to perform at the Mirage casino in the week before Klara—who has not told her husband the date she was given—is destined to die.

Part 3 concerns Daniel Gold between 1991 and 2006. A military physician who has risen to the rank of major, Daniel has enjoyed a long career. By 2006, however, he is suffering from a crisis of conscience. He has worked for several years at the Military Entrance Processing Station (MEPS) in Albany, New York, and he feels increasingly uneasy approving recruits with normally disqualifying mental or physical conditions for combat in Iraq or Afghanistan. When told by his youthful commanding officer to lower his standards of acceptance because military enlistments are down, Daniel balks and is promptly suspended for two weeks for insubordination. During his suspension, Daniel receives a call from Eddie O'Donoghue, now a special agent with the Federal Bureau of Investigation (FBI), whom he first met in the early 1990s while Eddie was investigating Klara's death. Based on a tip Daniel had given him about the fortune-teller, Eddie has been researching a Romani family involved in fortune-telling fraud. He shows Daniel pictures of suspects to see if he recognizes anyone from long ago. Among the mugshots is that of the old woman who predicted the Gold siblings' deaths: her name is Bruna Costello. Daniel conducts further research and locates a possible spot in small-town Ohio where her twenty-year-old mobile home might be located. Just before the predicted date of his death, he collects his handgun and begins driving west, intending to confront the old woman.

The final part of the novel follows Varya Gold between 2006 and 2010. She is working with marmosets at the Drake Institute for Research on Aging in northern California. Over several days, Luke Van Galder, a young freelance writer, interviews Varya about her work, which is aimed at extending human longevity. During the course of the interview, details of her daily routine and life experiences are revealed, raising the issue of quality versus quantity of life. Luke asks Varya increasingly personal questions that distract her from her tasks. Overcome with suppressed emotions, she violates laboratory protocol, putting twenty years of research—and her career—in jeopardy.

The Immortalists is, at its core, the history of a family—a Jewish family, with unique, interesting individuals who exhibit a wide range of personal philosophies and different degrees of commitment to religious tenets and traditions—over a half-century. Members mature, drift apart, and gather periodically in sometimes warm, sometimes contentious reunions, just like real people. Besides an intricately plotted, unpredictable story that skillfully builds tension, the novel gives readers much to contemplate. With each section, Benjamin explores how the different characters react to knowing the date of their deaths and how they approach living with that knowledge. Overall, *The Immortalists* received a positive critical response, debuting in the top ten on the New York Times Best Sellers: Hardcover Fiction list. Multiple critics praised the depth and individuality of Benjamin's characters, as well as the involved visuals used to create the settings and histories within the novel. Some critics, however, felt that Benjamin undertook too much, leaving the novel unbalanced and parts of the plot feeling forced.

Jack Ewing

Review Sources

Clark, Clare. "'The Immortalists by Chloe Benjamin Review—Is it Better to Know Your Own Fate?" Review of *The Immortalists*, by Chloe Benjamin. *The Guardian*, 30 Mar. 2018, www.theguardian.com/books/2018/mar/30/the-immortalists-by-chloe-benjamin-review. Accessed 20 Aug. 2018.

Duffy, Bob. "Book Review in Fiction: 'The Immortalists: A Novel.'" Review of *The Immortalists*, by Chloe Benjamin. *Washington Independent Review of Books*, 16 Jan. 2018, www.washingtonindependentreviewofbooks.com/index.php/bookreview/the-immortalists-a-novel. Accessed 20 Aug. 2018.

Review of *The Immortalists*, by Chloe Benjamin. *Publishers Weekly*, 23 Dec. 2017. *Literary Reference Center Plus*, search.ebscohost.com/login.aspx?direct=true&db=lkh&AN=125843323&site=lrc-plus. 20 Oct. 2018.

Tsouderos, Trine. "'The Immortalists' by Chloe Benjamin: What Would You Do if You Knew When You Were Going to Die?" Review of *The Immortalists*, by Chloe Benjamin. *Chicago Tribune*, 12 Feb. 2018, www.chicagotribune.com/life-styles/books/sc-books-immortalists-chloe-benjamin-0214-story.html. Accessed 20 Oct. 2018.

In Extremis
The Life and Death of the War Correspondent Marie Colvin

Author: Lindsey Hilsum
Publisher: Farrar, Straus & Giroux (New York). Illustrated. 400 pp.
Type of work: Biography
Time: 1956–2012
Locales: New York, London, the Middle East, Sri Lanka, Eastern Europe

The turbulent personal and professional life of internationally acclaimed journalist Marie Colvin is chronicled by a friend, fellow journalist Lindsey Hilsum, who examines Colvin's contributions to unmasking atrocities in several conflicts between 1987 and 2012.

Courtesy of Farrar, Straus and Giroux

Principal personages

MARIE COLVIN, American journalist, foreign correspondent for London's Sunday Times
ROSEMARIE COLVIN, her mother
KATRINA HERON, her lifelong friend, an American journalist and editor
JANE WELLESLEY, her close friend, a British television producer
PATRICK BISHOP, her first husband, a British journalist
JUAN CARLOS GUMUCIO, her second husband, a Bolivian journalist
RICHARD FLAYE, her partner at the time of her death
SEAN RYAN, her editor at the Sunday Times
YASSER ARAFAT, Palestinian leader
MUAMMAR GADDAFI, dictator in Libya until 2011

On February 22, 2012, Marie Colvin, foreign correspondent for the London *Sunday Times*, was killed in what was later determined to be an attack by Syrian government forces on the media center in Baba Amr, a district in the city of Homs, Syria. At the time, Colvin was reporting on the plight of civilians trapped inside the rebel-held city, where she saw firsthand the savagery with which President Bashar al-Assad's troops pursued their campaign to retake Homs. As fellow correspondent and friend Lindsey Hilsum makes clear in her book *In Extremis: The Life and Death of the War Correspondent Marie Colvin*, the civil war in Syria was the last of numerous conflicts that Colvin would bear witness to during her long, distinguished, and turbulent career as a war correspondent.

The outline of Colvin's life is the stuff of which superhero comics and action films are made (indeed, the 2018 film *A Private War* is a riveting biopic based on her career).

Born in 1956, Colvin grew up in an Irish Catholic family in New York, the eldest child of a conservative father who she loved but rebelled against constantly. His death in February 1977 left a hole in her life that she never filled, and may explain why, throughout her career, she sought approval from others. A class at Yale University with internationally acclaimed reporter and novelist John Hersey convinced her to become a journalist. While Hersey became one model for Colvin, the other was Martha Gellhorn, whose reporting during the Spanish Civil War in the 1930s and World War II focused on the impact of war on common soldiers and civilians. Gellhorn's work inspired Colvin to dedicate her own life to reporting on the plight of the victims of war. When she finally received assignments to cover overseas conflicts, she carried a copy of Gellhorn's *The Face of War* (1959) with her when she traveled into combat zones.

After brief stints working for a labor union and United Press International, in 1986 Colvin landed a job as a foreign correspondent with London's *Sunday Times*. Long fascinated with the Middle East, in 1988 she began to cover the first Palestinian uprising, or intifada, against Israel. For the next quarter century she roved the world from one conflict zone to the next. She was in Baghdad when the American-led coalition launched the first Gulf War and in Kosovo during the conflict with Serbia in the late 1990s. She went to Chechnya to report on the Russians' crackdown on dissidence. She interviewed rebels in Sierra Leone during an uprising in that country. Colvin was wounded and lost sight in one eye while covering the Tamil uprising in Sri Lanka. Undeterred, she covered her sightless eye with a patch and headed off to report from Afghanistan, where US troops were trying to oust the Taliban and turn a ragtag Afghan army into a credible fighting force. She was in Iraq again when US forces invaded the country to depose Saddam Hussein. She reported from the Middle East as Palestinian-Israeli clashes foiled attempts at a permanent peace settlement. She was on the ground in Tunis and Cairo to cover the Arab Spring uprisings, and in Libya to witness the fallout from the fall of that country's dictator, Muammar Gaddafi. Unfortunately, her insistence on covering the civil war in Syria in 2012—against the advice of her family and longtime *Sunday Times* editor Sean Ryan—proved to be a fatal choice.

Colvin's intrepid on-scene reporting made her a celebrity among international correspondents. In 2000, the Foreign Press Association named her Journalist of the Year and the International Women's Media Foundation honored her with a Courage in Journalism Award. She was also a repeat winner of the British Press Award for Foreign Reporter of the Year. After her death, she was honored with the 2012 Anna Politkovskaya Award, named for the Russian journalist assassinated, in part, for her work in reporting on the conflict in Chechnya. For her posthumously published collection of reports and essays, *On the Front Line* (2012), Colvin was recognized by the judges of the Orwell Prize, the United Kingdom's most prestigious prize for political writing.

Hilsum gives ample space to discussing the nuts and bolts of Colvin's career as an international correspondent, tracing many of the personal associations Colvin formed while on assignment. For example, during her work in the Middle East, Colvin developed working relationships with a number of international leaders, most notably Libya's Gaddafi and Palestine Liberation Organization (PLO) chairman Yasser Arafat. So impressed was Colvin with Arafat that she worked for years on a biography of him;

© ITN Channel 4 News

Journalist and editor Lindsey Hilsum has reported on armed conflicts around the world. Her book Sandstorm: Libya in the Time of Revolution *(2012) was nominated for the Guardian First Book Award. Her work has been featured in publications including the* Guardian *and* Granta.

it remained unfinished when she died. Her ability to get these leaders to open up earned special praise from one of the *Sunday Times* editors, who noted how she "got inside them, showing that they weren't identikit monsters, but real people."

Colvin's journalistic focus, however, was seldom on the leaders of countries from which she reported. Rather, she wrote principally about the ordinary people who became collateral damage in the never-ceasing rounds of armed confrontation across the globe. Working for a weekly publication gave Colvin the opportunity to develop stories that captured the pathos and heroism of men and women in the conflict zones. Colvin's detailed, sometimes passionate, first-person accounts earned her a reputation as the voice of the voiceless and the conscience of humanity; she spoke truth to power, even at the risk of her own safety.

At the same time, Hilsum does not try to gloss over Colvin's less admirable qualities, which were often on display in both her professional and personal life. From an early age, she was at times irresponsible. She had a habit of being late, ignoring deadlines, or determining for herself what she should be doing, rather than taking assignments from editors. She resented others benefiting from her work, showing her displeasure directly to colleagues sent by *Sunday Times* editors to assist in covering the fall of Hosni Mubarak in Egypt. In later years, the constant strain caused by working under threat of injury, kidnapping, or death took its toll, and Colvin's habit of drinking to excess burgeoned into a serious problem, compounded by feelings of depression.

Alongside Hilsum's portrait of Colvin as a brave professional reporter, the reader gets a frank discussion of Colvin's constant desire to gain the security of marriage and family while still being able to maintain the freedom she felt necessary to pursue her career. Hilsum laments the fact that Colvin was never able to find the right life partner; she always seemed to choose men like herself—wanting a stable relationship but retaining the freedom to stray when they felt the urge. Nevertheless, Colvin's marriages to Patrick Bishop and Juan Carlos Gumucio, her long relationship with Richard Flaye, and her many other romantic liaisons are treated honestly but also with sympathy. Colvin had better luck in forging bonds with women, particularly her mother Rosemarie (though not always a congenial relationship) and sister Cat, her former Yale classmate Katrina Heron, and her British confidante Lady Jane Wellesley. Hilsum wisely avoids psychoanalyzing her subject, restraining from speculating too deeply about the implications of Colvin's many failed attempts to forge lasting ties to others. Although

Hilsum frequently finds a way to justify Colvin's constant drive to be in the midst of armed conflict despite the risks to her personal safety, even Hilsum has to admit that, on occasion, Colvin was reckless.

As a fellow journalist who knew Colvin and worked alongside her in various hot spots, Hilsum is well qualified to judge the wisdom of Colvin's constant insistence on reporting from the most dangerous places on Earth. Hilsum presents Colvin as someone who lived up to her ideas of journalistic ethics. Not everyone, however, has found Colvin's reporting as free of bias as Hilsum would suggest. One can find comments scattered on the internet accusing Colvin of supporting the conservative, capitalist agenda of her employer, Rupert Murdoch, owner of the worldwide media empire News Corp. Critics have accused that corporation of promoting armed conflict for personal gain by the military-industrial complex and its media cronies. On occasion, Hilsum provides fodder for these critics by citing instances when Colvin was required to write articles that seemed to be solely for the purpose of promoting sales of the *Sunday Times*. Hilsum also points out that, especially in later years, Colvin saw her work as a form of advocacy, giving voice to the powerless so that world opinion could be swayed and international leaders convinced to change policies in order to ease suffering and privation on victims of military conflicts.

Hilsum's book is based on numerous interviews with people who knew Colvin and relies heavily on Colvin's journals and her published work. To give a wider scope to the conflicts on which Colvin reported, Hilsum consults numerous published sources, including journalists' accounts and scholarly studies. Hence, Hilsum is able to give a detailed, sympathetic, yet balanced portrait of a complicated, driven woman who was never able to reconcile for herself the demands of a career with the yearning for a stable personal life. The numerous photographs enhance readers' ability to visualize Colvin and those in whose circles she moved. One might be skeptical about the objectivity of those Hilsum interviewed, but wherever possible she has sought—in good journalistic fashion—to find additional sources to corroborate not only what happened but how Colvin reacted to events in her life. Hence, it is easy to agree with Hilsum's assessment of Colvin's contribution to the role of journalism in combat: "She was the champion of bearing witness so that even if no one stopped the wars, they could never say they had not known what was happening."

Laurence W. Mazzeno

Review Sources

Feigel, Lara. Review of *In Extremis: The Life and Death of the War Correspondent Marie Colvin*, by Lindsey Hilsum. *The Guardian*, 3 Nov. 2018, www.theguardian.com/books/2018/nov/03/in-extremis-by-lindsey-hilsum-review-life-war-correspondent-marie-colvin. Accessed 11 Feb. 2019.

Fox, Robert. "Marie Colvin, a War Reporter Who Thrived on the Edge." Review of *In Extremis: The Life and Death of the War Correspondent Marie Colvin*, by Lindsey Hilsum. *Evening Standard*, 25 Oct. 2018, www.standard.co.uk/lifestyle/books/

in-extremis-the-life-of-war-correspondent-marie-colvin-by-lindsey-hilsum-re-view-a3971261.html. Accessed 11 Feb. 2019.

Hammer, Joshua. "She Reported from the World's Combat Zones, at the Cost of Her Life." Review of *In Extremis: The Life and Death of the War Correspondent Marie Colvin*, by Lindsey Hilsum. *The New York Times*, 2 Nov. 2018, www.nytimes.com/2018/11/02/books/review/in-extremis-marie-colvin-lindsey-hilsum.html. Accessed 11 Feb. 2019.

Review of *In Extremis: The Life and Death of the War Correspondent Marie Colvin*, by Lindsey Hilsum. *Kirkus*, 20 Aug. 2018, www.kirkusreviews.com/book-re-views/lindsey-hilsum/in-extremis-marie-colvin/. Accessed 11 Feb. 2019.

Indecency

Author: Justin Phillip Reed (b. 1989)
Publisher: Coffee House Press (Minneapolis). 112 pp.
Type of work: Poetry

In his debut poetry collection, Indecency *(2018), Justin Phillip Reed presents an exhilarating political poetry, experimenting with an elaborate formalism that impinges on its content. Implied by the book's title, Reed's incisive methodology transforms insolence into a fine art. Reed casts the constitutive tensions between body, identity, and their social and political determinants in sharp— and then even sharper—relief.*

Courtesy of Coffee House Press

Exemplifying the ways that the personal always has political implications, without the political ever becoming too personal, Justin Phillip Reed's debut poetry collection, *Indecency* (2018), boldly pushes back against what Fredric Jameson once accurately described as "the uniquely apolitical atmosphere of Anglo-American literature." Packed into Reed's poetic formal compressions are stark instances of pressure, stress, tension, and violence, along with poetic formations that map onto an inimitable subjectivity, with all its securities and insecurities. *Indecency* is thus candid, incendiary, shrewd; neither less political nor historical than it is poetic or personal. It should come as no surprise, then, that this indelible collection of poems earned the 2018 National Book Award for poetry.

In "Witness the Woman I Am Not," the second of more than thirty poems, Reed's words take on a dizzying life of their own. Their tropic movement is mercurial, labile, borne along by subjective vagaries. The fluctuation of imagery and address is made manifest by a deliberate repetition of large gaps, completely lacking in text, that both separate and link each stanza to the next. In the third poem, "Pushing Up onto Its Elbows, the Fable Lifts Itself into Fact" (dedicated to poet and producer Tafisha Edwards), Reed laments the "absence-presence of taken Black girls," referring to how black women go unnoticed daily unless taken hold of by predominantly white, Western agents of power and interest. Here, Reed repeats the same formal gestures found in the previous poem, but the gaps appear within lines, not between stanzas. For example: "The soil turns as _____ turn away from / loud Black girls and their cacophonic insistence on Black girls." Such repeated swaths of textual silence not only expose, but also bring into critical examination the vacuous whiteness of the page, while throwing into acute relief the literal blackness of the words printed on it. As Luiza Flynn-Goodlett, writing for the *Adroit Journal*, aptly puts it, Reed "illuminates the contours of whiteness in ways that undercut and deftly dismantle it . . . turn[ing] the white, heterosexual, gaze back toward itself, revealing the void at the heart of those identities, while simultaneously reveling in black queerness and expounding on the vast universes contained therein." The acute repetition of such absences of particular formal features, in turn, begin to exert their own effects as they interact with the text's present formal features. Thus, Reed makes both absence and repetition into formal features themselves.

In each poem of this collection one will also find that Reed carefully organizes and punctuates his sentences with, and around, stylized slashes and square brackets, em dashes and parentheses, inverted commas and strange indentations. He places and activates these devices in novel ways, creating textual hippogriffs, as it were, giving odd shape to, and *in,* the bodies of text, inspiring these fantastic creations with spirit and temper. Reed inflects the syntax with cadences that do not simply contrast legato with staccato; the former and latter also imbue each other in uncanny ways. If, then, the reader finds it challenging to parse metrical rationality from absurdity, that is perhaps because Reed does a fabulous job vexing the boundaries between the two. In effect, sense and meaning is deferred and rendered acute; pause delays movement and vice versa; all this pointing up *not only* the confusion out of which order is constructed, but also the way that order confuses and obscures the intent behind linguistic constructions. The confusion whence order derives, Reed seems to demonstrate, solicits, only to be supplanted by, an order in which confusion thrives.

This is poetry that not only transposes the impersonal situations that seem both to define and refine the author; it also imposes, page after page, his own situations back onto a variety of perpetually formative conditions. For example, in "A Statement from No One, Incorporated," Reed makes use of the "royal we" to bewail and damn, in the same collective breath, a world that evinces an irate sadness, a world in which there seems never to be consequences for one's actions; a kind of consequence itself, nonetheless. And in "Slough," Reed anguishes over the ambivalent impurities that constitute the excruciating and intractable distance between substance and self, two diametrically different, and thus irreducible, axioms. Therein, his chosen words combine subject and object to evoke associations of pain, solitude, and anguish: words like "mouth," "wrist," and "scar" conspire with "railroad " and "sink" to deliver such intimately honest lines as:

> Here is my wrist where the dream was
> flayed off, the scar once as stark and embossed
> as railroad laid to make nowhere a place.
> I've scrubbed my own maroon out of the porcelain
> mouth of a pedestal sink upon
> request, forced such distance between
> substance and self.

© Nicholas A. Nichols

Born and raised in South Carolina and living in St. Louis, Justin Phillip Reed is the author of Indecency *(2018), his debut poetry collection published by* Minneapolis's Coffee House Press *and winner of the 2018 National Book Award for Poetry. Reed's work has appeared in the* New York Times Magazine, Best American Essays, Boston Review, Callaloo, *the* Kenyon Review, Obsidian, *and other publications.*

If there is any universal political principle to be distilled from Reed's work, it is that one's own set of vulnerabilities, never simple, but rather a complex multitude of incommensurate worlds, is a fertile source of productive, salvific strength.

The elaborate formalism displayed throughout *Indecency*, then, may be viewed as intensively productive, powerful. In fact, the *Rumpus*'s Brian Spears called Reed's poetry "formally inventive"; and Alexandra Alter, reporting on the 2018 National Book Awards for the *New York Times*, noted that its judges "praised the collection as a 'formally explosive' work that makes 'intimacy both refuge and weapon.'" The poem "About a White City" invokes the twentieth-century New York School poet James Schuyler, who wrote a poem called "A White City." The reference may just as likely be an homage to Schuyler's friend W. H. Auden, whose own elaborate formalism was viewed by Schuyler as inhibiting. But for quite some time now, the academic verdict has been that Schuyler's opinion failed to acknowledge how, much like Reed's, Auden's poetry was, *is*, vigorously constitutive—precisely because of his penchant for form and the latter's seemingly inhibiting constraints. Single words, for example, transform the pressures of the stanza, and some words are expressly transformative at the level of the stanza. It is against such tried and true formalism, albeit a formalism that is at times extravagant and boldly experimental, that Reed's verses sculpt and figure the personal, the poetic, and the political all at once.

But addressing Reed's poignant and creative exercises in style and form, and his tasteful ability to maintain disjunctive syntheses between the personal and the political, reveals only part of a bigger picture. Reed's poetry also tends at times to reach beyond the page to blend the personal with an outside world with which he enters into multifarious conversation. Beneath many a poem's title—not just "About a White City"—he pays tribute to an eclectic lineup of people: to gay porn star Rogan Hard in "Exit Hex"; to American artist Rashid Johnson in "Orientation"; in "Paroxysm," to Ezell Ford, a young African American male who, like countless other young black men, was shot and killed by police officers; and in "Theory for Expansion," to Michael L. Johnson, who was criminally charged for transmitting HIV to his partner. Reed's poetry is therefore uniquely ecumenical; he not only experiments with content and form, he also "experiments with language to explore inequity and injustice and to critique and lament the culture of white supremacy and the dominant social order," wrote the National Book Award judges.

While reading *Indecency*, one is likely to be provoked to experience what its title seems to imply: an urge to rebuke the conventional and the customary. Thus, if *Indecency* evokes for its reader a sense of insolence, it is only insofar as insolence, as Maurice Blanchot once cleverly wrote, "is a way to be equal to oneself and superior to others in all the circumstances in which others seem to have the advantage of you." One will of course also experience the granular mutations of single sentences, the subtle shifts in rhythm, and the wild deformations in which content and form infect each other. In the end, all this and more gather together vertiginously, and dazzlingly, to press the poetic voice into the service of what *Publishers Weekly* has described a "visceral and teasingly cerebral" discourse about "black identity, sexuality, and violence."

Frank Joseph

Review Sources

Flynn-Goodlett, Luiza. "Nothing Is Ever Itself Only: A Review of Justin Phillip Reed's *Indecency*." Review of *Indecency*, by Justin Phillip Reed. *The Adroit Journal*, 4 Oct. 2018, www.theadroitjournal.org/blog/2018/8/22/nothing-is-ever-itself-only-a-review-of-justin-phillip-reeds-indecency. Accessed 30 Dec. 2018.

Review of *Indecency*, by Justin Phillip Reed. *Publishers Weekly*, 16 Apr. 2018, www.publishersweekly.com/978-1-56689-514-9. Accessed 30 Dec. 2018.

Spears, Brian, "Why I Chose Justin Phillip Reed's *Indecency* for the Rumpus Poetry Book Club." Review of *Indecency*, by Justin Phillip Reed. *The Rumpus*, 16 Mar. 2018, therumpus.net/2018/03/why-i-chose-justin-phillip-reeds-indecency-for-the-rumpus-poetry-book-club/. Accessed 30 Dec. 2018.

Indianapolis
The True Story of the Worst Sea Disaster in U.S. Naval History and the Fifty-Year Fight to Exonerate an Innocent Man

Authors: Lynn Vincent and Sara Vladic
Publisher: Simon & Schuster (New York).
  Illustrated. 592 pp.
Type of work: History
Time: 1932–2017
Locales: The Philippine Sea; Tinian, Mariana Islands; Mare Island, California; Washington, DC

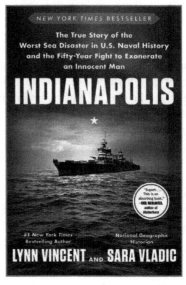

Lynn Vincent and Sara Vladic offer a vividly thrilling and meticulously researched look at the deadliest maritime disaster in US naval history. Drawing on extensive survivor testimonies, this history focuses heavily on the story of Indianapolis's *final captain, Charles B. McVay III, who was unfairly court-martialed for the ship's sinking.*

Courtesy of Simon & Schuster

Principal personages

CHARLES B. MCVAY III, the final captain of the USS Indianapolis (CA-35)
MOCHITSURA HASHIMOTO, the commander of the Japanese submarine that sank the Indianapolis
WILLIAM TOTI, a retired US Navy veteran who captained the USS Indianapolis (SSN-697)
WILBUR "CHUCK" GWINN, an American bomber pilot
ADRIAN MARKS, a US Navy pilot who helped rescue Indianapolis survivors
HUNTER SCOTT, an eighth grader who became involved in efforts to exonerate McVay

From its beginnings as a ceremonial ship of state for US president Franklin D. Roosevelt in the 1930s to its decorated and crucial service in numerous decisive battles during World War II to its tragic sinking by a Japanese submarine in the early hours of July 30, 1945, the USS *Indianapolis* (CA-35) has one of the most storied histories of any naval vessel that ever sailed the high seas. It is, however, only the latter part of that history—one that is anchored by harrowing and almost incomprehensible tales of survival in shark-infested waters—that has received the bulk of public attention. Interestingly, many Americans did not even hear of the *Indianapolis* until the release of director Steven Spielberg's 1975 blockbuster film *Jaws*, in which the grizzled shark hunter Quint (played by actor Robert Shaw) offers a fictionalized account of one of the ship's real-life survivors.

One of the most famous monologues in the history of cinema, the USS *Indianapolis* speech, as it has come to be known, helped catapult the heavy cruiser and its fate into the mainstream consciousness. Among those to first learn about the *Indianapolis* from *Jaws* was William Toti, a US Navy veteran who served as the final captain of its namesake nuclear attack submarine (SSN-697), which was decommissioned in 1998 after approximately eighteen years of service. Toti would form a lasting and impactful relationship with survivors of the attack on the *Indianapolis* cruiser, which is examined closely in Lynn Vincent and Sara Vladic's enthralling, exhaustively researched book Indianapolis: *The True Story of the Worst Sea Disaster in U.S. Naval History and the Fifty-Year Fight to Exonerate an Innocent Man* (2018).

Vincent, a US Navy veteran and best-selling author, and Vladic, an award-winning documentary filmmaker and historian, draw on interviews with more than one hundred survivors and eyewitnesses—conducted over more than a decade—to present a complete and thorough history of the legendary ship and its final crew. As its subtitle suggests, the book not only delves into the complex unfolding of events that preceded and followed *Indianapolis*'s sinking, but also ventures into a largely untold chapter of the ship that centered around its last commanding officer, Charles McVay III. A distinguished combat commander, McVay was among the ship's survivors, but he was court-martialed soon after the war's end for losing the vessel. He was ultimately convicted of endangering the ship by failing to steer a zigzag course—a standard submarine evasion technique—in dangerous enemy waters. Vincent and Vladic focus heavily on the decades-long efforts to clear McVay's name, in which Toti, working in collaboration with *Indianapolis*'s remaining survivors and others, played a pivotal role.

Their book begins with a detailed chronicle of the Japanese kamikaze attack on the *Indianapolis* in March 1945. Fresh off priming the beach for landing marines at the Japanese island of Iwo Jima, the *Indianapolis* had proceeded to do the same at Okinawa, firing on targets there for a week in preparation for the full-scale invasion of the island. During this time, the ship fended off repeated attacks by Japanese aircraft, but on March 31, it suffered structural damage and lost nine crewmen after being hit by a kamikaze pilot. The ship subsequently headed back across the Pacific Ocean to the Mare Island Naval Shipyard in Vallejo, California, for repairs.

McVay, whose father was a highly regarded US Navy admiral, had arrived on the *Indianapolis* with a strong reputation. In mid-July 1945, while the ship was docked at Mare Island, McVay was informed that it would be carrying out a top-secret mission: to deliver the components of the first atomic bomb, dubbed Little Boy, to Tinian in the Mariana Islands. Those components, two small but heavy canisters containing fissionable uranium and a large wooden crate holding miscellaneous classified materials related to the bomb, were escorted on the ship by two Manhattan Project officials who posed as artillery officers. The contents of the cargo, though, were kept a secret from McVay and his crew, several of which were new, inexperienced enlistees who had joined the ship during the holdover, replacing men who had been rotated out. This only triggered outrageous rumors about what the cargo might contain, which included everything from special scented toilet paper for General Douglas MacArthur to the Hollywood starlet Hedy Lamarr.

Still, recognizing the importance of the mission, McVay helped ensure that the *Indianapolis* transported its classified cargo quickly and without incident. The ship, which, despite its age, was one of the fastest in the US Navy, did just that. After offloading the cargo, the *Indianapolis* set sail for Guam before heading off to Leyte in the Philippines, where McVay was expected to get in much-needed training exercises for his crew. Much of this early section of the book, though filled with information, almost reads like a spy thriller, as Vincent and Vladic imbue their meticulous reportage with writerly flair. Describing the trip to Tinian, for example, the authors write, "By day, flying fish leapt like dancers along Indy's southwestern track toward the Marianas. At night, her screws spun a luminous green wake that ribboned from the stern like the trailing robe of a queen."

© Holly Hepburn

Lynn Vincent, a veteran of the US Navy and a longtime investigative journalist, has authored or co-authored several nonfiction books.

Sara Vladic, an acclaimed documentary filmmaker and historian, is widely regarded as one of the foremost authorities on the USS Indianapolis.

Once the *Indianapolis* embarks on its fateful course to Leyte, however, Vincent and Vladic's book soon descends into a realm of incalculable horror. Just a few minutes after midnight on July 30, 1945, the ship, traveling unescorted, was struck by two torpedoes launched from a Japanese submarine. The torpedoes almost tore the ship in half, causing fiery explosions that instantly knocked out its power and radio communications. Consequently, the ship sank in just twelve minutes, with an estimated three hundred crew members going down with it. The authors cover this part of the book in excruciating detail, giving a blow-by-blow account of the ordeal from both the American and Japanese sides. It is their chronicling of the horrific events that followed, however, that will likely linger in the minds of readers.

Although approximately nine hundred men survived the torpedo attack and sinking, nearly six hundred died in the water over the next four days, making the *Indianapolis*'s sinking the worst sea disaster in the history of the US Navy. The majority died of exposure, exhaustion, thirst, starvation, and salt-water poisoning. However, scores of them were also eaten by predatory sharks, with men's blood and corpses eliciting a feeding frenzy that would result in the worst mass shark attack in recorded history. Others, meanwhile, fell victim to violent delirium and hallucinations, which included diving down beneath the surface of the water to imaginary ships, hotels, and beverage stands. It was ultimately "a raw case of survival of the fittest," and the authors' survivor scenes cross the full spectrum of human behavior, from heroic self-sacrifice to unvarnished savagery. One sailor, for instance, even recalls bearing witness to acts of cannibalism, catching "glimpses between swells" that played out "like a stop-frame film from hell."

The sad truth of the matter, explored in the book, is that much of this horrifying ordeal could have been avoided. As Vincent and Vladic illustrate, there were a series of monumental missteps by high-ranking naval officials, including not making Mc-Vay aware of intelligence that indicated Japanese submarine activity along the *Indianapolis*'s route and not reporting the ship missing after it failed to arrive in Leyte as scheduled on July 31, 1945. It was only by sheer chance that Lieutenant Junior Grade Wilbur "Chuck" Gwinn spotted survivors in the water on August 2 while piloting a bomber on a routine antisubmarine patrol. Gwinn's "one in a billion" sighting sparked a massive rescue operation involving several ships and other military personnel, the most notable of whom included Lieutenant Adrian Marks, who, as the first rescuer on the scene, bravely defied orders by landing his seaplane on the open ocean to take in survivors.

Leading a small group that had drifted the furthest south from the attack sight, Mc-Vay was among the last of *Indianapolis*'s 316 survivors to be rescued. However, it was not long before he found himself at the center of an accelerated and highly publicized court-martial, one that even included the testimony of the Japanese submarine commander Mochitsura Hashimoto, whose own attack efforts are given in-depth treatment by Vincent and Vladic. McVay, as it turned out, became the only World War II captain to be court-martialed for the loss of his ship, and his conviction for failing to zigzag was widely viewed as a cover-up by the US Navy. Notwithstanding this sentiment, in the aftermath of his conviction, McVay received a steady stream of vitriolic hate mail, much of it from the families of lost crew members. This and other circumstances would contribute to McVay's suicide, at the age of seventy, in 1968.

Toti's involvement in clearing McVay's name comprises the last section of Vincent and Vladic's book, which also includes several pages of useful notes and back matter. Urged by *Indianapolis* survivors to respond to the late captain's "call" during the de-activation ceremony for his namesake submarine in February 1998, Toti spent the next two years rallying support for McVay's cause. Further awareness about McVay's case was raised by a precocious eighth grader from Florida named Hunter Scott, whose interest in the *Indianapolis*, like Toti, was first sparked after watching *Jaws*; Scott received national television attention after interviewing over one hundred survivors on his own for a school history fair project. In 2000, thanks to the combined efforts of Toti, Scott, and *Indianapolis* survivors, McVay's case was finally reopened before Congress, which exonerated the captain in a joint resolution.

While the story of the *Indianapolis* has been the subject of numerous other books, including Richard Newcomb's *Abandon Ship!* (1958), Dan Kurzman's *Fatal Voyage* (1990), and Doug Stanton's *In Harm's Way* (2001), Vincent and Vladic arguably deliver the definitive account of the ship and its crew. Their book ends, fittingly, with an epilogue chronicling the discovery of the *Indianapolis*'s wreckage in the Philippine Sea in August 2017 by a search team financed by Microsoft cofounder Paul Allen, thus giving the story a sense of finality. For Vladic, who directed an acclaimed 2015 documentary about the *Indianapolis*, titled *The Legacy*, it represents a culmination of a fascination with the ship that began when she was thirteen years old. It is safe to say that the authors' book will only continue to spark interest in the tragedy among new generations of readers. Most importantly, it will serve as lasting tribute to the ship's survivors and victims, as well as to the captain who guided them during one of the most fascinating episodes to emerge from World War II.

Chris Cullen

Review Sources

Review of Indianapolis: *The True Story of the Worst Sea Disaster in U.S. Naval History and the Fifty-Year Fight to Exonerate an Innocent Man*, by Lynn Vincent and Sara Vladic. *Kirkus*, 16 May 2018, www.kirkusreviews.com/book-reviews/lynn-vincent/indianapolis. Accessed 22 Sept. 2018.

Review of Indianapolis: *The True Story of the Worst Sea Disaster in U.S. Naval History and the Fifty-Year Fight to Exonerate an Innocent Man*, by Lynn Vincent and Sara Vladic. *Publishers Weekly*, 14 May 2018, www.publishersweekly.com/978-1-5011-3594-1. Accessed 22 Sept. 2018.

Kopper, Philip. "Remembering a Storied Warship and Its Tragedy." Review of Indianapolis: *The True Story of the Worst Sea Disaster in U.S. Naval History and the Fifty-Year Fight to Exonerate an Innocent Man*, by Lynn Vincent and Sara Vladic. *The Washington Times*, 20 Aug. 2018, www.washingtontimes.com/news/2018/aug/20/book-review-indianapolis-by-lynn-vincent-and-sara-/. Accessed 22 Sept. 2018.

Perry, Tony. "A Secret Mission, Torpedoes, Sharks and the Men Who Survived: The Story of the 'Indianapolis.'" Review of Indianapolis: *The True Story of the Worst Sea Disaster in U.S. Naval History and the Fifty-Year Fight to Exonerate an Innocent Man*, by Lynn Vincent and Sara Vladic. *Los Angeles Times*, 6 July 2018, www.latimes.com/books/la-ca-jc-indianapolis-20180706-story.html. Accessed 22 Sept. 2018.

Insane
America's Criminal Treatment of Mental Illness

Author: Alisa Roth
Publisher: Basic Books (New York). 320 pp.
Type of work: Sociology, current affairs, history
Time: Mainly twentieth and twenty-first centuries
Locale: United States

Alisa Roth investigates police departments, courts, jails, and psychiatric facilities across the country to expose how the criminal justice system provides care—or lack of it—to people with mental illness.

Courtesy of Basic Books

Principal personages

JASON ECHEVARRIA, a Rikers Island, New York, detainee who died of neglect after poisoning himself

TERRENCE PENDERGRASS, a Rikers Island corrections officer who ignored Echevarria's pleas for help

JAMIE WALLACE, a prisoner at the Donaldson facility in Alabama who killed himself after being denied transfer to the state mental hospital

TOM DART, a prison reformer and sheriff at the Cook County Jail in Chicago, Illinois

SAM COCHRAN, a retired police officer and cofounder of the Crisis Intervention Team in Memphis, Tennessee

STEVE LEIFMAN, a Miami-Dade County judge and founder of the Criminal Mental Health Project

In April 1882, the *Boston Globe* reported that Somerville, Massachusetts, resident Edwin R. Prescott murdered his mother-in-law, Mrs. Philemon Russell, by repeatedly hitting her with a brick and shovel, and then slitting her throat with a case knife. For some time, he had complained of his head feeling "strangely" and begged his wife to commit him to the Danvers Asylum in Danvers, Massachusetts. His wife was away to get his committal papers signed when the murder occurred. When his wife returned to the house they shared with his mother-in-law, he confessed to the crime and was sent to Danvers Asylum without trial. Danvers State Hospital, as it later became known, was run according to the revolutionary Kirkbride Plan, conceived by mental health reformer Thomas S. Kirkbride Initially considered a leader in the humane treatment of the mentally ill, Danvers Asylum adhered to British reformer William Tuke's philosophy that "lunatics would be treated as sick people, and where gentleness and patience would be exercised towards them," as the *Boston Medical and Surgical Medicine* summarized it in 1910. When the hospital opened in 1874, the state-of-the-art building featured wards that were light, airy, and uncrowded. The patients were encouraged to work in the hospital-owned gardens and farm as part of their therapy. Unfortunately, by the turn of the century, Kirkbride's innovative model was undermined by over-crowding and inadequate staffing, which, in turn, limited treatment opportunities.

Over the ensuing years, state psychiatric hospitals across the country experienced a similar situation, as Alisa Roth reveals in her sobering exposé *Insane: America's Criminal Treatment of Mental Illness* (2018). During the 1960s and 1970s, deinstitu-tionalization emptied most of the nation's state mental hospitals. That trend, in addi-tion to "new medications, new funding for outpatient treatment, and the creation of Medicaid," enabled many former patients to live in the community. However, some with mental illness, often lacking access to resources, committed crimes and had to be institutionalized elsewhere. Eventually, prisons essentially substituted for state hospi-tals. Roth notes that as of 2017, up to half of inmates in America's jails and prisons had psychiatric disorders—a stunning statistic. In lieu of asylums, Rikers Island in New York City, the Cook County Jail in Chicago, and the Los Angeles County Jail in Los Angeles are now the three largest providers of mental health care in the country. However, although the place of institutionalization has changed, the treatment of the mentally ill has not. Indeed, Roth notes that the criminal justice system has "replicated the appalling conditions of the asylums in our contemporary jails and prisons."

Drawing on personal interviews and detailed research, Roth offers numerous and frequently horrific case studies of the degradation people with mentally illness of-ten suffer in today's penal institutions. For example, in a chapter titled "Sanctioned Torture," she relates the tragic story of Jason Echevarria, who had been diagnosed with bipolar disorder and repeatedly jailed for various offenses. A robbery charge sent the pretrial detainee to Rikers Island, where he was kept in solitary confinement in a special mental health unit. Abuse and neglect of inmates by corrections officers were common. In Echevarria's case, he ate a caustic soap ball and became ill. When his worsening condition was reported to Terrence Pendergrass, the supervising captain, Pendergrass repeatedly brushed off the complaint. Echevarria was found dead in his cell the next day. Other examples of abuse include a Virginia prisoner who died of starvation and a Florida man with schizophrenia who died when officers put him a 160-degree shower for two hours. His infraction? He had smeared his cell with feces.

The dehumanizing conditions in prisons harm the psychological states of both guards and inmates alike—and are often responsible for prisoners taking their own lives. Roth notes that in spite of products such as suicide-prevention mattresses, stain-less steel toilet-and-sink combinations, and even toilet-paper holders, inmates regu-larly find creative ways to kill themselves. At some prisons, corrections officers have even been known to encourage inmates' self-harm. Roth reports that she interviewed an officer now retired from the Donaldson Correctional Facility in Bessemer, Ala-bama, who told her that he had witnessed his coworkers hand razor blades to suicidal inmates and tell them how to use them. At that facility, although mandated suicide watch checks should be performed every fifteen minutes, the reality is that checks are carried out every three to four hours—which gives prisoners plenty of time to harm themselves.

In one of many gripping case studies, Roth tells the story of Jamie Wallace, an inmate with multiple disabilities and mental illnesses who was jailed at Donaldson. From an early age, he had experienced severe conditions including inherited bipolar disorder, schizophrenia, and possibly post-traumatic stress disorder, in addition to attention-deficit hyperactivity disorder. He frequently cut himself and had been hospitalized multiple times. His family situation was unstable, which exacerbated his fragile condition. At sixteen, he shot his mother to death. Entering prison only worsened his condition. He knew he needed help, but the counseling staff was often in flux, so he was unable to form a consistent bond with one therapist. Moreover, when Wallace did see a therapist, it was for only five to ten minutes. Roth lays the blame for Wallace's suicide squarely at the door of the criminal justice system. She writes: "Most of all, however, it could be said that Wallace was a victim of the system: of the mental health system that failed to get his illness under control . . . and of the prison system that failed to provide the treatment that he needed and that it was constitutionally required to provide, until he died by suicide at age twenty-four."

These examples of abuse and neglect highlight one of Roth's major themes—prisons were instituted to punish, not restore, and are therefore ill-equipped to rehabilitate mentally ill inmates. On the surface, the roles of staff members seem clear cut. The primary job of corrections officers is to keep order, while the purpose of therapists is to treat and counsel. However, as Roth describes affectingly, the roles become blurred in the difficult and often-brutal conditions that define prison life. For example, a corrections officer may be called upon to deal with a suicidal inmate who possesses a sharp object and threatens to kill themselves in their cell. The officer must decide whether to stay outside the cell for self-protection or go into the cell to save a life. On the other hand, the mental health professional also faces a conundrum. Delivering therapy to hundreds of inmates is often unfeasible because of severe staff shortages. The only "treatment" available is to prescribe psychiatric drugs, which may alleviate symptoms but often do little to help inmates improve long-term.

From the variety of people Roth interviewed—inmates, their family and friends, corrections officials, and mental health professionals—there seems to be agreement that the treatment of the mentally ill in America is broken. However, Roth reports on the development of a few viable, humane alternatives to conditions that she calls "fundamentally immoral." For example, Roth offers a profile of a "trailblazer," Sheriff Tom Dart, who runs Chicago's Cook County Jail, where an estimated 20 to 30 percent of the nine thousand inmates have a mental illness. To ensure they receive appropriate treatment, they are screened for psychological disorders *before* they enter the prison, unlike other jails where such screening may be done after the person is already in the system. Once processed, those inmates enter a comprehensive program overseen by Dart that includes individual and group therapy, as well as special housing where corrections officers are specially trained to work with a mentally ill population. A transition center offers counseling to help outgoing prisoners adjust to life in the community, which includes participating in job training, navigating Medicaid and mental health services, and having access to a crisis hotline.

Training community law enforcement personnel is often crucial in getting help for the mentally ill before a crisis occurs. The 1987 police shooting of a Memphis, Tennessee, man with paranoid schizophrenia and the subsequent community outcry made it clear to then lieutenant Sam Cochran and his colleagues that he and his fellow officers needed more intensive special training than the eight hours the department allotted. They and Memphis's mental health professionals went on to inaugurate the forty-hour Crisis Intervention Team program (CIT). Developed with the intent of shifting the focus of law enforcement from "professional crime fighters" toward social service, CIT is what Cochran calls "slow policing." Instead of perceiving a person with mental illness as a threat, CIT trained officers view the individual as needing help. Officers are taught techniques that can help de-escalate and defuse a potentially dangerous situation without the use of force.

Reporter Alisa Roth has worked for Marketplace, *covered stories for* NPR, *and contributed to the* New York Review of Books *and* New York Times, *among other news outlets. As a 2014 Soros Justice Fellow, she researched jails and prisons' role as the de facto mental health care system in America.*

Although the CIT program has been criticized for its "hug-a-thug approach," Roth comments that the program "has become the cornerstone of police policies for dealing with people with mental illness" in some metropolitan areas and notes that Miami has combined its CIT program with a county-wide diversion program. In 2000, pioneering reformer and Miami-Dade County judge Steve Leifman developed the Criminal Mental Health Project to keep the mentally ill out of prisons. If a person with mental illness is arrested on a misdemeanor, or perhaps a nonviolent felony, he or she has a choice either to go through the criminal justice system or to enter the program. Of the roughly six hundred people referred annually, Leifman estimates that 80 percent choose the program. Once clients join, they receive mental health care and housing, with the provision that they periodically appear in court to confirm that they are compliant. Few participants reoffend. In fact, the jail closed a wing of its building because so many had been diverted from incarceration.

The efforts of these twenty-first-century successors to Kirkbride offer hope that contemporary patients and prisoners will get the treatment they need to get better. In spite of their work and others like them, however, there is much more to be done. Readers of Roth's scathing denunciation of the criminal justice system may wonder, as did the reviewer for *Kirkus Reviews*, whether administrators and policy makers will see this issue as important enough to move forward with necessary reforms.

Pegge Bochynski

Review Sources

Brinkman, Antoinette. *Review of Insane: America's Criminal Treatment of Mental Illness, by Alisa Roth. Library Journal, vol. 143, no. 10, 1 June* 2018, p. 102. *Literary Reference Center Plus*, search.ebscohost.com/login.aspx?direct=true&db =lkh&AN=129811219&site=lrc-plus. Accessed 4 Dec. 2018.

Dolnick, Sam. "Locked In: How The American Prison System Became a De Facto Warehouse for the Mentally Ill." *Review of Insane: America's Criminal Treatment of Mental Illness, by Alisa Roth.* The *New York Times*, 27 May 2018, p. 11.

Review of Insane: America's Criminal Treatment of Mental Illness, by Alisa Roth. Kirkus Reviews, vol. 86, no. 3, 2 Feb. 2018, p. 391. *Literary Reference Center Plus*, search.ebscohost.com/login.aspx?direct=true&db=lkh&AN=127646706&sit e=lrc-plus. Accessed 4 Dec. 2018.

Oshinsky, David. "Should We Reopen the Asylums?" Review of Insane: America's Criminal Treatment of Mental Illness, by Alisa Roth, et al. The *New York Review of Books, vol. 65, no. 16, 25 Oct.* 2018, pp. 37–39.

Junk

Author: Tommy Pico
Publisher: Tin House Books (Portland, Oregon). 80 pp.
Type of work: Poetry

Courtesy of Tin House Books

Poet Tommy Pico brings his Teebs trilogy to a close, with a third book-length poem, reflecting on love, Native American identity, and the detritus of daily life

The "junk" alluded to in the title of Tommy Pico's new book-length poem of the same name has several meanings, all rich in metaphorical import. The book, the third in a trilogy that began with 2016's *IRL* and continued with 2017's *Nature Poem*, is loosely modeled on A. R. Ammons's 1993 poem *Garbage*, aping that book-length work's form (composed entirely of couplets) and its concern with the detritus of life. But Pico is quick to distinguish "junk" from "garbage" (and *Junk* from *Garbage*). On the third page of the book, Pico writes, "Junk gets a bad rap because capitalism Junk / isn't / garbage It's not outlived its purpose—Junk awaits its / next life." In this formulation, garbage exists in a state of finality, but junk stands in a liminal state, a sort of limbo where it has ceased to function in its original intended purpose but will soon be repurposed and thus continue in its new life.

With the terms of junk established early on, Pico is then free to riff on the various meanings of the word, all of which suggest this state of limbo, as well as items (and people) who have been seen as superfluous by the larger world. The poem begins with a reference to junk food, one of the various meanings of junk and one that continues to be referenced throughout the book. This craving for junk food is entwined with the erotic, suggesting that erotic attachments can be as superfluous as no-nutrition food or, conversely, that both can be more significant than they are given credit for being. The book's opening lines read:

> Frenching with a mouthful of M&M's dunno if I feel
> polluted
> or into it—the lights go low across the multiplex Temple
> of
>
> canoodling and Junk food A collision of corn dog bites
> and
> chunky salsa to achieve a spiritual escape velocity . . .

Here, in this opening, Pico gives the reader a sense of his own ambivalence about his romantic/gustatory pursuits, conveyed in language both humorous and a little disgusting, while simultaneously suggesting that the combination of junk food and casual kissing in a movie theater can have surprisingly strong spiritual uplift.

These first lines also establish Pico's unique style, which is heavily influenced by internet and text-messaging shorthand and is saturated with pop-culture references, but which mixes in more elevated poetic diction as well. The use of the shorthand "dunno," which is echoed by dozens of other abbreviations (such as "b/c" and "af") throughout the work and the opening of the book with the slang term "Frenching" establish the work as one that speaks the language of the internet and of the twenty-first century, while the phrase "spiritual escape velocity" hints at something more universal and traditionally poetic. The phrase "Temple of canoodling and Junk food" encapsulates this combination of high and low, as well as being a surprising and effective turn of phrase, one of many surprising word combinations that enliven the book throughout its duration.

© Niqui Carter

Tommy Pico is the author of three books, IRL, Nature Poem, *and* Junk, *which form a trilogy. He has won multiple prizes for his work, including the Whiting Award in 2018. He is a contributing editor at the website* Literary Hub.

With the opening lines, then, Pico establishes his aims and milieu, which he goes on to develop throughout the work. Essentially a free-floating meditation on what it means to be a person (specifically a queer Native American person) adrift in the world of twenty-first-century America, the book is loosely structured around a breakup. The narrator, known as Teebs, alludes to and addresses a former lover throughout the work, providing fragments of details. In between, he has numerous random sexual encounters (another meaning of junk Pico teases out is "penis") and reflects on his position in the world. Essentially, the narrator is both comfortable in his pop-cultural milieu (he fluently speaks the language) and, at the same time, at sea. This double bind, which allows him to read a cultural landscape that he also distrusts, is often manifested in the question of language. While the narrator greedily absorbs the slang and shorthand of his times and saturates his text with it, he also calls out many of the phrasings of his contemporaries, phrasings that hide a sinister meaning. For instance, he dissects the buzzwords "content" and "brand" as the reductive, inhuman terms and concepts that they are.

If capitalism is a force that attempts to transform human identity and creation into pure profit, then it is also an entity that leaves behind its share of detritus in its wake. "The engine of / capitalism: / dope, dicks, misc bulls——t Junk is its accumulation," writes Pico.

Not as

> indistinct as 'thing' not as dramatic as 'trash' It's
> important
> to value the Junk, Junk has the best stories

This passage, which provides three meanings of the book's title (in addition to garbage, it represents slang terms for drugs and male genitals), posits junk as both a product of capitalism and a possible means of, if not salvation, as least of recouping some positive values in the form of a good laugh or yarn. In fact, *Junk* is filled with plenty of the "best stories" and lots of good humor besides. An intensely pleasurable book, *Junk* teems with clever wordplay that is not merely clever for its own sake but allows the reader to see the world in fresh ways.

It is necessary, Pico suggests, to see the world in fresh ways because it is in such a sorry state, and only humor and the transformative power of language wielded correctly can help combat despair. This is necessary because of the catalogue of ills that Pico outlines throughout the book, tying a personal sense of uncertainty to the uncertain state of the wider world. Whether it is African American men being killed by police, right-wing militias taking over public land in Oregon, or the Russians interfering in a US election, it is a tough world.

But, the narrator illustrates, it has always been tough, a state of affairs that is especially clear to Pico as a Native American who grew up on a reservation. Pico writes,

> American 'Freedom' is such historical propaganda
> Indigenous
>
> and black lives remind American exceptionalism that
> slavery,
> theft, and genocide are its founding institutions

A good portion of the book is dedicated to Pico's reflections on his Native American identity and the ways in which the Native people have themselves been treated as disposable, as another form of "junk." As someone with this historical background, Pico is able to see through much of contemporary American life in a way that other people cannot.

This perspective is compounded by the narrator's identity as a gay man, but it also differentiates him from many of the men that he takes up with. The speaker is frequently critical of a superficial, largely white, "homonormative" culture that he keeps finding himself involved in but is continually kept at an arm's length from. He says to his ex:

                            you

said you
were in a viral video dancing on a patio with a group of
gay

norms (of course) on Fire Island (of course) in a thong (of
course) and it made me want to punch a pigeon . . .

This disgust with what he considers the more obvious expressions of gay life is maddening to him on an intellectual level, but there is also a strong element of jealousy at play, both of the way his lover fits into a world that he cannot and of his lover's having fun with other men. Not belonging, in *Junk,* is something like an existential state.

But if the narrator is frequently at sea in the world, his language (Pico's language) is in firm control throughout. Pico uses the couplet form but does not employ rhyme, meter, or really any other traditional poetic device. He simply lets his language flow throughout the work, spilling over from one line to the next, the only breaks coming courtesy of capitalized words that indicate the start of a new sentence. (There are no periods.) This technique gives the poem a headlong rush, which, rather than feeling undisciplined, registers as excitement, the words of a man who has so much to say that he cannot be contained. That Pico *is* extremely disciplined is evident in the skillful ways in which he mixes modes and makes connections. Running between the colloquial and the elevated, associating words to further his thought, Pico proves himself a master of collage. He offers up fragments that rush together so well that they do not even seem like fragments but like complete thoughts.

Another element that Pico carefully collages into the text are a number of italicized segments that involve the narrator's alter ego reprimanding him, always with the term "dummy." In one passage, the alter ego comes to, in a sense, question the whole project. "My kink is holding / hands on the way to the deli I hate musicals so gd much," the narrator says, to which the italicized voice responds, *"Not / every revelation deserves a stanza, dummy."* Here, he reproaches himself for the potential superficiality of his thoughts. Since the poem largely consists of these thoughts, Pico here questions his whole project in a way that is striking but with whose skepticism the reader is unlikely to agree.

Pico carefully works these self-interrogating segments into the mix throughout the book, dosing them out at just the right intervals so that they provide continuity but do not seem overdone. These segments hint at the sense of dissociation that Pico alludes to on occasion in his poem, a sense that the reader comes to understand is born of his identity, not only as a queer man or a Native American man, but as a man out of time, a man who, while understanding the context in which he exists, can never fully embrace or feel comfortable in that context or in a world that aims to break down imagination and any form of contradiction.

Andrew Schenker

Review Sources

Ardam, Jacquelyn. "Canoodling with Junk Food: On Tommy Pico's 'Junk.'" Review of *Junk*, by Tommy Pico. *Los Angeles Review of Books*, 10 May 2018, lareviewofbooks.org/article/canoodling-with-junk-food-on-tommy-picos-junk. Accessed 19 Nov. 2018.

Hart, Michelle. "One Man's Trash." Review of *Junk*, by Tommy Pico. *O*, June 2018, p. 83. *MasterFILE Complete*, search.ebscohost.com/login.aspx?direct=true&db=f 6h&AN=129438969. Accessed 19 Nov. 2018.

Review of *Junk*, by Tommy Pico. *Publishers Weekly*, 19 Mar. 2018, www.publishersweekly.com/978-1-941040-97-3. Accessed 19 Nov. 2018.

Kenny, Tara. "Tommy Pico's 'Junk' Is a Love Letter to Abandonment." *Kajal*, 2018, www.kajalmag.com/tommy-picos-junk-native-poetry. Accessed 19 Nov. 2018.

The Kiss Quotient

Author: Helen Hoang
Publisher: Berkley (New York). 336 pp.
Type of work: Novel
Time: Present day
Locale: Northern California

In The Kiss Quotient, *Helen Hoang explores the developing romance between Stella, an econometrician with autism spectrum disorder, and Michael, the escort she hires to teach her about sexual and romantic relationships.*

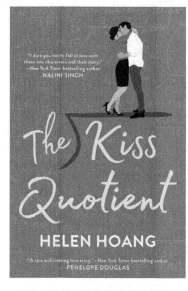

Courtesy of Penguin

Principal characters

STELLA LANE, a thirty-year-old econometrician who has autism spectrum disorder
ANN LANE, her mother
EDWARD LANE, her father
PHILIP JAMES, her coworker
MICHAEL PHAN, a.k.a. Michael Larsen, a twenty-eight-year-old tailor and clothing designer who works a side job as an escort
QUAN, his cousin
KHAI, his cousin, who is on the autism spectrum
ANH LARSEN, his mother
JANIE LARSEN, one of his sisters, an economics student

A perennially popular genre, romance literature experienced a boost in popularity during the first decades of the twenty-first century as new authors who had grown up reading romance novels sought to celebrate the genre while also ensuring that its characters reflected the audience more, introducing greater diversity not only in terms of race, sexual orientation, gender identity, and body type, among other areas, but also in terms of neurodiversity and relationship dynamics. Such was the case for novelist Helen Hoang, who was diagnosed with autism spectrum disorder in her midthirties and sought to write a romance featuring characters whose approach to social situations, challenges in daily life, and family backgrounds in part reflected her own as well as those of many other readers. At the same time, as she explains in the author's note for her debut novel, she had long considered writing a book that inverts the narrative trope, popularized by works such as the 1990 film *Pretty Woman*, in which a man hires and eventually falls in love with a female escort. Hoang instead sought to explore what would happen when a successful woman hires a male escort as well as the woman's reasons for doing so in the first place. The resulting novel, *The Kiss Quotient*, was published to widespread interest among fans of the genre as well as critical acclaim in 2018, demonstrating the success of Hoang's approach as well as the appeal of romances that incorporate some of the expected elements of the genre while also presenting something new.

The Kiss Quotient begins by making protagonist Stella Lane's reasons for hiring an escort abundantly clear. A thirty-year-old successful econometrician from a wealthy California family, Stella is having breakfast with her parents when her mother announces that she and her husband are ready for grandchildren. However, Stella is not even in a relationship, and the prospect of dating or having sex makes her deeply uncomfortable, in large part because she has autism spectrum disorder and struggles with social interaction and intimacy. Hoping to win the approval of her mother, she considers initiating a relationship with a coworker, Philip James, who tells Stella that she would be more successful in relationships if she became more sexually experienced and knowledgeable. Although Stella doubts her ability to gain that knowledge through dating, as her past experiences have been unpleasant for her, she realizes that a paid escort would have the experience to teach her everything she needs to know and would not demand the same kind of social interaction expected by a date. She ultimately hires an escort named Michael and proposes an arrangement in which she would be his sole client for several months, during which time he would instruct her in a variety of sexual activities. Although Michael is initially opposed to the idea of taking on a repeat client due to some of his past experiences, he finds himself both attracted to and intrigued by Stella and agrees to schedule further sessions with her.

Throughout *The Kiss Quotient*, the narrative alternates between Stella's point of view and Michael's, showing both sides of their developing romance. While the use of alternating third-person point of view is relatively common in novels, and particularly within romances published during the second decade of the twenty-first century, that technique is an especially essential element of *The Kiss Quotient*, as it enables Hoang to present both sides of the developing romance while emphasizing the key differences in how her protagonists see the world and themselves. Those differences in turn form the root of the novel's primary conflicts. The chapters that reflect Stella's point of view highlight many of the sensory and social challenges she faces throughout her everyday life and the routines and coping mecha-

© Eric Kieu

The Kiss Quotient *is Helen Hoang's first published novel.*

nisms she has developed for dealing with them, providing nuanced insight into the life of one specific woman with autism. At the same time, Stella's chapters make it clear that autism spectrum disorder is simply a part of her life, not something needing to be changed but instead something that exists alongside her passion for work, her love of martial-arts films and Korean dramas, and the other traits and interests that make her who she is. Michael's chapters likewise explore the mind behind the handsome face that Stella sees, exploring his guilt and self-loathing as well as his deep love of and dedication to his family.

Allowing the reader access to both perspectives creates moments of dramatic irony at various points throughout the novel. For example, the reader learns that Stella has autism in the first chapter, while Michael does not realize that fact until about halfway through the novel. Michael's chapters likewise reveal his true reasons for working as an escort long before Stella learns of them and also hint at truths about his father that are not revealed until late in the book. At the same time, Hoang aptly balances hints and revelations with moments of straightforward communication that are both refreshing for the reader and necessary for the characters, who clearly benefit from forthright discussions of their emotions and needs.

Over the course of the narrative, the novel reveals that Michael put a promising career in fashion design on hold to take care of his mother, who had been diagnosed with cancer after being abandoned by his father. Although Michael works as a tailor in his family's shop during the day, he holds a second job as an escort to earn money to pay for his mother's treatment. While he works to hide his second job from his family, the line between his professional life and personal life begin to blur when he and Stella encounter Michael's cousin Quan while at a night club. Following the disastrous trip to the night club, where the lights and noise prove to be too much stimuli for Stella, she suggests that she and Michael switch their focus from sex lessons to relationship lessons and that Michael become her "full-time practice boyfriend." Michael agrees to the proposal, but their practice relationship is tested when Stella accompanies him to dinner at his mother's house. Overstimulated by the unfamiliar, noisy environment and struggling to navigate within a new social context, Stella accidentally brings up painful topics of conversation and insults Michael's mother by refusing to eat food that had been microwaved in a plastic container. The incident, along with hints from Quan and the realization that Stella shares some similarities with Quan's brother, who is also on the autism spectrum, prompts Michael to realize that Stella has autism and grants him a better understanding of the reasons behind her responses to social situations and the reasons she had hired him in the first place.

As Michael's feelings for Stella deepen, he feels increasingly guilty about the commercial nature of their relationship and vows not to take the money she has offered him, instead planning to help her learn to navigate the world of romantic relationships of his own volition. Meanwhile, Stella fears that Michael is not truly interested in her and hopes to seduce him. She becomes increasingly drawn into his family, accompanying him to more family meals and attempting to help one of his sisters, economics student Janie, secure an internship with her company. Although Stella and Michael have each fallen in love with the other, neither knows how the other feels, and their respective doubts about their own self-worth threaten to end their relationship before it can truly begin. Although the novel at times raises questions that it may not answer to the full satisfaction of all readers—the truth about Michael's father, for instance, is hinted at throughout the novel but ultimately explored in a relatively brief, albeit cathartic and revealing, moment—the core romance narrative and characters are strongly developed.

Reviews of *The Kiss Quotient* were largely positive, with many critics praising Hoang's fresh take on her genre. In a review for *Kirkus*, Bobbi Dumas described the novel as "breathtaking" and particularly highlighted the ways in which Stella and Michael's backgrounds and viewpoints shape their romance and the narrative's conflicts. Writing for the *New York Times*, Jaime Green commented positively on the "insight and empathy" Hoang displays with regard to Stella in particular. Although Green did note that the stakes of the novel "only feel serious when [the reader is] in them with Stella," she went on to note that Hoang's presentation of Stella's difficulties with social interactions and simultaneous recognition of those difficulties creates "heartbreaking tension."

Many of the novel's positive reviews focused significantly on the role Stella's autism plays in the narrative and Hoang's deft and personally informed handling of the topic, with critics such as the reviewer for *Publishers Weekly* noting that Hoang succeeds in presenting a complex portrait of Stella while "never reducing her to a walking diagnosis." Reviewers additionally commented on the strength of Hoang's prose as well as her handling of the romantic and sexual aspects of Stella and Michael's relationship. The novel also received positive attention for its depiction of Michael's large and tight-knit Vietnamese American family, which Hoang has noted in interviews was based somewhat on her own. In addition to proving popular among readers and critics, *The Kiss Quotient* captured the attention of film industry executives. Pilgrim Media Group acquired the film and television rights to the novel in August 2018, and in October of that year, the film studio Lionsgate announced plans to adapt the novel for the screen.

Joy Crelin

Review Sources

Dumas, Bobbi. "So Much to Love in Helen Hoang's *The Kiss Quotient*." Review of *The Kiss Quotient*, by Helen Hoang. *Kirkus*, 6 Sept. 2018, www.kirkusreviews. com/features/so-much-love-helen-hoangs-i-kiss-quotienti/. Accessed 30 Nov. 2018.

Green, Jaime. Review of *The Kiss Quotient*, by Helen Hoang, et al. *The New York Times*, 2018, www.nytimes.com/interactive/2018/books/review/summer-reading-romance.html. Accessed 30 Nov. 2018.

Review of *The Kiss Quotient*, by Helen Hoang. *Publishers Weekly*, 9 Apr. 2018, www.publishersweekly.com/978-0-451-49080-3. Accessed 30 Nov. 2018.

Nesa, Kamrun. "Sweet and Hot, *The Kiss Quotient* Really Adds Up." Review of *The Kiss Quotient*, by Helen Hoang. *NPR*, 10 June 2018, www.npr. org/2018/06/10/613466426/sweet-and-hot-the-kiss-quotient-really-adds-up. Accessed 30 Nov. 2018.

Ragsdale, Melissa. "*The Kiss Quotient* by Helen Hoang Is the Hottest Romance of Summer—and Its Main Character Is Autistic." Review of *The Kiss Quotient*, by

Helen Hoang. *Bustle*, 6 June 2018, www.bustle.com/p/the-kiss-quotient-by-helen-hoang-is-the-hottest-romance-of-summer-its-main-character-is-autistic-9175023. Accessed 30 Nov. 2018.

Walker, Aleksandra. Review of *The Kiss Quotient*, by Helen Hoang. *Booklist*, 1 May 2018, www.booklistonline.com/The-Kiss-Quotient-Helen-Hoang/pid=9470285. Accessed 30 Nov. 2018.